ECCENTRICITY AND THE CULTURAL IMAGINATION IN NINETEENTH-CENTURY PARIS

Eccentricity and the Cultural Imagination in Nineteenth-Century Paris

MIRANDA GILL

OXFORD

UNIVERSITY PRESS

OXFORD
UNIVERSITY PRESS

Great Clarendon Street, Oxford OX2 6DP

Oxford University Press is a department of the University of Oxford.
It furthers the University's objective of excellence in research, scholarship,
and education by publishing worldwide in

Oxford New York

Auckland Cape Town Dar es Salaam Hong Kong Karachi
Kuala Lumpur Madrid Melbourne Mexico City Nairobi
New Delhi Shanghai Taipei Toronto

With offices in

Argentina Austria Brazil Chile Czech Republic France Greece
Guatemala Hungary Italy Japan Poland Portugal Singapore
South Korea Switzerland Thailand Turkey Ukraine Vietnam

Oxford is a registered trade mark of Oxford University Press
in the UK and in certain other countries

Published in the United States
by Oxford University Press Inc., New York

© Miranda Gill 2009

British Library Cataloguing in Publication Data
Data available

Library of Congress Cataloging in Publication Data
Gill, Miranda.
Eccentricity and the cultural imagination in nineteenth-century Paris / Miranda Gill.
p. cm.
ISBN 978–0–19–954328–1
1. Paris (France)–Social life and customs–19th century. 2. Eccentrics and
eccentricities–France–Paris–History–19th century. I. Title.
DC715.G497 2009
944'.36106–dc22   2008036156

Typeset by SPI Publisher Services, Pondicherry, India
Printed in Great Britain
on acid-free paper by
the MPG Books Group

ISBN 978–0–19–954328–1

1 3 5 7 9 10 8 6 4 2

Acknowledgements

I would like to thank the Arts and Humanities Research Council for funding the doctoral thesis on which this study was based; Pembroke College, Cambridge for electing me to a research fellowship which enabled me to continue work on the project; and Emma Wilson and the Department of French at the University of Cambridge for assistance with aspects of the publishing process.

I am greatly indebted to the supervisors of the doctoral thesis from which this study emerged, Adrianne Tooke and Ruth Harris, for their patience and scrupulousness; the latter generously provided a historical perspective without which the project would have been much the poorer. I am grateful to Roger Pearson and Daniel Pick for their detailed and perspicacious comments. Malcolm Bowie advised on the project at an early stage and was unfailingly encouraging. Terence Cave's advice and insight over many years have proved utterly invaluable. In the course of my research I have benefited greatly from conversations with and feedback from many other individuals, including Peter Brooks, Felicity Callard, Elizabeth Fallaize, Tim Farrant, Alison Finch, Michael Finn, Bernard Howells, Ann Jefferson, Ralph Kingston, Jann Matlock, Edward Welch, and Emma Wilson. Victoria Carroll and Susan Pickford's expert knowledge of eccentricity has been the basis of some extremely helpful discussions. I would like to thank Anna Sysoeva for her research on Russian philology and Susanna Goldschmidt for her assistance with editing. The period spent working on the project has been enriched at different times by the company of Lisa Downing, Deborah Dukes, Linda Goddard, Mina Gorji, Agnieszka Gratza, Joe Harris, Katherine Lunn-Rockliffe, Lisa O'Sullivan, Bettina Varwig, and Susannah Wilson, some of whom have also commented on sections of the manuscript. I have been fortunate in the support I have received from my parents and extended family, and owe a debt of a very special kind to Sandra, Deborah, and my sister Susannah. Finally, I would like to thank Steffan for enduring more than his fair share of eccentricity over the years. This book is dedicated to him.

MG

Jesus College, Cambridge
March 2008

Contents

List of Illustrations

Illustrations are reproduced by kind permission of the British Library; copyright information is provided in each caption.

List of Abbreviations

The following abbreviations refer to texts in the Bibliothèque de la Pléiade series, Gallimard, Paris:

CB Charles Baudelaire, *Œuvres complètes*, ed. Claude Pichois, 2 vols. (1975–6).

GN Gérard de Nerval, *Œuvres complètes*, ed. Jean Guillaume and Claude Pichois, 3 vols. (1984–93).

HB Honoré de Balzac, *La Comédie humaine*, ed. Pierre-Georges Castex, 12 vols. (1976–81).

JB Jules Barbey d'Aurevilly, *Œuvres romanesques complètes*, ed. Jacques Petit, 2 vols. (1964–6).

JV Jules Vallès. *Œuvres*, ed. Roger Bellet, 2 vols. (1975).

The following abbreviations have also been used:

GD Pierre Larousse, *Grand Dictionnaire universel du XIXe siècle*, 17 vols. (Paris: Administration du grand dictionnaire universel, 1866–77).

GF Gustave Flaubert, *Œuvres*, ed. Bernard Masson, 2 vols. (Paris: Seuil, 1964).

TLF *Trésor de la langue française: dictionnaire de la langue du XIXe et XXe siècle*, 16 vols. (Paris: CNRS, 1971–94).

Introduction

Paris is the land of eccentrics, murmured Rocambole.

Ponson du Terrail

The street, like the salon, has its eccentrics and its heroes...I
return to them often, but history will return to them too.

Jules Vallès[1]

This study asks what it meant to call someone 'eccentric' in Paris
between the July Monarchy and the *fin de siècle*, and investigates why
eccentricity aroused such intensely ambivalent responses in bourgeois
readers, writers, and spectators. Originating in the terminology of
astronomy and geometry, the terms *excentrique* and *excentricité* were
used figuratively in France from the early nineteenth century to denote
people, acts, or objects that broke with convention. In sources as diverse
as etiquette manuals, fashion magazines, newspapers, novels, plays,
political pamphlets, and scientific and psychiatric treatises, eccentricity
elicited sharply divergent opinions. The scandal of 'standing out' evoked
both the aspirations of the bourgeoisie (its dreams of freedom, creativity,
and individuality) and its deepest anxieties (the threat of madness,
monstrosity, and sin). It was simultaneously desired and feared, incorporated into and rejected from bourgeois identity. Contrary to what
is often assumed, the meaning of eccentricity is neither timeless nor
self-evident. The very synonyms used to define it—bizarre, singular,
original, peculiar, odd—suggest the frustration of rationality and the
failure of the codes by which social and mental life is interpreted.
Indeed, the concept owed its success precisely to its ability to adapt to
new contexts. Eccentricity is always defined in relation to something it
is not, but the imaginary 'centre' (or 'centricity') from which it departs
is far from stable. The concept functioned as a barometer sensitive to

[1] Ponson du Terrail 1964*b*: 211 and JV1: 936–7.

the slightest traces of cultural change, as the boundaries separating the normal from the deviant were drawn and redrawn in the course of the century.[2]

The notion of French eccentricity may initially appear puzzling, since eccentricity is widely associated with a mythical vision of Englishness. The popular image of the English eccentric still disseminated in biographies, newspapers, and everyday speech is that of a harmlessly quirky individual. Amiable and somewhat ludicrous by nature, the eccentric is rarely seen as a tragic or fashionable figure.[3] This was not always the case. In the decades before Victoria's ascent to the throne, the terms 'eccentric' and 'eccentricity' were regularly used in the English courts, often to create a sense of the disturbing abnormality or outright insanity of the accused.[4] They had ambiguous connotations in other contexts: in Regency magazines aimed at lower middle-class readers they denoted human 'monsters' of prodigious appearance or abilities, whilst in Gothic and Romantic novels they were used to evoke the tempestuous character of the genius. Once eccentricity is reconceptualized as a shifting and often contradictory concept, a wealth of new meanings emerges.

If England has traditionally been seen as a tolerant refuge for nonconformists, France has been portrayed, in the same body of stereotypes, as a nation characterized by its exquisitely polite salon culture and its rigid definitions of good taste and elegance.[5] After Napoleon's defeat in 1815, however, French writers began to appropriate the concept of eccentricity together with a range of English artefacts and myths, as a wave of Anglomania swept through Paris. French perceptions of the unconventional rapidly mutated in response to successive political, social, and aesthetic developments. Though eccentricity was identified

---

[2] Unless a different cultural context is specified, I use the term 'eccentricity' to refer to the family of French terms comprising the personal nouns *un excentrique*, and *une femme excentrique*, the adjective *excentrique*, and the abstract noun *excentricité* as used by 19th-century writers and speakers themselves, though the study also considers related terms such as *bizarre*, *singulier*, and *original*. In my translations of source material, the terms 'eccentric' and 'eccentricity' are always direct renderings of *excentrique* and *excentricité*.

[3] This stance is equally evident in popular biographies and psychological studies of 'eccentrics', e.g. Jolliffe 2001 and Weeks 1995 respectively.

[4] Typical examples of legal reports in *The Times* include the following: on 3 January 1823 a woman termed an 'eccentric-looking creature' was acquitted of theft due to insanity (3); on 21 August 1823 a 'Melancholy Suicide' was deemed 'remarkably eccentric in his conduct and manners' (verdict: 'insanity') (2); on 7 August 1826 the son of a woman who 'appears eccentric to the world in general' successfully requested a legal inquiry into her 'lunacy' (2); and, evidence of a new trend, on 9 July 1827 the testament of a 'woman of eccentric habits' was called into question (3).

[5] See Magendie's classic study (1925).

with Englishness during the eighteenth century, by both continental observers and the English themselves, it had been 'frenchified' by the *fin de siècle*.

Eccentricity and French bourgeois identity

Debate about French eccentricity first emerged during the July Monarchy, and was closely linked to changing perceptions of class and identity.[6] Although eccentricity was attributed to individuals from many social strata—from stigmatized groups such as prostitutes and the Bohemian poor to the aristocracy, *parvenus*, and occasionally the bourgeoisie itself—discourse about eccentricity was produced primarily from the perspective of the urban middle classes. The relationship between eccentricity and the bourgeoisie is complex. July Monarchy society has traditionally been portrayed by historians as a period of increasing cultural self-confidence in the French bourgeoisie, exemplified by representations of Louis-Philippe as a bourgeois 'citizen king'.[7] Since the 1960s, however, it has been acknowledged that the entity now known as the 'bourgeoisie' is remarkably difficult to define, since it was characterized by both elaborate stratification and social mobility.[8] The middling ranks of society also proved unwilling to construct narratives of collective belonging in relation to the term *bourgeois*. Generally pronounced with hostility and ridicule, *bourgeois* almost invariably described 'what *someone else* was', and the alternative *classe moyenne*, or middle class, was never popular.[9] Across Europe as a whole, but in France in particular, the phenomena of 'bourgeoisophobia' and anti-bourgeois satire testifies to ambivalence within the middle classes about the language of self-designation. There was thus a strong tendency for the term *bourgeois* to be used in a pejorative manner.[10]

Nonetheless, the inability of historians to circumscribe the bourgeoisie as a sociological entity should not distract from the many ethnographical markers of middle-class identity that existed in practice for

---

[6] Unless otherwise specified, the subsequent analysis focuses on French views of eccentricity between *c*.1830 and *c*.1900.

[7] On representations of bourgeois self-confidence, see e.g. Morazé 1957.

[8] See esp. Daumard 1996: 214–17 and Le Wita 1994: ch. 2.

[9] Maza 2003: 5.   [10] See Gay 1998: 34–6 and Clark 1973.

those who were neither *paysans*, *ouvriers*, nor *nobles* (peasants, workers, or members of the nobility). A middle-class ethos was displayed in the innumerable rituals of daily life, including what individuals ate and wore, the districts in which they lived, the ways in which they furnished their homes, the books and newspapers that they read, their leisure activities, and the forms of conduct and speech they considered appropriate in particular situations.[11] It was against this backdrop that eccentricity was defined. For the desire of the middling ranks of society to assert a distinctive identity necessitated the construction of 'others' upon whom was projected much that was forbidden within their own social codes.

In a still unsurpassed analysis, Peter Stallybrass and Allon White have argued that the emergence of bourgeois identity in nineteenth-century England and France was linked to a twofold structural change in the nature of transgression. First, they propose that the period witnessed the tightening of strictures about acceptable behaviour, lowering thresholds of shame, and increasing anxiety about the body, filth, and deformity. These increasingly rigid standards of propriety, they suggest, generated deep fascination with forbidden areas of experience:

A recurrent pattern emerges: the 'top' attempts to reject and eliminate the 'bottom' for reasons of prestige and status, only to discover, not only that it is in some way frequently dependent upon that low-Other . . . but also that the top *includes* that low symbolically, as a primary eroticized constituent of its own fantasy life. The result is a mobile, conflictual fusion of power, fear, and desire in the construction of subjectivity: a psychological dependence upon precisely those Others which are being rigorously opposed and excluded at the social level.   (1986: 5)

Through the very intensity of its efforts to separate high from low culture, normality from deviance, and 'purity' from 'filth', the bourgeoisie paradoxically ended up being shaped by that which it sought to reject. Second, Stallybrass and White suggest that transgression was increasingly internalized in the nineteenth century and became located in the bourgeois psyche—in the phenomenon of hysteria, for example—rather than the social world of the carnival and marketplace (176–8).

Both arguments draw on Mikhail Bakhtin's influential theorization of the carnival, and in particular on what social anthropologists have

[11] See Le Wita 1994; on the taste formation of the leisure class, see Auslander 1996. Garrioch 1996 documents the emergence of a specifically Parisian bourgeoisie by 1830.

termed 'symbolic inversion' ('any act of expressive behaviour which inverts, contradicts, abrogates, or in some fashion presents an alternative to commonly held cultural codes, values and norms'),[12] a concept which overlaps with those of 'deviance' and 'norm violation'. Like a number of other historians and theorists, however, Stallybrass and White have criticized Bakhtin's optimistic view of the carnival's social function, suggesting that it constituted a form of 'licensed release' and noting that it was often aggressive towards marginal groups.[13] This criticism overlaps with the 'containment' theory of transgression popularized in much New Historicist criticism influenced by Michel Foucault, which similarly suggests that dominant ideologies can permit a limited degree of expression to deviance with the underlying aim of containing and controlling the threat it poses.[14]

Nineteenth-century representations of eccentricity in many respects conform to Stallybrass and White's theory of bourgeois identity. The ethos of the bourgeoisie was one of discreet, almost invisible mediocrity, in which *not* being considered eccentric was a key virtue.[15] The middle classes nonetheless came to project onto 'eccentric' figures—such as artists, criminals, the insane and the deformed—a variety of anxious fantasies which merely served to link them ever more firmly to their own identity. Moreover, eccentricity has a complex relationship to transgression, deviance, and symbolic inversion (Bakhtin explicitly cites eccentricity [*èkscentričnosti*] as a 'carnival category' which signifies 'the violation of the usual and the generally accepted, life drawn out of its usual rut').[16] Though Bohemians were notorious for provocatively eccentric behaviour, for example, their inversion of bourgeois norms was typically less radical than it seemed. In practice, the identities of Bohemians and the bourgeois citizens to whom they were ostensibly opposed remained inextricably linked.[17] Stallybrass and White's reformulation of Bakhtin's model of transgression is also better able to account for the ways in which certain types of deviance can be normalized, for instance in the Parisian fashion industry with its constant quest for novel and eccentric

[12] Babcock 1978: 14.
[13] Stallybrass and White 1986: 12–19; see also Burke 1988.
[14] This pessimistic 'containment' theory is criticized by many cultural materialists, who argue that transgression is possible and ubiquitous, and hegemony fragile (see Patterson 1996: 93–7).
[15] See M. Perrot 1987*a*: 271 and Le Wita 1994: 68.
[16] 1984: 126; Russian terms in the Introduction and Epilogue have been transliterated in accordance with ISO 9.
[17] See Seigel 1999: 5.

forms. Such examples highlight the importance of contextualizing the notions of norm and deviance in relation to specific cultures.[18]

Finally, the conclusions of Stallybrass and White are confirmed by a growing tendency amongst historians of nineteenth-century France, most recently Jan Goldstein, to emphasize the problematic relationship of the French bourgeoisie to social norms. In the one instance, the bourgeoisie desired order and conformism in the prolonged period of political instability which succeeded the 1789 Revolution; in the other, it sought to dismantle rules and constraints in the name of progress. This ambiguity at the heart of bourgeois identity, it has been suggested, generated a cultural need for 'margins' such as Bohemia, as well as for satire in which bourgeois conformism was mocked.[19]

Despite its usefulness as a theoretical model for understanding eccentricity, Stallybrass and White's analysis is in many ways incomplete. It does not, for example, address the significantly different attitudes towards transgression that arose within different sections of the European bourgeoisie; these emerge very clearly when French and English responses to eccentricity are contrasted. More precise exploration of the rhetoric and concepts used by nineteenth-century writers is also required in order to explain the internalization of transgression from a genuinely historicising perspective, and thereby avoid the anachronistic projection of subsequent terms and categories onto the past.[20]

The rhetoric of eccentricity

Perspectivalism is embedded in the linguistic structure of the term 'eccentric'. One of the linguistic functions of this and similar terms such as 'odd' and 'peculiar' is to allow those who implicitly frame themselves as 'normal' (and, by extension, healthy and virtuous) to stigmatize others.[21] Research in social theory has suggested that subjects' behaviour can be strongly influenced by the classifications and labels

---

[18] As Sirotkina argues (2002: 3–6). For a conceptual overview of norms and deviance in social theory, see Gibbs 1981.

[19] Seigel 1999: 10–11; Goldstein 2005: 180.

[20] For example, Stallybrass and White project Freud's model of hysteria backwards onto 19th-century culture, rather than analysing the concepts and terms used during this period itself.

[21] My own use of terms such as 'eccentric' and 'monstrous' is non-normative, adhering to 'agnostic' approaches to labelling; see Becker 1978: 15, 125.

they are given.[22] Terms used to denote forms of deviance, including 'eccentricity', may also be understood as instances of 'empathetic deixis', a linguistic concept which denotes speakers' sense of emotional proximity or distance from a given referent.[23] Many judgements of eccentricity are dissociative, often strongly so. It was unusual in nineteenth-century France for people voluntarily to identify themselves as eccentric; indeed, the threat of being designated eccentric often triggered self-regulatory mechanisms such as embarrassment and shame, together with anxiety at the prospect of inadvertent transgression.

The act of attributing eccentricity to oneself, or self-labelling, remained rare even for Bohemians, the social group most likely to do so. It too had complex rhetorical functions. In a letter to his alienist Dr Blanche, for instance, the writer Gérard de Nerval, who had repeatedly been incarcerated as a madman, writes: 'Please could you ask these women to forgive me for the prolonged eccentricity [l'excentricité prolongée] which has made me take too seriously poets' claim to descend from Jupiter and Apollo.' Nerval arguably uses the term 'excentricité' strategically in order not to use that of 'madness', in an attempt to reassure 'these women' and present his allegedly strange views from their perspective.[24] His well-documented struggles over labelling are evident in the following comment from 1854: 'I officially admit that I was ill. I cannot admit that I was *mad* or even suffering from hallucinations' (GN3: 900). As Nerval recognized, eccentricity played a key role in mediating between absolute categories such as sanity and madness. It was therefore implicated in the slippage between scientific and social categories which intensified after 1848. According to the historian Robert Nye, the opposition between the normal and the pathological which came to dominate French medicine by the mid century was 'conceptually isomorphic with so many other binary terms that regulate the perception of social life: moral–immoral, criminal–honest, sane–insane, violent–passive'.[25] Around the same time, scientists and doctors began to believe that the normal and the pathological were not clearly separated, but rather that they were situated on a continuum and linked through imperceptible gradations.[26] This made it impossible definitively to separate health from disease, or permissible

---

[22] This view is particularly associated with labelling theory, social constructionism, Foucault's analyses of classification, and Ian Hacking's theorization of 'dynamic nominalism' and feedback loops (1986).

[23] See Levinson 1983: 81.   [24] GN3: 836; cf. 853.

[25] Nye 1984: 48.   [26] See Canguilhem's classic account (2003: 18–51).

from eccentric behaviour, and generated widespread alarm at the 'infil-tration' and 'undermining' of society by scarcely perceptible forms of deviance.

The difficulty of attributing conscious intent to peculiar individu-als intensified the troubling uncertainty with which eccentricity was associated. Were such people involuntarily peculiar, perhaps the victims of full or nascent madness? Or were they, in contrast, self-consciously performing to an audience, even feigning their oddity? People could feign eccentricity for a wide variety of reasons: to become famous, signal political allegiances, register rejection of dominant values or adherence to a nostalgic vision of the past, proclaim superiority over the masses or appeal to the masses' love of novelty, engage in avant-garde experimentation, irritate a repressive family, attract trade, evade legal responsibility, or merely enjoy contemplation of the bafflement it provoked.

The anxiety aroused by bizarre behaviour is also evident from the rapidity with which a body of reassuring stereotypes about eccentricity proliferated after 1830. The label 'eccentric' responded to an urgent need to master the puzzling unreadability of strange behaviour, par-ticularly in Paris, the locus of much recent debate about urbanization and modernity. As many critics have argued after Walter Benjamin, the 'panoramic' literature which influenced much cultural production of the period helped anxious readers to decode and master the city's mutating inhabitants and institutions. It was an intrinsically performative genre, in that it acted upon the social world as much as it described it. Terms such as *excentrique*, *bizarre*, and *singulier* expressed a sense of being overwhelmed by an inexplicable phenomenon, but they simultaneously allowed the unknown to be linguistically circumscribed and thereby provided readers with a sense of reassurance. The prevalence of discourse about the unclassifiable and incomprehensible in writing about the city reveals much about readers' need for dramatic fantasies of control, in the face of the unsettling complexities of urban life.[27]

Despite its connection with social exclusion and pathology, eccen-tricity also had a range of positive semantic associations, including genius, innovation, and creativity. It consequently became attached to emergent cultural tendencies such as Romanticism, fashion, and modernism. Though these developments initially threatened traditional values, they rapidly passed into the cultural mainstream in the capital,

---

[27] See Sennett in Wechsler 1982: 8.

and found passionate defenders in both elite and mass culture. An article of clothing, painting, or pastime that evoked angry or disgusted responses in one person could evoke admiration and pleasure in another, or, more commonly, a fusion of conflicting emotions. The workings of such 'mixed feelings' have been of increasing interest to social theorists. One of the key sites of ambivalence, Zygmunt Bauman has suggested, is the 'tempestuous relationship' between security and individual freedom; other social theorists have similarly highlighted the tensions between 'yearnings for independence and inclusion, [for] autonomous individuality and heteronomous collectivity'.[28] The clash between the demands of the individual self and those of the community is a recurrent theme in the history of eccentricity, for the concept signifies both the creative possibilities of individual self-fashioning and anxiety-inducing departure from the certainties of communal life. In short, eccentricity was emblematic of both slippage between categories and the erosion of absolute oppositions, for it was able to retain both positive and negative connotations. Examining the ambivalent responses to which it gave rise, and the rhetorical strategies in which it was implicated, will be the central aims of this study.

Structure and approach

This volume examines eccentricity from a jointly historical and rhetorical perspective. Since eccentricity is context-dependent, figurative, and largely imaginary, however, it is difficult to create a 'grand narrative', or even a conventional historical narrative, of its evolution. To some extent, there is a clear shift in French attitudes on the subject. In the aftermath of the failed revolution of 1848, the dominant classes became more hostile towards deviance and by extension to even minor forms of eccentricity.[29] In important respects, however, the history of the concept does not follow a linear path. The meanings attached to eccentricity evolved at a different pace in each context in which it was discussed. Different meanings often coexisted in the same period,[30] and the imagery with

---

[28] Bauman 2001: 41–5; Robert Kegan cited in Weigert 1991: 146.
[29] See Klein 1976: 111 on the increasing semantic negativity of eccentricity after 1848.
[30] In line with Raymond Williams's model of dominant, emergent, and residual ideologies (1977: 121–7).

which eccentricity was described often travelled between disciplines and periods (for instance, parallels were drawn between the concepts of eccentricity and monstrosity in writing on fairground sideshows, Bohemia, genius, female individualism, and mental illness, during many decades of the century). Whilst this study emphasizes the importance of historically contextualizing discourse about eccentricity, it thus has a primarily thematic and rhetorical focus. Each chapter seeks to unravel the meanings that the term progressively acquired within one or two specific contexts, and the analysis at times departs from chronological progression in order to investigate pervasive metaphorical associations between disparate texts. The analysis focuses on the period in which eccentricity generated the most intense cultural interest, namely 1830 to 1870, though in the case of medical and scientific discourse which took up the term relatively late, this period extends to the early twentieth century.[31]

The introductory chapter in Part I, 'The Rise of Eccentricity', proposes that debate about eccentricity emerged in eighteenth-century England in the context of growing cultural interest in innovation and originality and a new emphasis on individual uniqueness. Questioning why originality was the object of hostility in pre-Revolutionary France, it charts the gradual shifting of French attitudes and the naturalization of eccentricity during the Restoration, amidst increasing bourgeois ambivalence about individual freedom and social norms.

Part II, 'Fashionable Society', focuses on representations of eccentricity in discourse about the wealthy social elite, particularly the bourgeois salon, high society, and the *demi-monde*. Chapter 2, 'Etiquette and the Public Gaze', draws on sources aimed at helping readers understand the changing codes of Parisian life, including conduct manuals and advice on beauty and fashion, to explore the ambivalent nature of 'standing out' and 'being noticed' (*se faire remarquer*) in polite society. Eccentricity of dress or appearance highlighted tensions between the ideology of etiquette, which advocated 'feminine' self-effacement and tact, and that of fashion, linked to self-assertion and a distinctively modern aesthetics of the ephemeral and bizarre. Chapter 3, 'Dandies and Lions', examines fictional and journalistic representations of Parisian life in order to reconceptualize the relationship between dandyism and fashionable eccentricity. Dandyism was a historically unstable concept

---

[31] Though the terms continued to be used in *fin-de-siècle* fictional texts, they generated few new meanings by this stage and are therefore in my view less revealing of cultural tensions. On a comparable case of semantic 'banalization', see Starobinski 1999.

encompassing both overt eccentricity, which was easily legible and designed to astonish, and covert eccentricity, which necessitated more subtle modes of interpretation. Both male and female social types were situated on this continuum, including the *lionne, femme à la mode*, and *fat*, but fashionable women were more likely to be pathologized since female individualism was considered aberrant or even impossible. Chapter 4, 'The *Demi-Monde*', examines the rhetorical role of eccentricity in the context of 'semi-prostitution', the upper ranks of women excluded from polite society, particularly courtesans (termed *femmes excentriques*) and fallen women. The increasing cultural visibility of the *demi-monde* in Second Empire society generated polemic about spectacle, luxury, and consumption. In many conservative critics, the desire for moral regeneration through asceticism led to the explicit repudiation of eccentricity. Eccentric fashions were nonetheless depicted as a crucial clue which enabled *demi-mondaines* to be differentiated from respectable women.

Part III, 'The Underworld', turns to Parisian Bohemia and the fairground, highlighting the narcissistic preoccupation of the Second Empire man of letters with images of his own eccentricity. Chapter 5, '*Saltimbanques* and Savages', analyses literary and journalistic accounts of eroticized fairground encounters, in which the imaginary boundaries separating human 'monsters', 'savages', and other *saltimbanques* from their observers were blurred. The freak show threatened to reveal the perversity of all who attended such spectacles, and at times, the potential humanity of the monster, known as an 'eccentricity of nature'. Zoological metaphors appropriated from natural history underpinned the Parisian fascination with human exhibitions. Chapter 6, 'Bohemia', outlines the progressively more negative meanings attached to eccentricity in the context of changing perceptions of Bohemia. During the Second Empire, impoverished Bohemian eccentrics became a popular topic for biographical and journalistic sketches. These inhabitants of 'the unknown Paris' were portrayed as mysterious erotic enigmas by the men of letters who 'hunted' and questioned them, and were exhibited in textual galleries which resembled both the fairground booth and the natural history museum.

Part IV, 'Science', examines the rhetoric and imagery of eccentricity within the discourses of natural history and alienism. Chapter 7, 'Monsters', argues that growing interest in teratological theories of heredity (the transmission of congenital malformations) led to the literalization of the previously metaphorical concept of 'moral monstrosity'.

The eccentric was construed in scientific and medical treatises as the victim of a monstrously deformed nervous system. In turn, imagery drawn from natural history and medicine played an important role in literary depictions of mental and physical eccentricity. Chapter 8, 'Madness and Medicine', traces the shifting relationship between eccentricity and madness from the July Monarchy to the *fin de siècle*. Eccentricity was initially linked to monomania and obsession in literary and popular culture. After 1848, it was increasingly incorporated into psychiatric taxonomies, where it was located within the shadowy zone between the normal and the pathological and described in relation to new categories such as 'lucid madness', 'moral insanity', and 'superior degeneration'. Eccentricity thus came to represent the initial moment of contamination by the forces threatening to destroy society, but it was simultaneously seen by French alienists as a necessary component of genius. The Epilogue, 'Eccentricity in European Perspective', contrasts nineteenth-century French perceptions of a recurrent cluster of conceptual associations, the relationship between eccentricity, madness, and extreme individuality, with contemporaneous attitudes in Victorian England and Imperial Russia, in order to underscore still further the cultural and historical relativity of the concept.

Relatively little scholarly attention has been devoted to the subject of eccentricity in any culture. One recent study notes a curious 'dearth of serious criticism on the subject',[32] despite the continuing success of popular collections of anecdotes and biographical sketches about eccentric characters (a trend inaugurated during the nineteenth century itself).[33] Of the small number of analyses thus far devoted to eccentricity, even fewer have sought to reconstruct eccentricity in relation to specific contexts and historical norms. Since eccentricity was defined as departure from convention, however, its significance can only be grasped once these conventions are understood. As Edward Said noted, 'What is the meaning of "difference" when the preposition "from" has dropped from sight altogether?' (1995: 106). Existing accounts of French eccentricity are predominantly literary and formalist in approach, focusing on eccentricity of form

[32] Schulman 2003: 11.
[33] The three main scholarly works on English eccentricity are Langford 2000: ch. 6 (the most helpful general account), Cowlishaw 1998, and Plaisant 1976*a* (esp. Levier's chapter). For recent research relating to other national traditions see the Epilogue below.

and language rather than the social and historical meanings of the category.[34]

A further tendency of existing scholarship is to stress the subversive characteristics of eccentricity, in line with poststructuralist attacks on the doxa or collective opinion.[35] But accounts which write the negative axis out of the history of eccentricity cannot explain (as the perspective offered by Stallybrass and White can) why the term elicited such ambivalent responses. They invariably produce anachronistic interpretations of nineteenth-century culture, in which eccentricity elicited confusion and distress more often than avant-garde celebration, and they overestimate the desire of most writers who praised eccentricity to challenge dominant norms. Other key issues have scarcely been touched upon in existing accounts, such as the relationship between eccentricity and gender. A large body of discourse was produced about *femmes excentriques*, however, and most discussions of eccentricity throughout the century were informed by heavily gendered conceptions of physical, mental, and social norms. Finally, nineteenth-century perceptions of eccentricity cut across contemporary subject boundaries, particularly those which separate science and medicine from literature, popular culture, and social life. They have, perhaps for this reason, proved peculiarly difficult to pin down.[36]

Willingness to look beyond traditional subject boundaries therefore proves essential in understanding eccentricity. This study approaches the subject in the light of recent methodological developments in the study of literary and historical sources. Three related approaches to the analysis of nineteenth-century Parisian culture have particularly shaped it: the interdisciplinary analysis of 'popular' culture; discourse analysis; and rhetorical approaches to intellectual history.

First, following the much-discussed 'cultural turn' of the 1980s, movements such as New Historicism, cultural materialism, and the New

---

[34] Most accounts of French eccentricity are written from a poststructuralist perspective (see Sangsue 1987, 1988, and 2000; Tyers 1998). Schulman's study of the 'modern' French eccentric (2003), which mainly focuses on the 20th century, does not contextualize the term sufficiently in relation to 19th-century culture, and takes as self-evident that eccentricity is voluntary and positive. Eichel-Lojkine's study of 'eccentricity' during the French Renaissance is avowedly anachronistic (2002: 12–13). The most useful historical analysis remains Leduc-Adine's article of 1984.

[35] On 'ex-centricity' as a postmodern category see e.g. Hutcheon 1988: 60–1; on critical hostility to the doxa, see Prendergast 1986: ch. 1.

[36] The phrase 'popular culture' is problematic (see Bourdieu 1983; De Certeau et al. 1993; Clark 2003: 205) but remains necessary in the absence of an alternative; this study seeks to use it in a non-normative sense.

Cultural History have promoted the interdisciplinary analysis of sources which have traditionally been labelled either 'literary' or 'historical'.[37] Popular culture has increasingly become a legitimate topic of enquiry for both historians and literary critics working on nineteenth-century Paris, significantly expanding the number of texts deemed worthy of attention. This tendency has led to a growing body of scholarship on what Marshall Berman terms 'modernism in the street' and 'low modernism' and what Mary Gluck describes as 'the humble and neglected regions of popular culture and everyday experience that found increasingly commercial articulation by the middle of the nineteenth century'.[38] Such criticism often draws, explicitly or implicitly, on the insights of Bakhtin and Benjamin, thinkers who were both preoccupied by the cultural significance of ephemeral, even banal artefacts, and by the dynamic interplay of popular and elite culture.[39] In the light of this research, this study seeks to reconstruct a range of conflicting and often neglected voices from nineteenth-century Parisian culture.

Many of the sources in which eccentricity is discussed, such as etiquette manuals, psychiatric treatises, and the sprawling journalism of Parisian life, have been largely neglected by literary critics; nonetheless, they were produced during a period in which the concept of 'literature' was still fluid, and in which literary and non-literary discourses intersected in often startling ways.[40] Part of the task of reconstruction involves the analysis of the images (often engravings) that were an integral part of popular writing of the period.[41] Just as literary criticism has typically marginalized 'popular' sources,[42] historians of nineteenth-century French culture have paid relatively little attention to the rhetorical structure of their sources, though their metaphors, tropes, and intertextual allusions frequently repay close reading. The approach of discourse analysis, now widely used within cultural studies, provides a helpful framework for the close reading of non-literary texts

[37] On the related but distinct aims of these movements, see Ryan 1996, L. Hunt 1989, and Chartier 1988.

[38] Gluck 2005: 2. On the polysemy of 'modernism', 'modernity', and *modernité*, see Descombes 1993: 46–64; Felski 1995: 3–8; and Gluck 2005: 12–15.

[39] On the latter, see Buck-Morss 1983. Prendergast outlines Benjamin's view of the 'small, individual moment' as a 'crystal' from which can be inferred the shape of the 'total event' (1992: 213).

[40] See esp. Goulemot and Oster 1992 and 1989: 31–7.

[41] The illustrations in the study are mainly drawn from source materials which discuss eccentricity.

[42] A point made by Mainardi 2003: 69.

in relation to broader cultural discourses such as those of etiquette or medicine.[43] For the meanings of eccentricity were primarily shaped not by individual authors but by collective usage and the process that Bakhtin termed 'heteroglossia'.[44]

Finally, discourse analysis overlaps significantly with intellectual history and the history of semantics. Jan Goldstein notes that the term 'monomania', immensely popular in France around the mid-nineteenth century, was remarkable for its 'porousness ... to cultural values and cultural changes' (1987: 158). This comment aptly describes the workings of eccentricity, whose many layers of historical meaning this study seeks to excavate in a form of 'historical archaeology'.[45] Intellectual historians affiliated with both the Cambridge school and with the enterprise of *Begriffsgeschichte* have proposed that concepts are intrinsically linguistic and historically variable, rather than having a kernel of unchanging meaning.[46] The related discipline of word history has moved from pure etymology and philology to the more challenging analysis of the tangled relationship between semantics, history, and culture.[47] Intellectual history also has a growing affinity with the 'history of mentalities' and the 'history of affect'. These approaches foreground the role of non-rational forces in history, particularly in relation to highly charged subjects such as sexual and racial alterity, class, and the body;[48] and they rightly insist that such 'imaginary' factors, much in evidence in the history of eccentricity, are no less historically influential than those that can be quantified.[49]

Given the sheer volume of printed material produced in the nineteenth century, it is evidently impossible to write a comprehensive account of eccentricity during this period. This study seeks to outline the main contexts in which eccentricity was discussed, and analyses

---

[43] See Barker and Galasinski 2001.

[44] On heteroglossia as a model of everyday language, see Bakhtin 1981: 273.

[45] Gluck's phrase (2005: 23).

[46] On the former, see e.g. Skinner 2002: chs. 9 and 10, and Pocock 1996; on the latter, see Koselleck 2004: ch. 5. On the non-teleological history of concepts see also Cave 1999: 17–19.

[47] See Raymond Williams 1983 and Bal 2002: 27 n. 7.

[48] Roger Chartier criticizes historians' vague use of the phrase 'histoire des mentalités' (1998: 9), but it remains useful in the absence of a clear alternative. On structures of feeling, see Raymond Williams 1977: 128–41. Lynn Hunt associates recent historical interest in 'long-range trends in the alteration of the structure of the psyche', with the legacy of Norbert Elias, Philippe Ariès, Michel Foucault, and Lucien Febvre (1986: 217).

[49] On the influence of non-rational factors in French political history, for example, see Girardet 1986.

textual examples (or 'cultural fragments', in Walter Benjamin's sense) chosen because they are particularly revealing of underlying ideological tendencies and tensions. It is possible to imagine other approaches that would focus in more exhaustive detail on any one context or author in which the term was used.[50] Yet eccentricity was characterized precisely by its ability to migrate from one domain to another. Its distinctive role in nineteenth-century Paris as well as in wider European culture, this study attempts to show, is therefore best elucidated by examining the often unpredictable connections it forged between discourses and genres.

[50] The study does not, for example, analyse at length eccentricity of narrative and artistic form, the aspect of French eccentricity which has received the most attention to date (see Sangsue 1987, Tyers 1998, and Leduc-Adine 1984).

PART I

CAUSES AND CONTEXTS

1

The Rise of Eccentricity

The world considers eccentricity in great things, genius; in small
things, folly.

Edward Bulwer Lytton[1]

Eccentricity cuts across the boundaries of tragedy and comedy, elite
and popular culture, masculinity and femininity. Both contradictory
meanings and ambivalent responses were already associated with the
concept in eighteenth-century England, the context in which the term
'eccentric' was first popularized in its modern sense. The identification
of eccentricity with Englishness has proved to be so entrenched that
the emergence of early nineteenth-century French perceptions of oddity
from English tropes and models must be charted.

Debate about eccentricity proliferated in England when two cultural
developments came to intersect: rising interest across both elite and
popular culture in 'originality', in its new sense of novelty and innovation, and the increasing value placed on 'character', in its equally new
sense of the uniqueness of the individual self. Both were implicated in
the increasing individuation of bourgeois society. Social marginals and
outsiders had long been important social and literary types in popular
and elite European culture, in the form of wise fools, holy idiots,
sad clowns, melancholics, and misanthropists. Writers in eighteenth-
century England both built on these traditions and departed from them,
as types such as the genius, original, and eccentric provided new ways
of conceptualizing individuals with a problematic relationship to social
norms. In contrast, the French cultural elite did not possess a direct
equivalent for the term 'eccentric' until the early nineteenth century, and
remained notably suspicious of any departure from convention. The
cultural energy generated by originality and eccentricity in Georgian
England thus overshadows the far more limited interest that originality

[1] 1828: II, 64.

aroused in French writing and thought of the same period. Even after the 1789 Revolution, the French bourgeoisie remained ambivalent towards individualism and unconventional behaviour; but a series of challenges to dominant norms led to the partial re-evaluation of originality and eventual 'frenchification' of eccentricity.

The revaluation of originality in eighteenth-century English culture

The emergence of eccentricity in its modern sense in eighteenth-century England is closely related to the affirmation of bourgeois identity and to increasing social individuation, which both form part of the wider history of modernity.[2] These developments are inscribed in the history of linguistic innovation. The terms 'eccentric' and 'eccentricity', like their French equivalents, derive from the Greek *ekkentros* and the medieval Latin *excentricus* and *excentricitas*. They were originally used only in a non-metaphorical sense in both English and French during the medieval and early modern period. In astronomy, they denoted the deviation of planetary bodies such as comets from a perfectly circular and predictable orbit; in geometry, they denoted a circle that is not concentric with another circle. Thereafter they were also used in the technical vocabularies of disciplines such as botany.[3] In the latter part of the seventeenth century, these spatial images began to be used metaphorically in England to denote entities, traits, or people considered to be irregular and capricious, though the term 'eccentric' remained rare until the mid-eighteenth century. Before this time, people spoke mainly of 'Originals' and of 'odd', 'uncommon', and 'singular' characters. As a spatial concept which implicitly invokes a norm or 'centre' from which it diverges, eccentricity differs from originality, a temporal concept which suggests at once a tradition from which something departs and the founding of a new tradition. Both, however, are inseparable from that to which they are opposed, just as the concepts of heterodoxy and paradox refer always to the 'doxa', or common opinion, which they reject.[4]

---

[2] See Bauman 2001.

[3] In French, 'excentrique' was used from 1375 and 'excentricité' from 1562. On the semantic history of eccentricity in English, see Carroll 2006: 16–24.

[4] Eccentricity thus does not refer more to what it is *not* than originality, as Langford suggests (2000: 300).

Attitudes to social norms and traditions altered considerably during the late seventeenth and early eighteenth centuries in England, a culture marked by the growth of individualism across a range of discourses and practices, the expansion of a middle-class reading public, and the rise of new forms of writing such as journalism and the novel.[5] These interrelated developments formed the crucible for the popularization of the term 'eccentric', increasingly used in place of, or together with, 'original'.

The cultural revalorization of originality was most immediately noticeable in poetic theory. Until the seventeenth century, the term 'original' mainly denoted a model to be imitated, or an artefact that was not made from a copy.[6] It was therefore implicated in ongoing European debates about the relationship between classical models and contemporary artistic production. The rhetorical category of *imitatio* required artists to conform to existing artistic models. Though poetic practice was more complex than such codified doctrines suggest, 'official' theories of imitation remained dominant during the early modern period.[7] Around the turn of the eighteenth century, originality began to be praised in English poetic theory, often, though not always, by marginal writers contesting the values of the Augustan elite.[8] The rise of lending libraries, coffee shops, private spaces, and silent reading habits encouraged the emergence of a new reading public. Typically unable to read Greek or Latin, these new readers 'sought a poetry which would reflect their immediate concerns' and favoured 'modern' genres such as the novel and journalism.[9] These genres represented a cultural 'commitment to contemporaneity' and a fascination with the 'physiognomy of the age'. A couplet by Robert Wilde, placed on the title-page of John Dunton's early newspaper *The Athenian Mercury*, evokes the addictive quality of novelty: 'We are all tainted with the *Athenian Itch* | News, and new Things do the whole World bewitch.'[10]

Opposed to 'Athenian itch', or curiosity, were boredom and indifference. Novelty was portrayed as a mental stimulant, able to arouse wonder and banish the dulling effects of repetition. But an imbalance

---

[5]　On the interrelationship of these developments, see Hunter 1990.

[6]　See Phillips 1984: 138.

[7]　See respectively Cave 1985: xi and Greene 1982: 171.

[8]　See Phillips 1984: xi, 1 n. 1. For a recent overview of evolving English attitudes towards originality, see Macfarlane 2007: ch. 2.

[9]　See Phillips 1984: 146 and Hunter 1990: 167–71.

[10]　Wilde cited in Hunter 1990: 15. On the 'anti-classical spirit' of early periodicals, see Phillips 1984: ch. 5.

between excitement and repose was considered dangerous. Observing the overheated social environment of the Georgian elite, some feared that society was 'running mad after innovation'.[11] Concern for the effects of modern life upon bodily economy was elaborated in medical works such as George Cheyne's *The English Malady* (1733), largely devoted to hysteria and hypochondria. The English were particularly susceptible to such maladies, Cheyne famously argued, owing to the country's unpredictable and damp climate and to the nervous strain occasioned by the nation's prosperity. The belief that the English people were prone to erratic behaviour, indeed were a 'nation of humorists', in Oliver Goldsmith's phrase, recurred in subsequent depictions of English eccentricity. Discussions of 'humour' often evoked the term's original medical meaning, namely an imbalance of bodily humours leading to temperamental excess.

The adjective and personal noun 'original' began to be commonly used in a psychological context to denote bizarre individuals from the early eighteenth century.[12] Perceptions of psychological abnormality altered significantly between the Restoration and the Regency, as originality began to play an important role in poetics. Psychological disorders previously attributed to demoniacal possession were given secular interpretations, and a fashion for introspection arose in educated circles. Affliction with the English Malady was interpreted by many as a sign of distinction: 'Freed from contamination by the demoniacal and the vulgar', Roy Porter writes, 'the elite could luxuriate in the self and toy with mental and emotional singularities.' This included, prominently, the art of being 'an original'.[13] Greater tolerance towards erratic and eccentric behaviour arose, he suggests, in response to the Europe-wide vogue of sensibility, which stressed the need for empathy towards those suffering from nervous disorders and madness; there was also a gradual relaxation in familial and religious strictures. The theory of demonic possession was not, of course, the only cultural model available for interpreting psychological oddity. The figures of the fool and idiot, depicted in an extensive body of literature and iconography as well as the popular carnival, shaped attitudes towards deviant individuals in medieval and early modern European culture.[14] Cultural representations of melancholia also emphasized voluntary rejection of collective

---

[11] Cited in Porter 1987: 90.
[12] The personal noun is first documented in 1676, according to the *OED*.
[13] Porter 1987: 108; see also Porter 1983.   [14] See McKnight 1993: 35–7.

norms and withdrawal from society, often in relation to the category of misanthropy.[15]

Poetics and psychology were increasingly conflated when theorists proposed that it was impossible to produce original works of art without having an original mind, or indeed without being an 'original genius'. Edward Young's *Conjectures on Original Composition* (1759) crystallized a century-long series of skirmishes about originality outside the literary establishment, and provided a focal point for subsequent debate about genius.[16] Young equated originality with genius and organic growth, and imitation with mere learning and mechanical production. He suggested, significantly, that the underlying source of artistic originality was the variation between minds:

Born *Originals*, how comes it to pass that we die *Copies?* That medling Ape *Imitation*, as soon as we come to years of *Indiscretion* (so let me speak), snatches the Pen, and blots out nature's mark of Separation, cancels her kind intention, destroys all mental Individuality; the letter'd world no longer consists of Singulars, it is a Medly, a Mass; and a hundred books, at bottom, are but One.

(42–3)

The tendency to connect originality of artistic production and 'mental Individuality' was evident in the emergence of a figurative discourse of eccentricity, construed henceforth mainly as a social and psychological attribute.[17]

Eccentricity as a figurative concept

The adjective 'eccentric' was first applied to people considered to be irregular or capricious in 1685, shortly after the personal noun 'original' was coined, though again it remained rare for several decades.[18] Throughout the eighteenth century, there was considerable overlap between the term's new metaphorical meaning and its earlier, literal use in astronomical discourse. Eccentric individuals were portrayed as comets deviating in a blaze of glory from a predetermined orbit

[15] See Lepenies 1992. [16] See Phillips 1984: 95.
[17] Recurrent links were made in subsequent German aesthetic theory between the *Originalgenie/Originalgeist* and the *Originalwerk*; see Mortier 1982: 94–112.
[18] It had been used from 1630 to denote entities. According to the *OED*, 'Eccentricity' was first used in a figurative sense from 1657, to denote an eccentric act, and in the 1780s to denote the habit of deviating from the usual; the personal noun 'an eccentric' dates from 1832.

representing the path of ordinary people. These connotations of wonder and the sublime are evident in a heroic poem of 1743 by Aaron Hill, dedicated to the Duke of Marlborough 'On The Turn of His Genius to Arms':

> Comets! that sweep new Tracks, and fright the Skies!
> Not to be measur'd, *These*, by War's *known* Laws:
> Form'd, for excentric Fame, and learn'd Applause!
> No *Gen'ral System* circumscribes their Ways.
> They move, un-rival'd: and were born, to blaze!
>
>   (27)

The term 'eccentric' was frequently linked to poetic genius, particularly in the debates which followed Young's polemic. In his *History of English Poetry*, for example, Thomas Warton praised the 'brave eccentricities of original genius, and the daring hardiness of native thought'.[19] Adherents of neoclassical values were naturally critical of the conjunction, but by the 1780s the notion of the 'eccentric Genius' was well known. Unlike later visions of the mad genius, neither concept was medicalized, though they soon became the objects of parody.[20] Eccentricity was thus caught up in the shift from a neoclassical model of impersonal imitation to a Romantic model of self-expression and in new currents of Gothic sensibility.

Both the cult of originality and the association between eccentricity and comets influenced German culture in the decades before the French Revolution. The Sturm und Drang movement which emerged in the late 1760s adopted Young's theories of literary and mental originality, and advocated nonconformism in lifestyle and political and religious beliefs.[21] A glut of self-proclaimed original geniuses came to irritate the German reading public, however, and, as in England, they elicited parodies and criticism.[22] By the last decade of the eighteenth century, the notion of the 'exzentrische Bahn' or eccentric path had become popular amongst German writers. The phrase denoted planetary bodies, most commonly comets, with an unpredictable and erratic course, and was

---

[19] Warton 1774–81: II, 46 (though elsewhere used the term critically); see also Duff 1767: 287.

[20] See e.g. Edgeworth 1801: I, 18–19. Congreve distinguished 'affected' from 'sincere' humours, a distinction that became prominent in writers who differentiated feigned from genuine eccentricity; see Levier 1976: 19.

[21] These views shaped the emergence of a German model of Romantic individualism in the late 18th cent.: see Swart 1962*a*: 82–3.

[22] Mortier 1982: 113–24.

used as a metaphor for the uncertainties of human destiny.[23] Though the concept of eccentricity was used in this case primarily in its original, non-figurative sense, its extension to refer to individual lives occurred around the same time that the concept was being popularized in a figurative sense in English.

Psychological oddity was a dominant motif in eighteenth-century fiction by authors such as Henry Fielding, Tobias Smollett, and Laurence Sterne. Though generally portrayed with tolerance and humour, these characteristics at times had rather more disturbing connotations of fraud and insanity.[24] In Sterne's portrait of Uncle Toby in *Tristram Shandy* (1761–7), which became a particularly influential representation of an 'original', the discourses of astronomy, humoral psychology, climate, and inheritance are all suggested by the narrator as possible explanations for the family's oddity:

His humour was of that particular species, which does honour to our atmosphere; and I should have made no scruple of ranking him amongst one of the first-rate productions of it, had not there appear'd too many strong lines in it of a family-likeness, which shewed that he derived the singularity of his temper more from blood, than either wind or water ... And I have, therefore, oft times wondered, that my father, tho' I believe he had his reasons for it, upon his observing some tokens of excentricity in my course when I was a boy,—should never one endeavour to account for them in this way; for all the Shandy family were of an original character throughout;—I mean the males—the females had no character at all,—except, indeed, my great aunt Dinah.   (1983: 53)

Toby's eccentricity consists in his 'hobby-horsical' disposition, namely his obsession with re-enacting the siege of Namur in which he was wounded. In his writings on the English malady, Dr George Cheyne recommended the cultivation of precisely this type of private 'hobby horse' in order to ward off spleen or melancholia.[25]

Sterne's text highlights cultural perplexity concerning the relationship between eccentricity and gender. By questioning whether women are capable of originality, Sterne's narrator evokes Alexander Pope's notorious assertion that women were not capable of having characters at all. (Dinah's originality consists in marrying a coachman and bearing his child.) In eighteenth-century England, female eccentricity typically evoked 'masculine' characteristics such as 'wild' or 'free' demeanour,

---

[23] See Brown 1978.   [24] See e.g. Smollett 1771: 1, 176.
[25] See Levier 1976: 20.

eliciting quite conflicting attitudes.[26] The early decades of this century saw growing interest in female eccentricity, in genres as diverse as the popular magazines which narrated the careers of women who disguised themselves as men, the annals of high society which documented the excesses of female aristocrats, and the fiction and poetry of women authors.[27] A certain number of English women 'established their right to be as eccentric as men, both in theory and practice'.[28]

A moralizing vocabulary nonetheless continued to intervene in relation to the behaviour of middle-class women. The rhetorical nuances of novelistic discourse repeatedly betray ambivalence towards female eccentricity. In a chapter of Maria Edgeworth's *Belinda* (1801) entitled 'Rights of Woman', a male character appears to present female eccentricity in positive terms: 'I thought her a dashing, free-spoken, free-hearted sort of eccentric person, who would make a staunch friend, and a jolly companion.' But he immediately qualifies this comment: 'As a mistress or a wife, no man of any taste could think of her' (II, 170–1). In the writing of Fanny Burney, one of the eighteenth-century novelists who used the term most frequently, eccentricity often has positive connotations for male and female characters,[29] but on other occasions is carefully qualified: 'Yet,—these eccentricities set apart,—how rare are her qualities!'[30] A negative evaluation of female eccentricity became increasingly prominent as codes of female propriety became more rigid in the Victorian period.[31]

In the literature of sensibility, the term 'eccentric' was used in descriptions of character in conjunction with adjectives of energy ('vivacious', 'lively', 'spirited', and 'enthusiastic') which marked out the man or woman of feeling. Though eccentricity threatened to veer too much into the grotesque for the liking of many late eighteenth-century writers, its opposite was 'Dulness' and boredom.[32] Eccentricity answered a growing cultural need for emotional intensity and unusual sensations: it was used to suggest violence and wildness, melancholia, and subsequently the provocative singularities of the dandy.[33] Lord Byron, for example,

---

[26] On the gender of English eccentricity around this time, see Carroll 2006: 41-7.

[27] e.g. Mary Robinson writes, in a poetic self-portrait: 'I'm odd, eccentric, fond of ease, | Impatient, difficult' (1806: III, 303).

[28] Langford 2000: 207.   [29] e.g. Burney 1782: v, 47 and 1796: III, 389.

[30] Burney 1814: I, 376–7; see also V, 394.

[31] For further examples of semantic ambivalence, see Hays 1796: I, 8, 169, and II, 81–2.

[32] More 1777: 204–5.

[33] e.g. in Maturin's *Melmoth the Wanderer*, eccentricity is associated with 'violence', 'wildness', 'pride', and 'unsearchability' of character (1820: I, 321; III, 280, 322, 330).

was considered eccentric by both his English and his French contemporaries.[34] After the 1789 Revolution, these meanings merged with
discourses of English Romanticism and the 'modern' age.[35]

The astronomical connotations of eccentricity faded around the end
of the eighteenth century, but the term retained its connotations of
celebrity and wonder. The term was democratized for a mass audience in
England in the period 1790 to 1830. A proliferation of cheap magazines
for lower middle-class audiences foregrounded the term 'eccentric' in
their titles or subtitles (examples include *Kirby's Wonderful and Eccentric
Magazine*, the *Eccentric Magazine*, and the *Eccentric Mirror*).[36] These
compendia, which both vulgarized the discourse of natural history and
mimicked the popular freak show, were filled with prodigious human
and animal specimens. Lurid adjectives of the type found in Gothic novels and popular romances were common ('dreadful', 'awful', 'mysterious', 'prodigious'). Biographical sketches of peculiar or grotesque individuals were particularly popular: the *Eccentric Magazine* claims it was
founded in order to satisfy the 'great scarcity, and consequent high price
of Portraits and Lives of Remarkable Characters'.[37] In a more elevated
context, periodicals began to portray odd characters in the context of
hunting and collecting,[38] as though to mimic both gentlemanly pursuits
and the figure of the amateur natural historian.

The growth of interest in eccentricity in England in the aftermath of
the French Revolution had complex ideological functions. It occurred
around the time that eccentricity came to be seen as a key sign of
Englishness. As the historian Paul Langford has shown, a diffuse body
of often unrepresentative anecdote and myths shaped foreign perceptions of Englishness as much as direct encounters with English people.
English national identity was contradictory: though its inhabitants were
granted an unusual degree of political liberty, for example, England
was also home to conformist institutions such as the gentleman's club.
Eccentricity focused attention on the paradoxes inherent in the status
of individualism as a collective social construct, evident in the view that
English national identity consisted in the fact that its inhabitants had,

---

[34] Hazlitt writes, of Byron, that in 'slovenliness, abruptness, and eccentricity . . . Lord
Byron . . . surpasses all his contemporaries' (1825: 163); compare 'Lord Byron . . . forced
upon the men of his age a style that was utterly *distinctive*, or *eccentric*, as the English say'
(Delécluze 1832: 77, emphasis in original). Both comments contradict Langford's view
that Byron could not be an eccentric since 'he was too dangerous' (2000: 306).
[35] See e.g. Hazlitt 1825: 284.
[36] Cowlishaw terms them 'freak books' (1998: 165); see also Carroll 2006: 34–8.
[37] Lemoine and Cauldfield 1812: I, p. v.   [38] See Levier 1976: 11.

precisely, nothing in common.[39] The rise of eccentricity, Langford proposes, represented a 'rear guard action' by the English original. The new
category of eccentrics defused the dangers of nonconformism always
inherent in originality, he argues, by persuading people that eccentricity, unlike originality, was ultimately inoffensive and 'servicable'.
Eccentricity, in short, constituted a type of 'safety valve' for expressions
of deviance.[40] Furthermore, Langford notes that 'Originals' were not
sharply defined by class, whilst in late eighteenth and early nineteenth-
century journalism eccentricity was frequently linked to the gentry and
nobility (though 'Eccentric magazines' continued to portray lowly social
types under this heading).[41] Portraits and anecdotes about eccentric
members of the upper classes, whether in newspapers or novels, were
often implicated in a nostalgic vision of the pre-Revolutionary period, in
which the wealthy individual exercised his right to a benign, if somewhat
emasculated form of despotism over his own possessions, home, and
person.[42]

Whilst Langford's demystifying analysis of 'anodyne' and 'amiable'
representations of eccentrics is persuasive, matters were at times more
ambiguous, since various conflicting models of eccentricity coexisted in
England during the same historical period. The anodyne eccentric was
certainly a widely circulated type, but in elite literary culture eccentricity
could have dangerous and strongly sexualized connotations (including
genius, energy, wildness, and the sublime) quite inimical to the harmless
figures that populated novels and newspapers. Moreover, it is difficult to
generalize about responses to behaviour deemed eccentric in everyday
life on the basis of cultural representations produced and consumed
at a carefully mediated distance.[43] By the late 1820s there was a new
willingness to see eccentricity as a harbinger of full insanity, particularly
in cases of contested inheritance, whilst the personal noun 'an eccentric',
introduced in the early 1830s, made eccentricity a more rigid category
and defined the entire person in terms of a single trait. Victorian

---

[39] According to Langford, eccentricity represents absolute idiosyncratic difference,
opposed to any dogmatic 'code' (2000: 305). Yet as his own analysis shows, eccentricity
related to a limited number of heavily codified stock types, e.g. the miser and the hermit.
See Sangsue's similar analysis of the paradoxes of idiosyncrasy (1988).
[40] Langford 2000: 309, 300, 303 respectively. The 'safety valve' argument is evidently
similar to Bakhtin's account of the carnivalesque (see the Introduction).
[41] Langford argues that all classes could be originals (2000: 285); Levier agrees that
eccentrics were rarely lower class than the gentry (1976: 21–2).
[42] Eccentrics' asexuality was emphasized by Edith Sitwell; see Langford 2000: 3007.
[43] See Levier 1976: 18–19.

attitudes grew steadily more ambivalent in the context of increasingly rigid social norms.[44]

Distrust of originality in pre-Revolutionary French culture

In Georgian England, the concepts of originality and eccentricity were explored in a range of conflicting cultural representations. The trajectory of originality in France was very different, owing in part to significant differences in the nation's political, religious, and economic organization. Other factors that impeded the development of interest in eccentricity were rooted in French cultural institutions, particularly the Académie Française and the absolutist court.

Before 1800 there were no truly figurative uses of the words *excentrique* or *excentricité* in French, and considerably less significance was attached to originality as an aesthetic and social category. Why was this so? French Renaissance writers had, like their English and Italian contemporaries, experimented with 'digesting' and rearranging classical sources so as to avoid slavish imitation.[45] Furthermore, during much of the seventeenth century, the values of neoclassicism appeared as firmly entrenched in Augustan poetics in England as they were in French culture. The subsequent divergence of attitudes towards originality in English and French culture was largely due to the latter's institutionalization of neoclassicism. Neoclassical precepts were promulgated by the influential poetic theorist Nicolas Boileau, known for discouraging innovation and stressing the unsurpassable perfection of the ancients,[46] and by the powerful Académie Française, established in 1635 by Cardinal Richelieu. Literature and the state became inextricably linked, and the Académie promoted a poetics of imitation for many centuries.[47]

The history of the Académie was, nonetheless, punctuated by repeated polemics in which tradition and innovation were publicly

---

[44] e.g. in *Tomkins v Brown*, reported in *The Times* on 6 March 1830, the judge concluded that the deceased's being 'eccentric from an early period' constituted a 'probable indication of future unsoundness' (4). His will was declared invalid on the grounds of insanity.

[45] See Cave 1985.

[46] These precepts were followed by English Augustan writers, hence English proponents of originality couched their criticisms of 'imitation' as a nationalistic critique of French influence (see Phillips 1984: 3–4).

[47] On the Académie's conservatism, see Merlin-Kajmann 2001: 16.

opposed. The most significant of these was the 'Querelle des anciens et des modernes' (Quarrel of the Ancients and the Moderns) (1687), in which Charles Perrault publicly asserted that the seventeenth century was in some respects superior to the ancient world. The Querelle marked the crystallization of a debate about tradition dating back over two decades. Both the rise of the novel and of the first French newspaper, *Le Mercure gallant*, established new 'interpretive communities' in which literature was opened up to individual as well as institutional judgement; they were implicitly anti-classical and present-centred in ethos, like their English counterparts. Although the Moderns won over public opinion to their cause, however, they failed to assume power in the Académie, which perpetuated the values of the Ancients as well as seeking to standardize linguistic usage.[48]

French suspicion of departure from classical norms in seventeenth-century poetic theory was inseparable from the prohibition on unconventional behaviour in the court and the salon, and the cultivation of an ideal of exquisite civility. Key terms—*honnêteté, bon goût, bienséance, bel esprit* (honourableness, good taste, decorum, wit)—hinted at the inextricable fusion of aesthetic and ethical values.[49] Dislike of self-assertion in a social context was also influenced by the marginalization of individual judgement in elite French culture, which was hostile towards Protestantism.[50] Social observers were alert for the slightest signs of individual self-interest; considered an anti-social blunder, or even evidence of sin, it provided endless opportunities for ridicule. Figures with peculiar obsessions were mocked in the drama of Molière and in La Bruyère's *Caractères*, portraits from courtly life modelled upon those of the Greek writer Theophrastus. The title of La Bruyère's work gestures towards the earlier meaning of the term 'caractère', namely the stock type. Its modern meaning was only beginning to be used in France around this time, just as the personal noun *un original* and related adjective 'un homme original' emerged.[51] In general, however, the personal noun 'un original' continued to be used by writers such as La Rochefoucauld to denote an exemplary (often classical) figure whose conduct should be imitated—a sense evidently opposed to its

---

[48] See DeJean 1997: 73.
[49] Moriarty stresses the interpenetration of literary *bienséances* and social norms (1988: 7).
[50] See Krailsheimer 1962 and Swart 1962*b*: 10.
[51] The first reference to the 'original' occurs in a section of Tallemant des Réaux's *Historiettes* (1657) entitled 'Extravagants, Visionnaires, Fantastiques, Bizarres' (1834: 324).

modern sense of 'unique' and 'inimitable'.[52] When the personal noun *was* used in its new sense, it was overwhelmingly negative in connotation. Attitudes softened slightly where the adjective was concerned: to have 'original' traits could be positive, particularly in connection with producing original works of art or ideas, but the phrase 'Quel original!' ('What an original!') was uttered disapprovingly in eighteenth-century France.[53] This tendency was still marked in 1844, according to Théophile Gautier: 'Only in France is the term *original* almost insulting when applied to an individual' (1853: 351).

Though originality remained suspect in French poetics throughout the eighteenth century in the writing of neoclassical critics, interest in innovation entered the cultural imagination in other, more covert ways. The period between 1730 and 1789 was marked by the opening up of French aesthetics to foreign influences, evident in a prolonged first wave of Anglomania. English freedom was contrasted positively with French order and restraint across an array of cultural practices, including politics, religion, fashion, and pedagogy. Nonetheless, French writers unwittingly revealed the persistence of different cultural attitudes to originality in their translations of English writing. Discourse on individual difference tended to be 'socialized' in French translations, blunting its transgressive edge.[54]

Two eighteenth-century writers particularly influenced a marked revaluation of originality in French culture. Denis Diderot, who coined the phrase 'originalité de caractère' in a letter of 1762,[55] was preoccupied throughout his career by the relationship between order and disorder. He associated the latter with madness, genius, and monstrosity— concepts subsequently attached to eccentricity. His novel *Jacques le fataliste*, written in 1773 and inspired in several respects by Sterne's *Tristram Shandy*, foregrounds the bizarreness of human nature through its depiction of two obsessive duellists who pursue each other throughout the narrative and who sink into melancholy when deprived of the opportunity to fight. Their 'hobby horse' constitutes an antidote to spleen, just like the siege reconstructions of Sterne's Uncle Toby. Both texts are, moreover, positioned within a tradition of self-conscious

---

[52] See e.g. 'Des Exemples' in La Rochefoucauld's *Maximes*.
[53] See Mortier 1982: 34 and Henningsen, cited in Langford 2000: 285.
[54] On this tendency see Grieder 1985: 116, Mortier 1982: 93, and Langford 2000: 293.
[55] Diderot 1938: I, 265 (La Bruyère had previously coined the phrase 'auteur original').

narration which may be traced back to Cervantes's *Don Quixote*, which creates strong parallels between peculiarities of character and oddities of narrative form.[56]

Diderot's philosophical dialogue, *Le Neveu de Rameau* (Rameau's Nephew) (1762–72) proved even bolder in its representation of psychological and social originality. Both the positive and the negative faces of disorder are incarnated in Rameau, a complex figure in the tradition of Menippean satire who hovers between genius and madness, wisdom and foolishness. Rameau is a socially marginal entertainer who lives in the shadow of his uncle, the famous composer, and earns his living from his ability to entertain the wealthy with his ephemeral musical and dramatic performances. The text probes, with evident fascination, the mixed emotions of the narrator, a *philosophe*, faced with this 'bizarre character'.[57] He views Rameau with both distaste and admiration, declaring: 'I do not respect these originals.' Rameau, in contrast, perceives his own originality as a value he can force his social superior to recognize: 'I wanted . . . to compel you to admit that I was at least original in my degradation.'[58] Originality is acceptable in artistic works, the comment implies, but being 'an' original is not, echoing the different nuances of the adjective and the personal noun in French usage. But Rameau represents precisely the impossibility of separating original artistic production and originality of character, since his art is centred upon his idiosyncratic performances. The *philosophe* further proposes that madness provides necessary respite from monotony, and that Rameau acts as a corrective against excessive conformity (1972: 33). In the *philosophe*'s ambivalent response, a socially acceptable judgement which rejects the unconventional is counteracted by a seemingly inexplicable and only partially acknowledged yearning for it. Such ambivalence would become *the* dominant model for French responses to eccentricity in the nineteenth century.

Jean-Jacques Rousseau also fostered more positive attitudes towards originality. His autobiographical writing famously emphasizes his own idiosyncrasies in a discursive tradition influenced by Montaigne. In his *Confessions*, Rousseau proclaims that nature has shattered the mould within which it fashioned him (1997: 33), a striking image of absolute originality, though his deliberate estrangement from the world

---

[56] Sangsue 1987 links 'eccentric' form and content.
[57] Curran's discussion of Rameau as an eccentric and monster is suggestive, if anachronistic (2001: 142–5).
[58] Diderot 1972: 32, 33, 99.

participated in a well-established tradition of misanthropy and melancholy. By relentlessly stressing his own singularity, Rousseau sought to redeem his failure to achieve the success that he desired. His repeated suggestion that genius and social marginality were naturally linked did not, however, convince many of his contemporaries, for the majority of eighteenth-century French writers identified success with the wealth and recognition enjoyed by many *philosophes* towards the end of their lives.[59] Both Rameau and Rousseau highlighted the double-edged nature of 'singularity', close to genius but also to the underworld of struggling artists and men of letters later known as Bohemia.

The 'Frenchifying' of eccentricity

The 1789 Revolution inaugurated a new period of political and social influence for the French bourgeoisie, as well as growing cultural interest in innovation and progress. Many French thinkers of the post-Revolutionary period were nonetheless hostile to the notion of untrammelled individual freedom. Given the strong existing association between eccentricity, novelty, and individualism in English culture, emergent French attitudes towards eccentricity were inevitably caught up in these tensions.

Between 1789 and 1871 the French population witnessed an unprecedented succession of political regimes, creating anxiety about social instability and a corresponding desire for order. Napoleon's programme of centralization and homogenization was designed to create ideological cohesion.[60] Similar impulses were evident across French social, political, philosophical, and psychological thought.[61] Intellectual historians have long noted that attitudes towards individualism, a term first coined in France in 1820, were markedly more hostile in mid and late nineteenth-century France than in contemporaneous England, Germany, or America.[62] The semantic field of nineteenth-century individualism included the potentially incompatible notions of egalitarian individualism, laissez-faire economics, and aristocratic and Romantic individualism (the last two being at times labelled 'individuality' to

---

[59] See Goulemot and Oster's analysis of the 'Bohème des lumières' (1992: 85–98).

[60] This was evident on the level of taste formation, as Auslander notes (1996: 25).

[61] As Goldstein 2005 argues, for example, Victor Cousin sought to create a new foundation for social order by popularizing a model of orderly and conformist male bourgeois selfhood.

[62] See Swart 1962*a*: 78–85 and Lukes 1971: 48–54.

differentiate them from the others).[63] In France, attitudes towards these distinct forms of individualism varied significantly, with notable consequences for the reception of eccentricity.

Egalitarian and economic individualism remained highly negative in connotation throughout most of the century across the French political spectrum, from theocrats to socialists, liberals, and early feminists. The term 'individualisme' evoked such negative concepts as self-interest, indifference to others, atomization, egotism, and anarchy, and was typically opposed to the ideal of collective stability and order. Female individualism was portrayed even more negatively, since the model of selfhood implicit in nineteenth-century philosophical, legal, medical, political, and psychological discourse was gendered as masculine.[64] Sentimental narrative, the most widely read literary form of the post-Revolutionary period, popularized for mass audiences the conflict between the desire for individual freedom and the obligation to promote collective welfare. This 'liberal bind', for which there was no clear solution, generated dramatic intensity in novels which generally had a tragic denouement.[65]

In contrast, the theories of Romantic individuality that were first elaborated in late eighteenth-century Germany celebrated idiosyncrasy and uniqueness, creating a cultural climate favourable to positive representations of eccentricity. The influence of Romanticism was initially slower in France than in other nations because the Restoration, with its association of throne and altar and its desire to reinstate the *ancien régime*, sought to dampen the cultural experiments more widely seen in Germany and England (often self-consciously framed in opposition to French Enlightenment values).[66] The French literary establishment insisted on retaining neoclassical dramatic conventions such as unity of time and place during the Restoration, just as the aristocracy attempted to reinstate a defunct model of sociability widely felt to be oppressive and artificial in a post-Revolutionary climate. Both types of hostility to innovation were challenged by the second wave of French Romanticism during the 1820s, which culminated in the 'bataille d'Hernani' of 1830. This time, those who comprised the modern faction were the symbolic

---

[63] See Swart 1962*a*: 84.
[64] For an overview, see Fraisse and Perrot 1992. On feminist hostility to female individualism see e.g. Moses and Rabine 1993: 9 and Mills 1991: 30.
[65] See Cohen 1999: ch. 1.
[66] French Romanticism certainly cannot be straightforwardly identified with liberal values, however, given the extreme conservatism of certain French Romantic thinkers.

victors. Interest in individual difference grew across a wide range of cultural discourses and practices in the early decades of the nineteenth century,[67] as bourgeois conformism became the object of increasing scrutiny and satire in the mass press.[68]

The decades following the 1789 Revolution witnessed the first incursions of the terms 'excentricité' and 'excentrique' into the French language, though they were rarely used before 1830.[69] Eccentricity was defined in terms of having a 'caractère original', and of thinking and acting in opposition to received ideas.[70] The noun 'excentricité' was first used in 1817 in a text by Germaine de Staël, who stressed its link to originality: 'There is no nation in which one finds as many examples as in England of what is termed *eccentricity* [ce qu'on appelle l'*excentricité*], that is to say a completely original way of being which takes no account of the opinion of others.' She nonetheless nuanced this statement by noting the English population's subservience to fashion and fear of ridicule, and concluded that the nation was characterized by 'a bizarre mixture of shyness and independence' (1862: II, 371). The antonyms of eccentricity were terms such as 'regular', 'balanced', 'normal', and 'common'; one nineteenth-century writer suggested 'reason', 'custom', and 'positivism'.[71] French usage prior to 1830 was generally in the context of discourse on England, often with anglicized orthography.[72] Connotations of Englishness proved most persistent in relation to the personal noun 'un excentrique': Larousse's *Grand dictionnaire universel* still claimed in 1874 that 'we call an *original* the man whom the English more rightly call an *eccentric*', though it conceded that the terms were effectively interchangeable.[73] In practice, many French

---

[67] Including, prominently, Romantic theories of the poet-prophet; the legend of Napoleon; the rise of the individualistic Bildungsroman; and the growing individualization of everyday life and social practices (on the last of these, see Corbin 1987*c*).

[68] On anti-bourgeois sentiment, see Maza 2003.

[69] In 1877 the Supplement to Émile Littré's *Dictionnaire* reversed its previous judgement that the term was a neologism and an Anglicism, on the nationalistic pretext that the noun 'excentricité' was used in 1736 in a figurative sense by a *French* writer ('excentricité des opinions'; Littré 1877: 149). 'Excentrique' was listed in a figurative sense in the eighth edition of Boiste's dictionary in 1834; see Leduc-Adine 1984: 151–3. Two early instances of *partially* figurative use have been cited: Rabelais writes in his *Tiers livre* of the 'fol lunaticque, fol erraticque, fol eccentrique', and there is an isolated example in Cotgrave's 1611 dictionary; see Eichel-Lojkine 2002: 23.

[70] The earliest fully figurative use of the adjective 'excentrique' occurred in 1803; see Mackenzie 1939: I, 196, 201.

[71] See respectively Littré 1885: 1552–3 and Champfleury 1877: 8.

[72] See e.g. Pichot cited in TLF8: 394.

[73] GD11: 1469; see also GD7: 1177–8.

writers used even the personal noun without reference to England, whilst the adjective lost its English connotations from the early 1840s.[74]

The pre-figurative connotations of comets were fairly infrequent in nineteenth-century French usage, but the geometrical meaning of the term was signalled by one early commentator:

> We speak of two *eccentric* circles; thus, if you compare a man to a *circle*, with the aim, so we are told, of giving to understand that he is *original* and *bizarre*, you cannot hold him to be *eccentric* unless he has an accomplice who agrees to perform the role of the other circle; for a *circle* cannot be eccentric all on its own. Once the two human circles have been found, and the problem is considered solved, well then, be so kind as to explain to us how these two men, with the best will in the world, can set about being *eccentrics*, and how we may recognize that they have succeeded in becoming so.
>
> (Wey 1845: i, 95–6, emphasis in original)

The relativity of perspective inherent in the term was not widely remarked upon, however, for the simple reason that the 'centre' generally appeared self-evident. Like normality, virtue, and common sense, it was invariably identified with a bourgeois perspective.

The term gained currency during a period of cultural ferment in which Englishness was the object of both loathing and admiration. During the 1810s, and particular after Waterloo, French public opinion was hostile towards the English. The decade saw savage caricatures of the English by Louis-Philibert Debucourt, the production of satirical plays such as Nicolas Brazier's *Les Originaux au café* (The Originals in the Café) (1818), peopled by three ludicrous English 'Milords', and the circulation of unflattering anecdotes about the English 'singularities' and 'originalities'.[75] From the early 1820s, French attitudes towards the English became markedly more favourable, culminating in a second wave of Anglomania.[76] The mass imitation and importation of English material culture into France coincided with a new appetite for the writing of Walter Scott, Byron, and Shakespeare, and the growth of cross-cultural contacts between travellers and diplomats. In the French imagination, England evoked the uninterrupted rule of the aristocracy. 'Silver fork' novels such as Lister's *Granby*, Disraeli's *Vivian Grey*, and

---

[74] On the history of the terms, see also Matoré 1951: 318, Sarcey 1860: 118–32, Ritter 1905: XXXVI, 418, Pavot 1897, and TLF8: 394–6.

[75] e.g. the anonymous *John Bull, ou Londoniana, recueil d'originalités et de singularités anglaises* (John Bull, or Londoniana, A Collection of English Originalities and Singularities), printed around 1820 in Paris.

[76] See Prevost 1957: 46, Stanton 1980: 32, and Elkington 1929.

Bulwer Lytton's *Pelham* were rapidly translated into French in the late 1820s, as elite English practices such as dandyism, gentlemen's clubs, horse breeding, and pigeon shooting became fashionable in the Parisian aristocracy.

In addition to this new vision of singularity as a mark of aristocratic distinction, the older, medicalized vision of English humour remained, reinforced by articles about strange English expatriates in the Parisian press. The 'English malady' was portrayed in plays such as *L'Ennui* and *Le Spleen*, both performed in 1820.[77] The English individual's love of eccentricity, it was alleged, was evidence of his or her vain desire to stand out and be noticed.[78] To many French writers, originality appeared close to madness, and visitors from other countries echoed the view that English culture represented a carnivalesque inversion of sanity.[79] Such comments highlight a persistent set of associations in the Continental imagination. As late as the 1860s, it was a commonplace that the English fled to Paris to commit suicide in bizarre ways such as hanging themselves from the Vendôme column (GD14: 1024–5).

The relationship between French stereotypes of English eccentricity and actual cultural practices must, however, be carefully evaluated. In *Le Mot et la chose* (The Word and the Thing) (1860), for example, Francisque Sarcey creates an anachronistic historical fantasy to illustrate different cultural attitudes towards eccentricity. His text portrays an Englishman who arrives in France in 1710 and is astonished by the conformist nature of courtly society. Sarcey represents the English attitude to eccentricity as a symbol of their humourless pursuit of utility and profit (a view shared by many French social theorists hostile to economic individualism): 'Is Eccentricity [l'*Excentricity*] what we call ridicule, then?—Yes, ridicule, but without the laughter' (1860: 130). Sarcey evidently reveals less about actual English or French attitudes to eccentricity than about the French need to assert a distinctive national identity, premised on the rejection of English mercantilism and belief in the superiority of French models of sociability.

The cultural functions of eccentricity in the aftermath of the 1789 Revolution were therefore complex. Post-Revolutionary political turmoil significantly undermined faith in the naturalness of custom: amongst political theorists of quite divergent ideological perspectives,

---

[77] See Elkington 1929: 163–5.   [78] See e.g. Walter Scott 1823: I, pp. vii–viii.
[79] See Verneur 1814: I, p. v and Langford 2000: 289.

the Revolution and subsequent decades of instability represented the
sweeping away of communal values—the *mœurs* or ethos of society—
leaving a potential vacuum and the threat of chaotic disorder.[80] Anxiety
about eccentricity was perhaps driven by the desire to repress the knowledge that collective beliefs were ultimately fragile and arbitrary, a view
supported by the emphasis on conformism in emergent psychological
theories of selfhood.[81] Indeed, eccentric behaviour was seen by some
as an illustration of the destructive anarchy and disregard for tradition found in revolutionaries. In 1845 the Catholic monarchist Barbey
d'Aurevilly described eccentricity as 'an individual revolution against
the established order, at times against nature' (JB2: 675), a conflation
of the social and natural orders typical of a tendency amongst English
conservatives to portray the French Revolution as an 'unnatural' and
'eccentric' aberration.[82]

   At the same time, both the Revolution and the subsequent collapse of
the Restoration allowed certain forms of originality and individual difference to be reappraised, particularly in the aesthetic field. This development was far from linear. The legacy of neoclassicism and *politesse*
continued to be felt in France, and, as Sarcey's comments demonstrate,
these values were harnessed to new nationalist ends; Romanticism was
criticized by influential French social thinkers for its 'egotistical' individualism;[83] and the experiments of Romantic dramatists were soon
displaced by the conformism of the *comédie-vaudeville* and thereafter
by sententious Second Empire drama.[84] Underpinning these divergent
tendencies was a fundamental conflict at the heart of bourgeois identity:
a desire to abolish restrictions on individual freedom and personal
development, and an opposing and incompatible desire to impose new
limits in order to prevent social fragmentation. In an era in which 'social
margins and frontiers' were being continually 'probed and tested' by
the bourgeoisie, eccentricity allowed this group to explore the tensions
which arose between freedom and conformism, the individual and the
collectivity.[85]

This chapter has questioned why originality and individual difference
were viewed more negatively in eighteenth-century France than in

---

[80] See Kelly 1992: 45–9.   [81] See Goldstein 2005: 180.
[82] e.g. Edmund Burke associated both monstrosity and eccentricity with the 'Republic of Regicide' in *The Times*, 20 Oct. 1796, 2.
[83] Swart 1962*a*: 83–4.
[84] On the conservative ethos of the vaudeville, see Hemmings 1987: 272–5.
[85] Seigel 1999: 10–11.

Georgian England, the culture in which the term 'eccentric' began to be popularized in its modern figurative sense. There was undoubtedly greater rhetorical tolerance of unconventional behaviour in English society throughout the pre-Revolutionary period, a phenomenon influenced by the relatively rapid demise of neoclassicism, growing interest in individual liberty and judgement, new medical and social understandings of oddity, and evolving perceptions of national identity. Nonetheless, certain forms of eccentricity were censured in England, and it was by no means always portrayed as harmless and anodyne. In contrast, eighteenth-century French attitudes towards originality were shaped by the institutional dominance of neoclassicism, courtly codes of *honnêteté* and *politesse*, and suspicion of individual judgement. A negative semantic charge continued to be associated with originality and eccentricity in France throughout much of the nineteenth century, owing partly to anxiety about social disorder in the post-Revolutionary period. The next chapter examines an ideological conflict which arose in France after 1830: adherents of traditional models of etiquette repudiated eccentricity as an assault on custom, whilst proponents of fashion promoted eccentricity as a symbol of modernity, in debates which reveal growing interest in the power of the public gaze to regulate subjectivity.

PART II

FASHIONABLE SOCIETY

2

Etiquette and the Public Gaze

> The eyes of others are responsible for the majority of cases we see
> in which people are ruined and suffer disastrous loss of fortune.
>
> Privat d'Anglemont[1]

In Parisian bourgeois society, eccentricity of appearance or behaviour
was synonymous with the phrase *se faire remarquer* ('standing out',
'being noticed', 'drawing attention to oneself'). It therefore raised
central questions about the relationship of the individual to public
opinion and the public gaze, which functioned as a form of social
control. Since eccentricity was often identified with individual self-
assertion, it attracted censure in a culture in which emphasis on the
self occasioned suspicion in everyday life and was vigorously attacked
in social and political thought. Drawing attention to oneself in the
context of polite sociability was seen by the Parisian bourgeoisie as a
disgraceful impropriety, and often as evidence of underlying vulgarity,
vanity, and even pathology. Social acceptance required self-discipline
and adherence to collective norms of the type increasingly formalized
in etiquette manuals. Eccentricity was particularly discouraged in social
climbers, who were uncertain of how to behave, and in women, since
it threatened to undermine a central pillar of bourgeois gender ideology, namely the view that women were incapable of innovation and
individuation.

Yet a new current of thought suggested that a degree of eccentricity
could be supremely stylish. Eccentricity symbolized the constant
mutation of new fashions, and by extension the logic of modernity
itself.[2] There was therefore a fundamental tension in responses to eccentricity. The violation of collective norms could result in either ostracism
or praise, depending on whether it was interpreted as an embarrassing

---

[1] 1861: 168–9.
[2] On the identification of modernity with fashion and its consequent feminization
see Felski 1995: 60–3.

social lapse or the self-conscious inauguration of a new style. This tension revealed a wider contradiction between the values of etiquette and those of fashion. Etiquette represented tradition and stability, necessitating the effacement of the self in the interests of social cohesion. Fashion, in contrast, represented the cult of novelty and the aesthetics of the bizarre that characterized advertising and emergent commodity culture. The concept of eccentricity was thus implicated in the transition towards greater social mobility which intensified from the July Monarchy, and was associated with a wide range of responses, from humiliation to narcissistic gratification.

Eccentricity in the theatre of good manners

A growing body of commentators guided Parisian readers of the July Monarchy through the intricate new rules of social life in the capital. These included *élégantologistes* and *modilogues*, Balzac's comic neologisms for those who dispensed advice on etiquette, fashion, beauty, and comportment;[3] journalists and men of letters, who documented the changing appearance and inhabitants of the city in 'codes', 'physiologies', and guide-books; and cultural commentators who discussed new cultural and artistic tendencies in journals and newspapers. This amorphous body of texts embodied the communal *mœurs* to which individualism was typically opposed by French social and political thinkers. Indicative of a new market-driven literary sphere aimed at a mass readership, it constituted a vast repository of the *idées reçues* of the bourgeoisie and an emblem of the social conformism of this class. Indeed, a quite literal tendency to take refuge in the safety of imitation is evident in the enormous prevalence of plagiarism, repetition, and discursive circulation within the literature of Parisian worldliness.[4]

The conduct manual became a particularly popular form of writing from the early decades of the nineteenth century, in response to the growth of unprecedented social mobility. It was designed to help aspirant bourgeois readers, uncertain of how to behave in polite company,

[3] HB12: 235, 250. Balzac extended physiognomic codes to include dress and bearing as signifying systems; see Rivers 1993: 145–6.
[4] My phrase 'the literature of Parisian worldliness' adapts and extends the title of Brooks 1969 to include non-literary material.

to master the codes governing social advancement.[5] The ideology of the genre remained remarkably homogeneous in the course of the century until the decline of the aristocracy: it advocated conformism and was intensely hostile to individual difference, a stance exemplified by its monotonous criticisms of eccentricity. Like the novel of education, however, conduct manuals were written from the premise that individuals had the power to shape their own destiny, rather than being trapped in immutable social hierarchies. The overtly conservative ethos of the etiquette manual was therefore in tension with its pragmatic function: the genre advocated the effacement of the individual self, but in the service of individual advancement.

In polite society, eccentricity was perceived as a theatrical phenomenon, since it involved becoming a spectacle for others. The interpretation of social life as a series of performances was pervasive in nineteenth-century French culture.[6] The theatre was central to Parisian social life and the cultural imaginary: both the genre of the Parisian physiology and Honoré de Balzac's 'human comedy', for instance, were premised on the concept of Paris as a stage or *theatrum mundi* upon which stock characters reappeared.[7] Assumptions about good manners were often framed in theatrical language, with eccentricity viewed as an unpredictable departure from the scripting of social life. It invariably provoked ridicule, a powerful form of social control. The 'ritualization of daily life' which played a central role in the construction of bourgeois identity was facilitated by etiquette and conduct manuals. These provided a script for each social occasion and promised to 'shield' the bourgeoisie from social blunders.[8] Commentators repeatedly exhorted their readers to avoid eccentricity: 'I recommend that you avoid any type of eccentricity or singularity whatsoever', counsels one, concluding with a warning: 'If you draw attention to yourself in a ridiculous fashion, you will never recover from it.'[9] Eccentricity was the object of distrust due to its many negative connotations, particularly vulgar ostentation, pathology, sinful pride, and female immodesty.

Avoiding eccentricity was particularly important for those seeking to progress through the social hierarchy. It was difficult for newcomers to

---

[5] They have received little analysis hitherto (the conclusion of Lacroix 1990 and Mainardi 2003: 69), and almost no specifically rhetorical analysis; see Montandon 1994 for an overview of the genre.

[6] This constitutes one of the ways in which this body of discourse constitutes a prehistory of concerns later taken up in social theory.

[7] See Sennett 1986: 34–5.   [8] Le Wita 1994: 142.

[9] Mortemart-Boisse 1858: 242.

judge the degree of individuality permissible in a given context, and they were liable to fail in a spectacularly public manner. Advice to those unfamiliar with the conventions of polite society remained essentially the same over many decades: 'A man of good sense will never stand out because of the eccentricity of his dress'; 'Your hat is not original. Your trousers are not eccentric . . . For you seek above all not to stand out'; 'Young people . . . must avoid eccentric fashions'; 'street attire must always be decent, never eccentric'.[10]

Hostility to eccentricity therefore served to defend an ideal of social distinction. In post-Revolutionary France, the aristocracy rejected the *ancien régime* ethos of ostentatious excess and appropriated instead the middle-class ethos of virtuous austerity. To ward off imitation by social inferiors, sartorial refinement was defined in terms of ascetic, almost invisible luxury,[11] and manners had to be effortless to distinguish them from those painstakingly acquired by the *parvenu* and *arriviste*.[12] When the author of one manual writes that 'the prerequisite of *savoir-vivre* is self-forgetfulness', he implies that not being conscious of one's body constitutes true breeding.[13] Social alienation and shyness were typical afflictions of the *parvenu*, for whom it was too late to naturalize the good manners which the aristocracy had internalized in childhood. The injunction to be natural was, however, self-defeating, for it merely exacerbated existing self-consciousness. Both male and female *parvenus* tended to overload their bodies with sartorial signifiers to compensate for their social anxiety; their extravagant attire and clumsy attempts to conform generally provoked ridicule.[14] *Parvenus* feared the public gaze, knowing that the body provided treacherous clues of social origins ('in a phrase, in a word, the sound of one's voice, a movement, a momentary lapse in one's appearance, everywhere').[15] Conduct manuals suggested that eccentricity provided one such clue by means of which interlopers could be identified and symbolically excluded.

Second, the term 'excentrique' was ambiguous, for it could denote both voluntary departure from custom and borderline madness. Etiquette manuals criticized the category of 'originals', held to suffer from ill-tempered spleen that disqualified them from polite society.[16] Propriety was invariably identified with good health. In his *Guide-manuel*

---

[10] Boitard 1851: 46; Fresne 1858: 37; Anon. 1882: 68; Burani 1879: 112.
[11] A hypothesis first propounded by Thorstein Veblen; see P. Perrot 1981: 162, 241.
[12] See Bourdieu's analysis of bodily 'hexis' (1980: 111–34).
[13] Chapus 1877: 203.   [14] See P. Perrot 1981: 237.
[15] Chapus 1877: 203.   [16] See Ronteix 1829: 15–16 and Meilheurat 1864: 98.

de la bonne compagnie (A Manual of Polite Company), for instance, Pierre Boitard notes that one acquaintance who worked for two years as a doctor in Charenton, one of Paris's hospitals for the insane, became increasingly eccentric: 'mental illness is contagious', he concludes, 'and since vices are nothing but a type of madness, do not be surprised that so many well raised young people, replete with virtues and good qualities, have gone so rapidly astray by dint of keeping bad company.'[17] The list of social vices included incorrect dress. In everyday life clothing both determined and reflected social identity, hence eccentricity of costume suggested potential eccentricity of character. A man appeared insane, one writer proposed, as soon as his tie was removed and clothes ruffled; conversely, sober clothing was felt to 'prove' that its bearer was decent and sane.[18] Etiquette was construed as a form of medicine, counteracting the spread of social pathology.

In reflexive asides, manuals proposed that the function of *savoir-vivre* was to form a bulwark against disorder, keeping the drama of history running smoothly. Madness and revolution merged as the 'other' of good manners: 'Let us remember that *savoir-vivre*, politeness, indeed the science of sociability constitute a bulwark against the ravings of the imagination. When one has made oneself agreeable in society, it is rare indeed that one wishes to destroy the foundations of the temple in which one has sacrificed.'[19] Encouraging salon-goers to seek emotional fulfilment in the rules of sociability, the passage implies, was a task of considerable political importance. Another author implicitly collapsed sartorial eccentricity into the chaos of post-Revolutionary society: 'There are rules for the appearance that we must try to uphold; they restrain enterprising and ambitious imaginations, which, under the pretext of progress, lead us into anarchy, and anarchy is the cause of destruction.'[20] The assertion implicitly conflates eccentric appearances with the demise of neoclassical values, social mobility, chaotic anarchy, and sinful pretension.

Thirdly eccentricity was often interpreted as a symptom of pride. Describing the truly polite person, one commentator writes: 'his dress is simple, for eccentricity borders on ridicule, and his modesty forbids him to stand out because of his appearance.'[21] Another criticizes the act of drawing attention to oneself: 'Consider this man who prides himself on acting in a way contrary to the accepted customs of society, and

---

[17] Boitard 1851: 18, my emphasis; see also 170–3.
[18] Respectively Chapus 1844: 80 and Meilheurat 1864: 20.
[19] Meilheurat 1864: 113.   [20] Dash 1868a: 61.   [21] Fresne 1858: 17.

who wishes to be noticed because of a certain originality in his tone, manners, and clothing...he believes that the singularity of his tastes distinguishes him from the crowd and attracts the public gaze.'[22] 'What is originality?—Pretension', states a typical maxim.[23] The authors of conduct manuals emphasized the self-delusion and vanity of those who cultivated eccentricity, for the discourse of etiquette was underpinned by a mistrust of self-love which had distinctly theological echoes. Negative perceptions of the individual self which recalled earlier forms of religious rigorism such as Jansenism remained relatively common in mid nineteenth-century French culture, despite the rise of more tolerant forms of Catholicism around this time.[24] Any behaviour or attire, however austere, could be interpreted as evidence of hidden vanity. Delphine de Girardin advised her readers to avoid women with 'Jansenist' toilettes, suggesting that their external austerity was likely to conceal insolence and lustfulness.[25] One of Honoré de Balzac's characters casts doubt upon the enterprise of writing about etiquette on similar grounds: 'To undertake a treatise on elegant life would require an unbelievably fanatical degree of vanity [amour-propre]; for it would entail wishing to dominate the elegant people of Paris, who, themselves, fumble, experiment, and do not always attain grace' (HB12: 228–9). In this critique (which reflexively implicates the work in which it occurs, Balzac's *Traité de la vie élégante* or Treatise on Elegant Life), the notions of self-love and grace have evident religious resonance.

Etiquette was designed to ward off the threat of self-love and the social antagonism to which this gave rise. It did so by advocating ritual self-abnegation: ' "to pass unnoticed"...this phrase sums up all my preceding advice', declares the author of one manual.[26] Striking metaphors were used to evoke *le bon ton*, which was compared to 'the chameleon which must assume the colour of the places through which it passes and the objects to which it comes near, and...water, which, to be drinkable, must have no taste at all'. Visual and gustatory metaphors overlapped with an olfactory image: 'to smell pleasant it is necessary to smell of nothing. Never wear perfume, therefore, and leave to courtesans this means of standing out.'[27] Anything that stood out from anodyne

---

[22] Bescherelle 1861: 53.   [23] Chapus 1877: 190.
[24] On negative 17th-cent. French perceptions of self-interest, see Krailsheimer 1962.
[25] Girardin 1856: II, 12–13 (plagiarized in Drohojowska 1858).
[26] Burani 1879: 31. See also Dash 1868*a*: 144.
[27] Respectively Bourgeau 1864: 43, 414 and Boitard 1851: 443–4.

neutrality—and nothing did so more than eccentricity—evoked a whole underworld of vice.

Finally, eccentricity was perceived as being incompatible not only with the discreet self-effacement taken to embody Christian morality and secular good manners, but also with femininity. These concepts imperceptibly merged, for it was believed that women possessed mysterious knowledge of the rules of propriety. Despite his repugnance at the thought of women wielding political power, the influential medical publicist J.-J. Virey conceded in 1815 in an encyclopaedia article on 'La Femme' that women 'directed' public opinion. He attributed their skill in this domain to their instinctive ability to civilize the *farouche*, or the wild and unsociable (implicitly men).[28] Such views were incessantly reformulated in subsequent commentary, such as Alphonse de Meilheurat's widely read etiquette manual:

There is an extreme delicacy in woman's taste, something exquisite, fine, and elegant completely unknown to our sex... They have perfect tact, and they learn the social graces whilst at play. At twenty, the age at which we are merely starting out in the theatre of good manners, they are already so knowledgeable that we could take them for our teachers.   (1864: 17–18)

The passage claims that women are more skilled in good manners than men due to differences in upbringing, but its vocabulary of delicacy simultaneously suggests that women's superiority arises from their physiological refinement. Some portrayed women's knowledge of social conventions as entirely innate.[29] The gendering of good manners as feminine implied that etiquette manuals were substitutes for the pedagogic guidance of tactful women, and indeed they were one of the few nineteenth-century genres in which female authorship flourished.[30] Despite the widespread perception that women were prone to irrationality, they were held to police social norms through their innate mastery of etiquette.[31]

Eccentricity was seen as incompatible with femininity partly because of its association with innovation. Since the seventeenth century, French women had achieved considerable symbolic power through their role in salon culture, and often influenced political developments behind the scenes. In the nineteenth century, however, the notion that women

---

[28] Virey 1815: 547, 558–9, 569.   [29] Raisson 1836: 15.
[30] See Corbin 1991: 91. Delvau proposed, in an ironic inversion, that *femmes galantes* initiated men into the 'diabolical' science of pleasure: 1867c: 66, 291.
[31] See also Donzelot 1997: 20–1.

were the guardians of custom contributed to the view that they were unsuited for public life and the competitive individualism it entailed. Their place was in the home and salon, where the summit of perfection had been attained and needed only to be permanently reproduced.[32] Women were believed to have a natural propensity to shun eccentricity because of a more general belief that they were unsuited for change. This perspective assumed that women, given their supposedly innate lack of individuality, were adept at conforming to the opinions of others (despite plentiful evidence of rivalry and competition in salon culture).[33]

Violating social conventions was therefore fraught with social and psychological dangers, particularly for social climbers and women. The mechanism used to censor eccentricity was primarily the threat of 'being looked at', with its connotations of shame and ostracism. This conjunction of concepts was investigated with considerable psychological subtlety by many nineteenth-century writers, though their writing on the subject has been generally neglected within subsequent debates on panopticism and the phenomenology of the gaze.[34] For in nineteenth-century polite society there was little respite from being seen, as the bourgeoisie was painfully aware: 'The omnipresent gaze of the other, which judges and punishes, never fails to remind them of the permanent and exhausting duty of self-control.'[35]

From ridicule to adulation: the never-closing eye

Public opinion, colloquially referred to as le *'qu'en dira-t-on?'* ('But what will they say!'), was scrutinized in a body of often highly metaphorical commentary on social life. In a pioneering analysis of fashion first published in 1904, Georg Simmel proposed that women in particular

---

[32] On the opposition of 'timeless' femininity to modernity and change, see Felski 1995: ch. 1.

[33] See e.g. Constantin 1854: 26 and Karr 1860: 286.

[34] An important exception is Simone de Beauvoir, whose historical analyses of the gaze in 19th-cent. French culture (1950) remain exemplary in their exegetical sensitivity. On panopticism, see Foucault 1976, though fear of punishment in a penitential context is evidently very different from fear of social ostracism in the salon. Foucault notoriously fails to examine the gender implications of panopticism, but the phenomenology of objectification underpins analyses of gender in Bourdieu (e.g. 1998: 73) and Bartky 1990, which are both highly pertinent to my arguments here.

[35] P. Perrot 1981: 172.

avoid nonconformism in social situations since they know they cannot defend themselves from the critical public gaze. Conforming to social norms, he suggests, function as a 'barricade of the soul' and an 'iron mask' enabling them to preserve their inner freedom.[36] Simmel's image of the barricade arose from a wider nineteenth-century tradition of ambivalence towards public opinion. Around the mid-nineteenth century, French commentators increasingly expressed dissatisfaction with invasions of privacy by its 'never-closing eye', symptomatic of a gradual strengthening of individualism. The distress caused by the social gaze was evoked in metaphors which recur across chronologically and ideologically disparate texts. These frequently dramatize the encounter between the individual and public opinion with imagery of cruelty, persecution, and rape.

In the *Physiologie du ridicule* (1833), for example, Sophie Gay proposed that 'ridicule is the most solid of all the ties that bind people together'. Selecting an individual to designate as ridiculous creates a sense of superiority and furnishes the group with an inexhaustible supply of anecdotes which function as social currency. Her text portrays a ridiculous man and woman being lionized in the salon, mistakenly inferring that they are a success. In reality, their audience is collecting evidence of their foolishness to 'hawk' around salons (6–10). Like the anonymous letters or newspaper society columns it resembled, gossip pierced the boundaries of private life, flourishing in the fluid spaces where public and private intersected, such as the salon, carriage, and theatre box.[37]

Indeed, the obsessive desire for knowledge was a striking feature of post-Restoration French society. Spaces such as the Bois de Boulogne functioned as a symbolic stock market where the fluctuating value of individual Parisians could be assessed.[38] One observer evoked its visual intensity: 'each person's attire is classified and filed away in memoranda. Capes, a new hat, singular fabrics, are registered from start to finish ... everything is noticed. . . . The slightest adventure, glances, conversations, and smiles are noted down and form a dossier which increases constantly in size until it is presented.'[39] The concluding image of legal prosecution hints at the hostility at the origin of such interpretive edifices. The victims of public opinion were disproportionately likely to be women, given the pervasive double standards for male and female

---

[36] Simmel 1971: 308, 311–12.
[37] See Corbin 1987c: 436 and Burton 1994: 63.
[38] Balzac cited in Gourdon 1841: 50. [39] Dash 1868b: 6–7.

conduct. The regulation of female behaviour was accomplished through the circulation of positive models to emulate and negative models to avoid, in texts such as cautionary tales, fiction, and comportment manuals. It was also a perennial topic of social and political debate.

Part of the early feminist Claire Démar's manifesto *Ma loi d'avenir* (My Law of the Future) (1833), for instance, was framed as a response to the socialist James de Laurence, who had claimed that female emancipation would best be furthered by the abolition of privacy. Women, Laurence asserted, echoing the post-Revolutionary rhetoric of civic citizenship, should make no distinction between their personal and public lives.[40] Démar responded by arguing that 'mystery' was particularly essential for women, but she turns this potentially reactionary idea to radical ends:

> What! Because a woman has not shared with the public her womanly sensations; because no other eye than her own is able to tell which man she prefers, because her female neighbour cannot spice up a malicious conversation with the details of her private life; because her nights of love are not transparent and illuminated; because she would not open her doors and windows if she wished to lavish kisses and caresses upon the man into whose arms she was sinking; would this necessarily entail . . . that the happiness of humanity would be forever destroyed?   (31)

Using the metaphor of the self as a home, her imagery of closed doors and windows presents 'mystery' as the deliberate frustration of a 'penetration' akin to rape (though she notes that women are as liable as men to perpetrate this form of symbolic violence). Démar concludes by reversing Laurence's premise, asserting the need for 'freedom without rules or limits . . . based on mystery, which I would make the foundation of this new morality' (32). Freedom requires a veil of secrecy to flourish, she suggests, just as Simmel later argued that women's inner freedom depended upon a 'carapace' of external conformism.[41]

Démar's imagery is echoed in Gustave Loüis's *Physiologie de l'Opinion* (1855), a text preoccupied with the notion that the public gaze is intolerable. Public opinion is personified with imagery of monsters and animals: it is in turn cunning Proteus, the shepherd of a herd of sea monsters; a spider, ensnaring its prey; a famished animal; and a beast dashing its victim against rocks. Loüis stresses the narrative subtlety of

---

[40] See L. Hunt 1987: 21.
[41] Her hostility towards the public gaze was perhaps shaped by her early experiences as a kept woman; see Moses and Rabine 1993: 53.

Opinion's operations: it lulls its prey into false security, toys with it, and then pounces. His descriptions of the passivity of Opinion's victims reinforce their femininity: 'Women are more vulnerable than us to the advances of Opinion, which first tames them and spies on every aspect of their conduct, then terrifies them with its cries, and dashes them here and there, distraught, into its abysses.' Medical metaphors suggest calculating cruelty (*le monde* is a sugared and gilded pill, concealing its poison, or a doctor numbing his patients with chloroform), whilst imagery of violent dismemberment translates psychological wounds into physical pain.[42]

In Loüis's text, women are permanently illuminated in the hostile social gaze, portrayed as a predator hovering above her: 'She feels malevolence hovering over her, interpreting her actions and tastes, analysing everything down to the air that she breathes; should she forget this, even in the midst of pleasure, she suffers a painful reminder.'[43] His work resonates with a wider tendency to resist objectification, whether as the object of neighbours' gossip or of the official gaze of reformers, police, and hygienists, all of whom sought to enter the domestic sphere to gain information and regulate family life.[44] Loüis shows Opinion attempting to penetrate the walls of the home: 'curiosity in search of nourishment is a famished wild beast; it sniffs under doors, and its gaze, as fine as the blade of a knife, insinuates itself through imperceptible cracks' (22). His imagery of penetration evokes the pervasive nineteenth-century equation of masculine virility with knowledge, the scientist's 'unveiling' of nature with the unclothing of woman, and women's bodies with truth.[45] The analogy between psychological interiority, the home, and the body recurs in commentary hostile to public opinion, though it is not restricted to women's bodies alone.

Privat d'Anglemont, a well-known Bohemian and cataloguer of the Parisian underworld, echoed the perception that women were disproportionately susceptible to the dreaded 'But what will they say!'. He noted, though, its ability to damage both sexes. In a passage entitled '*L'œil sans paupières et la langue des ON*' ('The lidless eye and the

---

[42] See Loüis 1867: 101–5, 22.

[43] Loüis 1867: 104. On hunting as a metaphor for hermeneutics, see Ginzburg 1990: 102–4.

[44] The drive for knowledge, termed 'epistemophilia' in Strachey's translation of Freud's *Wisstrieb*, was influentially analysed by Toril Moi (see 1999: 348–68) and subsequently by Peter Brooks, who relates it to scopophilia (1993: 98–106). Corbin writes of a 'fantasmatic desire to decipher' in 19th-cent. French culture (1987*c*: 435–6).

[45] See Moi 1999: 348–50 and Jordanova 1989: ch. 5.

language of the THEY'), he depicts a never-closing eye, again framed in mythological terms, invading a man's home in response to a hypothetical case of transgression:

If this worthy man ... were to go astray amongst us, even for just one day, the lidless eyes, a hundred times more numerous and vigilant than those of Argus, would point at him from all sides; they would penetrate into his house, despite the doors, the curtains, the shutters, the blinds; they would spy on him to the very depths of his conscience.   (1861: 170)

The eye, the passage reveals, is the internalized social gaze, or conscience, from which escape is impossible. Privat concludes that the voice of the multitude undermines the family and weakens social bonds (172).

The notion that the public gaze engendered anxious conformism emerges in a contemporaneous French review of John Stuart Mill's *On Liberty*, which exhorts the French to emulate the English in their tolerance of eccentricity:

We are far too fearful of originality and even of eccentricity. Each one of us, man and woman alike, certainly wishes to appear in society, to dazzle, and to rise in the world, but we cannot bring ourselves to break out of the circle in which custom confines us. Women, even more than us, are victims of this form of oppression. With unimaginable alacrity they enslave themselves to the latest fashion, whatever this may be. Custom and society weigh down on them like a leaden yoke. With this phrase, 'What will people say?', and this, 'That's how we do things here!', women are forced into the most constrictive and humiliating positions [passent sous les fourches caudines les plus humiliantes].

(Jourdan 1860: 294–5)

Imagery of leaden yokes and physical constriction again transposes the concept of emotional suffering into that of physical torture.

By suggesting that audacity is a prerequisite of social success and advancement, the passage also reveals a central paradox in discourse on female eccentricity. Women were taught to cultivate modesty and conformism, and to flee the individual self-assertion attendant upon 'standing out'. Yet they were simultaneously believed to be naturally coquettish, driven to differentiate themselves from their rivals and capture public attention. Though it often censured ridiculous behaviour, the public gaze was also capable of bestowing social rewards, in the form of adulation and envy. The objectification of women, according to the influential analysis of John Berger, constitutes a structuring feature of the Western visual tradition: 'From earliest childhood she has been taught and persuaded to survey herself continually. And so she comes to consider the *surveyor* and *surveyed* within her as the two constituent yet always distinctive elements of her identity as a woman' (1972: 46).

Women's preoccupation with the gaze of others was typically understood in terms of feminine vanity. Such vanity could be portrayed as innate, as, for instance, in this description of young girls from the *Physiologie de la femme*:

Does she walk or gambol? Has she a new dress or hat? Is she standing? Lying down? At the table? At the piano? At the theatre? Out on a walk? In all circumstances, in all places, you will see her casting artful, furtive, and anxious glances to the left and right, in order to judge the effect she is creating.

(Neufville 1842: 22)

Other commentators attributed a perceived increase in feminine self-consciousness to social corruption. They advised readers to deprive young girls of the attention they craved, echoing the promotion of modesty in pedagogic manuals for girls. 'Look at them amidst the most seemingly pleasant of their games', wrote Alphonse Karr of Parisian girls, 'they are always thinking that they are in a performance, and from time to time they cast little glances about them to judge if they are succeeding.' He described them flirting from the age of 6, his hyperbolic declarations of horror perhaps masking more complex responses.[46]

Since the concept of female vanity was associated with flirtation and eroticism, it was implicated in the pathologies of female sexual frustration. According to a common narrative, the neglect of respectable married women and their invisibility in the public gaze leads to sexual frustration; this causes hysteria; and this in turn results in infidelity.[47] In his *Petites misères de la vie conjugale* (Petty Annoyances of Married Life), for example, Balzac depicts as the first stage of adultery the disillusionment of one wife when confronted with *femmes excentriques*, a phrase used to denote fashionable courtesans:

But to show oneself, to be seen, to attract the looks of five hundred men! . . . For this precious harvest, reaped by one's pride, *a woman must be noticed*. But a woman and her husband are scarcely looked at. Caroline is distressed to see that the room is preoccupied by women who are not with their husbands, by eccentric women [femmes excentriques].   (HB12: 70, my emphasis)

---

[46] Karr 1860: 22. Compare Cavé's similar critique of the objectification of young girls, though written from a perspective sympathetic to her subjects (1863: 188–9).
[47] See Mainardi 2003: 68–72.

Fig. 1. A mirror in the eyes of others, by Grandville. (Grandville 1844: 102)
© British Library Board. All Rights Reserved. (1458.k.10)

He portrays dissatisfied wives yearning for a position of high visibility: 'I recognized in her this attribute of the eccentric woman: she likes to be noticed', he writes of another, noting more generally that 'vanity drives some women to wear strange fabrics in order to be noticed'.[48]

The theme of social visibility is illustrated in an engraving by Grandville, set in an imaginary 'other world' in which the tropes of this one are literalized (here the synecdoche of being 'all eyes'; see Fig. 1). Grandville's illustration constitutes a hyperbolic vision of feminine vanity. With her implausibly low décolletage and elaborate hairstyle, the woman monopolizes the total quantity of male desire and female envy in the theatre. The figure appears similar to the *femme à la mode*, portrayed in many novels and physiologies of the July Monarchy as an expert in inventing eccentric styles in order to capture the public gaze and gratify her vanity. Paris was a glittering arena of real and metaphorical

[48] Respectively HB7: 856 and HB12: 254.

reflections, Walter Benjamin noted; long before any man glimpses the Parisian woman, she has already seen herself reflected in innumerable mirrors and windowpanes: 'Even the eyes of passers-by are hanging mirrors.'[49] In the realm of fashion rather than that of etiquette, very different perceptions of the relationship between eccentricity and the public gaze prevailed.

Fashionable innovation

Fashion is inseparable from the concept of innovation, and by extension from that of modernity. The term 'fashion' has been contrasted by historians with 'dress', the latter denoting clothing in traditional, non-capitalist societies. Fashion is dress in which 'the key feature is rapid and continual changing of styles',[50] and dates to the late fourteenth century when sartorial self-fashioning became an important strategy in the pursuit of worldly power. During the nineteenth century, mass production, journalism, and increasingly fluid social hierarchies led to the democratization and acceleration of stylistic innovation, a concept with close semantic links to eccentricity.

Nineteenth-century fashion appears to confirm the polarization of gender identity which intensified after the Revolution. Throughout the early modern period, male and female clothing was relatively undifferentiated; flounces and lavish materials characterized the attire of both sexes in the social elite. From the eighteenth century, in contrast, fashion gradually became 'an important instrument in a heightened consciousness of gendered individuality'.[51] After the fall of the *ancien régime*, bourgeois and aristocratic men adopted the uniform black suit, which, particularly after the 1830s and abandonment of the male corset, evolved very little. Caprice and overt eccentricity were banished to the dressing gown and to accessories such as the cravat and cane. Male attire ostensibly embodied the English ideology of comfort and utility, together with the mercantile value of austere self-control, though distinction could still be discreetly signalled. Female attire, in contrast, appeared unable to keep still, and symbolized extravagance, eccentricity, and spectacle. The corset was reintroduced during the Restoration, as

---

[49] Benjamin 1999: 536–8; I use Buck-Morss's translation (1986: 128).
[50] E. Wilson 1987: 3.   [51] Ibid.: 120.

though to provide somatic illustration of the ideology of sexual difference inscribed in the Napoleonic code.[52]

Fashion blurred the distinction between austerity and profligacy,
hinting that capitalism was not defined by the masculine values of production alone but also by consumption, framed in terms of 'feminine'
seduction and irrationality.[53] The department store, which imitated
a diverse array of institutions including the fair, church, opera, and
museum,[54] calculated its displays on the basis of a claim to understand
'feminine psychology'. In contrast, women's fashions were increasingly
described in terms of traits associated with masculine individualism,
including audacity and entrepreneurial innovation. The home was
'invaded' by commodities and trinkets, whilst tearooms in department
stores expanded women's ability to meet outside the home.[55] The cult
of innovation thus destabilized the divisions between public and private
spheres, masculine and feminine characteristics.

The function of eccentricity as a social phenomenon is closely par-
alleled by the logic of fashion, in which styles must constantly evolve
and can only be recycled after an interval in which they have been
forgotten. Simmel proposed, in his theory of fashion, that this cycle of
change symbolized the tension between conformism and individuality
(or, in his evolutionary vocabulary, heredity and variation). Nineteenth-
century Parisian fashion provided paradigmatic illustration of Simmel's
vision of a dialectic between doxa and paradox, norm and eccentricity.[56]
It also replicated the dynamic of capitalism, which functions by means
of built-in obsolescence. *Paris-Guide* aptly compared fashion to the
never-ending labour of Sisyphus (1867: II, 923).

Etiquette manuals insisted anxiously upon the timeless nature of elegance, opposing it to the vulgarity of fashion: 'True elegance is unaware
of itself. It is neither awkward, artificial, studied, eccentric, original,
whimsical, nor comic'; 'Naturally you will not adopt eccentric or bizarre
fashions, which are responsible for the disappearance of delightful simplicity from so many social circles, and which arouse the jealousy and
rivalry of so many women'.[57] Just as women had a natural grasp of social
conventions, it was proposed, they had an innate flair for elegance: 'To

---

[52] P. Perrot 1981: 182.
[53] See M. Miller 1981: 197–206 and Rosario 1997: 123–6.
[54] See M. Miller 1981: 165–78 and Saisselin 1985.
[55] See Felski 1995: 66–74.
[56] Uzanne aptly terms fashion a 'paradoxologie' (1894*b*: 242).
[57] Renneville 1852: 11 and Bourgeau 1864: 416 respectively.

please is the sole task of women's lives; a particular form of tact, a type of sixth sense reveals to them anything that could make them more attractive; hence it is as rare to see a women dressed without taste as it is to meet a perfectly well-dressed man.'[58] But such discreet good taste risked being anodyne and unremarkable, in a culture increasingly fixated on consumerism and spectacle. Moreover, nineteenth-century women's fashions were structurally opposed to ascetic understatement, for they represented all that was banished from male attire, such as bright colours, luxurious fabrics, feathers, jewellery, and elaborate hairstyles and hats.[59] The relentless succession of new styles exposed fractures in the ideology of self-effacement governing traditional ideologies of *politesse*.

Fashion disseminated the latest eccentric styles until they became the new norm, were no longer eccentric, and had to be replaced by some fresh novelty.[60] By abolishing aristocratic costume, the Revolution had, as in many other spheres, highlighted the arbitrary nature of social conventions, in this case undermining belief in timeless models of beauty and elegance. Several outrageous fashions came into vogue during the 1820s—the inflated leg of mutton sleeve, the toque, even giraffe accessories, following the arrival of the first giraffe in Paris in 1827—which symbolized the capricious eclecticism of fashion. Choosing a hair ornament during the July Monarchy, a Parisian woman might deliberate between Armenian toques, Catalan bonnets, Algerian fringes, and Jewish turbans.[61] Aided by advances in manufacturing and the circulation of fashion magazines, the rate of change became increasingly rapid over the following decades: 'The extreme diversity of outfits, the ease with which they can be adapted and modified according to personal caprice, the rapid invention and discarding of styles are the most remarkable characteristics of fashion', an analyst of fashion noted in 1866.[62]

The perceived eccentricity of the past became a source of re-enchantment and creative inspiration. The relativity of custom was emphasized by colonial expansion and the increasing interest in historical difference prompted by Romanticism.[63] The practices of French culture were increasingly juxtaposed with their eccentric counterparts in

[58] Raisson 1853: 142.
[59] On the rigours of fashionable life, see e.g. Despaigne 1866: 58.
[60] See Challamel 1881: 217.
[61] See e.g. La Bédollière 1858: 174, Challamel 1881: 212, Maigron 1911: ch. 2.
[62] Despaigne 1866: 14.   [63] See Rigolot 1994; Blum and Chassé 1931: 22.

alien cultures, the clash creating 'bizarre pleasure' (*bizarre jouissance*).[64] Geographical and historical alterity intersected, for exotic influences such as Bedouin sleeves, Greek togas, medieval jewellery, and Renaissance doublets were incorporated into new, heterogeneous styles. Many histories of French fashion were published in the latter part of the century, whilst historical dramas, paintings, and *tableaux* disseminated historical costumes to a wide audience. All were used as inspiration for new fashions. Delphine de Girardin wittily remarked in her chronicle of Parisian life that one might learn the history of France and England as well as geography merely by reading fashion magazines (1856: I, 255). Writing just after 1900, one journalist explained that when he looked back at fashion of the July Monarchy it seemed as implausible as the panniers worn by Marie-Antoinette, 'something of a farce, a piece of nonsense, almost an act of madness'.[65] Another writer catalogued 'eccentric hairstyles' from the realm of Louis XVI, made deliriously strange through the passage of time.[66]

Indeed, the vagaries of fashion highlighted the arbitrary nature of *all* customs, including those of the present. In the introduction to his *Tableau de Paris*, Edmond Texier portrays Parisian fashions as so irrational that they can only be evoked through a series of negations: 'assorted specimens of the most bizarre, unheard of, incoherent, inexplicable, and impossible fantasies.' They constitute an antidote to conformism, and the tendency of Parisians to be as indistinguishable from one another as coins worn smooth through constant circulation.[67] Others cultivated a defamiliarized perspective for the purposes of satire, drawing on the same semantics of impossibility: 'the eccentricity of fashion knows no obstacles; it attempts the most impossible and insane ventures, and often it succeeds.'[68] Foreign visitors had a naturally estranged vantage point from which to contemplate the strangeness of Parisian fashions, upon which they regularly remarked.[69]

Fashion, or *la mode*, was commonly personified as a dominatrix, 'a monarch as absolute as she is bizarre'.[70] Her power was evident in her ability to naturalize the ugliest innovations, particularly the crinoline. The vocabulary of feminine irrationality which suffuses discourse about

---

[64] See Said 1995: 103.   [65] Bouchot 1901: 334.   [66] Uzanne 1895.

[67] Texier 1852: p. iv. Larchey subsequently adapts the coin metaphor to describe the need for eccentrics (1867: p. ii).

[68] Drohojowska 1858: 24; for many further references to eccentricity in the context of fashion, see chs. 3 and 4 below.

[69] e.g. Morgan 1831: II, 303–20 and I, 388–96.   [70] Ronteix 1829: 13.

fashion in nineteenth-century culture has, indeed, continued to under-pin subsequent theories of fashion. Echoing the ambivalence of Parisian writing, twentieth-century theorists of fashion have often portrayed the cycle of constant innovation as morally absurd, a narcotic linked to the false consciousness permeating capitalist society.[71] The extravagance of Parisian fashion may be read in other ways. Walter Benjamin, for instance, proposed that it provided French society with escape from arid rationality and utilitarianism and a 'collective medicament for the ravages of oblivion'. Partially echoing nineteenth-century terminology, he praises the 'eccentric, revolutionary, and surrealist possibilities of fashion', suggesting that fashion provided Parisians with a means of imagining future cultural transformations.[72] Despite these connota-tions of visionary creativity, fashionable eccentricity could paradoxically become a new source of conformism.

The paradox of compulsory eccentricity

Fashion encouraged individual self-expression, particularly for women. Before the rise of the *prêt-à-porter* and Charles Worth's *haute cou-ture*, women were responsible for creating their own outfits from a bewildering array of potential combinations. Women's costumes were analysed by journalists with the air of connoisseurs discussing a work of art, and those who dared to innovate were often rewarded: 'She uses nuances and contrasts to good effect; she experiments, invents, im-agines, does what no dressmaker would dare to try, and creates an effect of positively aristocratic originality.'[73] Success required time, money, and intelligence, and was described as a form of 'alchemy' in which the combination of the occasion, the latest styles and materials, and the individual woman's features and social status had all to be taken into account. Others termed it 'an entire science, a science of choice, taste, and harmony'.[74] If fashion represented one of the few contexts in which the creativity of nineteenth-century women was seen as both legitimate and praiseworthy, a carefully judged dose of eccentricity was one of their most important tools.

[71] This tendency, which belittles a long tradition of female creativity, continues in most 20th-cent. theories of fashion from Veblen to Baudrillard and Barthes, as Elizabeth Wilson demonstrates (1987: 53–7).
[72] Benjamin 1999: 68 and 80 respectively.
[73] Renneville in *La Corbeille*, 11 February 1853.
[74] Chapus 1844: 84–5 and Despaigne 1866: 14 respectively.

For the middle- and upper-class women who could afford it, fashion
thus provided a vicarious outlet for the individualism denied to them
in the political sphere. Simmel saw it as 'the valve through which
woman's craving for some measure of conspicuousness and individual
prominence finds vent, when its satisfaction is denied her in other
fields' (1971: 309). His view resonates with a statement by the *fin-de-
siècle* historian of women's fashions, Baron Octave Uzanne: 'Fashion is
the literature of woman, each outfit her individual style' (1894*a*: 31).
Simmel, however, concludes that the pleasures of 'standing out' from
others through their dress ultimately distracted women from their actual
social powerlessness.

Despite its association with daring creativity, then, many nineteenth-
century commentators noted that fashion promoted its own type of
conformism. '[A]lmost every woman adorns herself neither for her
husband nor even for her lover', wrote Alphonse Karr; 'her appearance is
the altar that the Greeks raised to an "unknown God" ' (1860: 64). This
unknown deity was, of course, public opinion, simultaneously everywhere and nowhere and, it was feared, usurping the rightful authority
of the husband. A cautionary tale from the early 1840s shows a husband
teaching his wife a lesson about her misguided pursuit of fashionable
eccentricity. She slavishly adheres to the latest fashions, despite being
plain and over forty. When her husband tampers with her fashion
magazine by inserting a picture of a carrot, she insists upon wearing a
carrot in her hair to the Opera and is publicly humiliated. She thereafter
learns to dress more moderately (see Fig. 2).[75]

Eccentricity was therefore perceived in seemingly opposed yet closely
related terms in the discourses of etiquette and fashion. In the salon, the
language of *on* ('they', 'one', 'people') enforced conformity to tradition
and the rejection of eccentricity. In the world of fashion, in contrast,
'on' dictated permanent change and the deliberate pursuit of the bizarre
and eccentric. In both cases, women were construed as fundamentally in
thrall to social norms or doxa. Privat d'Anglemont writes, in his critique
of the conformism of the salon: '*They* say this; *they* say that; *they* repeat
it; *they* hawk it from the salon to the porter's lodge.' He notes that even
courtesans, symbols of freedom from constraint, have to obey 'they'.[76]
Alphonse Karr's criticism of ridiculous fashions echoes his terminology.
'*THEY* seem to be the great tyrant of women', he states, attempting in an
imaginary dialogue to reason with a typically irrational woman:

[75] Kock 1844: I, 206–8.   [76] Privat d'Anglemont 1861: 172, 173 respectively.

Fig. 2. 'Oh! What a singular hairstyle…How original…*carotte naturelle.*' (Kock 1844: I, 207) © British Library Board. All Rights Reserved. (010169.k.16)

—But what do you mean by 'they'?
—That's simple: everybody.
—But aren't you part of this 'everybody'?
—That's true, but *they* don't ask me for my opinion.
—*They* are quite appalling! What an atrocious tyrant *they* are![77]

Eccentricity was one of a range of interlinked adjectives which domi-nated descriptions of fashion. A number of terms were used largely pos-itively (*whim, fantasy, piquant, contemporary, fashionable, modern*). Oth-ers were used largely negatively (*loud, showy, monstrous, brash, unbridled, shameless, vulgar, exaggerated, ridiculous*). A large number of commonly used terms, however, remained strongly ambivalent. The adjectives *eccentric, singular, extravagant, unusual, original, strange, bizarre, start-ling,* and *unheard-of* could be used either to denounce or to praise the latest tendencies, depending on the observer's attitude towards

[77] Karr 1860: 65 and 253 respectively.

innovation.[78] The semantic instability of the term 'excentrique' thus illustrates the double-edged nature of the public gaze when confronted by disregard for convention.

Maladies of visibility

Fashion advocated eccentricity as a key component of modernity, whilst custom prohibited it in the name of tradition. This contradiction was implicated in a number of maladies associated with the public gaze, extreme cases which nonetheless illuminate the everyday logic of nineteenth-century French social life. Malaise centred on two tendencies: fear of passing unseen, and fear of being noticed in a negative manner, incarnated for many in the fear of public ridicule. Balzac had repeatedly cautioned his male readers that married wives were liable to be eclipsed by fashionable courtesans, with potentially disastrous social and emotional consequences. Commentary on Parisian life suggested that such unwanted invisibility was particularly liable to afflict unmarried older women, unattractive women, and ageing society women. Those who departed from the code of discreet invisibility by actively seeking public attention were portrayed as a social menace.

The *femme célibataire* (unmarried woman) and *vieille fille* (spinster), for example, were described with a vocabulary of monstrous aberration. One journalistic sketch depicts a typical spinster in pathetically elaborate attire, whilst Comtesse Dash disapprovingly evokes the supposedly ubiquitous *vieille fille à prétentions* or 'spinster with pretensions': 'Her attire is eccentric; she continues to dance, even though she ceased to be invited a long time ago.'[79] Like other commentators, she posits an analogy between the eccentricity of the spinster's appearance and that of her mind. The unmarried woman was depicted as a spider at the centre of a web of malice, a metaphor also used in descriptions of eccentric female types such as the *femme libre* and bluestocking. The segregation

---

[78] The original French terms are, respectively: *caprice, fantaisie, piquant, actualité, à la mode, moderne; tapageur, voyant, monstrueux, à effet, effréné, effronté, vulgaire, exagéré, ridicule; excentrique, singulier, extravagant, insolite, original, étrange, bizarre, étonnant,* and *inédit.*

[79] Dash 1860: 202. Fanny Trollope noted in 1836 that French attitudes to unmarried women were more intolerant than English ones (1985: 259–65).

of spinsters at social gatherings was believed to protect others from their disturbing presence, but it created, in the cultural imagination, an underworld of spiteful women plotting to destroy the lives of others. Their archetypal illustration was Balzac's Cousine Bette, described as suffering from eccentricity so severe it verges on madness.[80]

Alphonse Meilheurat argued that those who had never succeeded in mastering the codes of politeness might well seek to destroy the 'temple' from which they were excluded.[81] Ugly women were felt to be similarly threatening, for they could have no investment in the rewards of sociability; they were compared to monstrous errors of nature, and reviled like the old prostitutes pointed at in the street.[82] In their own way, perhaps, they were as fascinating as beautiful women, who were also portrayed as monstrous exceptions to the norm: 'every beautiful woman is a monster, and like all monsters is therefore suited above all to exhibition and display.'[83]

The prohibition on 'being noticed' extended even to fashionable and attractive women as they aged. Women were exhorted to retire from society shortly after the age of 30, or 40 at the most; this necessitated adopting a different wardrobe reflecting their dignified status, and no longer participating in activities such as dancing. Comtesse Dash advised women to adopt a hermeneutics of suspicion: they should regularly scrutinize their face in the mirror, and test whether people responded to them differently in public—for instance, noting whether men still turn to stare after them in the street (1868*a*: 162–3). Older women's fear of becoming invisible made them a danger to others and themselves, according to the journalist Nestor Rocqueplan, himself a well-known dandy:

After ten or twelve years of splendour and agitation, a woman nowadays begins a life of private rage and the denigration of the entire human race. She is envious of young women starting out in society and copies their fashions . . . In the salon, she attacks celebrated individuals, discusses the beauties of the day, criticizes everyone's teeth and hair, denounces the worthy as stupid, surprises and betrays glances, alarms husbands, interferes with lovers, destroys, spoils, and damages everything around her, and seems to say: 'look at me!' [me voilà!] . . . She will not resign herself to growing old. (1857: 7–8)

---

[80] See respectively Soulié 1846?: 64 and HB7: 207, 80 and 85.
[81] Meilheurat 1864: 113.
[82] See e.g. Neufville 1842: 20, Kock 1844: II, 321, and Dash 1860: 4–5.
[83] Frémy 1861: 307.

His accumulation of verbs evokes the feverish energy such women devote to the pursuit of destruction; they evidently prefer being disparaged to being invisible.

Indeed, for fashionable women, being abandoned by the public gaze upon which their identity was premised could be equivalent of the death of the self, as Arnould Frémy argued:

What becomes of dethroned idols? Even yesterday they were adored, drowned in a perpetual incense of tributes and favours; tomorrow they will be ugly, spurned for this very reason, exposed to ridicule, without any right to commiseration from society, treated, in short, as worthless creatures. What becomes of them, I repeat? Society, *high society* ... is wholly indifferent to their plight. Once one's face is dead, the whole person is dead; the woman who is old or ageing is nothing more than a *corpse* ...   (1861: 290, emphasis in original)

Again his rhetoric enacts the drama of the dethronement; by multiplying passive constructions he stresses the woman's status as a helpless object, thrown to and fro on the vagaries of public opinion.[84]

Second, fear of being objectified in a negative manner could lead both men and women to avoid exposure to the gaze of others. Though women were more liable to be defined through their appearances, men who refused to grow old were also mocked, particularly dandies whose attention to their appearance continued beyond the age of 40. In a manual on elegance which seeks to privilege this concept over the vulgarity of fashion, Eugène Chapus portrays the public gaze being used as a weapon. The youthful rival of an ageing *femme élégante* invites her to a social gathering during the morning ('akin to suicide for most women'), calculating that revelation of the latter's ravaged complexion will secure her triumph. The older woman retaliates by inviting her rival to a soirée held by candlelight, where she dazzles with her witty conversation whilst the foolish younger woman is reduced to silence (1844: 147–8).

Despite Chapus's attempt to prove the supremacy of conversation over the gaze, women's appearances assumed greater importance towards the middle of the century as the ideal female body mutated.[85] From 1825 to 1835, the ethereal romantic heroine was in vogue. Self-starvation and the cultivation of pallor were common in the fashionable

[84] See also Karr 1860: 28.
[85] Bourdieu notes that women are 'condemned to constant awareness of the gap between their real bodies, to which they are chained, and the ideal body which they tirelessly strive to resemble' (1998: 73).

class, including men, and it was considered unseemly to eat more than tiny quantities in public.[86] Between 1835 and 1848 there was a brief cult of physical exercise and strength, ceding to a Second Empire ideal in which the ideal woman displayed voluptuous quantities of flesh through low *décolletés*. The purpose of the crinoline, introduced during the latter part of Napoleon III's rule, was to enlarge body shape; contemporary writing suggests that women who were insufficiently youthful or plump dreaded exposure to mockery when wearing evening dress.[87]

The spectre of being pointed at in ridicule was, for both sexes, an ordeal akin to exhibition in a fairground booth: 'True wisdom consists in not standing out because of any kind of excess. Every eccentric act which is not motivated by a wager is an attack of madness…Let us submit to the laws of society so we are not pointed at in ridicule.'[88] Anxiety about one's appearance and fear of being judged negatively could culminate in a desire to flee the public gaze, even in debilitating forms of neurosis. Though French psychiatrists did not fully medicalize social anxiety until the *fin de siècle*, their writing on this subject casts light on the role of sexual difference in determining attitudes towards the social gaze in earlier French culture.

Medical recommendations for those suffering from social anxiety overlapped significantly with the advice previously dispensed in etiquette manuals. Shyness was consistently gendered as feminine in both discourses: the timid were perceived as sensitive and easily wounded, traits at odds with definitions of masculine identity in terms of stoicism and courage.[89] The malady of *éreuthophobie* ('ereuthophobia') was considered the most common of *fin-de-siècle* social anxiety disorders: it consisted in a phobia of blushing in which merely worrying about the possibility of an attack could be enough to trigger one. The cure depended upon the quasi-theatrical connivance of family and friends: by pretending not to notice anything, they made the afflicted individual feel that she was not the object of general scrutiny. Once this imaginary 'invisibility' was achieved, symptoms rapidly receded. Psychiatrists noted that the majority of their patients suffering from social anxiety were male. In practice, however, disorders relating to shyness were far more likely to result in medicalization in male sufferers, due to

---

[86] Maigron 1911: 32–48.   [87] Challamel 1881: 212.
[88] Poisle-Desgranges 1869: 7.
[89] See e.g. Hartenberg 1901: 47; on masculine identity, see Nye 1998: ch. 10.

underlying gender assumptions. One doctor, for instance, proposed that one of the main causes of the malady was concern about standing out and being judged by the gaze of others; he adds as a caveat that 'there is no being more concerned by her external appearance than woman, a beautiful ornament made to please and a beautiful creature made to adorn herself'.[90] Others echoed this refusal to pathologize shyness or blushing in women on the grounds that they were quintessentially feminine tools in the game of seduction.[91]

Anxiety about social interaction was discussed in a resolutely pragmatic manner in advice manuals. As part of her instructions on preparing young girls for their entry into society, Baronne Staffe outlines a treatment for anxiety very similar to that proposed by doctors, with a similarly gendered subtext: 'delicious awkwardness' and 'shy astonishment' are positive assets for a young girl, she suggests, whilst 'unflinching composure' is unseemly (1891: 280). The cure for blushing entails avoiding all potential accusations of eccentricity: 'She should be persuaded that young girls will remain unnoticed if they are simple, modest, and do not offend against convention.' On no account must victims be warned not to be ridiculous, a self-defeating tactic liable to increase their self-consciousness (1891: 272). Doctors agreed that blushing was an extreme example of the self-monitoring inherent in bourgeois sociability: 'If a woman suddenly realizes that she is ugly, badly dressed, and that this is noticeable, she will immediately lose her natural poise and grace, and will become *disconcerted*. But she could equally be disconcerted to start with, and only suddenly realize afterwards that she is ugly, badly dressed, and that this is noticeable.'[92]

The conventions upheld by conduct manuals were, however, perceived as increasingly stifling as behavioural codes were relaxed around the turn of the twentieth century. Béatrice Dangennes published many conduct manuals for women on the cusp of the transformation of the genre, as the First World War led to the decline of the *grand monde* that had underpinned its reproduction for over a century. She continues to advise her female readers to distrust eccentricity ('so very difficult to contain within the limits of good taste'), but fuses this traditional view with a new interest in emancipation.[93] Women's old roles were disappearing, she suggested, dismissing the self-effacing and conformist woman of preceding generations as 'soft wax', 'a colourless substance',

---

[90] Régnier 1896: 18   [91] See Hartenberg 1901: 128–9.
[92] Dugas 1898: 41; see also 72.   [93] Dangennes n.d. (*a*): 104.

'a white page'.[94] But the script for their new life had not yet come into existence:

> Ready to breech the solid fortifications of custom, prejudice, and habit, she contemplates the largely open fields of emancipation stretching before her with feelings of desire not wholly devoid of anxiety. No obstacle can be seen. And yet she hesitates, for these same obstacles which at times weigh down on her are also places of refuge. All along the horizon, now stripped of its barriers, she searches in vain for the shelter that she was accustomed to finding in the tepidness [tiédeur] of her past life.   (1919: 5–6)

Dangennes's imagery revolves around the traditional dichotomy between public and private spheres: shelter takes the form of a fortified building, locking women in even as it excludes their enemies, whilst emancipation requires emergence into open spaces, exposing women to attack. The term she uses to describe the old world, 'tepidness' is curiously ambiguous. It signifies that this world is dying, but simultaneously implies that it still has a degree of comforting warmth, in comparison with the cold and uncertain expanses ahead.

This chapter has examined the rhetoric of 'standing out' and 'being noticed' in polite society, an arena in which eccentricity was associated with self-assertion, spectacle, and departure from the rigid scripts which regulated bourgeois sociability. Etiquette manuals, fashion magazines, novels, and much writing about urban life were preoccupied by the relationship between the individual self and public opinion, personified as a hostile and never-closing eye. The amorphous and often repetitive body of texts which set out the codes of Parisian worldliness for their bourgeois readers constitutes part of the prehistory of issues subsequently taken up in social theory and philosophy, including panopticism, the phenomenology of the gaze, social control, and norm violations.

Contradictory interpretations of eccentricity arose in the discourses of etiquette and fashion, revealing underlying fractures in the relationship between tradition, associated with community, and modernity, associated with individualism. In conduct manuals, eccentricity was censured, for it was incompatible with the pragmatic ethos of discreet mediocrity which marked out the bourgeoisie from both *arrivistes* and *parvenus*, in the one instance, and the image of *ancien régime* aristocratic excess, in the other. Despite their attempt to facilitate

---

[94] See Dangennes n.d. (*b*): 8, and 1920: ch. 4. The tropes were clichés; Brachet, for instance, uses a very similar metaphor (1847: 86–7).

individual self-advancement, conduct manuals thus counselled their readers against any manifestation of individual difference, perceived to be a high risk strategy. A network of semantic and cultural associations linked departure from the norms of the salon to madness, revolution, and vice. For fashionable women, however, the public gaze was shown as adoring and potentially addictive, rewarding those who dared to create an individual, slightly eccentric style. The rhetoric of female vanity thus contradicted the dislike of female self-assertion shared by etiquette manuals and much social and political discourse, though it restricted female creativity to a narrow range of activities relating to self-presentation and display. The next chapter further examines the tensions surrounding eccentricity, gender, and the public gaze in relation to two icons of fashionable individualism: the male and female dandy.

3

Dandies and Lions

> When Buffon depicts the lion, he finishes off the lioness in a few words, whereas in Society, woman is not always the female of the male [la femme ne se trouve pas toujours être la femelle du mâle].
>
> Honoré de Balzac[1]

Members of high society were less influenced than the bourgeoisie by the conduct manual and its code of anodyne invisibility. In the literary culture of the July Monarchy, fashionable eccentricity was often associated with dandyism, a concept that was considerably more historically mutable than has often been recognized. Dandies exemplified an ethos of aristocratic individualism founded upon audacity, contempt for bourgeois mediocrity, and a desire to differentiate oneself from others. They were also characterized by emotional indifference, a sign of their alleged superiority, though they were nonetheless portrayed as being dependent upon recognition from an adoring or simply astonished audience. Representations of a now largely neglected figure, the female dandy, also flourished in the new atmosphere of gender experimentation which arose after 1830, and in the typological imagination of one of the period's most characteristic forms, the literary physiology.

Dandies were invariably defined in terms of their 'singularity', but opinions differed as to how overtly this singularity could be expressed. This chapter draws on two neglected nineteenth-century distinctions in order to illuminate the relationship between eccentricity, dandyism, and gender. First, the masculine 'ruffian' and the feminized 'exquisite' were two types of English Regency dandy. The former was known for his desire to shock his audiences with his audacious exploits and appearances, and incarnated flamboyant eccentricity; the latter, a dandy who followed the dictates of Beau Brummell, cultivated ascetic, almost invisible refinement and eschewed external eccentricity. Second,

---

[1] HB1: 8.

this distinction was echoed by the *tapageuse* ('loud woman') and the *mystérieuse* ('mysterious woman'), Delphine de Girardin's terms for fashionable women who represented overt and covert distinction respectively.[2] The former was exemplified by wealthy Parisian figures such as the *femme à la mode* (woman in vogue, lady of fashion) and *lionne* (lioness), who attained celebrity status through their strategically bizarre attire and audacious exploits. In contrast, figures such as female *fat* (a vain, pretentious individual) and the *femme froide* (cold woman) represented concealed and ultimately more destabilizing forms of eccentricity. Literary and medical discourse both portrayed exceptional women as monstrous yet strangely fascinating exceptions to the norms of femininity.

Dandies and lions in the vocabulary of Parisian life

The literary culture of the July Monarchy was greatly influenced by the *physiologie*, a moderately priced small book aimed at petit-bourgeois and bourgeois readers and often sold directly on the street.[3] Immensely popular during the period 1830 to 1845, the genre attained its zenith during 1841 and 1842, during which time, it has been estimated, around 500,000 copies were in circulation.[4] Each physiology treated a different social type or aspect of Parisian life in the humorous manner of the expert. Multi-volume compendia such as *Paris ou le livre des cent-et-un* (Paris or the Book of the Hundred and One) (1831–4) and *Les Français peints par eux-mêmes* (The French Painted by Themselves) (1840–2) were aimed at wealthier bourgeois readers. The physiology was linked to popular forms of mass entertainment such as the diorama and panorama, and, following Walter Benjamin, is often discussed under the heading of 'panoramic literature'.[5]

The genre has generated much recent commentary, particularly in the wake of Benjamin's theorization of the *flâneur* or urban stroller as the exemplary interpreter of urban life, as well as the meditations of cultural theorists and geographers on the 'legibility' and 'readability'

---

[2] Girardin 1857: IV, 193.
[3] See Lhéritier 1958: 7–8; Sieburth, who notes their affinity with etiquette manuals and tourist guides (1984: 165); Wechsler 1982: 31–4; and Goulemot and Oster 1989: 22–6.
[4] Pichois 1958: 63.   [5] Benjamin 1997: 35.

of the modern city.[6] The relationship between the physiology and the medical imagination has elicited far less attention, though the very term 'physiology' testifies to the prestige of the medical profession in nineteenth-century French culture. The genre implicitly claimed to be an anatomy of the social body and a diagnostic reading of its symptoms; similar metaphors underpinned much realist fiction of the period.[7] The concept of the physiology also evokes the notion of the body politic and imagery of pathology, a polysemic term often conflated with vice and immorality.[8] More specifically, the physiology, according to one reading, emerged in response to the mental pathologies of its bourgeois readers. Like Georg Simmel, Benjamin portrayed the city as a pathogenic arena which induced nervous shock in those who traversed it.[9] He suggested that the jovial tone of the physiology reassured its readers that the strangers they passed in the street were innocuous rather than threatening (1997: 36–9). The physiology thus attempted to neutralize a 'series of eccentric or simple, attractive or severe figures'—or, adapting Benjamin's metaphor, to 'inoculate' Parisian readers against all forms of social difference.[10]

Though dismissed by many literary critics as a banal compendium of received ideas, 'virtually devoid of genuine social insight',[11] the genre was as important for its social functions as its content. In addition to reassuring and orienting city dwellers, it was highly sensitive to novelty, registering ephemeral developments in contemporaneous Parisian culture. It helps to elucidate the many literary texts which drew on its concepts and typologies, and provides valuable information about bourgeois ideologies.[12] Finally, the physiology was connected to the rise of sociological and anthropological thought, which, prior to 1914, overlapped with literature.[13] For like sociology, the physiology attempted, in however clumsy a manner, to analyse social life reflexively; the act of (self-) portraiture was repeatedly portrayed, for instance in the *Physiologie des physiologies* which appeared in 1841 and in the reflexive

---

[6] See Benjamin 1997: 35–66; Schwartz notes that the notion of urban legibility now seems rather clichéd (1998: 1–2).

[7] See Matlock 1995: 50–3 and Rothfield 1992: ch. 2.

[8] e.g. three of Balzac's works of social analysis are grouped together as the *Pathologie de la vie sociale* or Pathology of Social Life (HB12: 185–87), whilst Boitard's manual contains a 'Pathological Tableau of Parisian Life' representing the 'vices' of different social groups (1851: 170–3).

[9] See Benjamin 1997: 117–18, 131–4 and Simmel 1971: 325–6.

[10] Benjamin 1997: 37.   [11] Sieburth 1984: 170.

[12] See e.g. Gluck 2005: 83.

[13] See Lepenies 1988 and Cowling 1989 respectively.

illustrations of the physiologist in *Les Français peints par eux-mêmes*.
Though the genre declined during the late July Monarchy, it continued
to influence the documentary rhetoric of realist and naturalist fiction,
journalism, photography, and the social sciences: 'The physiology no
longer existed because it was everywhere.'[14]

The proliferation of social types in the Parisian physiology signalled
a wider fascination with the notion of types in scientific and literary
culture. The terms 'stéréotype' and 'cliché' began to be used in French in
the two decades following the 1789 Revolution, when they were mainly
associated with the printing press and the mass-produced impressions
drawn from metal plates; they soon began to be used in a metaphorical
sense to denote commonplaces and received ideas. The notion of type
was closely related to that of 'character', in its earlier sense of dramatic
stock type. The term 'type' played an important role in Honoré de
Balzac's discussion of his enterprise as a novelist, and in the debates of
contemporaneous zoologists upon whose work he claimed to model his
fictional analyses.[15]

The notion of a typology of unique specimens, whether literary
or scientific, raises an apparent paradox. The critic Daniel Sangsue
has suggested that it was impossible for nineteenth-century writers to
analyse eccentricity in the physiology, citing the absence of a *Physiologie
de l'excentrique*. The inherently singular phenomenon of eccentricity, he
suggests, was unrepresentable within a genre devoted to generalities and
classification. He nonetheless acknowledges two historical vogues for
eccentricity in French literary culture, imitative phenomena which
undermine the view that oddity is incompatible with collective trends.[16]
Nineteenth-century writers were themselves aware of the paradox of
generalizing about unique cases. Some natural historians, for example,
disputed the possibility of a general taxonomy of 'monsters' or 'eccentricities of nature', since each was *sui generis*.[17] Similar difficulties arose
in conceptualizing a culture of individualists: one French journalist
described the English as a 'vast museum of eccentrics' whose common identity consisted precisely in the fact that they had nothing in
common.[18] The trope was reformulated in Georg Simmel's notion of

---

[14] Goulemot and Oster 1989: 23. In 1852 Théophile Gautier described one compendium as 'moving daguerreotypes' (cited in Goulemot and Oster 1989: 25 n. 7).
[15] On typology and fiction, see Bly 2004: 7 and Prendergast 1986: 32–6; on typology
in 19th-cent. zoology, see Farber 1976.
[16] See respectively Sangsue 1988: 53–5 and 1987: 33.
[17] See Ch. 7 below.   [18] Texier 1853: 245.

the 'club of club-haters' and Arthur Conan Doyle's Diogenes Club, a refuge for 'the most unsociable and unclubable men in town'.[19]

Nonetheless, not all eccentric behaviour was associated with the figure of the eccentric or the personal noun *un excentrique*, a subtle but important linguistic distinction which explains how physiologies did in practice manage to discuss eccentricity. Many figures in Parisian culture, including the stock type of the collector, the bluestocking, and the dandy, were linked to eccentric behaviour or appearances yet not described as *excentriques*. Even where the figure of 'the' eccentric is concerned, writers drew on characters such as Cervantes's Don Quixote, Sterne's Tristram Shandy, and Diderot's Neveu de Rameau (themselves variations on traditional stock types such as the wise fool) as archetypes for 'original' and 'eccentric' fictional characters.[20] Nothing, in short, prevents eccentricity from becoming stereotypical and codified.

The mastery of the city promised by the physiology required mastery of the city's shifting terminology, since social types were inextricably linked to linguistic innovation.[21] Only briefly fashionable, many nineteenth-century neologisms were fossilized in ephemeral texts such as the physiology. The prolific Parisian commentator Alfred Delvau later compared Parisian jargon to tides of silt engulfing the capital, and to the muddy depths of the ocean, both images suggesting the preservation of ephemeral forms of life.[22] Though often portrayed by modern critics as a monolithic category, the dandy was situated by most nineteenth-century commentators on elegance within a fluctuating historical genealogy of fashionable types, whose precise relationship to eccentricity varied. Polemic concerning the relative merits and 'true' meaning of individual terms proliferated, as writers vied to impose their own definitions and thereby establish their authority as experts on Parisian life. There was nevertheless a degree of consensus: the *fat*, *muscadin* (idle, well-dressed youth), and *petit-maître* (fop) flourished during the *ancien régime*; the *incroyable* (incredible) and *fashionable* during the 1790s; the *gentleman*, *merveilleux* (marvellous), *dandy*, and *fat* during the Restoration; and the *homme à la mode* (man of fashion) and *lion* during the July Monarchy. The derided *gandin*, *cocodès* and *petit-crevé*, all types of ridiculous dandy, were seen as their vulgar

---

[19] Simmel 1971: 307 and Doyle 1981: 436. [20] See Bly 2004: 11–20.
[21] See Matoré 1951; Klein 1976; and Lhéritier 1958: 56–8.
[22] Delvau 1867*b*: 13; 1867*a*: p. x. Balzac uses similar imagery in *Le Père Goriot*.

Second Empire successors.[23] As terms such as 'gentleman' and 'dandy' suggest, the influence of English culture permeated French fashionable life.

Ruffians and exquisites

The concept of dandyism was introduced to Parisian culture during a second wave of Anglomania in the late 1820s, though the term 'dandy' was first used in French as early as 1813. In English culture after 1789, the dandy and the wealthy eccentric were often considered to belong to the gentry or nobility, in the context of the defensive reassertion of aristocratic identity in the wake of the French Revolution.[24] Such figures thus appealed to those in France who also sought to reinvigorate an increasingly fragile aristocratic ideal.

English Regency culture inherited its own typology of male elegance, which included the categories of 'buck', 'beau', and 'fop'. It differentiated between several varieties of male dandy, including uncouth 'ruffians' and urbane 'exquisites'. The former, who exemplified a male-only ethos of sporting prowess and spent much of their time at gentleman's clubs, astonished people with their pranks and were distinguished by their noisily ostentatious behaviour. The latter cultivated ascetic, almost invisible forms of distinction.[25] Discourses of French dandyism were similarly nuanced, and the dandy was associated with quite diverse models of masculinity. Appropriating the Romantic ideology of 1830, for example, dandies affiliated to the Jeune-France movement strove for exuberant singularity and revelled in disconcerting the bourgeoisie; some emulated the unkempt, melancholic dandyism of Byron, at a time when the figure of the 'fatal man' enjoyed considerable prestige; others harboured nostalgia for the eighteenth-century French libertine exemplified by Laclos's Vicomte de Valmont; and others still copied the antics of English 'ruffians', putting itching powder in people's coats and careering up and down public promenades on their racehorses.[26]

The last of these types was often described as a 'lion' in the vocabulary of French elegance. Imported from English culture, this type was often

---

[23] See e.g. GD8: 117; CB2: 711. For examples of polemic, see e.g. Ronteix 1929: 16–22 and Chapus 1844: 134. On the semantics of dandyism, see Stanton 1980: 30–62.

[24] Levier 1976: 21–3.

[25] On 'ruffians' and 'exquisites', see Prevost 1957: 22–3.

[26] On the historical diversity of dandyism, see Prevost 1957 and Stanton 1980: 30–62.

Fig. 3. A Parisian lion with his page, by Grandville. (Hetzel 1842: I, 374) © British Library Board. All Rights Reserved. (C.155.h.21)

connected with fashionable eccentricity during the July Monarchy (see Fig. 3).[27] This usage of the term 'lion' derived from the popularity of rare animals at the London zoo, the English courtesan Henriette Wilson claimed in 1825; part of the French translation of her memoirs was entitled *Les Lions de Paris et les tigres de Londres* (The Lions of Paris and the Tigers of London).[28] The *Physiologie du lion* portrays the figure puffing cigar smoke into respectable women's faces, splattering passers-by with mud, and whipping his horses; it terms him a 'ferocious dandy' with 'eccentric tastes' and a love of audacious fashions.[29] A men's fashion

[27] See Rostaing (n.d.: 26). The term 'lion' also denoted the celebrity of the moment, not necessarily a fashionable individual; see Girardin 1856: I, 61–2.
[28] Wilson 1825: VII, 1 n. 1. On animal metaphors and human exhibitions, see Ch. 5 below.
[29] Deriège 1842: 17.

magazine first published in 1842 was entitled *Le Lion*, on the grounds
that this figure was the ultimate expression and model of the fashionable
society gentleman.

The flamboyantly eccentric English gentleman, close to the figure of
the lion, was also popularized in French sensation novels of the late July
Monarchy by writers such as Alexandre Dumas, Paul Féval, and Eugène
Sue. The term 'excentrique' was used in a highly codified manner in
this genre, often to signify the fabulous wealth and high life to which its
readers aspired. The term also contributed to creating an atmosphere of
melodramatic intensity. Both tendencies are evident in the hyperbolic
rhetoric of texts such as Alexandre Dumas's *Le Comte de Monte-Cristo*
(1844–5): 'He thought about the plan of going to Paris, which the
Count had already mentioned several times, and felt sure that with his
eccentric character, his distinctive countenance and his colossal fortune,
the Count could not fail to cause a sensation there.'[30] The trope was so
well known that in 1848 George Sand could write of one Englishman:
'he was one of those eccentrics whom one sees more often in novels than
in real life' (1971: 558). A stereotypical association between eccentricity,
Englishness, and aristocratic excess was thus known to a wide French
audience from the early 1840s, and persisted in some sensation fiction
of the Second Empire.[31]

Nonetheless, the figure of the 'exquisite' also found strong champions
in France. This ascetic figure, loath to advertise his distinction due
to his dislike of vulgarity, was interpreted in relation to the French
tradition of courtly *honnêteté*. His dominant English model was Beau
Brummell, whose sartorial philosophy was summarized in a simple
aphorism: 'If John Bull turns round to look after you, you are not
well dressed; but either too stiff, too tight, or too fashionable.'[32] The
dictum was ceaselessly invoked in subsequent French commentary.[33]
For this type of dandy, any type of overt eccentricity was banned.[34] An
influential proponent of this model, Barbey d'Aurevilly insisted upon
distinguishing dandyism from eccentricity, arguing that a 'Pascalian

---

[30] Dumas (père) 1956: 527.
[31] See e.g. Ponson du Terrail 1963: 194, 416, and 1964*a*: 93, 103, 136; see also
Schulman 2003: 22–4.
[32] Cited in Laver 1968: 21; compare Jesse 1854: 32. See Frémy 1836 on the French
vogue for Brummell.
[33] e.g. HB12: 256, CB2: 710; JB2: 690.
[34] Many critics divide dandyism from eccentricity on the basis of an unstated pref-
erence for Brummellian dandyism, defined normatively as 'true' dandyism (e.g. Wilson
1987: 180–4; Carassus 1971: 39, 100–6, 176; Kempf 1977: 85–91).

point of intersection' divided eccentricity from originality (JB2: 689). He considered eccentricity too radical to be in good taste:

> one of the consequences of Dandyism, one of its principal characteristics—or rather, its most general characteristic—is that of always producing the unexpected, that which the mind accustomed to the yoke of rules cannot logically expect. Eccentricity, that other fruit of the English soil, also produces the unexpected, but in a different way, in an unbridled, wild, and blind fashion. It is an individual revolution against the established order, at times against nature: here we verge on madness. Dandyism, on the other hand, scoffs at the rules yet still respects them. (JB2: 675)

Different writers situated Barbey's Pascalian point in different places, however. There was little agreement about whether eccentricity necessarily denoted violent rejection of social conventions or whether it might not include more subtle forms of deviance—and conversely, whether dandyism could denote more extreme forms of rupture with convention. In practice, dandyism and eccentricity were often perceived to overlap.

The term *excentrique* was a close synonym of *singulier, original, bizarre*, and *étrange*. In an attack on the etiquette manual as a bourgeois genre advocating mediocre conformism, the Baron de Mortemart-Boisse celebrated the dandy's desire to affirm his distinction: 'See how he exaggerates the rules and renders them ridiculous: what he desires is the triumph of the bizarre and singular over the natural.'[35] Charles Baudelaire's comments on dandyism and eccentricity similarly highlight widespread uncertainty about exactly how eccentric a dandy could be without relinquishing his self-control. Initially close to a Bohemian model of dandyism, flouting convention with his green hair and pink gloves, the poet later adopted a code of austere simplicity, part of a broader cultural rejection of the excesses of the Jeune-France movement. He could therefore have been describing himself in the following passage from 1846: 'as for the eccentrics who were once easily identifiable by dint of the intense and violent colours they wore, they today limit themselves to nuances of design and cut rather than of colour' (CB2: 494). Baudelaire's final, unfinished project on dandyism nonetheless hints at a return to more violent rupture with social norms: the nouns and adjectives that dominate his notes include 'astonishment, curiosity, singular, surprising, original, bizarre, haughty, gracious, wild,

---

[35] Mortemart-Boisse 1858: 50 (the quotation is misattributed by P. Perrot (1981: 250) and subsequently Steele 1998).

hot-tempered, violent'—several of which are evidently drawn from the semantic field of 'overt' eccentricity.[36] Representations of dandyism thus oscillated between the masculine pole of the 'ruffian' (overt singularity) and the feminized pole of the 'exquisite' (covert singularity).

It is commonly asserted that female dandyism did not exist during the nineteenth century. In the words of Roger Kempf, 'women are of little importance in the universal history of dandyism' (1977: 157). Even feminist critics have suggested that female dandyism only emerged in the interwar period with the arrival of wealthy American avant-garde women artists in Paris.[37] The figure of the female dandy was discussed in both English and French commentary, however, even if the two figures often had different connotations in a culture marked by sexual double standards. In England, for example, a novel by a male author entitled *The Charms of Dandyism, or, Living in Style* (1819), claimed to be written by 'Olivia Moreland, Chief of the Female Dandies'. It narrates the life of an extravagant courtesan, followed by her edifying repentance.[38] Approximate French equivalents to male fashionable types, such as 'merveilleuse', often denoted the courtesan; others such as 'lionne' and 'cocodette' did not invariably have such negative connotations. More generally, recent analyses of the *flâneur*, the figure that has dominated recent analyses of Parisian culture, have suggested that there can be indirect rather than direct equivalences between male and female social categories. The suggestion that *flâneuses* might have gone 'botanizing on the asphalt' alongside their male contemporaries has been much debated by feminist critics.[39] But subtler homologies arose, for instance, between the *flâneur* and the neglected figure of the *portière*, whose role as guardian of the apartment block made her a 'personification of urban observation' akin to both the *flâneur* and the omniscient realist narrator.[40] A similarly nuanced relationship existed between male and female forms of dandyism.

Representations of female dandyism were inseparable from both the emergence of the physiology and the gender ideologies of the July Monarchy. The 1804 civil code sought to enshrine a monolithic model

---

[36] Kempf's reconstruction of the project, based on the poet's notes (1977: 57).

[37] See Fillin-Yeh 2001: 10–22 and M. Perrot 1987*b*: 302. The 'artificial' prostitute and actress have been described as the real equivalents of the male dandy by Natta 1991: 160–1 and Garelick 1998: 3; both too hastily dismiss direct equivalents.

[38] See Ashe 1819.

[39] Walter Benjamin's metaphor (1997: 36). On the *flâneuse*, see Buck-Morss 1986: 113–17, Felski 1995: 215 n. 18 and Parsons 2000: ch. 1.

[40] See S. Marcus 1999: 42–50.

of feminine identity, defining women as dependent upon their fathers and husbands and devoted to domestic pursuits. Differences between women were often reduced to those of national temperament, summarized by Flaubert's philistine Homais: 'The German woman was dreamy, the French woman a libertine, the Italian woman passionate.'[41] Both models, which simplified female identity as a means of burying the disturbing memory of Revolutionary feminism, were inadvertently called into question by the panoramic literature of Paris. Social observers became aware of the wide range of female types; indeed, 'female identities seemed to proliferate'.[42] In comparison with both the Restoration and the Second Empire, when attitudes towards sexual difference were more rigid, the literary culture of the July Monarchy encouraged experimentation with gender boundaries.[43] Fiction addressed topics such as homosexuality and cross-dressing, and there was a surge of journalistic interest in women considered to be eccentric, including Saint-Simonian feminists, bluestockings, spinsters, and certain categories of courtesans. If Parisian life was often described as a *theatrum mundi*, two female types linked to eccentricity seemed particularly adept at taking centre stage: the *femme à la mode* and the *lionne*.

Calculating eccentricity: the *Femme à la mode*

Delphine de Girardin, a perceptive analyst of Parisian life, effectively reformulated the English distinction between the 'ruffian' and the 'exquisite' by differentiating between two types of women: *tapageuses*, or 'loud women', stun their audience through their flamboyant appearances, whilst *mystérieuses*, or 'mysterious women', present themselves as enigmas, hinting at their concealed depths.[44] Her distinction echoes the paradoxical role of eccentricity in discourses of etiquette, analysed in the previous chapter. Women were officially enjoined to avoid standing out, which was considered inimical to feminine self-effacement; yet they were simultaneously encouraged to exploit their supposedly innate coquetry in order to attain fashionable status.

[41] GF1: 669. On temperament, see Virey 1815: 508–31.
[42] Fraisse and Perrot 1992: 16. Prostitution also flourished in the typological imagination; see Ch. 4 below.
[43] See V. Thompson 1996: 121 and Wing 2004.
[44] Girardin 1857: IV, 193–200; see also Uzanne 1894b: 213–15.

Certain female types were particularly associated with the pursuit of celebrity. During the July Monarchy, symbolic dominance of Parisian society was the aim of the *femme à la mode*. None 'reigned' for very long: celebrity might last several months, weeks, or even days. The public's attention span appeared to be decreasing at a time when commodity culture was encouraging objects to be perceived as expendable. The *femme à la mode* and public opinion were dependent upon each other, the former for adulation, the latter for entertainment and distraction. Both were implicitly pathologized. The *femme à la mode* was portrayed as narcissistic and cold, fixated upon gaining maximum exposure; the public, in turn, suffered from dulled nerves. Eccentricity was referred to with metaphors at once culinary and erotic—*ragoût, assaisonnement, piquant* (spicy, highly seasoned, piquant)—which suggested the need for strong sensations to stimulate the flagging libido.

The writer and fashion journalist Eugénie Foa analysed the phenomenon in a physiological sketch of 1833 and in a novel published the following year. Her sketch proposed that the typical *femme à la mode* was a *parvenue*, the wife of a stockbroker whose shifting fortunes left her vulnerable to a sudden return to poverty. Public opinion was similarly precarious. Not necessarily the youngest, the prettiest, or the wealthiest, the *femme à la mode* calculated her public appearances carefully, appearing briefly at a number of events in one evening, 'like a flash, just long enough to dazzle, then she's gone' (1833: 277). In her mastery of theatrical self-presentation, she exemplified the recommendations of fashion manuals, which advised their readers to appear at gatherings like fairies and sylphs, 'like queens of the theatre, never leaving sufficient time for one to notice their imperfections or the artifices of coquetry'.[45] Such theatricality could be daunting, creating permanent anxiety that one's artifices might be 'discovered';[46] but the public's boredom threshold was a more serious obstacle. Foa's character has a strategic attitude towards costume, initially adhering to the code of simplicity but turning to eccentricity when she ceases to captivate: 'the most excessive luxury, the most stylish attire, *will still get her noticed*.'[47]

In her novel, Foa paints a rather different picture of the fashionable woman. Her heroine Marguerite is portrayed as passive and alienated from worldly life. Prevented by her family from marrying her beloved cousin George, she is forced to accept the ageing businessman Surgenne, who compels her to live ostentatiously in order to profit from

---

[45] Renneville 1852: 39.   [46] See De Beauvoir 1950: II, 129.
[47] 1833: 279; my emphasis.

her fashionable aura (he becomes furious when she attempts to wear the same dress on successive evenings, warning her it will damage his prospects). She throws herself into quasi-hysterical pursuit of fashionable life to distract herself from her misery, becoming the leading *femme à la mode* in Paris (1834: 207). Following illness, her husband's bankruptcy, her family's cruelty, and her cousin's betrayal, however, she dies in abject poverty in a fire. Tormented in every conceivable manner, Marguerite is a sacrificial victim to the coldly impersonal workings of finance and fashion. The narrator defuses the potentially alienating aspect of female narcissism by portraying Marguerite's social success as a form of self-imposed penance. The paradoxical juxtaposition of luxury and spiritual wretchedness became a central strategy in subsequent moralizing critiques of consumption: 'The luxury of society women is the mourning garb of their widowed hearts: their external riches are the mark of their internal destitution.'[48] A description of a *femme à la mode* first published around the same time as Foa's novel similarly shows her weeping behind the scenes, desperate for the love and friendship enjoyed by normal women. It compares her to a butterfly, a weather vane, and the figure of the wandering Jew.[49]

In a sketch of the *femme à la mode* by Virginie Ancelot published eight years later, the reader is introduced to Emma, Comtesse de Marcilly in a typical narcissistic scene: socially isolated and on the brink of falling from grace, she voices her secret fears to her mirror: 'Have I forgotten the art of creating an elegant outfit, bizarre enough to attract attention, but without coming close to that singularity which borders on the ridiculous?' (1840: 58). Far from turning to eccentricity when her reign is threatened, Emma's costume is designed from the outset to manifest the precise dose of singularity required to capture public attention:

In her eyes, women were no longer anything other than rivals; society, but a theatre in which she was constantly playing a role; and its diversions an opportunity for her to be seen! Her attire was no longer the chaste dress of a modest woman … First of all, with no expense spared, it represented luxury, variety, magnificence, and splendour; then came bizarre ideas and racy inventions to capture the public's wandering attention.   (1840: 59)

Fashionable women had to rewrite the rules of propriety, rejecting the codification of femininity in terms of demure self-effacement in order to initiate new trends.

[48] Loüis 1867: 116.   [49] Girardin 1856: II, 282–4.

Innovation was fraught with dangers: 'Only women reputed to be *ladies of fashion* may allow themselves the eccentricities of fantasy [les excentricités de la fantaisie]', warned the Comtesse de Renneville in her beauty manual (1852: 43). Comtesse Dash, the prolific novelist and author of conduct manuals, explains to her readers why they have to proceed carefully:

> I do not forbid you eccentricities where dressing gowns are concerned, provided, however, that you are in a position in which eccentricity is permitted: for not everyone who wishes to be eccentric may be so.—For some, it is a hideous absurdity. Only a very pretty, very rich and very prominent woman of uncontested wit and talent may risk such escapades. In a humble housewife or an unknown *bourgeoise*, they are the mark of flagrant conceitedness.
>
> (1868*a*: 67–8)

Her moralizing terminology evokes the suspicion of individualism widespread in discourses of *politesse*, and hints at the different rules governing bourgeois and aristocratic behaviour. The pursuit of eccentric fashions is seen as a dangerous, potentially immoral strategy to be deployed only by the expert.

Aware of these unspoken rules, Emma is tormented by the precariousness of her position. She has a pragmatic relationship to her image, and abandons eccentricity if necessary, for instance when a fashionable English rival appears: 'Lady Morton's delicate countenance could indeed have captured the capricious attention of society, but her outfits were so bizarre that their singularity bordered too closely on bad taste; they were *eccentric*, it is true, but without grace; in her presence, the simplicity of my clothing brought out the absurdity of hers.'[50] The qualification of 'eccentric' ('it is true') illustrates the term's ambiguity. The 'bizarre' and 'singular' are homologous with 'bad taste', it is implied, but 'eccentricity' is—just—an asset rather than an impediment. Success sways precariously upon the brink of vulgarity, since the sublime and the grotesque both give rise to astonishment.

Being a *femme à la mode* was a full-time career. Providing an outlet for female ambition, it required manly characteristics such as an 'iron constitution'; one caricature represented an executioner strangling a woman by her waist with the caption 'How one becomes a *femme à la mode*'.[51] Fashionable women's disregard for conventionally feminine behaviour linked them to courtesans, who were notorious for their

---

[50] Ancelot 1840: 59.
[51] Respectively Dash 1868*b*: 15; unpublished text cited in Maigron 1911: 184.

quasi-masculine insolence. In 1836 one commentator wrote that the term *femme à la mode*, formerly a compliment, ran the risk of insulting the *honnête femme* or decent woman; by 1855, the honour of such a woman was described as 'problematic'.[52] Why did this devaluation occur? The *femme à la mode* and the courtesan were both seen to be narcissistic and cold (the courtesan was sometimes termed a *femme sans cœur*, a woman without a heart, even a *femme sans âme*, a woman without a soul); both deployed eccentricity as a weapon; and both achieved only ephemeral celebrity. Such semantic similarities led to the eventual conflation of the two categories.

This tendency was always implicitly present in discourse on female celebrity. The demonic heroine of Balzac's *La Peau de chagrin* (The Wild Ass's Skin) (1831) is introduced as 'the beautiful Countess Fœdora, a *femme à la mode*': 'her movements, whilst walking or at rest, were neither gentle nor loving, despite their apparent sensuality . . . I discovered in her a type of intimate and secret briskness, a certain jolting and eccentric quality. There is nothing tender in the movements of a woman without a soul.'[53] Balzac glosses one of these terms in one of his discursive texts: 'Jolting movements are evidence of vice, or bad upbringing' (HB12: 284). Eccentricity too appears morally tainted. Fœdora is an archetypal literary *femme froide*, a key figure in the typologies of Parisian femininity. Her abrupt gestures evoke imagery of machinery, and she is repeatedly compared to a statue.[54] Emotionally indifferent to the point of sadism, her inner life retains a hieroglyphic opacity, enabling men to project upon her a range of fantasies.[55] Though she was able to dominate public opinion, the *femme à la mode*, it was suspected, was tainted by hidden vice. An ambiguous figure, she called into question distinctions by means of which nineteenth-century readers made sense of their world: between the social classes, between the male and female psyche, between virtue and vice.

The *lionne*

The *femme à la mode* represented eccentricity harnessed to the service of neurotic self-scrutiny. In contrast, the *lionne* or lioness, a subcategory of the *femme à la mode*, was associated with imagery of bodily vitality

[52] Respectively Raisson 1836: 191 and Loüis 1867: 139.
[53] Respectively HB11: 145, 169.   [54] HB11: 159, 184.
[55] Compare Sand 1960: 201n1.

Fig. 4. A *lionne* in riding costume with whip and gun, by Grandville. (Hetzel 1842: I, 378) © British Library Board. All Rights Reserved. (C.155.h.21)

(see Fig. 4). The emergence of the term to denote an icon of fashion dates from the first decade of the July Monarchy, between the decline of the ethereal heroine of Romanticism and the advent of the voluptuous Second Empire ideal.[56] Whilst the *lionne* rejected dreamy introspection and suffering, she embodied Romanticism's more life-affirming values such as exoticism and the thirst for novelty; since she was married, her sexuality could legitimately be stressed. Both *lion* and *lionne* were glossed, in the words of a commentator looking back from the 1860s on this outdated category, as 'an eccentric or extra-noticeable individual'.[57]

<hr/>

[56] Maigron 1911: 48. See Girardin 1856: I, 61–2. Stern dates the *lionne* to 1830 (1880: 335).
[57] Chapus 1877: 177 (first published 1861).

Like male dandies, fashionable female eccentrics were first described in the context of Anglophilia; in a fictional narrative of 1831, for instance, Prosper Mérimée refers to 'the women, and there are many of them, who lay claim to an original and *eccentric* character [*caractère original, eccentric*], as they say in England'.[58] A French physiological sketch from 1840 depicts the *lionne* as an aspirant member of the anglophile male elite of the July Monarchy. It suggests that she strove for originality in her lifestyle as a whole, rather than merely her toilette:

Madame Dureynel's name was soon mentioned amongst the divinities of Parisian fashion, and today she figures prominently in that elite of *merveilleuses* whom one meets at all elegant society functions; indefatigable amazons, spurning the peaceful recreations of their sex, and abdicating the gentle influence of their discrete charms to follow our dandies to the races and join in the large and small-scale schemings of the Jockey's Club; queens of the equestrian world, who have been dubbed 'the *Lionnes*' in recognition of the strength, intrepidity, and inexhaustible ardour which they daily evince.   (Guinot 1840: 10)

The surrogate masculinity of the *lionne* is expressed in her love of strenuous physical exercise such as horse riding, pigeon shooting, and swimming, her eating with a hearty appetite (unlike the self-starving Romantic heroine), and her manly habits such as drinking and smoking. But reference to 'inexhaustible ardour' hints at her femininity, and ambiguity is created by the term *merveilleuse*: the equivalent of *merveilleux*, a precursor of 'dandy', it had been used in the immediate post-Revolutionary period to refer to courtesans.[59]

The figure raised a central paradox in relation to female eccentricity. She was eccentric in relation to the norms of femininity, yet by virtue of this she conformed to, rather than departed from, the norms of masculinity. The paradox is foregrounded in Balzac's *Physiologie du mariage*, an advice manual for husbands. The narrator describes the 'first symptoms' that herald the married woman's decision to embark upon her first affair:

the first symptom in a woman is great eccentricity [*une grande excentricité*] . . . She dresses with great care, in order, so she claims, to flatter your vanity by attracting all eyes to her at parties and social engagements. Back in the

---

[58] Mérimée 1957: 256, emphasis in original. English-style clubs and 'masculine' behaviour in French women were linked from the late 18th cent. (Grieder 1985: 26–7).
[59] For additional descriptions of the *lionne* see Deriège 1842: 2; HB1: 916–17 and 12: 167; and Dash 1868*a*: 248–53.

tedium of home and hearth, you occasionally find her sombre and thoughtful; then suddenly she is laughing and gay as if striving to drown her sorrows; or she adopts the grave air of a German marching into battle.   (HB11: 991)

In this passage, Balzac summarizes the symptoms of mild hysteria, according to the medical codes of his time. In their emotional changeability, hysterics were often considered to be quintessentially feminine, hence the wife's *grande excentricité* merely exaggerates the norms of femininity.[60]

The passage also resonates with a medical tendency to frame women's identity in dramatic terms.[61] The medical publicist J.-J. Virey concluded his analysis of female nature with a panegyric to *la femme*: now she is a frolicking nymph, he writes, now an inconsolable widow, a tousled bacchante, a seductive Circe, and a cruel Medea.[62] Many of the characteristics ascribed to female nature were transferred onto the malady of hysteria itself, which was repeatedly described as a 'proteus' and 'chameleon'.[63] The symptoms of moderate hystericism were close synonyms of eccentricity. Emotive yet vague terms such as *bizarre*, *étrange*, *capricieux*, *fantasque*, *incohérent*, and *extravagant* proliferate in medical treatises, from eighteenth-century doctors to dozens of doctors and alienists writing before Charcot.[64]

Female eccentricity could also, however, denote the diametrically opposed phenomenon of departure from the mildly hysterical *female* norm, as, for example, in the image of female self-possession. By the late eighteenth century, the medical sciences had come to posit radical incommensurability between the sexes. Figures such as P. Roussel and J.-J. Virey argued that sexual difference permeated every aspect of mind and body: 'a woman is a woman not merely in one aspect, but rather from all the possible angles from which she can be contemplated.'[65] The ideal of sexual complementarity became deeply entrenched in the

[60] See e.g. Virey 1815: 570 and B.-A. Morel 1860: 728.
[61] Though Balzac's wife is sincere in this passage, she begins acting once embarked on an affair.
[62] Virey 1815: 572; see Roussel 1775: 26–7, 29–30.
[63] e.g. Brachet 1847: 257; Briquet 1859: 554. Hysteria was framed as a 'neuromimetic' malady in the *fin-de-siècle*, able to mimic the symptoms of other illnesses (see Micale 1995: 182 and Smith-Rosenberg 1986: 200). On the dramatization of hysteria, see Didi-Hubermann 1982: 139–45.
[64] e.g. Louyer-Villermay 1816: 1, 57, Sandras 1851: 1, 11–27, Brachet 1844: 35–7, 52–5; Briquet 1859: 201.
[65] Roussel 1775: 2. Thomas Laqueur has influentially described the shift from the Galenic 'one sex model' to modern views of 'two incommensurable sexes' (1990: 154–61, 194–8), though his positing of absolute epistemological rupture is controversial.

medical and cultural imagination. The male norm consisted in stoicism, courage, and aggression; men were held to have a stronger sense of self and to be more energetic than women, for 'vital fire' was located in the seminal fluid.[66] Conversely, the female norm consisted in sensitivity and timidity. Women were believed to be naturally sluggish,[67] to have an innate instinct for servitude, and a weak sense of self (hence their ability to move rapidly from one mood to another). Medical science framed women as lacking in sexual desire—even if popular culture continued to affirm their sexual voracity.[68] Men were thus considered eccentric in relation to the male norm and disparagingly labelled 'femmelettes' ('little women') when they manifested excessive sensibility, often linked to hypochondria, in some respects the male equivalent of hysteria.[69] Women, in turn, were considered eccentric in relation to the female norm, and termed 'homasse' ('mannish'), when they manifested coldness or self-control.

The *lionne* exemplified the second, more alarming form of eccentricity in which women appropriated male physiological norms. She is portrayed in one sketch as disdainfully dismissing women who suffer from vapours and migraines as *femmelettes*.[70] Female participation in sporting pursuits was discouraged during the early nineteenth century in the belief that it damaged women's complexion and delicate constitutions. By the *fin de siècle*, though, gymnastics commonly formed part of young girls' education, whilst outdoor sports such as bicycling became popular for both sexes.[71] The *lionne* rejected the model of female weakness many decades before such attitudes became widespread. She was also remarkable in meeting with male approval, despite her 'masculine' qualities. Pretty and accomplished, she was situated at the pinnacle of fashionable life.[72] One illustration depicts the *lionne* in a dressing gown; it thereby highlights uncertainties in masculine identity, for this item was one of the few refuges of *ancien régime* luxury and 'feminine' caprice in nineteenth-century male clothing.[73] Her bold gaze directed towards the viewer hints at erotic availability, since women who did not modestly lower their gaze were often assumed to be prostitutes (see Fig. 5).[74]

---

[66] Virey 1823: 96–9. See e.g. Nye 1998: 118–26.
[67] See Jaton 1984: 15–19.
[68] See Brachet 1844: 298–303 and Laqueur 1990: 161–3, 181–92.
[69] Brachet 1844: 291.   [70] Guinot 1840: 12
[71] See E. Wilson 1987: 160–6.   [72] Guinot 1840: 15.
[73] See P. Perrot 1981: 201.   [74] See Clark 2003: ch. 2.

Fig. 5. The *lionne*: 'Her attire is utterly ambiguous.' (*Les Français peints par eux-mêmes*, 1853–9: I (1853), 373) © British Library Board. All Rights Reserved. (12355.k.4)

In contrast, equally eccentric female figures such as the bluestocking were the target of unrelenting hostility. 'Her attire is as eccentric as her mind', wrote the author of one conduct manual, whilst another warned that eccentricity provided a fatal clue to even the neatest blue-stocking's identity: 'Though she may be well-groomed ... there is always something singular, eccentric or indeed original about her toilette by which she may be recognized.'[75] Perceived as a usurper of male privilege, the bluestocking was defeminized—as many approvingly noted, the grammatical gender of the term *bas-bleu* was masculine—and relegated to a realm of disgusting monstrosity. The label 'excentrique' was pre-dominantly used critically in descriptions of women with artistic or

[75] Constantin 1854: 86, Boitard 1851: 177.

intellectual aspirations. A notable exception was George Sand, who repeatedly laid claim to the creative connotations of the term in her autobiography, and at times used it to designate her female characters.[76] This was, however, largely in relation to her self-consciously Bohemian persona, which her supporters and detractors alike acknowledged was quite exceptional in a woman.

Despite her ostensibly radical lifestyle, the *lionne* was complicit with the social hierarchies of her time. In order to create astonishment, the July Monarchy *lionne* had to be an exception: 'this taste for a pleasure generally little known to the weaker sex lent them something of the zest of the exceptional, a halo of eccentricity [une auréole d'excentricité].'[77] She could not, therefore, be a feminist. The early 1830s saw the emergence of the *femme libre* (free woman) or *femme nouvelle* (new woman) associated with Saint-Simonian feminism, as well as George Sand's fictional portraits of rebellious women. In one sketch of 1842, the author assured his readers that the *lionne* was not related to such women, since all she wanted was to 'remain a woman', leaving the 'banal' task of wielding political power to men.[78] In her memoirs, Daniel Stern described the *lionne* as a symbol of 'l'excentricité tapageuse' (noisy eccentricity), explicitly linking her to Sand's heroines:[79]

In imitation of George Sand's heroines, the *lionne* pretended to disdain the feminine graces. She wanted neither to delight others with her beauty nor to charm them with her wit, but rather to surprise and astonish them with her audacity. Horsewoman and huntress, her riding crop raised aloft, spurs at her heels, a rifle over her shoulder, a cigar in her mouth, a glass in her hand, all impertinence and bluster, the *lionne* took pleasure in defying and disconcerting gentlemen with her extravagant behaviour. (1880: 355)

Whilst her description stresses the *lionne*'s brutishness, the multiplication of phallic imagery strongly eroticizes her. Stern also implies that the *lionne*'s masculine persona is contrived, essentially a coquettish strategy. During the *fin de siècle*, Octave Uzanne retrospectively sought to connect the emergence of a generation of eccentric women with that of the Vésuviennes, a movement of radical feminist socialists (1894*b*: 194). The conflation of *lionne*, Sandean heroine and radical, however, is implausible, and it is equally mistaken to view the *lionne* as

---

[76] Sand 1879: 106, 334, 375, 385; see also 1993: 182.
[77] Émile Blavet in 1887, cited in Goulemot and Oster 1989: 277.
[78] Guinot 1840: 10.
[79] Stern's original phrase was 'fantaisie tapageuse' (Klein 1976: 111).

a Bohemian.[80] The *lionne* of the July Monarchy was, in the cultural imagination, a wealthy woman enacting transgression in the sphere of lifestyle and self-presentation. The feminist and bluestocking had different concerns and often different class affiliations.[81]

Androgynous women were typically perceived as threatening: 'A woman who is too mannish and masculine will never be loved by a man; he would believe himself to be sinning with her as if with a member of his own sex, and would feel the same sense of repugnance', J.-J. Virey wrote (1815: 551), conceding that such women were well suited to effeminate men, since complementarity between the sexes creates equilibrium. Subsequent critics such as Alphonse Karr agreed that men who found the *lionne* attractive were effeminate and perverted (1860: 14). Nonetheless, cross-dressing and lesbian tableaux were also staples of the brothel and the heterosexual male imaginary of the period, again problematizing attempts to appropriate the *lionne* as an early feminist.[82]

A vogue for animal terminology was evident in many physiologies, finding its best-known expression in Balzac's Foreword to the *Comédie humaine*, in which the author compares his enterprise to the zoological taxonomies of Étienne Geoffroy Saint-Hilaire (HB1: 7–9). Animal metaphors placed the *lionne*'s body at the centre of commentary.[83] The bourgeois erotic code dictated that women hide their desire, that they feign being prey forced to 'yield' to concerted male assault.[84] Difficult to tame, the *lionne* appealed to men's desire for more challenging conquests.[85] The *lionne*'s unconventional qualities could be inscribed within both reactionary ideologies of women's closeness to nature and the looser behavioural codes applied to prostitutes and courtesans.

The virtue of this figure was inevitably called into question, like that of the *femme à la mode*. In a sketch of 1842, a mother-in-law criticizes her son's fashionable wife: 'She does not want (please note!) her son's wife to be too much of a *lionne*, for she claims (see how prejudiced she is!) that being very much of a *lionne* leads a little too far.'[86] Scandalous women held to be the *lionne*'s role models included the actress Virginie Déjazet, a Parisian *rat* or pre-pubescent performer immersed in sexual

---

[80] As E. Wilson does (2000: 50), following Richardson 1969.
[81] See Moses 1984: 128–34.
[82] As the success of Théophile Gautier's salacious *Mademoiselle de Maupin* in 1835–6 demonstrates. See also Coffignon 1888: 312. *Lorettes* were portrayed applying for permission to cross-dress in Alhoy 1841: 88, but official permits were rarely granted; see Steele 1998: 162–4.
[83] Uzanne 1894*b*: 195.   [84] Corbin 1987*b*: 530.
[85] See e.g. Arago 1841: 32, Uzanne 1894*a*: 293.   [86] Marie 1842: 255.

Fig. 6. A *lorette* cross-dressing and wearing a false moustache. (Neufville 1842: 55) © British Library Board. All Rights Reserved. (1094.g.8)

scandal from the age of 10,[87] Fanny Essler, a dancer who performed on the Parisian stage dressed as a man, and Lola Montès, an Irish dancer and 'eccentric adventurer' known for her masculine attire, promiscuity, and horsewhipping men who irritated her.[88] The *lionne* was also seen to have certain affinities with the *lorette*, the July Monarchy term for a middle-ranking kept woman. One physiology details the latter's 'eccentricities', terming her a *lionne*; another shows her cross-dressing and sporting a moustache (see Fig. 6).[89] Accounts ritually evoked the *lorette*'s love of flouting public opinion.[90] If overt female eccentricity was often suspect during the July Monarchy, however, covert eccentricity proved even more threatening to the regulation of female identity.

[87] See Colin 1942: 239–47.
[88] Mirecourt 1857: 40–3, 54, 82; see also Anon. 1841*a*: 302 and Delvau 1867*b*: 312.
[89] Alhoy 1841: 85–96, 94 and Neufville 1842: 55; see also the subtitle of Anon. [n.d.].
[90] Delvau 1848: 59, 75, 81; also Texier 1853: 53.

Concealed eccentricity

The eccentricity of the *lionne* was expressed externally, through bizarre clothing and behaviour; she was framed as a 'ruffian' and 'tapageuse'. To the male dandies who adopted Beau Brummell's prohibition of external eccentricity, there corresponded a female 'exquisite', a 'mystérieuse' who concealed her singularity behind an inscrutable exterior.[91]

Barbey d'Aurevilly, who had championed the more discreet model of male dandyism, portrayed the latter type in a novella entitled *L'Amour impossible* (1841). Written shortly before Barbey produced his influential essay on dandyism, *Du dandysme et de George Brummell* (1845), it recounts a psychological battle between a young man, Maulévrier, and an emotionally cold older woman, Mme de Gesvres. Each seeks to seduce the other whilst preserving his or her autonomy. Failing in his attempt, and having sacrificed to Mme de Gesvres his 'feminine' lover Mme d'Anglure, who consequently dies of grief, Maulévrier is contaminated by Mme de Gesvres's inability to love, and the narrative closes with a depiction of their joint emotional sterility. An anonymous review, probably written by Sainte-Beuve or Philarète Chasles, explicitly interprets the text in relation to the rhetoric of the physiology and the figure of the *lionne*: 'It concerns a *femme à la mode*, a *lionne* who steals the lover of one of her friends yet barely derives any pleasure from her actions, for both she and he are jaded … The style, language, costumes and manners of this novella follow the most modern tendencies; fashion plays a large part, and fashionable jargon is not absent' (JB1: 1252). The review compares Mme de Gesvres to a *panthère*, a wealthy kept woman, again situating the novella within the taxonomic framework of the physiology. (Barbey knew this discourse well, for much of his writing on dandyism first appeared in women's fashion magazines.) Mme de Gesvres embodies both the narcissistic coldness of the *femme à la mode* and the self-confidence of the *lionne*, but this combination, elaborated by Barbey into one of the earliest French models of female dandyism, was more threatening than either element alone.[92]

Just as they reworked themes from the literary physiology, Barbey's texts presupposed that their readers would grasp the cultural meanings

---

[91] See Coblence 1988: 134–66.

[92] In his discussion of prostitution in Barbey's writing, Charles Bernheimer opposes women, prostitution, and animal passion to men, dandyism, and emotional coldness, but this ignores the existence of female dandies who, precisely, undermine such stereotypical polarities (1989: 75–88).

sedimented around medical concepts such as coldness, hermaphrodism, and melancholia. First, and in line with the models of national temperament which retained their prestige well into the century, Barbey associated dandies with the phlegmatic and cold north, as opposed to the sanguine and passionate Latin south (JB2: 671, 705 n.). Female coldness was more likely to be pathologized within the medical codes of the period. Doctors believed that civilization cooled down women's innately hysterical tendencies and made them wiser; excessive female coldness such as that of the *femme froide* was explained in terms of frigidity and 'manliness'.[93] Upon meeting the Marquise de Vallon, the woman on whom Mme de Gesvres was closely modelled, Barbey placed her in the category of female exception: 'Despite certain senseless desires and the need for tenderness, rooted in the hearts of women, she is protected by a male spirit and an unshakeable coolness. She desires more with her mind than with her heart' (JB2: 853). He evokes Vallon's austere coldness with imagery of snow, and Gesvres's name hints at her iciness, since *givre* means frost. Mme de Gesvres's deviance is particularly subtle. The narrator remarks that she is not fixated upon her image in the mirror like the feminine coquette, thus apparently exempting her from accusations of vanity (JB1: 45); in the course of the narrative, however, it emerges that she is convinced of her own aristocratic superiority. Barbey considered this a central feature of dandyism, and included it prominently in his own self-descriptions.

Second, Barbey stressed the dandy's androgyny; this predominantly spiritual and psychological category often overlapped with 'hermaphrodism', its biological corollary, in nineteenth-century writing. His essay on dandyism closes with a lyrical invocation of dandies' transcendence of sexual difference, in which he terms them the 'androgynes of history' (JB2: 718). Though critical discussion has focused upon the androgyny and feminization of the male dandy, Barbey's comment simultaneously refers to the androgyny of the *female* dandy, associated with her 'virilization' and hence her eccentricity in relation to the norms of feminine psychology. Mme de Gesvres represents psychological hybridity: 'it was a hermaphrodism which blended together so thoroughly the charming and the imposing, the subjugating and the intoxicating, that nothing like it had ever been produced in all of art and its incomparable flights of fancy' (JB1: 46–7).

---

[93] See Edelman 2003: 52 and C. W. Thompson 1997: 20–1.

Barbey's image of the monster draws on an aesthetic trope of Romanticism, the monstrously original work emerging from the male artistic imagination.[94] It also evokes a topical medical debate. The most important nineteenth-century analysis of malformations, Isidore Geoffroy Saint-Hilaire's *Traité de tératologie* (Treatise on Teratology) (1832–7), cites as an example of the female pole of the hermaphroditic spectrum the cold and frigid woman.[95] French doctors were intrigued by the problem of the hermaphrodite's desire. J.-J. Virey's description of the hermaphrodite was typical: '[it] would no longer have any desire; it would be neuter and, as it were, sated. It would not therefore love and would be incapable of being loved. It would be an equivocal, ambiguous, indifferent individual, cold in all senses of the word' (1815: 551). For Virey, hermaphrodites are condemned to emotional indifference since they cannot be propelled towards a member of the opposite sex with complementary characteristics; they already contain inner equilibrium. His metaphors resonate with Barbey's depiction of dandyism, and specifically to the inability of the androgynous Gesvres and Maulévrier to experience love.

Finally, the historically specific category of melancholia lay behind many nineteenth-century representations of problematic desire. It was discussed during the first half of the century in terms of *mal du siècle*, *ennui*, and *spleen*, terms often used loosely. Gesves and Maulévrier are portrayed as suffering from pervasive ennui, and are linked to a social type characterized by the absence of desire for anyone other than himself: the *fat*. This figure, a vain individual who exudes a type of arrogant indifference to others, was known to a wide audience from the Parisian physiology.[96] Barbey claims that he was tempted to place as the epigraph to his essay on dandyism '*Of a* fat, *by a* fat, *for* fats' (JB2: 1438), and evinces strong identification with the type in his autobiographical writing. Barbey's depiction of Mme de Gesvres as a female *fat* departs strikingly from the cultural convention that the *fat* was a male subject, symbolized by the absence of a female form of the term. He even subsequently experimented with approximate equivalents such as 'femmes fates', or women *fats* (JB2: 700 n.).

In the preface to the second edition of *L'Amour impossible* in 1859, Barbey portrays himself as being embarrassed by his earlier depiction of female singularity. He justifies it against charges of implausibility

---

[94] See Huet 1993.   [95] See Nye 1998: 59–65.
[96] See Ancelot 1840: 61 and Foa 1841.

on the grounds that Mme de Gesvres was typical of the fashionably melancholic Parisian women of the late July Monarchy (explicitly, again, termed *femmes à la mode*): '[They] used to pride themselves on their coolness, like aged *fats* who boast of their jadedness even before they are old. These singular female hypocrites would *take on roles*; some played angels and others demons, but all, angels or demons, would *claim* that they loathed emotion' (JB1: 1254, my emphasis). By creating a female *fat*, Barbey was transforming a literary model with strongly masculine associations. This bold move accounts for his subsequent embarrassment, as well as his attempt (like many of the writers who portrayed the *lionne*) to argue that such women were merely feigning their unfeminine absence of emotion. Similarly rewriting the male malady of melancholia for a female character, George Sand had portrayed female *mal du siècle* in her partially autobiographical novel *Lélia*, published in 1833. This forms an important intertextual reference at the end of Barbey's novel when a momentarily guilty Mme de Gesvres claims to identify with Sand's impotent heroine. An unpublished section of Barbey's novel explores this theme at length.[97] Yet Barbey subsequently dismissed Sand's impotent heroine as 'an impossibility', echoing the cultural doxa which posited a necessary link between femininity and sensibility (1979: II, 21).

Despite Barbey's later discomfort with *L'Amour impossible*, he returned to the theme of female coldness, particularly in 'Le Dessous de cartes d'une partie de whist' (The Story Behind a Game of Whist), originally published in 1850, and 'Le Bonheur dans le crime' (Happiness in Crime) (1874).[98] The first recounts the psychological impenetrability of Marmor de Karkoël and Mme de Stasseville.[99] The latter is, like Mme de Gesvres and the figure of the hermaphrodite, cold and emotionally indifferent:

Her nature was of the stagnant sort; a woman dandy [une espèce de *femme-dandy*], the English would have called her ... 'She belongs to the class of cold-blooded animals,' her doctor used to whisper confidentially to his intimates, thinking to explain her by a simile, as a disease is diagnosed by the symptoms. Though she always looked ill, the baffled doctor declared that there was nothing

[97] See JB1: 133–5 and 1247–8. On the masculinity of French romantic melancholia, see Waller 1993.
[98] The former was first published in *La Mode* in 1849 as 'Ricochets de conversation I: le dessous de cartes d'une partie de whist'.
[99] Stasseville was also modelled on Mme Franqueville Dupoirier, as Barbey's letters attest.

the matter with her. Was this discretion? or was he really blind? At any rate, she never complained of discomfort, whether physical or moral. She had not even that shade of melancholy, as much physical as anything else, that usually broods over the mortified features of women of forty … She seemed determined to falsify her reputation as a woman of strong mind [femme spirituelle] by refusing altogether to accentuate her behaviour with any of those individual ways of behaving that we call eccentricities.

(JB2: 148; 1986: 146–7, trans. modified)

Through his suggestion that the doctor might be incompetent, the narrator seems to posit illness as the explanation. But this is qualified by recognition that the main symptom consists precisely in the absence or ambiguity of conventional symptoms.

The passage suggests various explanations for her singular character, including temperament and humour,[100] melancholia, and an unspecified pathology; but it simultaneously calls them all into question. The frenetic conclusion of the narrative, which reveals Mme de Stasseville's monstrous infanticide, adds the moral categories of perversity and sin to this list. In contemporaneous medical theory, the condition described in this passage is typical of moral insanity and lucid madness, maladies which increasingly preoccupied alienists in the latter part of the century in the context of a growing tendency to medicalize unconventional behaviour.[101]

Mme de Stasseville's explicit dissociation from eccentricity symbolizes her dissociation from the 'overt' peculiarity of figures such as the July Monarchy *lionne*; it echoes Barbey's theoretical dissociation of the understated singularity of dandyism from its 'unbridled', 'wild', and 'blind' English relative, eccentricity. Mme de Gesvres was initially exempted from overt vanity only to have her covert aristocratic self-love subsequently affirmed. So too Mme de Stasseville is arguably dissociated from 'vulgar' understandings of melancholia and eccentricity only for more subtle aristocratic variants of these qualities to be reinscribed in her identity.[102]

Barbey's vision of female dandyism was elaborated during a surge of literary interest in female singularity and coldness. He highlighted the affinities of Hauteclaire, his female dandy, with Stendhal's idiosyncratic heroine Mathilde de la Mole, again referring to the latter in one

---

[100] See JB2: 671, 705 n. and Gill 2007.   [101] See Ch. 8 below.
[102] For a more detailed discussion of these issues, see Gill 2007.

of his theoretical texts on dandyism.[103] Though Stendhal never used the term 'excentrique' to describe his characters, his male and female protagonists are described repeatedly with the term's closest synonyms ('singular', 'original', 'bizarre', 'strange'). The latter are at times termed *femmes originales*, and characters such as Mathilde, Lamiel, and Mme Grandet subvert medical conceptions of female temperament in very similar ways to the female dandy.[104] Cold and self-possessed, they are described with the language of exception; Lamiel, for example, is dubbed 'Mlle Autrement' ('Miss Differently').[105] Their anarchic energy relates them to the *lionne*, a figure who, Daniel Stern proposed, typified young women's thirst for dangerous sensations in reaction to the monotonous 'comme il faut' of the Faubourg Saint-Germain around 1830.[106] Mathilde suffers from *ennui* and requires 'anxiety' to stimulate her nerves, and was famously described by Stendhal as an 'impossible' figure in an ironic narratorial aside.[107] Balzac's portrait of the aristocratic Lady Arabelle Dudley in *Le Lys dans la vallée* (The Lily of the Valley) (1836) explored similar themes, drawing on the discourses of national temperament. Lady Dudley is prone to boredom and spleen, is described as having a typically English need for shocking and extraordinary sensations, and is explicitly compared to a lioness.[108]

Referring to *all* singular women, the alienist Jean-Louis Brachet asserted in 1847 that women were naturally undifferentiated: 'women seem to have been cast from a common mould … exceptions are an error of nature' (64). The ambiguous appeal of the *femme froide* intensified in the latter part of the century, as the *fin-de-siècle* 'idol of perversity' became an important cultural model of femininity, echoed in the medical image of the perverse and scheming female hysteric.[109] In contrast to this growing cultural fascination with women who appropriated masculine qualities such as coldness and self-control, representations of male dandies produced towards the *fin de siècle* increasingly emphasized their feminine traits, such as nervous sensitivity, and often hinted at sexual perversion or homosexuality. This new model of male dandyism was equally at odds with the early French dandies who emulated the exquisite but nonetheless virile and stoical persona of Beau Brummell, and with the stereotypically masculine ruffian. Huysmans's novel *À Rebours*

---

[103] JB2: 724, 1281.   [104] See C. W. Thompson 1997: 20–1.
[105] Stendhal 1971: 132 n.   [106] Stern 1880: 355.
[107] Stendhal 1948: 513. On 19th-cent. critical debates on her plausibility, see Prendergast 1986: 120–5.
[108] HB9: 1142–3.   [109] See e.g. Richet 1880: 344.

(Against the Grain) (1884), for example, constitutes an extended portrait of this new model of feminized dandyism, though the reclusive central character of the novel, Des Esseintes, simultaneously reworks many of the themes elaborated since the July Monarchy: he suffers from melancholia, is intrigued by Englishness, and fantasizes about the circus acrobat Miss Urania, a virile woman who complements his weak and sickly persona in precisely the manner predicted by J.-J. Virey. The eccentricity of Des Esseintes is repeatedly highlighted, in relation to his deliberately shocking attire, interior decoration, and social performances, of which he is acutely self-conscious.[110] The mythologies surrounding real life dandies such as Robert de Montesquiou popularized a similarly flamboyant and implicitly homosexual model of male dandyism.

In conclusion, the vocabulary and typologies of fashionable individualism expanded significantly during the July Monarchy, as new terms such as 'dandy' and 'excentrique' were given wide currency in genres such as the literary physiology. All dandies needed to diverge from bourgeois norms in order to signal their distinction, even those who avoided allegedly 'vulgar' sartorial and behavioural eccentricity. The difference lay primarily in the hermeneutic skill required of their audiences. The ascetic 'exquisite' was designed to appeal to a small group of initiates able to decipher the most subtle of nuances, whilst the public persona of the 'ruffian' was aimed at a broader public which required more obviously codified signs such as those found in the sensation novel. The figures of the cold and dissimulating woman and the feminized *fin-de-siècle* male dandy represent perhaps the two most culturally challenging of many possible combinations between two sets of conceptual oppositions: dandyism as overt or covert eccentricity, in the one instance, and 'feminine' or 'virile' dandyism, in the other. These axes, I have suggested, allow the shifting relationship between dandyism and eccentricity to be plotted as it evolved over time and fluctuated according to context and genre.

Unconventional women were more likely to be pathologized than their male counterparts, since female singularity was incompatible with the dominant medical view that normal women could not be individuated, on the grounds that the essence of femininity was self-abnegation. The *lionne* was associated with unfeminine qualities such as physical

[110] Huysmans 1907: 16, 165; 106.

strength and audacity, but she met with greater approval than equally eccentric figures such as the bluestocking owing to her affinity with aristocratic anglophile culture and her erotic appeal. However, the meaning of female eccentricity was fundamentally ambiguous within the cultural codes of medicine. The behaviour of hysterical women was described as 'eccentric', 'bizarre', and 'singular', implicitly in relation to the norms of masculinity such as stoicism and self-control. In contrast, types such as female dandies, female *fats*, and *femmes froides* were portrayed as psychologically androgynous and prone to dissimulation, hence were perceived as eccentric in relation to the norms of feminine psychology. During the Second Empire, the metaphorical connections between female eccentricity, enigma, and coldness persisted, though they became attached predominantly to the cultural sphere of the *demi-monde*.

4

The *Demi-Monde*

For women, eccentricity is akin to depravity. How great a hold
upon her she grants to evil, by wanting to be noticed at any price!

Henri Nadault de Buffon[1]

The range of meanings attached to female eccentricity narrowed considerably after the demise of the Second Republic. In the panoramic
literature of the July Monarchy, various female types were termed eccentric, from bluestockings and spinsters to fashionable female aristocrats,
dandies, and *lorettes*. Though all these figures were unconventional, only
some were portrayed negatively. During the Second Empire, in contrast,
female eccentricity was almost invariably associated with the *demi-
monde*, the 'half-world' separating respectable women from prostitutes.
The dialectic between overt and covert eccentricity which played a key
role in representations of dandyism was reformulated in discourse about
courtesans. Certain courtesans flaunted their difference from respectable
women; indeed, the courtesan was widely referred to as a *femme excentrique* on account of her extravagant attire and her role at the centre
of the fashion industry. Others sought to emulate society women and
proved notoriously difficult to differentiate from them. All, though,
lacked the defining quality of the respectable woman: 'honour', equated
in nineteenth-century French gender ideology with chastity before marriage and subsequently with avoiding even the slightest suspicion of
adultery.[2]

The different degrees of openness with which courtesans signalled
their identity generated a complex and widely discussed hermeneutics
of female appearances. Eccentricity was portrayed in Second Empire
drama and social commentary as an important though not infallible
clue to deciphering the truth about women's social status and honour.

[1] 1869: 75.   [2] On the honour ethic, see Nye 1998: 29–30.

The cultural prominence of the *demi-monde* became the subject of conservative polemic designed to generate moral panic in its readers and thereby halt the perceived undermining of the social order. Eccentricity was also implicated in criticism of the luxury industry by Catholics and neo-Stoic moralists during a period of growing materialism and industrial expansion. Cultural critics and some politicians alleged that the pursuit of eccentric fashions encouraged respectable women to abandon their domestic duties, in favour of narcissism and hysterical consumption. Underlying these debates were wider social anxieties about the blurring of boundaries between the social classes, and physical and national decline.

'Semi-prostitution' and the typological imagination

The literary culture of the July Monarchy was tolerant of gender fluidity in comparison to both the Restoration and the latter part of the century, evident both in the emergence of 'eccentric' female types after 1830 and in fictional depictions of gender ambiguity and transgressive desire. During the Second Empire, ideologies of sexuality and gender became increasingly rigid, at the same time that courtesans and *demi-mondaines* gained unprecedented cultural influence. 'People thought at first that it was exceptional and eccentric to Parisian life,' wrote Jules Castagnary of venal sexuality in 1866, 'but they now realize that in Parisian life, everything, or almost everything, leads towards it.'[3] The cultural panic evident in such comments was echoed in a wide body of commentary, including official reports by doctors and hygienists, guides to urban pleasure written from a perspective of male complicity, and drama and journalism designed to influence middle-class attitudes towards female sexuality.

Discourse on female eccentricity was inseparable from the shifting typologies of the *demi-monde*. Ritualized expressions of astonishment were common in analyses of the complex hierarchies of venal sexuality. 'How many fine distinctions and varieties of fallen women are to be found in the world of semi-prostitution, which is often worse than that of open prostitution!' wrote the journalist Arnould Frémy; a former police officer repeated this observation in a lower register: 'How many

---

[3] Cited in Burton 1994: 60.

shades of mud there are in this mire!'[4] Frémy's term 'semi-prostitution' was designed to encompass the large class of women who, though not 'respectable', were not technically considered prostitutes by the police, including courtesans and kept women, fallen women, *demi-mondaines*, actresses, and bourgeois wives engaging in clandestine sexual encounters for financial gain.[5] As his comment suggests, this realm was the focus of considerable bourgeois anxiety, for it threatened to undermine class boundaries, spread venereal disease in the social elite, and dissipate the wealth and sexual energy of bourgeois husbands.

To a greater degree than in any other nation, French venal sexuality formed an intricate counterpart to the hierarchy of polite society, giving rise to an array of categories and terms which descended from the *grande cocotte* (courtesan) to the lowly *fille publique* (common prostitute). Such minute differentiation reflected the mania for typologies in the literary physiology, itself influenced by medical imagery, natural history, and the hygienist's report. It also recalled the displays of commodities in the Parisian arcades, since, as Walter Benjamin notes, 'prostitution opens a market in feminine types'.[6] Finally, linguistic profusion sought to master two powerful symbols of irrationality: female sexuality and fashion.[7] The vocabulary of venal sexuality evolved considerably between 1830 and the *fin de siècle*. Like defunct fashions, it rapidly appeared nonsensical; from the perspective of 1848, for example, the early July Monarchy *grisette* seemed as 'implausible' and 'incomprehensible' as a dinosaur.[8]

The ambiguous realm that Frémy termed 'semi-prostitution' was considered intensely difficult to define throughout the century.[9] Though it technically denoted any woman of suspect morals, the term 'prostituée' was in practice restricted to women financially dependent upon paid sexual encounters, and who could not choose their clients.[10]

---

[4] Frémy 1861: 502, Lecour 1870: 17; see also Lecour 1874: 51.

[5] I use 'demi-monde' as an equivalent of 'semi-prostitution', though it also had the more restricted sense discussed below.

[6] See Goulemot and Oster 1989: 28; Benjamin 1999: 515.

[7] On the former, see Matlock 1994: 26.

[8] Delvau 1848: 4; see also 1867*c*: 263.

[9] Historical and literary analysis has tended to focus on the issues surrounding the regulation of prostitution, rather than specific issues relating to courtesans and the *demi-monde* (e.g. Matlock 1994, Harsin 1985, Bernheimer 1989); even Corbin's illuminating comments on the *demi-monde* mainly serve to contextualize his analysis of prostitution (1978: 190–203).

[10] See Corbin 1978: 190–2.

Nineteenth-century commentators who sought to distinguish prostitutes from 'semi-prostitutes' placed their taxonomic divisions in different places: between *les filles* and *les femmes entretenues* (kept women) or *les femmes galantes* (women of loose morals); between *les soumises* and *les insoumises* (registered and unregistered prostitutes); or between *la prostitution avouée* and *la prostitution clandestine* (overt and clandestine prostitution).[11] The most important factor was the presence or absence of police regulation. The legal status of courtesans and ordinary prostitutes differed markedly during the mid- and late nineteenth century, with important implications for their association with eccentricity. Unlike *filles publiques*, courtesans were not required to register with the police or to submit to medical examinations, even though legislators and hygienists continued to assert the need to differentiate them from respectable women (in the 1870s, officials were still discussing whether to force *femmes galantes* to wear obligatory ribbons to mark out their status).[12] Though the temptation of luxury was frequently adduced as a cause of women's descent into prostitution, unregistered prostitutes had to be careful not to stand out too explicitly, for they risked arrest. The courtesan and *demi-mondaine*, in contrast, were free to wear what they pleased; indeed, their status often depended upon their strategic harnessing of conspicuous consumption and their association with fashionable eccentricity.

Key categories proved unstable, intensifying the bourgeois determination to classify and master 'semi-prostitution'. The term 'courtisane' could be used to denote the extensive middle and upper ranks of kept women, for example, but it often had a more restrictive sense, designating a wealthy elite whose most prominent members included celebrities such as Alice Ozy, Mogador, Cora Pearl, and La Païva.[13] The term *demi-mondaine*, in its original meaning, referred to refined women of mysterious origins, including widows, foreigners, and the *femme déchue* or *déclassée*, a woman forced to leave polite society following a scandal. Its semantic field gradually became wider to encompass courtesans and kept women as well, though Alexandre Dumas fils argued

[11] See Klein 1976: 63–3, and 77; Lecour 1870; Du Camp 1875: III, 315–65; Uzanne 1894*a*: 265.

[12] On the regulation of prostitution, see Harsin 1985: 18–19. On differentiating courtesans, see Parent-Duchâtelet 1857: I, 642, Lecour 1870: 45, and Clark 2003: 108–9.

[13] See Richardson 1967.

Fig. 7. 'The *fille publique* is the pariah of civilization; she is its leper. . . . Let us penetrate the secrets of this extraordinary life, this eccentric existence.' (Kock 1844: II, 321) © British Library Board. All Rights Reserved. (010169.k.16)

strongly against this change in meaning, which he claimed ignored the different class backgrounds of *demi-mondaines* and courtesans.[14] The phrase 'clandestine prostitution' similarly cut through class distinctions, forming a spectrum which ran from the overtly respectable bourgeois wife to the the working-class *insoumise* who risked arrest.

The *fille publique*, a target of constant opprobrium in the literature of Parisian life, was 'eccentric' mainly in the sense of being socially ostracized (see Fig. 7). The courtesan and kept woman were perceived as 'eccentric' in a much broader sense, for their clothing, morality, behaviour, and even minds were held to diverge from the norms of their sex. These qualities allowed them to function as potent cultural symbols. As 'the incarnation of personal freedom in an age of repression, constraint, and conformism', for example, the courtesan became a metaphor for

---

[14] See Dumas fils 1898: II, 9–11; see also Delvau 1867*c*: 213.

the new writing of urban modernism promoted by figures such as Jules Janin.[15]

Courtesans were, paradoxically, defined more than anything else by their absence of defined qualities. A strong metaphorical connection between female sexuality, eccentricity, and enigma arose during the July Monarchy and persisted for over half a century. Balzac, for example, described wealthy courtesans in 1846 as 'eccentric women [femmes excentriques], these meteors of the Parisian firmament who are so difficult to classify' (HB7: 1210). In 1891 Edmond and Jules de Goncourt noted in their journal that the Jardin des plantes in Paris was full of 'bizarre, original, eccentric, exotic, unclassifiable women, who seem inclined to sensual adventures as a result of their contact with the animals of the place'.[16] Whilst they are strongly associated with animality (drawing on the fact that animal terms such as *poule*, *cocotte*, and *biche*, or hen and doe, were commonly used in French to designate courtesans), the women portrayed by the Goncourt brothers evade the classificatory impulses of the zoologist, leaving them free to play the most diverse erotic roles. An important characteristic of the *femme excentrique*, these and many similar phrases suggest, was to have no fixed identity. Like the figure of the actress, she functioned as an empty cipher upon which both men and women could project their fantasies, including that of epistemological mastery.[17]

The *lionne pauvre*

Cultural disquiet about the instability of the boundaries separating bourgeois society from the *demi-monde* focused during the early Second Empire upon the *lionne*, a figure generally portrayed during the July Monarchy as an elegant and eccentric aristocrat. In 1856 Émile Augier and Édouard Foussier wrote a play entitled *Les Lionnes pauvres* (The Poor Lionesses); censored for two years, it was performed only after the personal intervention of Napoleon III.[18] The play drew attention to clandestine prostitution in the Parisian bourgeoisie. It depicts a marriage between Pommeau, an older notary's clerk of modest means, and Séraphine, an extravagant young bourgeois wife in thrall to her

---

[15] Gluck 2005: 40.
[16] Edmond and Jules de Goncourt 1959: IV, 107. See also III, 1175, and compare the association of eccentricity, enigma, and female sexuality in Zola 1960: 421.
[17] On this trope, see Chambers 1971*a*.   [18] See Danger 1998: 149–60.

marchande de toilette (a combination of moneylender and procuress), who has drawn her into debt by supplying her with expensive clothing on credit. Séraphine seduces her husband's younger friend Léon in an attempt to raise funds, and subsequently attempts to entrap Léon's cynical friend Bourgnon, the 'philosopher' of the play. He describes her in the following terms:

What's a *lionne* in the slang known as society language? A fashionable lady, wouldn't you agree, that's to say one of those female dandies whom one invariably meets in all the places where a fashionable person would do well to be seen: at the races, at the Bois de Boulogne, at opening nights . . . Add a touch of eccentricity and you have a *lionne*: take away the fortune, and you have a poor *lionne*. (Augier and Foussier 1884: 45)

The concepts of eccentricity and dandyism are used purely as markers of sartorial extravagance. Rather than being psychologically androgynous and impassive, like some models of the female dandy, Séraphine is portrayed as hyperbolically feminine, and is dominated by her narcissistic rivalry with other women.

When Séraphine attends a ball in her lavish new clothing, rumours circulate. Female clothing provided a series of clues to the knowing observer, as one conduct manual warned:

more than one woman, happily displaying her regal costume, is quite unaware that, aside from a handful of foolish admirers, the extravagance of her attire is provoking smiles and the kinds of commentary which, by wounding her own character, also damage that of her husband and harm the future of her family. Some luxuries can only be obtained at the price of the greatest sacrifice and, we shall say it again, in society, everything is known, or everything can be guessed!

(Chapus 1877: 130)

The ending of Augier's play was required to be edifying, since the representation of vice was only acceptable to Second Empire censors if nominally punished. When Séraphine's vice is revealed her husband offers her an opportunity to repent, but she decides it would be more lucrative to join the *demi-monde*. Leaving her husband's reputation in ruins, her own fate remains uncertain. Other characters prophesy a swift decline in the hierarchy of prostitution and death in the Salpêtrière hospital, where some former *femmes galantes* went to die; the courtesan's lifestyle was held by doctors to have a ravaging effect on her health.[19]

---

[19] See Delvau 1867*c*: 124–9, 142–9.

There was a strong element of wishful thinking in the positing of moral and medical retribution.

The ostensible moral of Augier's play was that fashion disseminates immorality. Raised amidst the spectacle of unavailable luxury, one character comments, was too much for the penniless Séraphine to bear. By implicitly pathologizing Séraphine, the play thereby absolves her of some responsibility: like all social climbers, she has a 'mania' for luxury; like all women, she has a weak conscience and a hysterical thirst for consumption. Fashion contained the antidote to its own poison, however, for it displayed women's hidden vices in public, allowing observers to decipher the truth. Séraphine's clothing speaks the truth: 'her luxury is a confession, her wardrobe a dossier' (1884: 42). The play was most unsettling in its representation of women's vulnerability; indeed, critics stressed Séraphine's sheer ordinariness.[20] On how many occasions might a bourgeois wife of modest means be tempted? Heavily in debt because of her addiction to fashion, Flaubert's Emma Bovary had refused to yield to the advances of Guillaumin, the local notary, but not all women had her romantic scruples.[21]

By the early Second Empire, the terms *femme à la mode* and *lionne* thus belonged in the realm of semi-prostitution. Their previous connection to a model of aristocratic distinction nonetheless lingered, creating a sense that the boundaries which demarcated respectable from fallen women were being undermined.[22] The *lionne* was retrospectively held responsible for Second Empire moral decline by conservative commentators. Comtesse Dash, one of the most vociferous critics of the *demi-monde*, argued that by imitating the boyish manners of the *lorette*, the *lionne* had initiated a series of fatal category confusions:

They became female centaurs, they smoked cigars, they adopted the manners of horsemen and they were happy to be treated in an offhand manner . . . The result is what we now see: a motley intermingling of all the social spheres, an assembly of monstrosities in which we can no longer recognize one other.[23]

The concept of monstrosity was an important rhetorical device used by conservatives to suggest the proximity of eccentric fashions to

---

[20] Saint-Victor terms her 'a monster with nothing eccentric or fabulous about her' (1889: 102–3).

[21] GF1: 677; a similar plot occurs in Dumas fils's *L'Affaire Clemenceau* (1866).

[22] The cultural specificity of the *lionne* undermines Clark's claim that although courtesans' *names* were legion, 'they all meant much the same thing' (2003: 109).

[23] Dash 1868*b*: 114–15. Dumas fils uses identical metaphors: 1898: II, 12; see also Rocqueplan 1857: 32.

immorality and perversion. The very terms 'demi-monde' and 'semi-prostitution' evoke boundary confusion similar to that associated with the figure of the monster.[24] According to the critic Paul de Saint-Victor, the *demi-monde* was characterized by a disgusting form of indeterminacy ('the anomaly and eccentricity of amphibian things').[25]

A satirical Second Empire poem which similarly blames the July Monarchy *lionne* for moral decline describes this figure as a monstrous hybrid of actress and centaur:

> The dove becomes a *lionne* in a trice
> And vulgar ways soon become elegant ones...
> How skilful our women are at being uncouth!
> Their ardour would defy the conquerors of the Kabyles.
> They smoke fearlessly and drink with temerity.
> *Lorettes*, they are even more brazen than you...
> Our rough horsewomen would be the envy of the hippodrome,
> And, with their lively eyes, loud voices, and outlandish gestures,
> They transform our salons into perennial circuses.
> Their language neighs with raucous words:
> Actresses of life, they overplay their parts.
> God's law no longer lives in these iron hearts:
> On leaving church they go in search of hell.
>
> (Belmontet 1858: 11–12)

The critique implicitly depicts the *lionne* as a variant upon the diabolical *femme froide*, distinguished by her skills at dissimulation and her emotional coldness.[26]

Category confusion was exacerbated by the practice of excluding women from polite society after any hint of sexual transgression. The class origins of the *femmes déchues* (fallen women) whom Séraphine joined were inscribed on their bodies, evident in their refined manners and accents. Many writers emphasized the psychological difficulty of adjusting to a new rank: 'The fallen woman [femme déchue] is thus always ill at ease, rejected from a sphere which she both misses and hates, little suited to the other sphere to which she belongs but which she despises.'[27] In his play *Le Demi-monde*, first performed in 1855, Alexandre Dumas fils depicts the pervasive anxiety of such women: condemned to narrative indeterminacy, they cling on to their position,

---

[24] See Ch. 7 below.
[25] Saint-Victor 1889: 243 (he himself frequented the salon of La Païva).
[26] See also Uzanne 1894*b*: 288–9 and Carlier 1887: 21.
[27] Rocqueplan 1857: 40.

wanting to climb back up, but frightened at the prospect of falling
further still (1898: II, 104). His play, like many others, attempted to
show that such women became morbidly fixated upon regaining a sense
of respectability, scheming to lure naive men into marriage. Their skill
at acting was implicit in their names: Dumas's anti-heroine is called 'la
Baronne d'Ange', close to Augier's 'Séraphine'.

Other forms of dissimulation played a prominent role in the cultural imagination of the latter part of the century, owing to a mutation in sexual sensibility. Middle-class men increasingly abandoned
brothels during the July Monarchy, felt to be degraded and impersonal. The remaining, more specialized brothels catered for perverse
sexuality, whilst new forms of venal sexuality emerged that were modelled upon bourgeois domesticity. The latter was exemplified by the
femme entretenue, intermediate between mistress and prostitute,[28] and
the *maison de rendez-vous*, which created the elaborate pretence of a
chance meeting between a client and a prostitute masquerading as a
middle-class married woman.[29] Dramaturgical metaphors were central
to descriptions of clandestine prostitution (known as 'la comédie de
l'amour' or 'la comédie du vice') during the Second Empire and early
Third Republic.[30] The pursuit of women for hire was often metaphorically associated with hunting, but it was also claimed that men were
in fact the prey: the *persilleuse* and *raccrocheuse* ('hookers') lured men to
part with their money by means of *ficelles* (ploys).[31] Bourgeois readers
were warned in lurid reports that procurement could take a 'thousand
forms'. Its stage might be a *boutique à surprises*, a shop staffed by women
who had nothing but themselves to sell; in the *pièce à femmes* (women's
theatrical play), prostitutes pretending to be actresses sought to set up
meetings by means of signs to the audience. The respectable theatre had
its own system for communicating the price of an actress,[32] and was also
a favourite haunt of the *insoumise*. Portrayed arriving late in 'eccentric'
costumes and moving around noisily to attract attention, she provided
an alternative spectacle that continued after the play had finished.[33]

Even by the *fin de siècle* the term 'lionne pauvre' still had theatrical connotations: '[clandestine prostitution] sometimes creates scenes
which would mislead even the subtlest observer as to the nature of the

---

[28] Corbin 1978: 182–9; see Lecour 1874: 18 and 1870: 102.
[29] Corbin 1978: 257–73; Coffignon 1888: ch. 14.
[30] Carlier 1887: 34; Uzanne 1894*a*: 264. See also Maugny 1892: 279–88.
[31] Delvau 1867*c*: 275–91; Virmaître 1893: 126.
[32] See Carlier 1887: 28, Hemmings 1993: 202–3.   [33] Lecour 1870: 146–7.

play to be performed shortly afterwards', writes Baron Octave Uzanne
in a typically titillating account: 'It recruits its leading ladies amongst
lionnes pauvres, actresses who give private performances, women "from
a certain sphere" who have been caught short, girls who sell themselves
having found no-one to give themselves to, in short all the needy'
(1894*a*: 266–7). The relationship between external appearance, social
status, and female virtue thus remained ambiguous throughout the
latter part of the century. In the mythologies surrounding bourgeois
sexuality, both husbands and wives provided conduits for the infiltration
of vice into respectable society, the former through their liaisons with
kept women, the latter through clandestine prostitution. One anecdote
narrates a husband suddenly recognizing his wife in the darkness of a
hired room; another tells of a near escape from incest, when a son abandoned as a child by his mother, a fallen woman, encounters her many
years later at a ball.[34] Though implausible, such narratives symbolize the
sense of disquiet that arose from the replacement of stable social roles
by class fluidity and an eroticism based on performance.

Equivocal signs

Fear of dissimulation gave rise to a body of writing with a clear pragmatic function: to help readers differentiate between virtue and vice,
appearance (or performance) and reality. Eccentric clothing and behaviour were repeatedly cited as important clues enabling the correct distinctions to be made. Discourse on Parisian life suggested that although
the Second Empire *femme galante* was marked out on certain occasions,
at least to the practised eye, she often remained indistinguishable from
the respectable woman. Category confusion was believed to arise from a
three-way process. The refined manners of the fallen woman or *déclassée*
contrasted with her actual social position, undermining attempts to
quarantine her; the wealth of the most successful courtesans allowed
them to emulate the habits of high society women; and 'respectable'
middle-class women appeared increasingly willing to emulate both courtesans' eccentric fashions and their allegedly impertinent manners.

   Some courtesans were skilled in the accomplishments of the respectable woman, such as singing, dancing, and conversation; others failed,

---

[34] Coffignon 1888: 184–5, Dumas fils 1898: II, 8–9.

or did not attempt to conceal, their working-class origins.[35] The most important cultural code through which courtesans signalled their identity was that of dress and appearance. In *Les Toilettes tapageuses* (Showy Attire), the playwrights Dumanoir and Barrière compare women to commercial establishments, likening their clothing to the external shop sign which describes the wares sold within (1856: 9). Courtesans played a key role in the luxury trade. Every season, and particularly at the April races at Longchamps, they initiated the new styles subsequently disseminated across Paris, France, and abroad, since Paris was the centre of the world fashion industry. Dressmakers, journalists, and society women gathered to scrutinize and copy their innovative eccentricities.[36]

In an inversion of the advice to respectable women to create elegant harmony between their costume and their manners, critics argued that the courtesan's audacious costume was meaningless without her unfeminine character: 'After having prepared their own outfits, courtesans bring them vigorously to life with their nonchalant manners and impudent expressions. Take away these two spices and the latest fashions seem nonsensical.'[37] Courtesans typically hinted at forbidden parts of the body through close-fitting or translucent fabrics, and used cosmetics liberally in a way not permitted to respectable women. The *Moniteur de la mode* warned its readers that the slightest detail could be compromising: 'Hats should be worn completely horizontally: positioned in such a way as to cover the forehead and rise up at the back, they would betray a most ambiguous form of eccentricity [une excentricité de toilette des plus équivoques].'[38] Courtesans flaunted their luxury in social spaces such as the Bois de Boulogne, Champs Elysées, theatre, and opera. The carriage functioned as a semi-private, semi-public stage on which women could model their clothing. Even respectable women would allow themselves liberties in their carriage that they would never emulate on foot: 'in a carriage one may follow all the latest caprices of fashion: it is the very pedestal of eccentricity.'[39]

The tendency of society women to emulate the courtesan's fashions was repeatedly highlighted by contemporaries, often in satirical mode, as in this description of the Bois de Boulogne published in 1865 in *L'Illustration*: 'The same fabrics, same dresses, same skirts, same earrings, same colours, same plumes, same feathers, and same lorgnettes

[35] See Delord 1840: 247; Parent-Duchâtelet 1857: I, 174.
[36] See P. Perrot 1981: ch 9.   [37] Loüis 1867: 233.
[38] 20 April 1843: 3.   [39] *La Corbeille* 1 July 1853: 101.

everywhere ... I must say, however, that the elegant people who in-habited this paradise outdid their neighbours with respect to their eccen-tricity, luxury and inventiveness.'[40] Eccentricity, the article suggests, still enables a crucial distinction to be made. The Baron de Mortemart-Boisse argued that only those newly arrived in Paris could fail to under-stand the symbolic significance of eccentricity: 'It is the duty of one and all to warn them against any error, to ensure they know that all the *eccentric costumes, gaudy colours* and bold looks that they encounter do not belong to women of good company.'[41]

Writers suggested tests for the uncertain: if you follow an honest woman and a courtesan and speak loudly to them, only the courtesan will turn around; if you make a comment with a double meaning, the virtuous woman will look at you with astonishment and appear not to understand.[42] The bestselling novelist and playwright Ernest Feydeau imagined watching two women with the aim of differentiating between them, turning the objection that the respectable woman imitates the courtesan's fashionable appearance to his own advantage: 'even in her eccentricities, for she is sometimes eccentric,—and why should she be any less so than you or I?—she knows how to remain herself and com-mand respect' (1866: 105–6). In contrast, the courtesan is portrayed as unable to make subtle distinctions, and her attempts to copy the elegance of the society woman as horribly exaggerated.

Not all Parisian observers concurred with Feydeau's view that the courtesan aimed to pass for a society woman.[43] One of the main weapons deployed by the courtesan, already exploited by the July Monarchy *lionne*, was her ability to provide a stimulating contrast with normal women and appropriate certain masculine characteristics. She relied on her novelty to mark herself out from others. Esther Guimond, a celebrated Second Empire *cocotte* known as 'le lion', rose to prominence after racing her carriage against a duchess whilst loudly singing an insulting ditty; endlessly rehearsed in the press, her audacity provoked much admiration.[44] Far from blending in with the norms of high society, the courtesan often subverted the ideology of the ruling classes by exaggerating their habits to the point of absurdity. A 'parody

---

[40] Cited in Vanier 1960: 192.
[41] Mortemart-Boisse 1858: 39; on strangers' misinterpretations, see also Dash 1868*b*: 8.
[42] Gourdon 1841: 95–8; see Drohojowska 1858: 31–2.
[43] e.g. Girardin 1856: I, 254.　　　[44] Richardson 1967: 76.

of a duchess',[45] she might turn her apartment into a temple of vulgarity, thereby implicitly mocking the theatricality and ritual at the heart of aristocratic identity itself.

The courtesan's cultivation of ironic distance mirrored the dandy's hyperbolic pursuit of a bourgeois ethics of self-restraint: both figures aimed to undermine a system of values through exaggerated and parodic compliance. In a speculative comment, Georg Simmel proposed that the desire for revenge underpinned the courtesan's pursuit of fashionable innovation:

> The pariah existence to which society condemns the demi-monde produces an open or latent hatred against everything that has the sanction of law, of every permanent institution...In this continual striving for new, previously unheard-of fashions, in the regardlessness with which the one that is most diametrically opposed to the existing one is passionately adopted, there lurks an aesthetic expression of the desire for destruction.   (1971: 311)

By creating and destroying eccentric fashions, he implies, *demi-mondaines* enact endless symbolic parricide. The trajectory of the wealthiest of Parisian courtesans, La Païva, illustrates this dynamic: humiliated as a young woman by being refused entry to a salon of the *grand monde*, her subsequent disloyalty to French society culminated in alleged spying for Prussia and marriage to a Prussian aristocrat who welcomed the occupying army into Paris in 1871.[46]

Other commentators suggested that it was impossible to distinguish courtesans from respectable women, owing not to the former's simulation of respectability but rather to the latter's increasing effrontery. Meilhac and Halévy's play *La Vie Parisienne* (1867), for example, dramatizes the confusion of virtue and vice by depicting the confusion of an observer faced by two elegant and seemingly undistinguishable women, a 'cocotte' and a 'cocodette'. The former is a courtesan and the latter a countess (1867: 86). The term *cocodette* was generally used to denote the Second Empire successor to the *femme à la mode* and *lionne* of the July Monarchy. All three were ostensibly respectable, but shared a dangerous fascination with courtesans. The *cocodette*'s 'morbid curiosity' about the courtesan's lifestyle threatened to blur the fragile boundaries which separated them.[47]

Comtesse Dash proposed that responsibility for confusion lay with respectable women: 'it's not the fault of the *lorettes*: they are copied

---

[45] Chapus 1877: 129.   [46] Loliée 1920: 34–5; Boulenger 1930: 30–1.
[47] Baguley 2000: 303.

by others, but they themselves do not copy anyone' (1868*b*: 8). She portrays courtesans and actresses infiltrating the protective boundaries of the bourgeois home through newspaper accounts and the complicity of husbands, brothers, and sons (1868*b*: 147), and suggests that respectable women allow themselves to be magnetized by the courtesan:

[N]ext to the pleasure of seeing them, they know of nothing sweeter than talking about them . . . these ladies are devoured by curiosity for anything related to the forbidden fruit; they demand to be told the biographies of rising stars. They have their own preferences and dislikes; they are interested in every break-up and reconciliation,—they are like penniless gourmands who can only watch whilst others eat.   (Dash 1868*b*: 274)

Her rhetoric of erotic obsession was echoed in other texts:

The respectable woman loves to penetrate the secret mysteries of the courtesan's life, and asks her husband and brother to initiate her into its customs . . . One sees her copying the movements, bearing, language and dress of the courtesans and, if need be, surpassing their eccentricities. She dreams of the pleasure that one's vanity must enjoy when one yields without restraint to one's most ruinous fantasies! Finally,—the last sign of her blindness,—she hastens to the theatre to weep at sentimental accounts of courtesans' adventures.

(Nadault de Buffon 1869: 108)

The metaphor of penetration places the *honnête femme* in the position of an infatuated lover.

The simultaneously erotic and gustatory imagery which permeates discourse on courtesans hints at the ambiguity of the French term 'consommation', which denotes both the consumption of commodities and food and sexual consummation. Oral metaphors and the vocabulary of voracity were used in nineteenth-century discourses of both fashion and reading. The devouring of fiction, for example, was believed to trigger hysterical crisis in women, owing to their propensity to strong identification with imaginary characters and the instability of their moods.[48] Exposure to courtesans, these passages suggest, could provoke uncontrollable curiosity in respectable women, mirroring the uncontrollable profligacy of the courtesan. The writer Privat d'Anglemont suggested that courtesans' symbolic status depended on their ability to encourage the circulation of gossip: 'they live entirely off this fictitious

---

[48] See Matlock 1994: ch. 6; for a discussion of reading as devouring, see Felski 1995: 79–87.

merchandise.'[49] Both wives and courtesans are represented nourishing themselves upon narratives of sexual transgression, poisonous stories which circulate in oral and written form.

The Comtesse Drojohowska claimed, following Delphine de Girardin, that there was a test capable of discerning the true character of a woman on the basis of her clothing, but refused to reveal it on the grounds that it could be misused to conceal vice (1858: 31–2). Émile Augier's play *La Contagion* (1866) takes up the theme in its depiction of the fashionable courtesan–actress, Mlle Navarette, giving acting lessons to the respectable Marquise Galeotti; both are attempting to secure marriage with the same man. The courtesan is dressed austerely and the Marquise in an eccentric outfit (1866: 38, 34). The moral message of the scene is clear: actresses, adept at manipulating the codes governing female appearances, contaminate respectable women and teach them to dissimulate in all areas of their lives.

The drama of female eccentricity

Acting threatened to undermine the foundations of social life by destabilizing the link between appearance and reality. The bourgeoisie was both disturbed and fascinated by the spectre of imposture, of particular concern during a period of social mobility in which wealthy appearances did not invariably signify social distinction. Dramatists who wished to avoid censorship were obliged to show dissimulating women being expelled from polite society. Nonetheless, their overt moralism concealed a number of performative contradictions.

First, the role of the theatre in Parisian life greatly facilitated the cultural prominence of the *demi-monde*. Theatre censorship was as ineffective as proposals to regulate courtesans, since the dominant class 'could never quite make up its mind whether it preferred to be titillated or bored'.[50] The plots of the most successful plays of the period revolved around semi-prostitution, whose vocabulary greatly expanded in consequence: Augier's play disseminated the phrase 'lionne pauvre'; Alexandre Dumas fils popularized the terms *camélia* and *demi-monde* in plays performed in 1852 and 1855; and the term *fille de marbre* (girl of marble) came to denote the courtesan following Theodore Barrière's play of 1853. Second, the dramaturgical language with which clandestine prostitution was framed further undermined the distinction between the stage and real life. Finally, theatrical representations of the *demi-monde* generated dramatic irony. Most actresses were obliged to find 'protectors' in order to pay for their expensive costumes, and women who entertained in public were banned from polite company.[51] Both courtesans and respectable women were therefore portrayed on stage by actresses known to belong to the *demi-monde*, and whose private lives were often reported in the mass press.

In Second Empire drama, eccentric fashions are portrayed as the cause of both category confusion and social disintegration. In Victorien Sardou's *La Famille Benoîton*, for instance, a poor young relative uses casuistry to justify her extravagant clothing, which, she fails to realize, frightens off potential suitors: 'Alas, insofar as eccentricity is concerned, God knows that my attire is hardly comparable to that of the Benoîton girls, which didn't stop Martha from making a very good match.'[52] Associated with the rise of ugly Parisian neologisms, eccentricity appears in Sardou's play emblematic of everything distasteful about modernity. In Ernest Feydeau's unpublished one-act play *Deux coqs pour une poule* (Two Roosters for One Hen), the naive Roger de Lerigny muses over the character of his fiancée Cora, a liberty-loving American who, like the *lionne*, pursues masculine activities such as shooting: 'just because she is a little eccentric, they immediately conclude that I am marrying a *déclassée*' (1988: IV, 811–12). Only at the last minute does he avoid marriage with Cora, who is revealed to be the mother of an illegitimate child; but an unsuspecting male rival soon takes his place. The message remained the same for all virtuous women: 'beware of eccentricity'.[53] Yet such alternately stern and satirical depictions had the unintentional effect of glamorizing eccentric fashions. During the first performance of *Les Toilettes tapageuses* in 1856, Maxime Du Camp noted, the leading actress wore a ludicrously inflated crinoline to convey the play's moral point; the next day, dozens of society women asked the actress for the pattern, and the size of the Parisian crinoline expanded dramatically.[54]

The tendency to conflate courtesans and actresses, the latter characterized by their protean ability to take on new identities, confirmed the stereotype that all such women lacked 'normal' female emotions

---

[51] See Hemmings 1993: 201–9 and Maugny 1892: 143–212.
[52] Sardou 1889: 10; see also 68–9.
[53] Feydeau 1988: I, 262. For further usage, see e.g. Dumas fils 1898: I, 27–8 and Meilhac and Halévy 1867: 54.
[54] Cited in Benjamin 1999: 66.

and were thus psychologically eccentric. Though Alexandre Dumas fils's 'dame aux camélias' was a courtesan with a heart of gold, the Second Empire *cocotte* was generally defined in explicit opposition to her predecessor the *grisette*, romanticized as a decent seamstress supported by her student lover. Barrière's play *Les Filles de marbre*, conceived as an explicit critique of Dumas's narrative, multiplies imagery of Pygmalion to frame its female protagonist as an insensible statue who torments her devoted lover Raphael to death. The actress at the centre of the play has a masculine name, Marco; she is described as both a 'lionne' and a 'femme à la mode' (1883: 70). As in *Les Lionnes pauvres* and other plays centring on semi-prostitution, the playwright creates a moralizing contrast between the cold anti-heroine and an emotional heroine, Marie, who embodies all the domestic virtues her demonic double lacks. Marco's malice is held to be unrelated to either desire or financial gain: she accepts Raphael as a lover, the play reveals, purely in order to inflict suffering upon the innocent Marie.[55] Motivated by wanton destruction, her actions conform to the image of the *demi-mondaine* as a vengeful pariah.

Courtesans symbolized the 'feminine' aspects of the psyche, ostensibly repressed by the masculine code of self-restraint which underpinned capitalism and the pursuit of utility and profit. Like the fashion that defined their identity, they represented the last refuge of what Walter Benjamin termed 'the most parched and imagination-starved' century.[56] In the words of a Second Empire analyst of fashion:

What strikes you are these ingeniously ostentatious costumes, against which your thrifty, austere nature protests; what seduces you is the splendour which surrounds them. The insolent coquetry of their fluttering eyelashes and adornments, the artifices of their make-up, their lack of regard for what other people may think, their strange but real radiance: all these things fascinate your eyes and your imagination. (Despaigne 1866: 8–90)

Nonetheless, the feminine values of irrationality and phantasmagoria were also an intrinsic component of capitalism, for they motivated consumption and were implicated in what Marx described as the magical aura of the commodity. Simultaneously a producer of new fashions, a consumer, and a consumable item, the courtesan undermined the opposition between production and consumption, masculinity and femininity. She also overcame the dimorphism that split the male and female

---

[55] Barrière 1883: 86–9.   [56] Benjamin 1999: 64.

spheres, for she was permitted to express sexual pleasure, drink, gamble, and swear like a man, and had masculine characteristics such as coldness and insolence. The cultural panic generated by the *demi-monde* was caused in part by the ability of courtesans to undermine the structuring principles of bourgeois identity.

Dreams of asceticism

The view that society women had begun to model their manners upon those of the courtesan inverted the traditional model of the etiquette manual, which advised its readers to emulate the aristocracy. To some extent the accusation was rooted in changing patterns of social interaction. In traditional salon culture, which strictly policed birth and quality, married women wielded considerable symbolic power, and the respect they gained from transmitting their knowledge of etiquette to the next generation was viewed as compensation for the humiliation of the ageing process.[57] But the popularity of sporting pursuits and the introduction of male clubs during the late Restoration, modelled on those of English high society, tended to deprive both the salon and society women themselves of their cultural influence.[58] During the Second Empire, furthermore, the entertainments attended by the male elite were often hosted by actresses and courtesans, and therefore excluded respectable women.[59] Conservative critics attributed social deregulation and increasingly ostentatious materialism to the decline of the salon as an institution. The dominant forms of entertainment during Napoleon III's regime, which revolved around lavish masked balls and tableaux, favoured the audacity of the courtesan.

The balance of symbolic power thus appeared to be shifting away from the figures of the *femme comme il faut* and the *femme honnête*, even as the ideological supremacy of wives and mothers was endlessly rehearsed in social and political discourse. Anxiety about the increase of inherited pathology in the latter part of the century, it has been suggested, may have been exacerbated by male guilt at the knowledge that sexuality had become severed from marital life, resulting in a decline in the birth rate.[60] The spurned *honnête femme*, framed as the persecuted female victim of the stage melodrama, haunted polemic

[57] See Virey 1815: 567.   [58] See Prevost 1957: 45.
[59] See e.g. Dash 1868*b*: 274 and Saint-Victor 1889: 138–9.
[60] Nye 1998: 125–6 (following Roudinescu); see Du Camp 1875: III, 353.

on the *demi-monde*. One anecdote portrays the courtesan choosing a box opposite the wife of her protector, and flaunting her extravagant clothing in order to cause her rival as much distress as possible.[61]

In addition to highlighting the humiliation of virtuous women, conservative criticism of the *demi-monde* emphasized the moral and financial dangers which courtesans posed to the bourgeois family. Eccentricity thus became enmeshed in wider debates about consumption and luxury during a period of industrial expansion. The theme of financial ruin resulting from male involvement with courtesans had been highlighted by Balzac in his *Petites misères de la vie conjugale*, in which two wives agree that it is better to lavish money on a fashionable lifestyle with their husbands than for the latter to spend it with courtesans: 'one can devour one's entire fortune with eccentric women' (HB12: 68). With incomes of tens or even hundreds of thousands of francs at their disposal, Second Empire courtesans created inflation in the economy of fashion. Though aristocrats could compete, adopting successive new styles was prohibitively expensive for many middle-class families.[62]

Whilst some cultural commentators sympathized with the alleged 'demoralization' of respectable women,[63] others portrayed them as narcissistic monsters, willing to let their husbands and children starve in order to indulge their love of consumption. Criticism came from two other sources. The Second Empire witnessed the collapse of the July Monarchy alliance between socialists and feminists, replaced by left-wing patriarchs such as Michelet and Proudhon who deployed brilliant rhetorical techniques to disseminate their views about the radical alterity of female nature and the need for unconditional female submission. The misogyny of these thinkers united them in some respects with their ideological enemies, reactionaries and Catholics, who devoted considerable energy to the critique of luxury.[64] This occurred around the time that disquiet about venereal disease was increasing, and the two debates came to overlap. 'In my opinion, the police should apply itself to curbing the real scandal, namely eccentric costumes and behaviour,' wrote one doctor in 1868, though the police were quick to point out the impracticality of his demand.[65]

---

[61] Arago 1841: 23; see e.g. HB12: 70, Girardin 1856: I, 253–5.
[62] See e.g. Dash 1868*b*: 24.   [63] Nadault de Buffon 1869: 61.
[64] Feminists contested their propaganda; for the former, Juliette Adam and Jenny d'Héricourt; for the latter, Olympe Audouard and Maria Desraimes, amongst others.
[65] Jeannel, cited in Lecour 1874: 23–4.

In 1858 the Catholic author Comtesse Drohojowska published a moral tract entitled *La Vérité aux femmes sur l'excentricité des modes et de la toilette* (The Truth Revealed to Women About Eccentricity in Fashion and Dress). It went through several editions, though its content was largely unoriginal. Her strategy was to deny the appeal of eccentricity, just as Feydeau had denied the courtesan's ability to imitate the respectable women convincingly.[66] Others echoed her main argument: 'a woman is strangely mistaken if she believes that the eccentricity of her attire is pleasing; she does attract attention, that much is true, but she loses respect.'[67] Such comments sought to reinterpret fashion as an addictive narcotic creating delusional states in women. Distinct theological undertones emerged in the championing of asceticism and repudiation of eccentricity. Drohojowska depicts a typical contemporary woman torn between devotion and luxury, in the language of monstrous category confusion ('a lady, half-young, half-old, half-devout, half-worldly, with one foot in church and the other at the ball'). She asks her confessor whether her soul can still be saved if she follows the latest fashions; he replies that she would have to dress half of herself in luxurious clothing and the other half with chaste simplicity, since one cannot serve two masters.[68]

Her comments betray the influence of Catholic rigorism.[69] The latter part of the nineteenth century saw a shift away from the strict Tridentine moral code and its 'God of fear' towards the sentimental codes of ultramontane piety, as the Church sought to retain believers amidst an increase in anti-clericalism. Nonetheless, a rigorist vocabulary continued to inform the polemic surrounding eccentricity and luxury during the Second Empire.[70] Luxury was interpreted in terms of both sinful greed and cultural decline. This was partly due to its widespread association with courtesans, but it had other causes. Economic discourse had a peculiarly moralizing tenor in France. Despite clashes between exponents of economic liberalism, who supported the luxury trade, and its critics, who drew upon a mixture of classical Stoic philosophy and Christian asceticism to oppose it, the parameters of the debate remained that of the public good. Luxury and *la morale* were considered to be closely linked, so even defenders of luxury were obliged to

---

[66] Drohojowska 1858: 19.   [67] Bourgeau 1864: 189–90.
[68] Drohojowska 1858: 20, 10. See also Baudrillart 1878: I, 90.
[69] Gibson 1989: 28.   [70] See Gibson 1989: ch. 8.

justify it in moral terms that would have been considered irrelevant in other nations. A school of economist–moralists who championed asceticism over luxury took inspiration from the writings of the Catholic social scientist Frédéric Le Play.[71] H. Baudrillart, a nineteenth-century historian of luxury, revealed the theological assumptions informing discussions of consumption when he differentiated between the 'rigorist school' and the 'apologists of luxury'.[72] A set of binary oppositions dominated discourse on eccentricity: worldliness–spirituality, ephemerality–eternity, self-assertion–self-effacement, greed–asceticism, excess–austerity, eccentricity–simplicity. Respectable women were paradoxically censured for lacking the moral strength to reject the sartorial influence of the *demi-monde*, by the very commentators who tended to decry female self-assertion in all other contexts.

During the 1860s the dimensions of the crinoline were at their most extreme, with a single dress requiring around seventeen metres of fabric. The tensions arising from the role of the *demi-monde* in the fashion industry were highlighted during a controversy that occurred towards the end of Napoleon III's regime. In 1865 Procurator-General Dupin presented a speech at the Senate entitled 'Du Luxe effréné des femmes' (On the Unbridled Luxury of Women), following a petition aimed at abolishing prostitution. Many of Dupin's arguments are unoriginal, but his piece had an important function in crystallizing public debate.[73] He claimed that respectable women had allowed themselves to be contaminated by the *demi-monde*:

> People talk of courtesans parading about in public places. Yes, this one or that has a dazzling coach and horses, able to attract everyone's attention. What does high society do? It watches, it takes the courtesans as its model and soon it is these young girls who decide upon what is fashionable, even for society ladies; people copy *them*, such is the example given by high society.
>
> *Several senators.* It's true! It's true![74]

Dupin also blamed luxury for the proliferation of prostitution and pornography, and implicitly attacked the failure of the Restoration to impose both medical and sumptuary regulation upon courtesans. (The possibility of reinstating sumptuary laws in order to establish a necessary

---

[71] See Rosalind Williams 1982: 220–2, 236–40, and P. Perrot 1995.
[72] Baudrillart 1878: ch. 2 and ch. 4 respectively.
[73] For a description of the resulting polemic, see Aubert 1865: 1.
[74] Reproduced in Meugy 1865: 69.

link between class origins and appearances was widely discussed, though never enacted.[75]) The petition concludes by calling for the establishment of a league of virtuous wives and mothers, akin to a temperance society.

Dupin's speech met with enormous acclaim. His language was partly responsible: the adjective he chose to describe the behaviour of respectable women—'effréné' or unbridled—evoked an underworld of vice. The *Grand dictionnaire universel* entry for 'Courtisane' lists the following adjectives to describe this figure: 'free, lively, bold, shameless, brazen . . . lascivious, lewd, cynical, insolent, lustful, unbridled, vile, infamous' (GD5: 393). Responses to Dupin's comments rehearsed wider debates about eccentricity in the fields of fashion and etiquette. Some respondents portrayed bourgeois wives as vainly obsessed with the public gaze, neglecting the rightful audience of their husbands and family:

It is this feverish desire to dazzle, to make an impression, to be noticed; it is this need for splendour which does all the harm. Half of all women feign an impossible level of luxury; they go beyond their rightful sphere. The home and family no longer provide a satisfactory stage on which to display this deceptive splendour. Twenty years ago, the ultimate achievement was to be respectable [comme il faut]. Today, the phrase no longer even exists.   (Aubert 1865: 6)

Others who conceded that respectable women copied courtesans sought to defend them by recasting them as the victims of male hypocrisy. By dressing in bizarre and elaborate styles, they argued, wives could avoid the humiliation of being ignored by their husbands.[76]

Most respondents who criticized Dupin were sympathetic to the dilemma of middle-class women; indeed, ritually denigrating courtesans served to establish their own moral credentials. Olympe Audouard, one of the first women to give public lectures on the 'woman question' and subsequently a prominent advocate of divorce,[77] produced two pamphlets on the Dupin affair from a perspective unusually sympathetic to courtesans. Narcissism was typically coded as feminine; Audouard reversed this assumption in her second pamphlet, *Du luxe effréné des hommes* (On the Unbridled Luxury of Men), by suggesting that men

[75] Rosalind Williams 1982: 229–30 (though she does not specifically relate the issue to the *demi-monde*).
[76] Saint-Céran 1865: 4–5, Audouard 1865*a*: 30; Coffignon 1888: 324.
[77] See Moses 1984: 195.

were themselves dominated by their obsession with conforming to a certain model of masculinity:

Man is devoured by his desire to appear in public; he wants his horses, dogs and mistresses to be the subject of our conversations. He showers gold upon prostitutes whom he doesn't even like... out of generosity? No, out of ostentation... This woman is nothing but an advertisement for his wealth; she is a mechanical doll invented to satisfy his pride; she has to get dressed up, show herself off, paw the ground and splatter those around her. Monsieur would drag her to the Bois de Boulogne the day after her mother's death... It has to be this way: isn't she the plaything of Monsieur?   (1865*b*: 11–12)

She concluded by countering Dupin's notion of a female temperance society with that of a 'society of good fathers', which would require men to break with their mistresses, live frugally, and support their illegitimate daughters.[78]

The Dupin debate occurred at the height of controversy over the crinoline: introduced in 1853, it grew ever wider until suddenly shortened by the couturier Charles Worth in 1867 and abandoned the subsequent year. Though the cultural influence of courtesans during the Second Empire was indisputable, conservative commentators undoubtedly exaggerated the links between polite society and the *demi-monde* for rhetorical effect. By generating in their readers a sense of outrage at the humiliation of virtuous women and the insolence of *nouveaux riches*, they sought to shock them into reaffirming traditional class distinctions. An analysis published in 1900 proposes that the illustrations of magazines such as *La Mode*, popular during the mid century, were unrepresentative of what respectable women actually wore:

In practice, when prepared for a society lady or, as we used to say, 'a respectable person' ['une personne comme il faut'], these costumes changed in appearance and became more aristocratic. This was effected through the slightest of changes, little touches, shades of colour, a cut which was more or less daring, adornments which were added or rejected... There was no eccentricity whatsoever amongst those from reputable circles.   (Bouchot 1901: 335)

The most commonly cited evidence of complicity between the two spheres, the widespread emulation of the new fashions invented by the courtesan, was thus more complex than polemical accounts suggest.

The Franco-Prussian war contributed to the demise of Second Empire fashions, as well as the period's notoriously extravagant forms

---

[78] Audouard 1865*b*: 19 (emphasis in original).

of entertainment. The increasing democratization of luxury in an era of standardized mass production generated a desire for more discreet forms of luxury in the upper classes:

Since 1870, eccentricity has disappeared from fashion...With the popularization of certain outfits mass-produced by department stores, it has become impossible even for the most elegant society lady to escape from the democratic uniform created by all the department stores of the capital, save by seeking out a seemingly unpretentious outfit, but one which is impeccably styled and at least six or ten months ahead of the ready-made items of the warehouses frequented by the Parisian bourgeoisie.[79]

Uzanne later revised the date of eccentricity's disappearance to 1880. Whilst the notion of sartorial eccentricity undoubtedly generated the most vehement debate during the Second Empire, the reality was less clear-cut than either of Uzanne's dates suggests. Emulation of the social elite's fashions by the lower classes was far from new; most of the major department stores had opened during the Second Empire; and sartorial eccentricity continued to be discussed in fashionable society well into the twentieth century.[80] Paris long retained its image as 'the capital of stupefaction and strangeness',[81] a realm of fantasy in which eccentric fashions, enigmatic appearances, and illicit eroticism were closely entwined.

The legacy of the *demi-monde* was felt in other genres which drew on the rhetoric of eccentricity for specific purposes. Pornography published during the *belle époque*, for example, used terms related to 'excentrique' in a sensational manner to attract readers. Victor Léca's volume *De l'amour et du sang: volupté excentrique* (1908) (On Love and Blood: Eccentric Ecstasy), catalogues perversions such as sadism and paedophilia. It publicizes a forthcoming work entitled *Chez Satan* with the claim that 'the author leads us...into the bizarre world of the eccentrics of love [les excentriques de l'amour] who cannot achieve satisfaction without the most outlandish of practices'.[82] Alphonse Gallais's *Les Enfers lubriques: curiosités, excentricités et monstruosités passionnelles* (1909) (The Hells of Lust: Oddities, Eccentricities, and Monstrosities of the

---

[79] Uzanne 1894*a*: 36; compare 1910: 64.
[80] Proust opposes the austere attire of the Duchesse de Guermantes to the eccentric attire of the Princesse de Guermantes, as Steele notes (1998: 208–10).
[81] Delvau's phrase (1867*a*: p. xi).
[82] Unpaginated advertisement at the end of the text.

Passions), uses a pseudo-anthropological focus to justify its voyeuristic catalogue of sexual practices in cultures such as Africa and the Far East, taken, bizarrely, to include childbirth rituals. Though the term 'excentricité sexuelle' is used in contemporary French as a euphemism for sexual perversion, *fin-de-siècle* French sexologists tended to avoid the terms 'excentrique' and 'excentricité'. They had perhaps accumulated too many frivolous connotations after half a century of association with the *demi-monde*, and scientists preferred ostensibly neutral-sounding terms such as 'aberrations', 'perversions', and 'anomalies'.

In summary, the most persistent strand of discourse about female eccentricity in the French cultural imagination, particularly after the reputations of the July Monarchy *femme à la mode* and *lionne* were called into question, concerned courtesans. For they combined to a high degree many different connotations of the terms 'excentrique' and 'excentricité': extravagant fashions, spectacle, and luxury, above all, but also nonconformism, perversity, exclusion from polite society, and the appropriation of culturally masculine characteristics such as coldness and arrogant self-assertion.

The underworld was increasingly central to the social elite during the Second Empire, generating moral panic. This was exacerbated by the ambiguity of the categories in terms of which the 'amphibious' realm of semi-prostitution was understood, and by the numerous connections believed to exist between respectable wives, courtesans, and unregistered prostitutes. Eccentric fashions were the most frequently mentioned evidence of this type of connection, to the extent that some critics proposed banning eccentricity in female clothing as a means of lessening the influence of the *demi-monde* on middle and upper-class society. Conservatives exaggerated actual patterns of influence for rhetorical effect, seeking to generate anxiety in readers about the infiltration of polite society by pathological elements in order to re-establish definitive class boundaries.

The *femme excentrique* was typically portrayed as an enigma whose identity was permanently open to conjecture. Even in this respect, courtesans had much in common with bourgeois wives. Both types of woman were perceived to lack fixed identity: the courtesan was defined in relation to the fantasies of her protector, whilst the ideal wife was self-effacing and focused on the needs of her husband. Both were portrayed as being liable to uncontrolled and pathological behaviour, exacerbated by the circulation of poisonous narratives of sexual transgression in everyday anecdotes, the press, and theatrical representations. In Second Empire fashionable life, eccentricity was synonymous with women of high visibility and the commodification of sexuality. In the fairground of the same period, it denoted an equally eroticized and commercial form of human exhibition, but one which focused on anomalous *bodies*: the sideshow.

PART III

THE UNDERWORLD

5

Saltimbanques and Savages

I sing the mangy dog, the pitiful dog, the dog without a home,
the roving dog, the *saltimbanque* dog, the dog whose instinct, like
that of the gypsy and the strolling player, has been so wonderfully
sharpened by necessity, marvellous mother and true patroness of
native wit!

Charles Baudelaire[1]

The rhetoric of eccentricity played an important role in representations
of the Parisian fairground and sideshow. Such spectacles can only be
understood in the context of a culture of human exhibition that pervaded the French literary and scientific imagination for over a hundred
years. The exhibition of human beings for entertainment and profit
was a central though until recently largely neglected feature of French
cultural life. Drawing on the rhetoric of natural history, the genre of
the physiology transformed Paris into an enormous zoological garden
of exotic human specimens; during the July Monarchy and Second
Empire, Parisians of all classes paid to visit freaks and other human
and animal 'eccentricities'; and from the 1870s until the 1930s, mass
spectacles transformed the techniques of the fairground to create human
zoos in which the natives of distant countries were displayed as tokens
of anthropological difference, receiving millions of visitors and shaping
attitudes towards colonial expansion.

The relationship between bourgeois observer and human exhibit
became a subject in its own right during the Second Empire. In one
sense, such encounters formed variations upon traditional themes of
the carnival analysed by Mikhail Bakhtin, such as the foregrounding
of grotesque bodies and social misalliances. During the nineteenth century, however, the fairground became the locus of quite new cultural
tensions in response to the evolution of the literary field. The writers

---

[1] 'Les Bons chiens' (CB1: 361; Baudelaire 1970: 105, trans. modified).

who documented their visits to the fairground sought to escape from bourgeois conformity, projecting fantasies of freedom onto *saltimbanques* and 'monsters'; but they simultaneously rediscovered their own sense of alienation in these figures, at a time when the social status of the man of letters was becoming increasingly problematic. Some writers took this sense of affinity further, and began to consider both the potential humanity of 'monsters' and the potential monstrosity of their own desires in the face of highly eroticized spectacles of deformity. What compelled paying customers to seek out deviant bodies? Both the doctrine of original sin and a persistent sense of guilt accompanied many into the fairground booth. The secret desires of fairground spectators became a spectacle as mysterious as the exhibits themselves, as writers explored their simultaneous sense of identification with and distance from the socially marginal.

From zoology to ethnography: exhibiting human beings

Fairground freaks exerted enormous and often underestimated influence on nineteenth-century visual culture.[2] They also shaped the literary culture of the period. In July Monarchy Paris, close connections began to be forged between popular culture, literature, journalism, and natural history, which later influenced understandings of the crowd and mass spectatorship. All were founded on the trope of humans as animals, to be divided into different 'species' and savoured by the Parisian observer, masquerading as an amateur zoologist.[3]

French scientists dominated the field of natural history from the Revolution of 1789 until around 1830, a period that saw the establishment of the Muséum d'histoire naturelle and the zoological gardens of the Jardin des Plantes.[4] Imagery from natural history was increasingly mapped onto the 'living museums' of boulevard life; Walter Benjamin's celebrated description of the *flâneur* as a figure who 'botanizes the asphalt' thus continues a well-established nineteenth-century theme.

---

[2] Bancel et al. 2002: 10.

[3] Since orthodox French natural historians denied any link between humans and animals until after 1870, the human–animal analogy was not perceived as threatening in the same way it was by the Victorian public after the publication of Darwin's theory of evolution.

[4] See Limoges 1980: 212–14.

The Parisian physiology repeatedly described social and professional types as animal species, the best known of which were *lions* (male and female dandies), *panthères* (kept women), *rats* (young dancers at the Opera), and *mouches* (government spies). The equivalence between zoological and social typologies received celebrated formulation in the Foreword to Balzac's *Comédie humaine* (1842) (HB1: 8). Vivid illustration of this theory was provided in the *Scènes de la vie privée et publique des animaux* (Scenes From the Private and Public Lives of Animals), published by Jules Hetzel in 1842. The latter modelled itself upon the great physiology compendia, but added a distinctive twist: its brilliant illustrator, Grandville, portrayed human types as animals, amidst interpictorial allusions to the illustrations of the eighteenth-century naturalist Buffon. Representations of human zoos proliferated: texts such as Louis Huart's *Muséum parisien: histoire de toutes les bêtes curieuses de Paris* (1841) (The Parisian Museum: A History of All the Curious Beasts of Paris), which evoked Buffon in its subtitle, catalogued dozens of anthropomorphic animal types, from the celebrated lion and panther to lesser-known specimens such as the cicada, duck, pigeon, bear, and frog. Indeed, in a typically 'mock-heroic' and parodic tone, the *Physiologie des physiologies* (1841) depicts the entire enterprise of physiology writing as an attempt to compensate for the absence of human beings in the writings of the natural historians Cuvier and Buffon.[5] The theme continued more diffusely in texts such as Gustave Doré's *Ménagerie parisienne* (1854), which illustrated a range of Parisian vices associated with well-known animal types.

The concept of the human zoo had a number of cultural functions. The legacy of the seventeenth-century writer Jean de La Fontaine was evident in allegorical representations of humanized animals, and provided readers with a comforting sense of detachment from human folly. Positing equivalence between humans and animals was also, perhaps, a psychic strategy for producing a sense of mastery in a rapidly evolving social environment. Walter Benjamin argued that the social types illustrated in the physiology were 'innocuous', attempts to neutralize the anxiety that permeated nineteenth-century Parisian street life (1997: 36–9). The analogy between humans and animals suggests a need to infantilize city-dwellers, transforming Paris into a fairy-tale world of talking animals. Though staring at humans was a cultural taboo

[5] Anon. 1841*b*: 19; Gluck 2005: 93.

regulated by the codes of propriety, staring at animals was not. In addition, since courtesans were described with a range of animal terms, humanized animals hinted at the raw erotic vitality concealed beneath the civilized exteriors of modern Parisians.[6] Finally, the concept of the human zoo merged with that of the urban jungle, a symbol of the ferocity of emergent capitalism. The jungle was also suggestive of violence and criminality, its inhabitants portrayed as 'savages' and 'barbarians'.[7] After 1848, the comic tone of July Monarchy experimentation with the human-animal trope ceded to a darker vision of innate perversity and atavistic regression to barbarism. Representations of the Parisian crowd habitually compared the masses to ferocious savages.[8]

During the July Monarchy, some writers experimented with potential reversals of perspective, a tactic that would recur in subsequent accounts of fairground encounters. The natural historian presided like a patriarch over the plant and animal kingdoms, his work of classification and naming synonymous with conceptual mastery. Struggles within the scientific establishment revealed anger at misuses of this power, often directed towards Baron Cuvier, seen as a scheming and pedantic reactionary.[9] Hetzel's compendium includes a satirical sketch by Balzac that represents the professors at the Jardin des Plantes as animals, and the work as a whole concludes with a reversal in which three contributors to the volume are exhibited in the Jardin des Plantes (see Fig. 8). Another anti-Cuvier satire written shortly afterwards by a dissatisfied student classifies natural historians themselves within the Linnaean model, terming Cuvier *Analyticus diplomaticus* and Geoffroy Saint-Hilaire *Transcendentalus honestus*.[10] Though it reserves its overt critique for Cuvier and his school, the text implicitly constitutes a more general carnivalesque reversal of power, in which all the thinkers who seek to subject the natural kingdom to their mastery are themselves categorized and placed on display.

The use of zoological terminology during the July Monarchy was a symptom of a wider set of connections between the emergent disciplines

---

[6] Monselet's *Musée secret* (1870) is specifically framed as an erotic museum.

[7] A trope linked to Balzac and Sue; see Benjamin 1999: 441, 443. The rhetoric of 'inner savagery' was echoed in alienism and criminology in the latter part of the century.

[8] Baudelaire suggested that 'bestial names' evoked Satanism (CB1: 660). On imagery of the bestial crowd, see Chevalier 1958: 458–60, Barrow 1981: 44, and Prendergast 1992: 86.

[9] On the cultural ramifications of the Cuvier–Geoffroy debate, see Appel 1987: ch. 7.

[10] Salle de Gosse 1847: 29–33.

Fig. 8. Observers observed: Grandville's image of Janin, Balzac, and Hetzel on display at the Jardin des plantes, being sketched by the artist himself. (Hetzel 1842: II, 388) © British Library Board. All Rights Reserved. (C.155.h.21)

of sociology, ethnography, and anthropology, in the one instance, and literature and journalism, in the other.[11] Of the many young writers

---

[11] See Lepenies 1988. On analogous developments in Victorian culture, see Cowling 1989: 1–6.

who arrived in Paris hoping for literary glory, most found themselves in the impecunious condition of the *homme de lettres*. One of the subjects most in demand was sketches of city life and its species, haunts, and habitats, turning the man of letters into an 'ethnographer' of urban life.[12] The similarity between the Parisian 'zoo' and the fairground is highlighted in an illustration by Honoré Daumier entitled 'La Grande ménagerie parisienne'. Social types commonly portrayed by writers in the physiology—the *panthère*, *lion*, and *mouche*—are presented here in the distinctive iconography of the fairground *parade*, designed to attract paying customers into an exhibit. The man of letters, Daumier implies, is a *saltimbanque* exhibiting Parisians as though they are the inhabitants of a sideshow (see Fig. 9).

The man of letters was increasingly positioned as an ethnologist who specialized in his own species. For he was particularly preoccupied by social types that reflected the difficulties of his own precarious existence: the itinerant performer, sad clown, ragpicker, and freak. Due to this 'metaphorical projection of the self into models of social marginality',[13] the marginals of Paris came to occupy a space in the cultural imaginary disproportionate to their actual influence. *Saltimbanques* were the practitioners of a derided form of art,[14] who exhibited their skills for others but themselves willingly exploited human 'monsters' for profit.[15] Their ephemeral performances mirrored the rapidly forgotten output of most men of letters. Journalists and *chroniqueurs* appeared to specialize in performing carefully orchestrated rhetorical tricks.[16] The fairground therefore had quite different functions. In the one instance, it provided a form of domestic exoticism, which revealed sides of Paris as mysterious as those found on distant travels and disrupted the monotony of bourgeois life in a manner analogous to alcohol and drugs.[17] Opposing this need for estrangement was a deep desire for identification in men of letters, who saw in circus performers their own image. The literary fascination with the fairground gave rise to a literary and iconographical genre that Jean Starobinski has termed the 'portrait of the artist as a

[12] See Goulemot and Oster 1989: 31–7.
[13] Goulemot and Oster 1992: 105, 109.
[14] See the introduction of Challamel 1875.
[15] As part of my efforts to reconstruct 19th-cent. ideologies, and for stylistic reasons, I have retained and not always placed in inverted commas the highly offensive personal noun 'monstre'; this is not to condone it in any way.
[16] On the *saltimbanque*–writer trope see Véron 1868: II, 8–9 and 1875.
[17] See Chambers 1985.

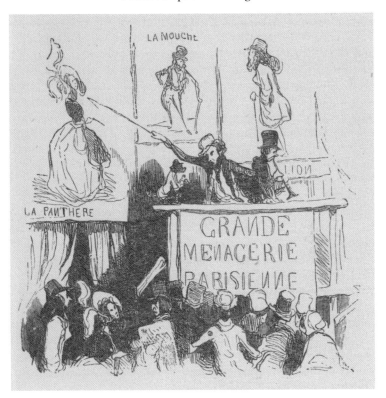

Fig. 9. Daumier's *parade*: Parisian social types on display like fairground specimens. (Champfleury 1871: 181) © British Library Board. All Rights Reserved.
(2262.a.5)

saltimbanque', an expression of writers' growing sense of social alienation
around the mid century.[18]

Urban spectators were allotted specific roles in the drama of
omnipresent exhibition associated with the notion of the Parisian
menagerie. Cultural criticism often assumes that types such as the
flâneur, *dandy*, and *courtisane* each correspond to a stable essence whose
meaning may ultimately be determined.[19] In practice, rival definitions

---

[18] See Starobinski 1970. On Flaubert's notable early use of monstrosity as a symbol
of alienation, see e.g. 'Un parfum à sentir' (A Perfume to Savour) (1838) and 'Quidquid
volueris' (Whatever You Want) (1837), both in Flaubert 2001; and, on the latter, Sartre
1971: I, 208–35.

[19] See Gluck 2005: 67.

proliferated without consensus, and practices changed from one decade to the next.[20] The term 'dandy', I have suggested, is used in a normative and elitist way by writers such as Baudelaire and Barbey d'Aurevilly, whereas in the literature of Parisian worldliness it has a more trivial sense, denoting anyone with pretensions to fashionable status.[21] In a similar manner, the term *flâneur* was defined relationally, and contrasted with figures such as *badaud* (gawper), *musard* (loiterer), and *oisif* (idler). All were used imprecisely. 'Do you take me for a *badaud*?' one *flâneur* asks in a physiological sketch, eliciting the narrator's gloss: 'A phrase tinged with a just sense of dignity, which saves me from having to dwell on the gulf which separates the *badaud* from the *flâneur*.'[22] Louis Huart's *Physiologie du flâneur* (1841) posits an eruption of false *flâneurs,* including Sunday strollers, foreigners, *musards, batteurs de pavé* (loungers), and tramps.[23] The importance such texts place on distinguishing true *flâneurs* from usurpers indicates the looseness with which the terms were generally deployed—together with writers' desire to assert their 'professional' hegemony as Parisian experts, warding off bourgeois amateurs and philistines.

The term *badaud* was typically used in the context of mass spectatorship.[24] It had more egalitarian connotations than the *flâneur*, and was used to evoke the Parisian crowds of different ages, sexes, and classes who would gather around any remarkable event, particularly on Sundays. The term suggested the act of staring open-mouthed ('gawping'), as is evident in a text from 1815:

The only Parisian trait that one might be permitted to regard as irremediable is that type of curiosity which, if we might risk saying so, is a little mindless, and for which the word *badauderie* has been invented. Here, this characteristic is not restricted to those who lack an occupation, as it is everywhere else; the entire population seems infected by it.[25]

Any Parisian could be a *badaud* when confronted with a marvellous occurrence, including workers, artisans, shopkeepers, and sales clerks.[26] The *badaud* was often portrayed as foolish, and denied the typological

---

[20] Parkhurst-Ferguson analyses the shifting semantics of *flânerie* during the early 19th cent., for example, but not the Second Empire (1994: 82), the period focused on by Gluck in 2005: ch. 3.

[21] See Ch. 3 above.   [22] Anon., 1832: 104.   [23] 1841*a*: 16–23.

[24] On the development of mass spectatorship in Paris, see Schwartz 1998 and Shaya 2004.

[25] Jouy 1815: 139–40.   [26] See Shaya 2004: 51.

talent of the *flâneur*, typically phrased in terms of the latter's 'philosophical' disposition.

There was some ambiguity about the position of the man of letters in relation to these types. For Baudelaire, the archetypal urban spectator was 'l'homme des foules', with reference to Poe's 'man of the crowd'. This figure experienced borderline states of consciousness verging on the epiphany in which self and crowd mingled, but could reassert his individuality when desired.[27] Baudelaire contrasts the flexible boundaries of the poet's self, able to contract and expand, with the bourgeois *égoïste* and *paresseux* who remain indifferent to the world of others (CB2: 291). Victor Fournel writes in similar terms of the dissolution of the self, but suggests instead that this defines the *badaud*:

The simple *flâneur* observes and reflects . . . he is always in full possession of his individuality. That of the *badaud* disappears, in contrast, and is absorbed by the external world which steals him away from himself, which overwhelms him to the point of intoxication and ecstasy. When under the sway of the spectacle, the *badaud* becomes an impersonal being; he is no longer a man; he is the public, he is the crowd . . . The true *badaud* is worthy of the admiration of all upright and sincere hearts.   (1867: 263)

Fournel also uses the term *flânerie* to define this activity, though, and at times reverts to *flâneur* (1867: 276).[28] His equivocation is evidence of contemporaneous linguistic fluidity, as are earlier references to the ragpicker as a 'flâneur prolétaire'.[29]

In short, though the figures of the *flâneur* and *badaud* had broadly different connotations, urban spectatorship was situated within a spectrum of popular and elite practices, and described with a shifting range of terms. *Saltimbanques* and itinerant performers were particularly successful at uniting popular and elite audiences. The cultural critic Tony Bennett has placed the fairground under the heading of the 'exhibitionary complex', together with museums, panoramas, international exhibitions, department stores, and arcades. In these new spaces, he suggests, the rules of what Foucault termed the 'carceral archipelago' were

---

[27] Baudelaire claimed considerable importance for this dialectic between 'vaporization' and the 'centralization of the *Self* [*Moi*]' in the man of the crowd (CB1: 676); see Howells 1996: 64–82.

[28] Forth's claim that the *badaud* was ridiculed by Fournel is misleading (2004: 110–16), since the latter laments the figure's demise (1867: 264–5). Burton distinguishes the July Monarchy *flâneur* from the Second Empire 'man of the crowd' in both Fournel *and* Baudelaire (1994: 1–2), as does Walter Benjamin.

[29] Anon. 1844 (unpaginated).

reversed: 'The panopticon was designed so that everyone could be seen; the Crystal Palace was designed so that everyone could see.'[30] Often designed for the display of commodities, the spaces used increasingly subtle 'techniques of behaviour management' to ensure that the bourgeoisie exercised a calming influence on the working classes. Though the concept of the exhibitionary complex usefully highlights the links between different practices, the metaphor of the panopticon cannot be applied to Paris and London without further contextualization. For French types such as the *flâneur*, *badaud*, and *homme de lettres*, urban life functioned as a permanent exhibition. Such figures were not merely observers like the guards in Bentham's panopticon or government spies. They were simultaneously subject and object, participants in the Parisian drama in their own right and material for the observation of others.

Conflating different exhibitionary spaces also blurs the specificity of different types of spectacle. Some exhibits belonged to an uneasy middle ground between the human and non-human, including allegedly erudite animals and wax figures that moved mechanically. The exhibition of live human 'specimens' generated peculiarly disturbing experiences, partly owing to spectators' residual sense of the buried humanity of the exhibits. Recent research on both nineteenth-century American sideshows and *fin-de-siècle* French colonial exhibitions has argued that 'monsters' and 'savages' were held up to the audience as triumphant proof of their own normality. This view underlies the most subtle accounts of the encounter, written from a psychoanalytic perspective: 'The viewer's horror lies in the recognition that this monstrous being is at the heart of his or her own identity, for it is all that must be ejected or abjected from self-image to make the bounded, category-obeying self possible.'[31] Nonetheless, audiences at American sideshows proved considerably more hostile to deviance than audiences attending similar displays at St Bartholomew's fair in London, suggesting that such theories must also be able to account for culturally variable responses.[32]

What factors shaped French responses to physical deviance? The French salon and its tradition of *politesse* was seen by both French and foreign observers to be particularly conformist, ensuring adherence to

[30] Bennett 1995: 65; see Foucault 1976.
[31] Grosz 1996: 65; see also Grosz 1990: 86–93. For a typical, if reductive, formulation of the 'normalization' argument, see Thomson 1996: 1–19.
[32] Youngquist 2003: 49.

social norms with the threat of ridicule. Nineteenth-century etiquette manuals suggest that many middle-class Parisians were brought up to feel that their demeanour was under hostile scrutiny from the never-closing eye of public opinion ('Let us submit to the laws of society so we are not pointed at in ridicule'[33]). When bourgeois observers saw monsters pointed at in the fair, or eccentrics in the street, they were perhaps gazing at images of their own potential ostracism.

In addition, although monsters aroused strong negative emotions they simultaneously exerted an incomprehensible and frightening attraction. The spectre of original sin, influential in rigorist tendencies within nineteenth-century French Catholicism, was often interwoven with responses to anomaly.[34] Since 'freaks' were held to be the product of unnatural couplings in the popular imagination, monsters appeared to be engendered amidst the same perverse desires associated with viewing them. Eccentric bodies elicited eccentric desires, threatening to turn fairground customers themselves into moral monsters. An aside in a *fin-de-siècle* novel formalizes the dynamic which underpinned the fairground culture of the Second Empire: 'I was a girl, but an eccentric one, which accounts for my melancholy', a hermaphrodite exclaims sadly after a medical examination, but a brothel-keeper later reassures her: 'Men are pigs: they're captivated by eccentricity. Once they find out you're a hermaphrodite, they'll queue up to spend half an hour in your company.'[35] Intentionally or not, the writers who left records of their encounters around the mid-century emphasized the channels of con-tamination, identification, and desire drawing bourgeois and 'monster' together.

Saltimbanques **and** *la vie excentrique*

Cultural representations of *saltimbanques* and 'monsters' occupied an ambiguous space in the bourgeois imagination. Fairground perform-ers appeared close to the dangerous classes yet, like Bohemian artists, evoked a realm of freedom and fantasy. Their itinerant lives rendered them a puzzlingly archaic exception to the laws of modernization.[36] The fusion of *saltimbanques*' mythical appeal and their ability to function as present-day political symbols captivated observers such as the Bohemian

---

[33] Poisle-Desgranges 1869: 7.   [34] See Gibson 1989: 28, ch. 8.
[35] Dubarry 1897: 35, 305. I am grateful to Michael Finn for this reference.
[36] See Privat d'Anglemont 1984: 83.

Jules Vallès: 'A strange and ancient race, which attracts me as do all those who struggle through battles and adventures. Life in the present age is so stupid! We are so hampered in everything we do that I turn with curiosity to those lives which escape our regimental classifications, which flee from rules across the fields and along the gutters' (JV1: 707). Vallès juxtaposes a residual Romanticism with a deflating realism that insists on bourgeois idiocy and the grotesque aspects of fairground life.[37] The tension between these two aesthetic modes dominated Second Empire discourse on *saltimbanques*.

During this period, literary interest revolved around 'la petite banque', small troupes in the process of being overtaken by commercial circuses. The authorities increasingly persecuted such troupes, part of a wider trend to restrict public spectacles to carefully regulated settings.[38] The courts often prosecuted *saltimbanques* for infringements of laws prohibiting vagrancy,[39] a crime perceived as so serious by the *fin de siècle* that recidivists were punished by transportation to the colonies for life.[40] Following the alleged involvement of *saltimbanques* with the production of Republican propaganda in the period before 1848, a raft of legislation was passed during the Second Empire regulating fairground performances, particularly the use of child labour, though laments for the decline of the *parade* preceded these events.[41] By 1863, restrictive laws signalled the demise of small troupes, part of a wider tendency to suppress anything resembling the popular carnival across Europe.[42]

Baron Haussmann's reconstructions of Paris occasioned mourning for a supposedly more colourful past. Semi-permanent circus tents were erected around the mid-century on the two most important sites for fairground shows: the Carré Marigny became the site of the Cirque des Champs-Elysées in 1835, and the Boulevard du Temple the site of the Cirque Napoléon in 1852.[43] Theatres and hippodromes doubling as circuses began to host exhibitions of human 'curiosities'. Awareness of the impersonal nature of mass spectacle sharpened writers' desire to catalogue their more intimate experiences of earlier popular culture.

---

[37] On Vallès's career, see Richepin 1872, Münster 1974, and Bellet 1977.
[38] See Faure 1978: 142, ch. 4 on the regulation of the *fin-de-siècle* carnival.
[39] See Seigel 1999: 146–7.   [40] See Nye 1984: 72–6.
[41] Du Camp and Flaubert express typical nostalgia in the late 1840s (1987: 507–8, 553–4); see Burton 1994: 52.
[42] See Clark 1973: 120–1 and Harper 1981: 32 n. 39 for a critique of his argument.
[43] The former became the Cirque national and Cirque de l'Impératrice, the latter the Cirque d'Hiver.

Fig. 10. The Carré Marigny in Paris in 1848. (Texier 1852–3: I (1852), 19) © British Library Board. All Rights Reserved. (574.m.13)

A nostalgic account of the Boulevard du Temple published in 1873, shortly after the demolition and reconstruction of the area, typically warned that it was impossible to imagine its previous role as a 'living encyclopaedia' of Parisian pleasures, 'the workers' land of plenty and the eccentric playground of the capital's richer inhabitants'.[44]

The fairground, like the carnival, suspended the normal rules of social segregation. Like London, Paris was a magnet for the strange and marvellous from all over the world, its exhibitions attended by a heterogeneous public.[45] 'Who doesn't know the carré Marigny? Which of us *flâneurs* of the city has not gone at least once to stroll around that vast area, with his idleness for sole company?' (see Fig. 10).[46] The frequently signalled desire for *ébahissement* (stupefied amazement) suggests that the fairground functioned as a popular sublime, providing escape from the constraints of everyday rationality. Noise, the 'music of the poor', played an important role, as did colourful posters and the smell of frying food: 'In this fantastic town . . . all one's senses are enchanted at once.'[47] Sensorial overloading encouraged psychic detachment from

---

[44] Challamel 1873: 6.
[45] See Privat d'Anglemont 1861: 148–9, Challamel 1873: 72, Pommier 1831: 200–1.
[46] Pommier 1832: 114.   [47] JV1: 707 and Texier 1852: 18 respectively.

habitual modes of perception. The term 'phantasmagoria', which Marx associated with the magical fetishism of the commodity and Walter Benjamin with Parisian modernity as a whole, originated in popular spectacle: the term *fantôme* denoted ghostly optical illusions displayed to paying customers.[48] The decline of the fairground was partially linked to the emergence of more seductive forms of phantasmagoria in the arcade and the department store.

The terminology of eccentricity was used in a range of contexts in the vocabulary of the fairground and subsequently the circus. Those who earned their livings in an itinerant manner, including acrobats, travelling salesmen, quack doctors, and street performers, were known as *industriels*, a term ironically hinting at their materialism. In 1859 Alphonse Esquiros included fairground life within the category of 'eccentric professions', whilst during the Second Empire, Bohemian gypsies were held to symbolize 'la vie excentrique'.[49] Many types of *industriel*, including sword-swallowers and charlatans, were described as eccentrics. Towards the end of the century, the personal noun *un excentrique* and related adjectives were also used on advertising bills for the circus and music hall, often to imply a daredevil approach (e.g. 'Three eccentric negroes', 'the true eccentric dancers').[50] Throughout the July Monarchy and Second Empire, though, the term was mainly used to denote the circus freak or 'live phenomenon',[51] and by extension the exhibitions themselves ('the most eccentric and absurd exhibitions').[52]

The Carré Marigny was, above all, a city of monsters.[53] The freak was valuable relative to other nineteenth-century performers, as the nineteenth-century historiographer Gaston Escudier noted, describing *saltimbanques* as 'this colourful, roaming Bohemia...which recognizes only one monarchy in the world: that of THE MONSTER in all its forms, for the monster ensures the livelihood of its courtiers, without their having to do anything whatsoever' (1875: 4). In a situation of intense competition, a single error could result in the crowd's attention

---

[48] See Parkhurst-Ferguson 1994: 108.
[49] Esquiros 1859 and Forgues 1862 respectively.
[50] See Hotier 1972: 51, and the *Catalogue de la Bibliothèque de l'Opéra*, 1969: 110–18.
[51] Though the term *phénomène* also denoted monstrous animals, I focus primarily on human performers. The archives of the Cirque Olympique and the Cirque Napoléon list as *excentricités* a 'liliputian', mixed-race conjoined twins, and an 'armless violinist', for example; see Thétard 1978: 500.
[52] Comte 1854: 39.   [53] Alhoy et al. 1854: I, 48.

being drawn by a rival troupe, leaving performers on the brink of ruin (JV1: 709–10). Marvellous beings were advertised carefully. Posters displayed around the city announced the 'phenomenon' in hyperbolic terms. The painted canvases hung over fairground booths provided free entertainment for those who could not afford to enter. A typical example depicted a 'savage' eating a child and a monstrous calf gazed at in astonishment by a sea captain and aristocratic lady.[54] Musicians then serenaded the audience with brass and cymbals until a large crowd had gathered. Finally, standing on makeshift trestles, the ringmaster would begin his tirade, known as *la parade*.[55] The speech was the culmination of a series of rituals designed to bypass everyday consciousness completely.

Eccentric specimens

The inhabitants of the fairground booth were shrouded in deliberately cultivated mystique. Social policies that encouraged the segregation of the mentally and physical deviant may have contributed to a hunger for public displays of abnormality.[56] In nineteenth-century France, deviance of every kind gave rise to a profusion of linguistic categories. From the multiplication of Parisian slang for different types of prostitute to the growth of fabulous psychiatric terminology for new phobias during the *fin de siècle*, linguistic activity hinted at a need for mastery that no amount of discursive inventiveness could satisfy. The epithets used to describe human monsters hinted at their resistance to interpretive codes. One of Barnum's human exhibits was dubbed ' "WHAT IS IT?" because this is the universal exclamation of all who have seen it' (when exhibited in Paris, it became known as 'Qu'est-ce que c'est que ça').[57]

The concepts of eccentricity and monstrosity are structurally similar: eccentricity entails departure from social and psychological norms, whilst monstrosity entails departure from physiological norms.[58] Highly polysemic, both terms lend themselves to metaphorical extension. The term *monstruosité* was, like eccentricity, vaguely defined in nineteenth-century dictionaries ('that which is violently opposed to

---

[54] See e.g. Pommier 1831: 204.
[55] On the iconography of the *parade*, see Harper 1981.
[56] Bancel et al. 2002: 9.   [57] Altick 1978: 265; Thétard 1978: 192–3.
[58] See Ch. 7 below for further discussion of the semantics of eccentricity.

received laws and customs').[59] Eccentrics were described as 'monsters' and 'prodigies', whilst monsters were known as 'eccentricities of nature', *merveilles, curiosités, bizarreries*, and *anomalies*.[60] Often such terms were accumulated, as though each synonym could explain the preceding terms. In his fictional evocation of one of the most popular Parisian fairs in 1879, Alphonse Daudet writes: 'All these living *curiosities* merged with those which were only represented in pictures: giant women . . . monsters, *accidents* of nature, all the eccentricities and peculiarities imaginable' (1879: 193). A French advertising bill for the touring Barnum and Bailey circus from the turn of the twentieth century promises, in similar terms, 'all circus freaks . . . all human anomalies; marvellous beings, bizarre creatures; the caprices and eccentricities of nature'.[61]

The enigma foregrounded by the proliferation of synonyms was at the centre of the sideshow's appeal. As with eccentricity, a category defined in relation to a shifting norm, there was no certainty about how different bodies had to be from the norm to qualify as a 'phenomenon'. Freakishness 'derived less from particular physical attributes than the spectacle of the extraordinary body swathed in theatrical props, promoted by advertising and performative fanfare'.[62] Above all, freaks had to be shocking in relation to the expectations of their audience. Novelty and eccentricity shared the same semantic field; both were linked to the built-in obsolescence typical of capitalist production. Unwanted 'monsters', it was rumoured, were bartered amongst *saltimbanques* for fresh specimens still able to shock.[63]

The freaks exhibited throughout France on public holidays were variations on the cast later popularized for the masses by Barnum,[64] including giants and dwarves, conjoined twins, hermaphrodites, bearded ladies, feral humans, and 'savages' purporting to be from distant countries. The cast was completed by working acts such as dislocation and sword swallowing, and monstrous and erudite animals. Severely malformed infants who died at birth and the corpses of deceased performers

---

[59] GD11: 475. Compare Eyma's comments: 'All the nations of the world have their ridiculous aberrations and their *eccentricities*, their exceptions which, at times, are actual monstrosities' (1860: 5).

[60] On American equivalents, see Bogdan 1988: 3; on the history of freaks see Fiedler 1981.

[61] Cited in Howard 1977: 42.   [62] Adams 2001: 4–5.

[63] Escudier 1875: 114–15; see also Delvau 1867*b*: 4.

[64] The opening of his 1898 tour to Paris was attended by senior officials and writers such as Zola; see Thétard 1978: 192.

were stuffed and displayed for an extra price; photography came to function as a metaphorical equivalent of pickling. Due to the rarity of severe
malformations, fraud was ubiquitous: 'At fairs, what stand out above
all are the inordinate numbers of female giants, savages . . . and Siamese
twins . . . and it is not uninteresting to observe that these eccentricities
are *manufactured* with the same ease with which we twist a piece of
paper into a bird or a little boat.'[65] As the definition of a freak is partly
contextual, the spectacle depended upon an unspoken pact between
performer, observers, and *saltimbanques*, similar to the implicit contracts
governing the mimetic illusions of realist fiction and the theatre. All
participated in a dramatic ritual in which roles were determined in
advance,[66] though the illusion proved fragile. Once the customer had
paid to enter, many *saltimbanques* were unconcerned if their deception
was discovered. Deception met with a variety of responses. Some viewers
emerged from the show with their illusions destroyed, pervaded by a
sense of shame reminiscent of descriptions of men leaving nineteenth-
century brothels.[67] At times the police had to be called in to control
angry crowds when fraud was discovered.[68] At others, deception was
tolerated by audiences, who took malicious pleasure in the thought that
others would be defrauded after them.[69]

That some viewers enjoyed being deceived was suggested by their
willingness to be hypnotized by the *parade* before entering the exhibition: 'they resemble animals that have let themselves be caught in the
same traps since the beginning of the world.'[70] In his description of
English fairgrounds, Alphonse Esquiros notes that the English know
they are being defrauded yet do not mind,[71] and French accounts
similarly suggest that observers could cynically relish the gap between
appearance and reality. The concept of the *coulisses*—the secret machinery upon which the appearances of social life depended—was a dominant theme in Parisian mythology, traversing Balzac's *Comédie humaine*
and many representations of the underworld. Watching performers
struggling to appear as ferocious savages, or erudite animals failing their
tricks, became a new spectacle at a meta-level, enhanced by a sense of
superiority over the naive.[72] Attending a fair in Normandy, Gustave

---

[65] Escudier 1875: 45–6; emphasis in original. [66] Adams 2001: 6.

[67] e.g. Pommier 1831: 206; see Corbin 1978: 71.

[68] Escudier 1875: 36 and Alhoy et al. 1854: I, 59–60. [69] Comte 1854: 40–1.

[70] Pommier 1831: 205. [71] Esquiros 1859: 134.

[72] Barnum, whose memoirs were widely read in France, argued that audiences actively
wished to be duped; see Jones 1984: 128–30, 140.

Flaubert and Maxime Du Camp admit to being disappointed when, upon entering a booth, they discover that a five-legged sheep is real.[73] In one of the most frequently cited examples of deception, a talking seal displayed on the Champs Elysées was impersonated by a bored student; at times he would recite poetry in Greek or Latin.[74] The figure of the talking seal appeared emblematic of the impoverished man of letters, who debased himself and squandered his talents for an ungrateful audience.

Fraud extended to the deliberate infliction of deformity. Writers suggested, with horrified fascination, that *saltimbanques* hoped for or even deliberately produced deformed children in order to improve their earnings.[75] The rituals of the fairground often facilitated the illusion of the observer's superiority: 'labelling a person a *freak* evacuates her humanity, authorizing the paying customer to approach her as an object of curiosity and entertainment.'[76] But fraud threatened to reverse the power dynamic, making a spectacle of gullible customers. Furthermore, the act of labelling was not always straightforwardly dehumanizing, given the potentially positive connotations of terms such as 'monster' and 'eccentric'. Jules Vallès, explaining his decision to enter a fairground booth, reveals conflicting motives:

> I entered, I always enter: throughout my whole life I have always loved *monsters*. There are very few heads of aztecs, hydrocephalics, cyclops or Arguses...that I have not touched or measured, on which I have not knocked to see what was inside...It is not that I like horrible things! But I wanted to know what God had left by way of souls in these ill-fashioned bodies, what there might be of MAN in a monster. I wondered how they lived, these strange anomalies, these male and female vestals of deformity.   (JV1: 264)

Vallès's denial of perversion hints at the guilt of many who attended freak shows. His professed love of monsters clearly consists, in part, in narcissistic love of his own experience of exploring deformed bodies with a sense of mastery, as though they were toys or objects of scientific study. Nonetheless, the passage also suggests that he is struggling towards a

---

[73] Du Camp and Flaubert 1987: 223–4. See also Du Camp 1984: 63–4.

[74] See Delord et al. 1854*b*: 82, Texier 1852: 18–19; and Eugène Sue's portrait of Léonidas Requin, a human fish ('homme-poisson'), in *Martin, l'enfant trouvé* (Martin, the Foundling) (1846–7).

[75] Vallès repeatedly makes this claim. Hugo's *L'Homme qui rit* (The Man Who Laughs) (1869) and Maupassant's 'La Mère aux monstres' (A Mother of Monsters) (1883) depict, respectively, the selling of mutilated and deliberately malformed children to *saltimbanques*.

[76] Adams 2001: 10.

perspective in which the 'humanity' of the performers is no longer unthinkable.

Voices from the fairground

Vallès's innovation consisted in giving human monsters a voice in the documentary setting of fairground life.[77] The link between talking monsters and political discourse had previously been explored in English Romanticism. In his autobiographical poem, *The Prelude* (1805), William Wordsworth describes St Bartholomew's fair, seen during a childhood visit to London, as a 'parliament of monsters'; though couched in the language of repugnance, his metaphor implicitly associates the fairground with democracy.[78] Mary Shelley's novel *Frankenstein* (1818) allowed the 'Creature', rapidly interpreted as a symbol of the dangerous classes, to speak for himself, thereby transforming Wordsworth's debased parliament into the Utopian possibility of the oppressed being given their own voice.[79]

That representations of the fairground were perceived as threatening by some French observers suggests similar awareness of a metaphorical link between monstrosity and the dangerous classes. Stéphane Comte, for instance, attacked the institution of the fairground in the tract *Les Saltimbanques jugés* (1854), or '*Saltimbanques* on Trial', subtitled 'Reflections on the pernicious influence exerted by charlatans, *saltimbanques* and travelling singers on social morals'. The work views itinerant performers as parasites and the 'chrysalis' of dangerous crime, and sternly recommends that they turn to useful professions such as agricultural labour. Comte criticizes the literary energy devoted to the fairground: 'in this day and age, we have so glorified *saltimbanques* that we have become infatuated with them and have made them the very height of fashion' (1854: 41). Vallès's portraits of *saltimbanques* constitute the culmination of this literary trend. A tormented and at times lachrymose sense of sympathy pervades his writing on the fairground, emblematic of a wider Bohemian preoccupation with *le vécu* or lived experience.[80] The enterprise remains problematic: his identification is linked to displaced narcissism and self-pity, and the power relationship

---

[77] In contrast, Victor Hugo was famous for his representation of fictional monsters and grotesques.
[78] See Youngquist 2003: 36–7.   [79] See Baldick 1987: 10–29.
[80] See Bellet 1977: 208–38, Goulemot and Oster 1992: 130.

is always tilted in his favour. Metaphors of hunting, seduction, and prostitution underlie his encounters with monsters and eccentrics.

One sketch is particularly revealing of his ambivalence: 'Le Bachelier géant', first published in *Le Figaro* during the summer of 1864 as 'Les Confessions d'un Saltimbanque'.[81] The narrative frame depicts Vallès's visit to a fairground booth in Montmartre, whose main attraction is a giant who has allegedly passed his baccalaureate. After the performance Vallès listens to his life story, described by the giant as a corrective to the misleading stories of fairground life circulating in literary culture (JV1: 276). The giant recounts a past of humiliation in his home village, but finds happiness for a time in a community of eccentric bodies, and his sense of shame diminishes at the thought of the audience's credulity: 'one soon starts to despise the crowd in this profession which requires it to be deceived' (JV1: 282). The troupe is obliged to refashion itself at regular intervals; one popular display is termed 'the living museum', and the giant sets up an *entre-sort*, a miniature sideshow comprising particularly repugnant preserved malformations. In describing the latter, he explicitly dissociates himself from monstrosity: 'God only knows what we sometimes see! What transactions between bipeds and quadrupeds, crustaceans and mammals! A string of plagiarisms and barbaric borrowings! . . . a hell paved with dreadful intentions and truncated bodies, these sinister orphans of which man, made in God's image, disavows paternity!' (JV1: 292–3). The giant's rhetoric of disgust mirrors that of the culture that in turn condemns him, and his own sense of bounded individuality is contrasted with the dissolution of identity and authorship. He nonetheless comes to believe that he is a failure and his life ends in tragedy. After his daughter is mauled to death by lions during a performance, he chooses a life of self-imposed humiliation by way of penance (JV1: 309).

Vallès's presentation of the narrative, in which it is difficult to ascertain the degree to which the narrator reworks the giant's story, exploits the discrepancy between the *saltimbanque*'s educational level and lifestyle. He is shown to be sensitive and acts in accordance with an honour ethic; Vallès's bourgeois readers, attempting to imagine life in the fairground, can readily identify with him. Second, readers are encouraged to interpret the giant's narrative within the framework of the melodrama, placing him in the feminized role of persecuted victim. Finally, neither Vallès nor the giant consider the latter wholly disgusting;

---

[81] Subsequently included in *Les Réfractaires* (1865).

abjection retreats to the stuffed and pickled inhabitants of the *entre-sort*. The giant's conscious embracing of shame at the end of the narrative highlights the extent to which he resisted identifying with his identity as 'monster' before.

Vallès returns to the theme of freaks in 'Une Poignée de monstres', embedded within a series of sketches entitled 'Les Saltimbanques' in *La Rue* (1866). The 'human museum' is here replaced by the more informal metaphor of the *poignée*, a handful or clutch, suggesting that they have been plucked at random from the 'sad army of Bohemians' (JV1: 289). A plump woman with no legs and only one arm, whose torso emits a mysterious ticking sound, fifty-year-old Césarine was a well-known fixture on the Parisian fairground scene.[82] Dressed in a revealing costume, she specializes in performing erotic dances on top of a stool. Like the giant, Césarine defiantly refuses to identify with her monstrosity, asserting, to the amusement of Vallès, that her children are as well formed as 'you and ME'.[83] Césarine was banned from the centre of Paris when a deformed child was born to the wife of an important government official whose arm she had touched. The remnants of a discredited doctrine of monstrous aetiology, which attributed malformations to the imagination of the mother at the time of conception, were evident in contemporaneous decisions to ban exhibitions of deformed bodies at theatres for fear of inducing malformations in the female audience.[84]

Césarine's erotic persona evidently transfixes Vallès, as it did several of his contemporaries, including Champfleury and Maxime Du Camp.[85] In the mythology surrounding her, she drives lovers to suicide and despair, marries, and has children by different fathers. Vallès portrays her as 'a piece of living flesh which jumps and quivers at the sound of the till and stops, breathless and perspiring, to talk to the crowd' (JV1: 719). The knowing, ironic tone of his sketch fully exploits the contrast between Romantic rhetoric and grotesque realism, for instance when she is described as warming her 'stumps' at the flame of passion,[86] or when her project to set up a school for monsters evokes images of perverse couplings in the narrator's mind.

Vallès's position thus remains ambiguous. He frames himself as a champion of the oppressed, and views the 'monster' as an icon of marginality, simultaneously sought out and shunned by bourgeois society.

---

[82] Césarine is sketched in *La Parodie*, 12–17 December 1869.
[83] JV1: 294 and 719.   [84] Howard 1977: 30; see also Huet 1993: 1–2.
[85] See e.g. Maxime Du Camp 1875: III, 26–8.   [86] JV1: 720.

Yet he also sees himself as historiographer of a way of life in the process of disappearing, and cloaks his analyses in melancholy and nostalgia (JV1: 723). One of the main themes of fairground discourse—*saltimbanques* profiting from gullible customers—informs his own persona as the manager of a textual sideshow from which he makes his income, his journalism resembling a living museum or *entre-sort* in which a procession of human oddities is paraded before the reader (JV1: 727). Finally, his overtly eroticized responses belie the theme of documentary investigation. The *bachelier géant* describes how his lover Rosita once took to performing lascivious dances: 'I saw them over the top of the canvass, those idle libertines, sons of good families wearing gold pince-nez, artists with long black hair, prowling around the female tightrope walkers and castanet players' (JV1: 295). Vallès's enterprise is inevitably tarnished by the image of his lecherous Bohemian peers.

Despite their limitations, Vallès's accounts of monsters are remarkable in their attempt to consider *saltimbanques* as biographical subjects. To many of his contemporaries, it seemed ludicrous, even indecent to devote time to writing about monsters or eccentrics.[87] The following passage from a review of *La Rue* by Charles de Mazade constitutes a typical reproach: 'I do not dispute the rights of these shabby characters to citizenship of the kingdom of eccentricity and misery; but the gallery is simply too long, and they end up being of little interest.'[88] Such comments were also representative of criticisms directed towards the realist movement as a whole. Around fifteen years earlier, the bestselling novelist and critic Champfleury had embraced the controversial revaluation of the insignificant in the name of verisimilitude in his portraits of Parisian eccentrics.[89] Most of his contemporaries considered his subjects to be 'hopelessly trivial and uninteresting...tedious if not absolutely disgusting'. Typical accusations included the claim that he attempted to make art out of material as hopeless as discarded orange peel.[90] Champfleury's portraits of Bohemian marginals were thus produced in opposition to dominant normative views about the proper subjects of art, and thus are emblematic of his wider realist project. At times, they resonate with Vallès's interest in the secret affinity between monster and bourgeois.

---

[87] Prarond 1852: 141–2.   [88] Mazade 1866: 764.
[89] See Hemmings 1971: 107–13.   [90] Cited in Weinberg 1937: 147.

Champfleury in the underworld

In a series of sketches published in 1852 as *Les Excentriques*, Champfleury investigated the boundaries between the observing self and a series of metaphorical monsters: the Parisian eccentrics of the late July Monarchy. These hungry figures, clad in rags, hovered perpetually on the brink of madness. As for Vallès, Champfleury's descent into the Parisian underworld was inseparable from the quest for material for his articles. His marginal subject matter appeared to correspond perfectly to the ephemeral nature of journalism: one eccentric is described as 'this singular individual, who did not deserve a biography but only a portrait' (1877: 16).

Champfleury's self-description as a pathologist, painter, and stenographer was intertwined with the realist movement and its scientific claims.[91] Nonetheless, his text reveals that the fairground could provoke perverse desires not easily mastered by the voice of reason. In the preface to the second edition, Champfleury portrays the experience of being struck by the eccentrics who pass in the street: 'everything is present in their physiognomy, which utopian imaginings, dreams and ideas have rendered strange... Swedenborg said it in an unforgettable phrase: "The outside of the man is moulded upon his inside"' (3). The scientific jargon of physiognomy, which permeated descriptions of Bohemian eccentrics,[92] fuses in this passage with imagery of supernatural metamorphoses.[93] Champfleury proposes that his subjects may even have contaminated him: 'It has happened more than once that I have penetrated too far into the ideas of eccentrics, which then started to affect my own *self*... Each new and strange being that I meet disrupts my life for several days; I put myself in his place, I suffer his pain, I delight in his joys, I invent his inventions' (1877: 199). One sketch, 'L'Homme aux figures de cire' (The Man with the Wax Figures) illustrates this contagion in narrative form. A foray into the Parisian underworld threatens to sweep away the narrator's protective carapace of rationality, placing *him* in the position of borderline madman.

---

[91] Champfleury's aesthetic manifesto *Le Réalisme* was published in 1857.
[92] See Yriarte 1868: 35; Fournel 1867: 279; and Delvau's subtitle for 1867*b*, 'Parisian physiognomies'.
[93] Champfleury argued that 'Every serious novelist is an impersonal being who, through a sort of metempsychosis, enters whilst still alive into the bodies of his characters' (cited in Weinberg 1937: 122).

The first section describes an itinerant wax cabinet before the 1848 Revolution; the second recounts Champfleury's visit in 1849 to the same exhibition in the company of his friend, the realist painter Gustave Courbet. Describing the eccentric *saltimbanque* who owns the collection as a 'figure who is odder than anything in his museum', Champfleury seeks to insert him into his own literary gallery, establishing a parallel between the two men. But the *saltimbanque*'s features have fused with the wax criminals in his gallery: 'his general physiognomy had nothing human about it: he seemed to have been shaped in the mould in which criminals are poured . . . one does not live amongst lifeless beings with impunity, without taking on their form' (316–17). The spectre of retribution hovers over the acts of collecting and exhibiting deviance, whether in wax museums or their virtual textual equivalents.

Champfleury's visit to the wax collection is analysed with a strange mixture of complacency and horror.[94] When the grotesque Césarine performs her erotic polka dance on a stool, Champfleury admits that she provides 'a seductive curiosity for even the least curious'; but when she invites him to verify the bizarre ticking sound inside her body by touching her, he, unlike Vallès, retreats: 'I recoiled; both wax monstrosities and flesh-and-blood monstrosities fill me with more disgust than curiosity.' The enigma of his response stimulates desire, however, for he returns several times as though under a strange compulsion (303). The wax figures replace the 'natural' association between death, boredom, and the absence of desire with the 'perverse' linking of death, curiosity, and desire, generating both masochistic and sadistic fantasies. His response to the gallery is troubling:

I had wanted to visit the exhibition for a long time, as I love to witness the agony of these spectacles. I am cruel enough to laugh at the misery, sickness and infirmity of those on show . . . These shows corrupt people and make them wicked, above all the sight of the wax cabinets. On setting foot inside these rooms, one is troubled; one has thoughts of murder and homicide.

(1877: 305)

Champfleury notes that shop-owners increasingly use moving female dolls to advertise their products. Displayed in provocative clothing, these new 'wax sirens' provide free phantasmagoria in broad daylight, exemplifying the forces drawing urban crowds away from sideshows and into arcades and department stores. The public responds to commercial

---

[94] On ambivalent responses to freaks, see Grosz 1996: 56.

spectacle with the same open-mouthed astonishment that recurs in discourse on the fairground. Some spectators remain mesmerized for hours; the dolls' owners fondle them lovingly, and men wait outside the shop windows at dawn to see the naked figures being dressed.

The notion of sexual intercourse with wax figures is strongly suggestive of necrophilia. Beset by disquieting emotions, Champfleury performs an improvised self-analysis, scrutinizing the memory of a traumatic childhood visit to a wax cabinet to discover the origins of his terror; he concludes that it lies in their similarity to statues and corpses. The wax figures, partly made of stuffed cloth, mirror both the morgue and the abattoir, since murderers often cut their victims into pieces to make them unrecognizable. Images of fragmented bodies fill Champfleury's sketch, including the truncated body of Césarine. The narrator concludes the first section on an optimistic note: 'This accounts for the terrible sensations and the nightmares in broad daylight to which cabinets of wax figures give rise' (308). This explanation skirts over the disturbing lure of the pathological. Champfleury's evocations of monstrosity, like those of many of his contemporaries, highlight a central similarity between the aesthetic category of the grotesque and eccentricity: both are premised upon unsettling ambivalence.[95]

The most hyper-real of all aesthetic products and close to the perfect simulacrum, the wax figure allows Champfleury to explore the consequences of realistic representation on the level of phantasmagoria—precisely that which is denied by the rationalistic language of the realist movement. His fascination echoes that of the hundreds of thousands of Parisians who later queued to visit more impersonal spectacles such as the Morgue, on the pretext of identifying corpses drowned in the Seine, or larger wax collections such as the Musée Grévin, a metaphorical extension of the *Gazette des tribunaux* in which the most brutal crimes were recorded.[96] The second part of Champfleury's sketch is set under the sign of saturnalia, in typically nostalgic mode. In the aftermath of 1848, it seemed likely that the carnival would be abolished;[97] the narrator resolves to visit the underworld with his friend, Gustave Courbet, before it disappears.

---

[95] Steig argues that the grotesque involves the 'managing' of the (frightening) uncanny by the (reassuring) comic (1970: 259).

[96] See Schwartz 1998: 43–83, 98–130 and Huet 1993: ch. 8.

[97] See Faure 1978: 114–23.

Weaving his way through violent drunkards late at night, Champfleury fantasizes about his own murder.[98] But horror, like terror, excites him: 'I left one of these terrible places, half-hallucinating and no longer recognizing myself, having noticed cases of sexual ambiguity and hybrid men and women, figures that the licentious sculptures and paintings of antiquity cannot even begin to evoke' (1877: 310). When Champfleury and Courbet enter the eccentric's house, this 'trouble' escalates into a temporary breakdown of reason which functions as the climax of the sketch. The eccentric *saltimbanque* leaves them in a dark room where they can sense inanimate bodies all around them, and they panic, fearing a plot to murder them. Once the room is lit by candle-light, they find themselves surrounded by disintegrating wax body parts suggestive of violent dismemberment. Again, a single visit is not enough (321). When they return, the old woman finally narrates to them the secret crime at the centre of the collection: her husband's sexual obses-sion with his favourite wax doll, Julie, whom he has placed on a pedestal. The image evokes Césarine dancing on a stool; both serve as grotesque caricatures of the Romantic vision of the idealized female beloved. In the closing scene the husband, termed a 'cruel monster', threatens to murder his wife. The reactions of Champfleury and Courbet are not stated, and closure evaporates into meditation upon the inexplicable nature of perverse desire.

Physical monstrosity repeatedly merges, in the narrative, with moral monstrosity, amidst a sequence of real or imagined couplings between the erotically deviant and 'cripples', hermaphrodites, wax figures, and corpses. Creating a strong impression of ontological indeterminacy, these unions disrupt the working of reason, and the narrator's stable sense of identity disintegrates in a type of negative carnivalesque ('night-mares in broad daylight', 'half-hallucinating, no longer recognizing myself'). Although it aspires to be a total replica of the human body, the wax figure is destined to remain disturbingly uncanny.[99] Portraying the narrator in the throes of the same mental disorder that normally characterizes his eccentric subjects, the text enacts a striking reversal of authority. The narrator had earlier attacked those who nourish the

---

[98] On the psychic functions of the underworld for the bourgeoisie, see Stallybrass and White 1986: ch. 3.

[99] E. Jentsch held that the *unheimlich* arose from doubts whether an apparently animate being were alive, or an apparently lifeless one inanimate, citing waxwork figures and automata, though Freud himself does not locate the uncanny in Hoffman's doll Olympia (see Freud 1955: 226–7).

public's hunger for vice, with implicit reference to Plato's banishment of poets from the Republic: 'the large band of false artists, false scholars, false poets, and false philosophers, who spend their time distilling poison and making the people drink it' (307).[100] The vocabulary of civic responsibility distances Champfleury from participation in criminal representations whilst granting himself and his readers covert access to them. Far from creating stable barriers between the bourgeois home and the underworld, the text holds a mirror up to the disavowed desires of the reader.

Two different interpretations of monstrosity in Champfleury's narrative thus emerge: first, that it is an unnatural poison, threatening to contaminate healthy male readers and requiring constant policing; and second, that the desires of the reader are intrinsically monstrous—according to a common narrative, the consequence of original sin. The dilemma was typical of the obsession with innate perversity in contemporaneous medical discourse.[101]

Spectacles of savagery

The women portrayed in Champfleury's sketch are uniformly grotesque; the wax collection includes a *femme disséquée* (dissected woman) and a *femme sauvage* (wild or savage woman). The latter particularly fascinated writers of the period, undermining fixed oppositions between human and animal, culture and nature.[102] If the Parisian literary physiology at times contained illustrations of performing animals dressed in waistcoats and top hats, exhibitions of 'savages' revealed writhing, dirty, human bodies reduced to the level of wild animals. Vallès tellingly described *femmes sauvages* as 'these girls whose calves and breasts are on display' (JV1: 709; see Fig. 11).

Expressions of erotic pleasure were common in fairground exhibitions, which functioned as extensions of both the brothel and the pornographic text. The audience's grunting was often echoed by performers, perhaps in an attempt to arouse, or mirror, their desire. In one visit to the Carré Marigny, in which he enters ten booths in succession, Victor Fournel watches an Arab dancer arousing her audience: 'Sybarites in blue smocks, who do not have the money to go and admire

---

[100] See Prendergast 1986: 9–12.　　[101] See Ch. 7 below.
[102] See Grosz 1996: 57.

Fig. 11. The *femme sauvage* performing in a fairground. (Escudier 1875: 26) © British Library Board. All Rights Reserved. (12330.i.l)

the dancers from the Opera, are plunged into ecstasy and utter little exclamations of pleasure while licking their lips delicately' (1867: 159). In a neighbouring booth a savage chieftain devoured raw carrots ferociously, 'rolling his wild eyes and grunting softly with satisfaction' (157). The eroticization of savagery was by no means restricted to a proletarian audience. Recounting a display of an exotic dancer in Normandy, Maxime Du Camp fantasizes about her bloodthirsty oriental ancestors, informing his readers that he 'sinned' that night whilst thinking of her.[103]

The contrast between raw and cooked foods, which symbolizes the clash between 'savage' and 'civilized', was ubiquitous in fairground rhetoric. Exhibitions centred upon performers' theatrical consumption of raw and revolting substances, most commonly live rabbits or poultry

---

[103] Du Camp and Flaubert 1987: 550–1; 554.

with its feathers intact, rats, cats, pebbles, or glass. The role of such drama in attracting custom is evident in a poster transcribed and annotated by Fournel:

FEMALE CANNIBAL

CAPTURED 4070 LEAGUES FROM FRANCE, BY CAPTAIN POLLAR,

A SPANISH MILITARY COMMANDER . . .

RECOGNIZED IN SEVERAL CITIES OF FRANCE

AND BY THE MEDICAL SCHOOL OF MONTPELLIER

FOR FEATS PERFORMED WITH HER REMARKABLY STRONG JAWS

SHE CRUSHES STONES BENEATH HER TEETH

AS WELL AS CHICKENS, DOGS, AND CATS

In huge red letters:

ADDERS AND SNAKES

In tiny black letters:

IF WE CAN OBTAIN THEM.

SHE FINISHES BY SWALLOWING FIRE AND PERFORMS

PEERLESS FEATS OF NON-COMBUSTION.

(1867: 168)

Obvious phallic symbols, serpents also hinted at woman's role in the fall. A circle of Parisian urchins hovers by this spectacle, gripped by feelings of anxious curiosity. The act of eating is etymologically present in the French term for disgust, 'dé-goût'.[104] This common response to all sideshow exhibitions was taken to hyperbolic extremes in spectacles of savagery.

The concepts of feral wildness and ethnological exoticism were frequently blurred, as in one account of a *femme sauvage*. Billed as an 18-year-old discovered living like an animal in the forests of Lithuania, she is described by the narrator as 'a poor girl dressed up as a cannibal and made to eat stones'.[105] Cynical accounts of the fairground elaborated numerous means for avoiding ingestion, including crunching on sweets, hiding flesh torn from live animals behind the trestles, and arranging for accomplices to create realistic sounds in the background by breaking glass bottles.[106]

Erotic attraction and disgust often fused with the desire for violence. Describing the highly popular feeding time at the zoo, the authors of

---

[104] Also evident in the English 'distaste' and 'disgust'.
[105] Pommier 1831: 206.   [106] Escudier 1875: 58, Thétard 1934: 5–6.

the *Physiologie du jardin des plantes* (1841) noted its similarity to the vicarious aesthetic of melodrama:[107]

Stationed in front of the ferocious beasts are, in general, those who love violent emotions that can be safely relished. One recognizes amongst them regular patrons of the Ambigu-Comique and the Gaieté theatres. They never fail to ask themselves...the following wholly philanthropic question: what would become of a child, a woman, a man...or at a pinch a little dog, faced with even the single most ferocious of those carnivores?

(Bernard and Couailhac 1841: 36–7)

Patterns of spectatorship mutated significantly around the mid-century, a symptom of the increasing regulation of bodily responses across social life. Theatre-going audiences who displayed their emotions became subject to disdain; a typical account of 1874 views the audiences of melodramas as 'primitive creatures', 'happy in their despair'.[108] Fairground exhibitions permitted Second Empire audiences, who were forced to conceal their responses when attending the theatre or opera, to indulge fantasies of cruelty and fear without any such strictures. Their faces smeared with walnut liqueur, fraudulent savages often performed surrounded by *saltimbanques* dressed as armed policemen. Crowds were informed that without the metal grilles on their cages, heated until they glowed, none would leave the exhibition alive: 'Inside, the savage abandons himself to every conceivable type of eccentricity, shouting and screaming with hunger.'[109]

Jules Vallès had asked how much of 'MAN' there was in the fairground monster; Champfleury's exploration of the underworld questioned the moral monstrosity of the viewer. Their contemporary Charles Baudelaire took self-interrogation further still in 'La Femme sauvage et la petite-maîtresse' (The Wild Woman and the Fashionable Coquette). This prose poem is framed as an address by the speaker to his mistress, towards whom he manifests an attitude of sadistic hatred culminating in fantasies of murder. Social preoccupations are closely entwined with private concerns in the text, typical of the 'markedly social thematic' of *Le Spleen de Paris* as a whole.[110] The speaker compares the complaints of his pampered lover, whom he suspects is simulating the mild hystericism expected of sensitive women,[111] to a supposedly more authentic world of misery incarnated in three female

---

[107] See Brooks 1976: 24–55.   [108] Cited in Sennett 1986: 205–6.
[109] Escudier 1875: 58.   [110] Monroe 1985: 179.
[111] See Edelman 2003: 46–7.

figures: an old peasant working in the fields, a beggar who gathers the crusts discarded outside cabarets, and a *femme sauvage* exhibited by her husband at fairgrounds. The speaker claims he will 'cure' his mistress of her fashionable malaise for the price of admission to the exhibition.

The body of the poem depicts an imaginary encounter between the two couples across the barrier, amidst references to zoological imagery in the form of an orangutan, tiger, and bear:

Now just observe, if you please, this solid iron cage, and see that hairy monster howling like one of the damned, shaking the bars like an orangutan maddened by exile . . . This monster is one of those animals generally called "my angel!"—that is, a woman. The other monster, the one yelling his head off and brandishing a stick, is a husband. He has chained his legitimate spouse as though she were an animal, and displays her at all the street fairs with, of course, the permission of the authorities.[112]

Covered with fake hair, the *femme sauvage* performs the ritual ingestion of live poultry, which her husband snatches away before striking her harshly. The narrator concludes his description on a metaphysical plane: 'Such are the conjugal customs of these descendants of Adam and Eve, these works of thy hands, O my God! This woman has certainly the right to complain, although after all the titillating delights of fame are perhaps not unknown to her.'[113] Erotic, political, and spiritual meanings intersect in the poem. The speaker's despair at the lot of the oppressed—the old female beggar, the caged woman—mingles with narcissistic self-pity; he projects his own marginal status as poet into such social pariahs, and his desire to punish the rich is channelled into the sadism he manifests towards his mistress.[114] The infliction of symbolic wounds upon the speaker is mirrored by both the violence of the husband towards the *femme sauvage* and his own cruelty towards his mistress. In turn, the poet's thirst for literary glory is reflected in both the incongruous vanity of the *femme sauvage* and in his accusation that his mistress resembles a young frog with her feet in the mud and her eyes on the 'ideal', an image typical of descriptions of the Bohemian poet.[115]

---

[112] CB1: 289–90; Baudelaire 1970: 17.

[113] CB1: 289–90; Baudelaire 1970: 18.

[114] 'Assommons les pauvres!' (Beat Up the Poor) in the same collection has generated very conflicting interpretations (see Burton 1991: 326–8); again, the speaker's ambivalence is evident.

[115] e.g. JV1: 154.

The speaker thus oscillates between the roles of victim and perpetrator, occupying all the dramatic positions of the poem.[116]

The poem echoes key tropes of Second Empire discourse on fairground exhibitions, including simulation, the link between external and internal monstrosity, reversals of perspective, the drama of ingestion,[117] the arousing of prohibited emotions, and vicarious cruelty. The rhetoric of vanity was at times used by nineteenth-century historiographers of the fairground to justify human exhibitions, in terms reminiscent of Baudelaire's poem: 'Sensitive souls should not be too overcome with pity on account of these delicate beings. Vanity inhabits the hearts of dwarves just as it does the hearts of men, and the Princess Paulinas of this world are happy to be exhibited.'[118] Such common themes are refashioned by Baudelaire in relation to the personal preoccupations of his later writings. Most notably, the relationship of both couples in the fairground mirrors the earlier drama of Adam and Eve.

In his autobiographical text *Fusées* (Rockets), Baudelaire frames a vision of post-lapsarian pessimism in terms of omnipresent savagery: 'man...is always in a state of savagery. Whether man snares his dupe on the Boulevard, or spears his prey in unknown forests, is he not eternal man, that is to say the exemplary animal of prey?'[119] Sceptical of the idea of progress, such comments invert conventional perceptions of the relationship between nature and artifice. Thus Baudelaire's lurid depiction of the *femme sauvage* appears only on a superficial level the expression of his hatred of the 'natural' (associated with woman, whom he notoriously views as remaining at the mercy of their bodies and appetites).[120] It expresses both a hatred of human nature, male *and* female, and a critique of the idea that its ostensible opposite, civilization, can escape from the taint of the fall. Despite Baudelaire's praise for the artificial woman in his critical essays,[121] civilization and animality

---

[116] A similar multiplication of perspectives is staged in Baudelaire's poem 'L'Héautontimorouménos' in *Les Fleurs du mal*.

[117] Compare the 'polyphagous monster' in Baudelaire's 'Portraits de maîtresses' (CB1: 347).

[118] Le Roux 1889: 50–1.

[119] CB1: 663. 'Savagery' is a key Baudelairian trope; see e.g. CB2: 325, 715, 720.

[120] Most notoriously in *Mon cœur mis à nu* (My Heart Laid Bare) (CB1: 677); the view that animality and femininity are viewed with unambiguous negativity in 'La Femme sauvage' (see e.g. Stephens 1999: 148–9) could therefore be modified.

[121] CB2: 714–18.

are here portrayed as disconcertingly easy to invert: the speaker's over-civilized mistress resembles a dog, whilst the *femme sauvage* is an artificial fabrication.

Despite the negative connotations of vanity within Catholic doctrine, furthermore, the poem hints at the speaker's compassion for the *femme sauvage*. The 'fame' to which the woman aspires is that of the artist, mutating into masochistic satisfaction with being despised typical of the Bohemian 'dramatization of need'.[122] Other poems from *Le Spleen de Paris* support the implicit identification of *femme sauvage* and poet, again drawing on zoological metaphors. In 'Les Bons chiens' (The Faithful Dog), the speaker describes the pampered dogs of the wealthy. Like the mistress in 'La Femme sauvage', these artificial creatures are depicted as 'tiresome parasites',[123] and contrasted with the stray dog, another emblem for the poet: 'I invoke the friendly, lively muse of cities to help me sing the song of the faithful dog, the mangy dog, the pitiful dog, the dog everybody kicks around because he is dirty and covered with fleas, except the poor man whose companion he is, and the poet who looks upon him with a brotherly eye' (CB1: 360; 1970: 104).[124] Wildness, such passages suggest, can be a marker of spiritual authenticity. In the imaginary Baudelairian bestiary, 'Les Bons chiens' testifies to an important shift during the poet's stay in Belgium: decreasing interest in the symbolism of cats, seen as self-contained and cerebral, and increasing fascination with dogs, portrayed as ambiguous and marginal creatures who incarnate the fault lines of class and wealth.[125] The polysemy of concepts such as savagery, animality, and vanity in 'La Femme sauvage' profoundly problematizes the poem's meaning. The association of the *flâneur* with smug visual mastery in July Monarchy representations is thus replaced, in 'Les Bons chiens', by more unsettling imagery. The 'roving dog, the circus dog' evokes the edgy wanderings of the unwanted, close to Nerval's compulsive travelling or Poe's man of the crowds, a 'werewolf restlessly roaming a social wilderness'.[126]

---

[122] Goulemot and Oster 1992: 128.
[123] CB1: 360; the mistress reclines on 'stuffs as soft as your own skin', the dog in 'silken and tufted baskets' (CB1: 290, 361; Baudelaire 1970: 18, 105).
[124] On the trope of the artist as a performing dog, see Chambers 1971*b*.
[125] See Kete 1994: 163 n. 2.   [126] Benjamin: 1999: 418.

Living museums in a colonial age

Towards the end of the century, public attention shifted from fraudulent specimens to 'genuine' savages imported from distant countries, as
these became more accessible. As early as 1800, Verniquet planned an
ethnographical-zoological park in Paris in which inhabitants would live
in reconstructed indigenous settings.[127] The 'Hottentot Venus', Sartje
Baartman, was exhibited in London and Paris and dissected by Georges
Cuvier in 1814, inspiring a popular French vaudeville. Yet compared
to London, at the centre of a colonial empire, authentic ethnological
exhibitions in Paris were relatively rare.[128]

By the 1850s, 'Londoners' taste for samples of primitive races...had
been abundantly satisfied, and showgoers once more were seeking new
sensations'.[129] In Paris, exhibitions of indigenous peoples were in the
process of expansion from the late 1860s, though mainly in well-
regulated institutional settings. This was linked to two developments.
First, *expositions universelles*, staged to great acclaim in Paris in the
context of rivalry with other capital cities, exploited colonial exoticism.
In the exhibition of 1867, for example, *tableaux vivants* of colonial
subjects in their native settings included an Algerian bazaar, a Tunisian
café, and a stable of camels in Cairo.[130] Such displays had a number of
functions, including inculcating a sense of racial and cultural superiority
in the Parisian audience, justifying French colonialism, selling colonial goods, and providing allegedly educational entertainment for the
masses.[131]

Second, human exhibitions were institutionalized through the re-
invention of the Jardin zoologique d'Acclimatation in the Bois de
Boulogne as a hybrid of natural history museum and sideshow.
Designed as a zoo, the Jardin was forced to diversify when all its animal
exhibits were eaten during the siege of Paris. The equation of animals
with savages lingered. With the enthusiastic backing of the Société
d'Anthropologie de Paris, the organizers began in 1877 by exhibiting
Nubians and Inuits, rapidly expanding to include natives from countries
such as Lapland, Argentina, and the Tierra del Fuego (unlike the villages
of the *expositions*, most 'exhibits' at the Jardin were not from French

---

[127] Baratay and Hardouin-Fugier 2002: 126.
[128] On Baartman, see Lindfors 1996: 208–9. Delvau can recall only three major
exhibitions of indigenous peoples in the previous forty years (1867*b*).
[129] Altick 1978: ch. 20.   [130] Bennett 1995: 76–9.
[131] Greenhalgh 1988: 82–4.

colonies). The extraordinary popularity of such spectacles is evident from attendance figures: in 1878 an exhibition of Lapps and Gauchos was seen by 985,000 visitors during one year.[132] For many in the audience, such exhibitions provided their first and only contact with non-Westerners. As in the fairground, there was a need for permanent innovation in order to draw crowds. Audiences were informed that natives indulged in shocking transgressions such as cannibalism, human sacrifice, and incest, and journalistic and advertising techniques were carefully deployed to draw in crowds of visitors.[133]

The legitimating fantasy underlying such exhibitions was that they contributed to knowledge; as the anthropologist Alphonse Bertillon claimed, 'The great success enjoyed by the human exhibitions at the Jardin d'Acclimatation shows that the public is becoming increasingly interested in ethnography, a science which enables us to contemplate things from a position outside the prejudices and customs of our own race' (1883: p. vii). The human exhibits became the objects of scientific enquiry, and were approached by members of the Société d'Anthropologie de Paris laden with tape measures, callipers, and cameras.[134] Tourists travelling from France to distant locations were encouraged to collect human measurements. The head of the Société d'Anthropologie de Paris, Paul Broca, compared individual measurements made on living 'specimens' to those taken by doctors, describing his aim as 'gathering *anthropological observations* in the same way that doctors are accustomed to gathering pathological observations' (1879: 26). Within the French medical philosophy that defined pathology as any deviation from the statistical average, the difference between the native and the European body was taken to confer pathological status on the former.[135]

More explicit parallels between the fairground freak and the ethnological specimen emerged when delegations of scientists were sent from the Société to examine Nubians, Inuits, and the freaks of Barnum's circus.[136] The positing of a parallel between 'monster' and 'savage' was partly rooted in a paradigm change in nineteenth-century natural history. From the 1830s, the doctrine of polygenesis became

[132] Schneider 1982: 132.
[133] Schneider 1982: 143; see also Coupin 1905 on the popular fascination with anthropological 'bizarreries'.
[134] See Ardagna and Boëtsch 2002: 59.
[135] See Canguilhem 2003: 18–51. On the links between anthropology and medicine, see E. Williams 1994: 246.
[136] In 1877–8 and 1899 respectively.

increasingly influential. Eighteenth-century monogenesists had asserted that the human races shared a common origin, ascribing human variety to the process of adaptation to milieu. Polygenesists claimed, in contrast, that there were as many as sixteen separate human races, all separated by rigid barriers, and drew on teratology, the science of malformations founded by Étienne Geoffroy Saint-Hilaire, to account for the variety between races. Thus in 1843 Armand de Quatrefages, professor at the Muséum d'histoire naturelle, asserted that the 'Negro' was '*an intellectual monstrosity*', his brain demonstrating arrested development.[137]

Like the Bohemian writer who projected his own marginality onto the human monster, ethnological difference tended to intrigue Parisian observers only insofar as it suggested potential similarity, as a passage by the journalist Alfred Delvau suggests: 'Civilization differs too much from Savagery for the latter not to excite the curiosity of the former every time it appears in books and in the street. We do not mind knowing what we would be like if centuries of civilizing had not lifted off the dust of barbarism that once covered our bodies and minds' (1867*b*: 155–6). Reversing Rousseau's model of the natural self obscured by the artifice of civilization, Delvau imagines savagery as a layer of dirt obscuring the civilized person within, who is granted ontological primacy. He suggests offhandedly that white people might be exhibited for profit in the New World, a visual trope already evident in Grandville's carnivalesque image of writers locked up in the Jardin des plantes and stared at by the animals. A cheap pamphlet published to accompany the exhibition of Fuegians at the Jardin d'Acclimatation expresses a similar sentiment: 'after all, put yourself in their place! How would you like it if the Chinese or Japanese came to take you away from your home to exhibit you as a curiosity in a public square in Peking or Tokyo?'[138] Fortunately, the author concludes, the human exhibits are too stupid to notice their condition, and are so credulous that they probably believe they have been taken to Paris so that *they* can examine the Parisians (64–5).

Some contemporaneous accounts suggest, however, that a 'powerful erotic fascination' was awakened on both sides of the barrier.[139] Audiences projected their desire for unconstrained physicality and eroticism

---

[137] Emphasis in original; cited in Blanckaert 1995: 34, 25. See also Lucas 1847: 317.

[138] Ginos 1889: 64.   [139] See Baratay and Hardouin-Fugier 2002: 128.

onto the 'savages', whose bodies were frequently foregrounded in ritual dances.[140] Despite the intimate relationship between scientific and popular exhibitionary practices, the similarity of some colonial exhibitions to popular fairground displays eventually threatened to diminish their scientific prestige. From the early 1880s, the scholars linked to the Société d'Anthropologie who had initially supported the displays began to criticize them; the managers were termed 'Barnums' by promoters and detractors alike.[141] The public's thirst for popular exoticism led to the spectacles becoming ever more violent, and the Society severed its links with the Jardin in 1886. Its legitimating function was soon taken over by the Colonial Ministry in Paris.

'Regardless of its motives', one historian writes, 'the anthropological community had invented a genre at the Jardin d'Acclimatation destined to debase and defile non-Western cultures in a way barely conceived of before.'[142] In an era in which French society was traversed by concerns about national decline, however, the pleasure of *fin-de-siècle* audiences and anthropologists in contemplating their own superiority perhaps concealed a latent sense of anxiety. The extreme contrasts afforded by the juxtaposition of savage and civilized bodies distracted from the legion of exhausted and malformed French bodies which medical theories of national decline situated in between these two poles.[143]

Human exhibitions cast little light on the 'savage'; their historical significance lies instead in the light they cast on the psychic structures of those who went to stare and measure.[144] The same is largely true for the other forms of 'eccentric' human exhibition this chapter has explored. *Saltimbanques*, freaks, and fabricated 'savages' furnished writers with material for articles and self-analysis. They were rarely considered as subjects in their own right, even in the writing of Jules Vallès, which gestures more than most towards their humanity. For pronounced differences in symbolic capital shaped all encounters between writers and monsters, including his own. This chapter has explored important connections between anthropological and medical discourse, literature, and popular culture, in the context of a Parisian cultural imaginary in which spectatorship and objectification were major models for conceptualizing human encounters, with far-reaching ethical implications.

---

[140] Bancel et al. 2002: 13.   [141] Schneider 1982: 145.
[142] Greenhalgh 1988: 87.   [143] Morel 1857: I, 74 n. 1, 46.
[144] See Blanchard, Bancel, and Lemaire 2002: 69.

The literature of Parisian worldliness often emphasized the phenom-enological consequences of 'standing out' and 'being looked at' in the context of the never-closing eye of public opinion. In the fairground, in contrast, the focus was invariably placed on the phenomenology of the spectator engaged in looking at others. In a society fascinated by novelty, human 'eccentricities' were seen as expendable. The same complaints that were voiced in descriptions of fashionable society against the fickle nature of public opinion arose in relation to the audiences of street performers. For the wealthy and eccentric *homme* or *femme à la mode*, seeking to capture the public gaze, narcissistic gratification was at stake; for the *saltimbanque*, the price to be paid for fading from sight was often ruin. Some sank into penury when their bodies were broken by their bizarre performances; others scraped a living on the margins of society; a small number became rich, usually from the exploitation of other performers. Their fate seemed to mirror that of the *hommes de lettres* and eccentrics who populated Bohemian Paris.

6

Bohemia

I, who have been saved, am going to write the history of those who have not.

Jules Vallès[1]

Attitudes towards eccentricity were notably unstable in Parisian Bohemia. This 'kingdom of eccentricity and misery' was home to artists and writers struggling to make their living, who, though they often adopted a stance of social opposition, were firmly linked to the bourgeoisie.[2] During the July Monarchy, eccentricity was generally portrayed positively as wilful nonconformism. An important performative strategy for artists and writers, it reflected a new political and cultural climate following the collapse of the Restoration, and was associated with the Romantic movement of 1830, the Jeune-France, and a new body of writing preoccupied with modern life and urban experience. During the Second Empire, in contrast, it became more common to perceive eccentricity as a shameful necessity than as a deliberate choice. Nostalgia for July Monarchy eccentricity remained as a strong residual ideology,[3] but the realities of poverty, social marginality, and alienation were documented in a growing body of texts. The shifting semantic nuances of eccentricity thus reflect wider changes to understandings of Parisian Bohemia, and by extension to the social role of the artist and the function of art in the modern age.

Bohemia became a favourite subject for writers and men of letters interested in all those who, like themselves, failed to conform to the norms of the bourgeoisie. A particular subcategory of Bohemians was described as *excentriques*, typically men whose lives were dominated by cerebral pursuits and mystical values.[4] They traversed certain parts

---

[1] JV2: 889.   [2] Mazade 1866: 764.
[3] The term of Raymond Williams (1977: 121–7).
[4] Almost all sketches of Bohemian eccentrics are of men; historical eccentrics are occasionally female, e.g. in Yriarte 1868.

of Paris like 'living hieroglyphs', each locked within a set of private obsessions. Displayed in journalistic sketches and textual galleries that resembled portable fairground booths, male eccentrics provided entertainment for bourgeois readers in search of the mysterious Parisian underworld. Whilst they were mainly thought to be amiable and harmless, their indigence implied proximity to the dangerous classes and they were liable to be pathologized. The difficulty of distinguishing between deliberate and fraudulent eccentricity, or between eccentricity and insanity, generated continuous uncertainty for the writers who portrayed peculiar individuals with a strange mixture of affinity and contempt.

The evolution of Bohemia

The phrase 'Bohemian Paris' has been applied to a period extending from the mid eighteenth to the mid-twentieth century, though the term 'Bohème' was popularized in its modern sense during the July Monarchy and its demise was announced from the turn of the twentieth century.[5] Bohemia denoted both a geographical space and an imaginary realm encompassing not only artists and writers but also *saltimbanques*, itinerant salespeople, and all those trying to make ends meet in ways not recognized by the courts.[6] Recent accounts have sought to disentangle the social structures of Bohemian life from the often misrepresentative self-descriptions of Bohemian writers, and to distinguish between the various functions of Parisian Bohemia in different decades of the century.[7] Whilst distinctions can be drawn in a number of ways, four broadly overlapping paradigms existed in the century before 1870, each characterized by a different relationship to social marginality and eccentricity: (1) the eighteenth-century literary underworlds which functioned as a precursor to Bohemia; (2) the early July Monarchy Bohemia exemplified by the Jeune-France and their peers; (3) the Second Republic Bohemia of Henry Murger; and (4) Second Empire Bohemia.[8]

---

[5] See e.g. Audebrand 1905.   [6] See Seigel 1999: ch. 1.
[7] Particularly Seigel 1999, Wilson 2000, Goulemot and Oster 1992, and Gluck 2005, whose approach as she acknowledges is discursive rather than socio-political (2005: 9).
[8] My analysis draws on a statement by Jules Levallois, a contemporary of Jules Vallès, who writes of 'three Bohemias, each characterised by a different attitude' (cited in Marotin 1997: 124). Gluck usefully distinguishes between the 'sentimental Bohemia' of Henry Murger and the 'ironic Bohemia' of the Jeune-France, though she does not address the disillusioned Second Empire Bohemia of Vallès and his peers.

The fields of art and literature underwent long-term structural changes from the early eighteenth century. Following the demise of aristocratic patronage, writers had to adapt to new modes of production and consumption, and were increasingly positioned within complex networks of printers, publishers, booksellers, and critics. The phrase 'Enlightenment Bohemia' has been coined retrospectively to designate the growing number of eighteenth-century writers who, like Louis Sébastien Mercier and Restif de la Bretonne, attempted to live from their pens. It was associated with the semantic prehistory of eccentricity, namely discourse about oddity and originality, in both England and France.[9] The spectacle of Rameau's degradation in Diderot's philosophical dialogue *Le Neveu de Rameau* incarnated a central feature of the eighteenth-century sphere of letters in France: the belief that social marginality was shameful. Working within strict symbolic hierarchies, descending from the author of poetry to the hack who produced pornography and satire, most men of letters sought wealth and recognition. Despite Rousseau's attempt to position the writer as a lone voice of truth, there was little sense of the paradoxical revalorization of misery that would emerge in nineteenth-century literary culture.[10] The nineteenth century witnessed two developments that shaped the emergence of cultural self-consciousness about Bohemia: Romanticism, which glorified the figure of the artist, and the expansion of print culture and the reading public. The former tempted many to aspire to the role of artist;[11] the latter increased opportunities for literary careers, but also the degree of competition and the subsequent failure rate.

The Bohemia of the July Monarchy was the subject of influential literary representations stressing its picturesque aspects. Texts such as Théophile Gautier's *Les Jeunes France* (1833) portrayed eccentricity as a key Bohemian value, like free love, friendship, and youth, and one able to ward off the 'prose' of bourgeois life.[12] Real-life gatherings of artists, including the house in the Rue du Doyenné inhabited by writers such as

---

[9] In relation to the mythology of Grub Street (see Plaisant 1976*b*) and Diderot 1972 respectively.

[10] On Rousseau, see Goulemot and Oster 1992: 91. Grub Street was revalorized earlier; see Plaisant 1976*b*: 119–20 and Mortier 1982: 75.

[11] See Bénichou 1973: 421–3 on the changing semantics of the term 'artiste' after 1800.

[12] The narrator of one of Gautier's texts writes of 'the magic circle of eccentricity with which Rodolphe had surrounded himself to ensure his protection from the reigning epidemic' (of bourgeois insipidity). Gautier 1995: 129; see also 94.

Gérard de Nerval, became the objects of almost immediate nostalgia.[13] The terms 'Jeune-France' and 'bousingots' (alternatively 'bousingos' or 'bouzingos') were used, at times with subtle distinctions, to describe this new species of flamboyantly unconventional Bohemian.[14] With its ideological connections to July Monarchy Anglophilia, Byronism, and dandyism, this second Bohemia was partially aristocratic in inspiration, though it simultaneously drew on the popular melodrama. Eccentricity thus became a badge of belonging, even a necessity, in this 'performative subculture' distinguished by its ironic self-consciousness and its efforts to invent and publicize the most extravagant excesses.[15]

The notion of sartorial eccentricity, I have noted, accumulated strong connotations of 'standing out' and 'being noticed' during the July Monarchy in the discourses of etiquette and fashion. These connotations were also important for constituting a sense of group identity in the Romantic movement of 1830, given its emphasis upon performativity. Gautier provided a retrospective account of this phenomenon in his influential *Histoire du romantisme* (1874), particularly in his extended description of the opening night of Hugo's play *Hernani*. The deliberately eccentric clothing of Hugo's followers at this event is seen as a simultaneously playful and agonistic effort to provoke the members of the establishment watching from their boxes.[16] Gautier underscores the extent to which eccentricity was normalized in this carnivalesque reversal of values, making occasional austerity, such as that of Gérard de Nerval, stand out:

In this period of eccentricity in which each person sought to mark himself out through some singularity in his dress, whether a floppy felt hat in the style of Rubens, a velvet panelled coat thrown over one's shoulder, a doublet in the style of Van Dyck, a frogged *polonaise*, a Hungarian riding coat with military decorations, or indeed any other exotic piece of clothing, Gérard dressed in the most simple and, as it were, the most invisible style, in the manner of one who wishes to pass unnoticed in a crowd.   (1874: 74)

Exploits catalogued by Gautier such as Nerval's alleged practice of walking lobsters in Paris on velvet ribbons (1875: 40) were subsequently widely circulated in anecdotes, though their accuracy is questionable. Indeed, both bousingots and Jeune-France used deliberate exaggeration

---

[13] On the Rue du Doyenné, see Steinmetz 1988: 61–6.
[14] See Larchey 1861: 47–8, Dondey 1875: 12–14, and Bénichou 1971: 428–9 on the relationship between the terms. On the Jeune-France, see Bénichou 1973: 427–34.
[15] Gluck 2005: 57; see 27–32 and 54–5.
[16] 1874: 113, 96; see also Maigron 1911: 57.

and black humour in order to alarm the bourgeoisie. Though the eccentricity of the Romantics was mainly associated with deliberately bizarre appearances and behaviour, it also extended to their poetics, for instance the use of fashionable neologisms and reflexive narrative and typographical techniques to startle readers.[17]

The relationship between eccentric Bohemians and the bourgeoisie was complex. The 'bourgeoisophobia' typical of much European discourse of the period was particularly pronounced in France; portrayed as foolish, materialist, philistine, and conformist, the bourgeoisie constituted the repressed 'other' by means of which Bohemians often sought to define themselves (and who consequently became, regardless of their intentions, an integral part of their identity). As historians have noted, Bohemia functioned as an imaginary outlet for the secret desires of the bourgeoisie as well as a rite of passage for young bourgeois students.[18] When suitably toned down, the Bohemian values of *fantaisie* and *excentricité* influenced the fashions of the established classes.[19] The two realms were not wholly opposed in economic terms either: just as free market capitalism was premised upon an apparently Bohemian love of risk, picturesque descriptions of Bohemian life concealed a realm of financial anxiety and unrelenting labour. The dark side of the Jeune-France movement consisted in a widespread sense of failure and the threat of madness.[20]

Henry Murger's *Scènes de la Vie de Bohème* (1848–52) departed from the carefree world of the Jeune-France in its depiction of widespread poverty amongst writers and artists, though it remained picturesque and often sentimental in its evocation of friendship and free love. A dialogue towards the end of the novel between the writer Rodolphe and the painter Marcel highlights the potential strain between these two perspectives. In a long tirade, Marcel announces his intention to repudiate Bohemian nonconformism, described as 'more or less eccentric revolts [rebellions excentriques] against those prejudices which will eternally rule the world'. Eccentricity, he claims, has no relationship to talent:

---

[17] See e.g. Matoré's study of Gautier's neologisms (1951) and Sangsue 1987: 19–30 on 'eccentric' literary strategies.

[18] Privat d'Anglemont 1846: pp. ii–iii; Seigel 1999: 5–30.

[19] See Maigron 1911: 88.

[20] See respectively Bénichou 1973: 431 and Gautier's narrative 'Elias Wildmanstadius' in *Les Jeune-France*.

Having talent is not just a case of wearing a summer coat in the month of December; one can be a true poet or artist whilst keeping one's feet warm and eating three square meals a day. Whatever one says and whatever one does, if one wishes to amount to anything, one must always follow the common path.

(1869: 286–7)

Underlying this apparent appeal to the bourgeois value of comfort is a nightmarish fantasy of the future, as he pictures the two friends aged 30, isolated, suffering from a pervasive sense of disgust and envy, and condemned to 'shameful parasitism' in their efforts to make ends meet. Marcel seeks to portray Bohemian life as a youthful episode which must be surmounted: 'it would make a nice novel', he notes, 'but . . . all this has to have a denouement' (286).

The bitterness expressed by Marcel was increasingly in evidence during the Second Empire, when imagery of suffering bodies and unstable minds became central to representations of Bohemian life. Bohemian writers unable to succeed in prestigious genres depended for their livelihoods upon writing for ephemeral publications such as newspapers and journals. This entailed humiliating dependence on editors, creating a tension between the Romantic glorification of the writer and 'industrial literature'. The book was a legitimate wife, a common saying held, and the newspaper a prostitute.[21] By extension, the journalist himself came to be seen as a prostitute, shamefully feminized through his lack of control over his labour.[22] During the regime of Napoleon III, critiques of Bohemia were increasingly voiced from within Bohemia itself, though there was considerable nostalgia for the ideal of Bohemian life elaborated before 1851. This shift represented a return of the eighteenth-century view that poverty was shameful. Discourse on Bohemia was also influenced by the aesthetics of truth-to-life, and political disillusionment in the aftermath of 1848. Melancholia and frustration became common themes across the French intelligentsia as a whole.[23]

It is tempting to read the evolution of Bohemia in terms of a progression from 'narcissism and exhibitionism' to 'seriousness and self-restraint', as, in Mary Gluck's words, 'the minority exchanged the individualistic excesses of Romanticism for the social restraint and

[21] Goulemont and Oster 1992: 125.
[22] On Balzac's exploration of this trope in *Illusions perdues*, see Prendergast 1986: 91–2.
[23] See Chambers 1987.

impersonality of the flâneur' (2005: 66). In practice, matters were rather more complicated. Whilst external presentation certainly changed, exemplified by the decline of the Jeune-France's sartorial eccentricity and the rise of the sober black suit, individualism remained much in evidence. A covert strain of narcissism traversed Second Empire depictions of Bohemia, with important consequences for writing about eccentrics. In the wake of the physiology and its thirst for social typologies, the day-to-day realities of life as a writer provided an ideal subject for much journalistic and literary production. 'Whether successful or downtrodden, the man of letters takes narcissism to its extreme limits', write Daniel Oster and Jean-Paul Goulemot; 'He inspects and examines himself, takes an inventory of himself, analyses and dissects himself.'[24] This self-absorption partly palliated the symbolic wounds inflicted in Bohemia. It also led to markedly increased interests in marginals and eccentrics as literary subjects. By sketching Parisian eccentrics whose social marginality mirrored his own, the man of letters appeared to be producing a series of indirect self-portraits. As for the inhabitants of the fairground with whom eccentrics had much in common, however, problematic differences in symbolic capital, and a constant fluctuation between distance and identification, determined their relationship.

Paris inconnu: hunting human oddities

Authors and readers from the July Monarchy onwards were intrigued by the activities of the menacing yet strangely thrilling 'dangerous classes'. Many of the plots of serial novels revolved around a Parisian underworld of criminals, prostitutes, and tricksters. Corresponding to the unleashing of anti-social energies was the increasing emphasis placed on the police and detective, tracking down the causes of unrest by means of ingenious interpretative efforts and networks of informers.[25] Fear of disorder thus coexisted with seemingly paradoxical resistance to the work of sanitizing and deciphering. A mournful sense emerged that *Paris inconnu*, the unknown Paris, was on the cusp of disappearance: 'it fascinated nineteenth-century readers, at once drawn and repulsed by the mysteries lurking beneath the surface of city life, and aware that new forms of industry and urban rebuilding projects threatened

---

[24] Goulemot and Oster 1992: 103, 109; see also 1989: 31–7.
[25] See Benjamin 1997: 36–41. The mythologization of the former criminal Vidocq played a key role in this development.

to do away with a world that still looked, behaved, and smelled like a remnant of the Middle Ages'.[26] The dangerous classes appeared one of the few remaining sources of intense emotion and fictional plots in an era of increasingly vicarious and homogenized experience. The Parisian spectator resembled Norbert Elias's image of *homo clausus*, the individual closed off from the external world.[27] Accounts of the underworld implicitly position their male audience in the home, reading of insalubrious events at a carefully mediated distance.[28]

Depictions of *Paris inconnu* took on an increasingly autobiographical cast during the Second Empire. Men of letters occupied a middle ground between the forces of order and subversion: in background and educational level they were of the bourgeoisie, yet the experience of poverty led some to greater awareness of the lives of the urban underclasses. Many journalists and novelists self-consciously invoked the techniques of the detective in their efforts to grasp their new habitat. The metaphors of 'hunting', 'tracking', and 'deciphering' eccentricity became ubiquitous, part of a wider preoccupation in Parisian culture with the legibility of urban life.[29] At the same time, the unclassifiable eccentric constantly thwarted this interpretive effort, encouraging escape into reverie. Victor Fournel terms eccentrics '[l]iving enigmas, the key to which I seek in my imagination, for I am unable to find it in history' (1867: 280).

This new type of writing had affinities with travel writing, though it focused on undiscovered proximity rather than distant cultures. Privat d'Anglemont suggested that the streets through which Parisians walked every day concealed mysteries as exotic as those found by ethnographers in distant lands (1984: 15). Charles Yriarte was thus summarizing a commonplace when he wrote, in the preface of his gallery of Parisian eccentrics: 'The truly unexplored country, the one in which the traveller's curiosity forever finds new sustenance, where the horizons before the *flâneur* are infinite, is the same Paris that we live in without ever really knowing it' (1868: 19). Allegedly still unknown in the 1860s, despite over thirty years of sustained investigation, the lure of the unknown Paris arose precisely from its ability to resist yielding its secrets. It provided a metaphor for the uncharted mysteries within the self, even the cultural unconscious. Essayistic accounts of this realm tended to

---

[26] Seigel 1999: 139–40.   [27] See Elias 1994: 370–81, Ebers 1995: 169–71.
[28] For a fine analysis of the genre, see Rieger 1988.
[29] See e.g. Prendergast 1992: 208–212. The use of hunting as a metaphor for hermeneutics was most influentially formulated by Ginzburg (1990).

shift social enigma onto the level of the psychological enigma. The concept of the 'mysteries of Paris', popularized by Eugène Sue in his bestselling novel of that title published in 1844–3, found a Second Empire counterpart in the mysteries of the Bohemian subject and his tenuous grasp of sanity, around the same time that interest in eccentricity was increasing amongst French alienists.[30]

Where was the unknown Paris? Champfleury noted that Parisian eccentrics lived around the Rue Judas and Montagne Sainte-Geneviève, seemingly an area of infinite literary potential: 'full of people whose strange, miserable, and problematic existences remain to be recorded in biographies' (1877: 156). His poor visionaries lived, ironically, in the shadow of the Pantheon, a symbol of the recognition denied to them. Privat d'Anglemont wrote in similar terms of the 'the large family of problematic existences', which he estimated as numbering some 70,000, who scraped a living from bizarre trades not officially recognized by society. With moral criteria resonating with bourgeois values, he suggested that these honest and entrepreneurial individuals congregated on hilltops, contrasting them with the lazy *misérables* living on lower ground (1984: 15–17).

The literary critic Ernest Prarond described Champfleury as the 'Baron of Bohemia' (1852: 156), and indeed the latter surveys his subjects rather like a feudal lord. The eccentrics that Champfleury portrays in *Les Excentriques* (1852) are also his imaginary sexual conquests. The language of eroticism pervaded descriptions of eccentricity as it did the fairground, fusing with the rhetoric of pathological anatomy. Medical terminology was a consistent element of realist doctrine in both England and France.[31] A coldly rational approach to grotesque subject matter was generally held to be the basis of the analogy, but the anatomical metaphor was in fact heavily sexualized.[32] Female wax Venuses figured prominently in anatomical collections, whilst metaphors of 'unveiling' and 'penetrating' a feminized Nature permeated French science (symbolized during the *fin de siècle* by Barrias's statue outside the École de Médecine in Paris, entitled 'Nature unveiling herself before Science'). The act of anatomy was framed as a virile act performed on an inert female body, akin to rape or necrophilia.

Champfleury positions himself as the dissector of eccentrics, deploying metaphors of striptease and prostitution. His male subjects initially

---

[30] Champfleury explicitly links underworld eccentrics to Sue's trope (1877: 4, 311).
[31] See Weinberg 1937: 193.   [32] See Matlock 1995: 28–30.

appear as 'genuine *bohemians*, difficult and despondent of humour, often as mysterious as sphinxes, and always as indecipherable as the obelisk' (1877: 8). The relationship between eccentric and his 'client', the *homme de lettres*, arises when the latter's epistemological desire is stimulated, followed by the need to decipher the hieroglyph of a mysterious existence. The eccentric can only be defined negatively through his intractability to social codes, like 'WHAT IS IT?', the mysterious wild man exhibited in Barnum's circus:

> You tell yourself that the unknown man is neither a tailor, nor a pharmacist, nor a lawyer, nor a poet, nor a merchant . . . What is it? This *what is it* becomes a puzzle more difficult to solve than a mathematical equation; but the question is interesting, it has become lodged in the brain and nothing will get it out.
>
> (1877: 5)

Obsessed by interpreting the 'enigma' of eccentricity, the man of letters comes to resemble his subjects, themselves often fixated upon solving 'impossible' problems. Champfleury's eccentrics are termed 'those poor seekers of the absolute', 'all of those, in short, who seek but never find'. They suffer from dual but related forms of interpretative dysfunction: obsessively pursuing insoluble problems in the belief they can find a non-existent 'key', they tend towards hypertrophy of interpretation, construing all signs in relation to their particular obsession, whether the squaring of the circle or the omnipresence of malicious sprites.[33]

Jules Vallès emphasizes the enigmatic nature of Second Empire social marginals in *Les Réfractaires* (The Rebels) (1865), using equally eroticized metaphors: 'These heterogeneous existences [existences hétéroclites] are always surrounded by an air of mystery that they do not themselves seek to penetrate' (JV1: 187). His terminology shifts between *réfractaire*, *irrégulier* (irregular individual), *déclassé*, and *paria*. The first term, whose literal meaning is that of the draft-dodger, derived historically from the men who refused to be conscripted into Napoleon Bonaparte's army. By extension, it denotes the qualities of rebelliousness and recalcitrance which make Bohemians refuse to conform to bourgeois norms. These figures are differentiated from the working classes by their learning and values, but again defined negatively:

> A *réfractaire* is a man who has lost his footing in life, who lacks a profession, a position, a trade, who cannot claim to be something, whether an bugle player, cabinet maker, notary, doctor or shoemaker, and whose only possession is his

---

[33] Champfleury 1877: 59, 261 n. 1, 63–7, 123.

mania...*Réfractaire*s are all those whose occupations are not listed in Bottin's directory: inventor, poet, orator, philosopher or hero.[34]

Despite Champfleury and Vallès's insistence on the unclassifiable nature of eccentrics, they fall into a number of distinct categories: charlatans and street performers; mystics and Utopian thinkers; and, for Vallès in particular, intellectuals, hacks, and private tutors. Champfleury refused to include 'true' poets and artists in his sequence, considering it insulting for them to be placed in such company—but he later relented, planning to include a sketch of his friend Gustave Courbet in a second series.[35] The eccentrics portrayed by both writers tend to be of questionable sanity.

Vagrancy trials sought to determine whether defendants had a legitimate profession, but the dominant assumption that there was a fixed number of professions or *états*, evidently at odds with the fluidity of urban life, made it difficult for them to succeed. The legal system refused to endow unconventional lives with moral legitimacy: 'To require that an activity be an *état* was to imply a standard of social membership that shaped individuals according to pre-existing ideas about what productive work was, and what activities society required.'[36] Many of the figures Vallès described work in the least prestigious forms of literary hackwork, as ghost-writers, copyists, and contributors to women's magazines, and many spend periods sleeping rough. The original title for 'Les Irréguliers de Paris' was 'Misères savantes' or 'The misery of the learned'.[37] The prevalence of struggling writers was a recurrent theme in writing on the city.[38]

Vallès portrays himself tracking individuals whom he considers potential specimens for his collection.[39] In one example, he is intrigued by a man at a public lecture, later revealed to be a historian suffering from delusions of grandeur: 'I wouldn't have let him go for all the world', he notes, hinting at the relationship between bourgeois and courtesan: 'I would have ruined myself for that man; I offered him the drink of his choosing, on the condition that he morally undressed himself before me' (JV1: 186–7). Both writers use the metaphor of undressing to characterize their encounters with eccentrics. Champfleury's implicitly feminized subjects prove pathetically eager to unclothe themselves, providing free spectacle for the *flâneur*: 'They are only too willing

---

[34] JV1: 138–9. Bottin compiled an *Almanach du commerce*.
[35] Troubat 1906: 215 n.   [36] See Seigel 1999: 146–7.
[37] See Bellet 1977: 71.   [38] e.g. Delord et al. 1854*a*: 7.   [39] JV1: 176.

to undress, and you see the naked man. They obligingly remove their skin, and you see the flayed man. They sell their flesh, skin and veins for very little, and you see the skeleton...these odd figures are quite artfully constructed, like artificial anatomical parts.'[40] Yet the flood of information that the eccentric offers to his observers has a hieroglyphic quality of its own, proving difficult to understand.[41] The 'consummation' of the relationship leads to an abrupt change of attitude: once the secret of the eccentric's 'system' is extracted, for instance, he is forbidden from boring Champfleury by returning to it. Though he includes more of the first-person discourse of his eccentrics in his text than any of his contemporaries save Vallès, this appears less as an attempt to allow their voices to be heard than a strategy of ironic citation, one which establishes a fantasy of complicity and superiority between the narrator and his readers.

Eccentrics are felt to be placidly amenable to their observers' demands, rather like human dolls. One critic suggested that Champfleury tracked each eccentric for days at a time with the aim of 'penetrating' and 'piercing' him with an invisible gaze and 'appropriating' him for himself, a comment that implicitly compares the writer to an animal magnetist and the eccentric to a suggestible patient.[42] Victor Fournel, who describes Parisian eccentrics such as the 'Persian of the Opera' as 'living enigmas' (see Fig. 12), models the observer's role upon two figures: the palaeontologist, who like the detective reconstructs vanished traces, and the puppet-master:

Each individual provides me, little though I care, with enough material for a complicated novel; and, just as Cuvier pieced together a whole animal from a single tooth, and a whole world from a single animal, I piece together all these scattered existences, I make this theatre of automata, whose strings I hold, move, think and act as I see fit.   (1867: 279–80)

The dehumanizing tendencies evident in such descriptions were presumably shared by the many readers of such texts. Champfleury portrays himself toying with eccentrics like a cat playing with a mouse (1877: 12). The pleasurable pastime of observing eccentrics, he argues, creates a strong link between a 'band' of eager and curious Parisians (5–6). This dynamic radiates outwards to include his bourgeois readers. Male

---

[40] 1877: 9. Champfleury returns to the image: 'Diderot would not have created his finest work had the young Rameau not agreed to perpetually undress himself before the great philosopher' (1877: 11).

[41] See Champfleury 1877: 57.   [42] Prarond 1852: 143.

Fig. 12. 'The Persian of the Opera.' (Yriarte 1868: 137) © British Library Board. All Rights Reserved. (12350.g.11)

eccentrics thus bind together members of an imaginary community of male spectators—just as the ridiculous individual of the salon creates bonds of complicity between his or her malicious observers, facilitating the circulation of gossip and anecdotes.

How overtly politicized were Parisian eccentrics? Marx and Engels framed the inhabitants of Parisian Bohemia as natural allies of Napoleon III, famously including in this monstrously heterogeneous category 'decayed roués' and 'ruined and adventurous off-shoots of the bourgeoisie', as well as assorted criminals, charlatans, and beggars ('the whole indefinite, disintegrated mass thrown hither and thither, which the French call *la bohème*').[43] In contrast, the historian T. J. Clark has argued that radical politics were prevalent within Bohemia, citing Champfleury's description of his subjects in *Les Excentriques*, some of

[43] Marx and Engels 1950: I, 167.

whom are radicals, as '*bohêmes* véritables'. The view that Bohemians had radically departed from middle-class norms is, however, unconvincing. In fact, Champfleury's text used the indefinite article to describe his characters ('true Bohemians' not '*the* true Bohemians').[44] Furthermore, many of them were apolitical. Champfleury's text juxtaposes figures such as the communists of Sainte-Croix and Jean Journet (a disciple of Fourier) with a vegetarian, a bird-collector, a fairground charlatan, and a mathematician obsessed with squaring the circle. The link between them is formed by their obsessive psychological traits and their indifference to wealth and status, rather than by any specific ideological stance. A similar ambiguity arises in the case of Jules Vallès, who, following his active role in the Commune, retrospectively sought to politicize the *réfractaires* he had depicted during the late Second Empire.[45] At the time they were first published, however, the texts were framed as an exposure of the phenomenology of misery from the perspective of the *homme de lettres*, rather than as a call to arms from that of the revolutionary.

Eccentricity in the mirror: Jules Vallès

During the eighteenth century, according to a common historical narrative, the urban poor were increasingly construed as culpable and as a dangerous menace to be contained, in contrast to the Christian model of exemplary poverty and the morally improving nature of charity. Though philanthropy evidently continued to be an important force throughout the nineteenth century, poverty was more likely to be attributed to individual moral deficiency, and vagabonds were the object of particular contempt.[46] Certain Second Empire representations of eccentricity, particularly those of Vallès and Baudelaire, attempted to recuperate a partially secularized version of charity for the dispossessed. Their

---

[44] See Clark 1973: 65 and Seigel 1999: 404, 412 n. 24. Seigel's rejection of Clark's political interpretation is correct, but his claim that Champfleury reserved the term 'Bohemians' for artists (implicitly *excluding* 'eccentrics') is not. Champfleury planned to include artists in a new series of 'eccentrics', and, more generally, Seigel's distinction between 'real' artists and the types of eccentrics portrayed by Champfleury and Vallès appears arbitrary, since the two categories frequently overlapped in representations of Parisian life.

[45] See Bellet 1977: 43–76 and Marotin 1997: 231–5.

[46] On the moral deficiency of the poor, for example, see Lawrence 2004: 212–14; on the vagabond, see Wagniart 1999.

compassion was nonetheless intertwined with narcissistic concern, expressing their own desire for social recognition.

A new documentary interest in the realities of urban poverty arose in both France and England in the nineteenth century. Henry Mayhew's pioneering investigation of poverty and social degradation in the Victorian capital, *London Labour and the London Poor* (1851–62), constitutes the most significant English counterpart to French sketches of the poor published during the Second Empire. Mayhew exploits the theme of domestic travel writing in very similar ways to the French texts, framing the underworld as a *terra incognita* and the vagabond as an exotic 'savage'. A key difference emerges, however, in its narratorial gaze which is redolent of middle-class distance and distaste: 'In the slum, the bourgeois spectator surveyed and classified *his own antithesis.*'[47] Though a dehumanizing gaze was also common in French responses to urban squalor, this was simultaneously countered by an opposing narcissistic gaze that transformed abject individuals into symbolic doubles of the writer, tending to create a sense of proximity rather than distance.

If Champfleury was the baron of Bohemia, Jules Vallès was indisputably the baron of misery. Vallès emphasizes his own sense of ugliness and monstrosity,[48] and identifies openly with figures such as circus performers and the hydrocephalus;[49] this 'monster' with a large forehead but small brain was perceived as a grotesque parody of the figure of the genius, to whom phrenologists attributed an enlarged cerebral cortex.[50] The latter's attempts to catalogue marginality were symptomatic of the Bohemian preoccupation with artists' lived experience (*le vécu*).[51] Vallès was often portrayed by his contemporaries as one of Victor Hugo's grotesque characters.[52]

Though they mirror his personal preoccupations, the eccentrics that Vallès depicts are simultaneously endowed with social and historical significance:

The street, like the salon, has its eccentrics and its heroes. The eccentrics of the great outdoors are those who as schoolboys had already gone astray, and who, upon leaving school, found themselves powerless and unable to earn a living;

---

[47] Stallybrass and White 1986: 128.   [48] JV1: 830, 966–8.
[49] See Bellet 1977: 209–37.   [50] See JV1: 516, 830, 958.
[51] Notably in his autobiographical 'Lettres d'un irrégulier' (1867) and trilogy of novels Jacques Vingtras. On the centrality of 'lived experience' in the rhetoric of Bohemia, see Goulemot and Oster 1992: 130.
[52] Marotin 1997: 182 n. 6.

the false direction in which their education had led them, the chance happenings of history and the crimes of fate threw them, distraught and famished, into adventures which it would make you sob and laugh to hear. I return to them often, but history will return to them too; they represent all of the hesitations and misfortunes of a society that has gone off the rails.   (JV1: 936–7)

In his vision, the typical *réfractaire*, who comes from a middle-class background and has shown great promise at school, is lured to the capital by the dream of fame as a writer; sinking into indigence, he squanders his talent and dies a slow death, his body and mind broken by his wretched living conditions. Vallès's hesitation about whether to narrate their lives in tragic or in comic mode echoes that of his contemporaries.[53]

The characters portrayed by Vallès differ most significantly from those of Champfleury in relation to their self-consciousness. For Champfleury, 'true eccentrics are unaware of themselves; they do not know that they are eccentric and, above all, do not say that they are; they believe themselves to be firmly rooted in positivism, in reason, in custom, and are astonished if they are stared at' (1877: 8). In contrast, Vallès's marginals are agonizingly conscious of the chasm between the life to which they aspire and feel entitled and their actual condition. In this, the *réfractaires* were indeed representative of wider social trends. During the mid-nineteenth century, social theorists began to differentiate between poverty and misery, the former absolute and typical of the rural poor, the latter relative and characteristic of the urban underclass. During the July Monarchy, misery became a topic of urgent concern, arising in discourses as diverse as the novel and theatre, socialist tracts, and the emergent social sciences. Interest crystallized around the amorphous category of *les misérables*, linked in the cultural imaginary to revolutionary turmoil and to the cholera epidemic of 1832. In 1840 Eugène Buret broke with previous attempts to define misery in objective terms. He proposed instead that '[m]isery is a phenomenon of civilization', and argued that migration to the city exacerbated awareness of the gap between rich and poor, leading to subjective feelings of misery.[54] The most original aspect of Vallès's writing on social marginality lies in its detailed investigation of what Buret emphasized

---

[53] e.g. Champfleury 1877: 17; Saint-Victor termed Vallès's text a 'tragi-comic novel' (cited in JV1: 1256).

[54] Buret 1840: I, 188; see Benchuza 1994.

Fig. 13. Dirty and despairing bodies: 'Between the Seine and hunger' by Gavarni, part of his series of Bohemians. (Gavarni et al. 1845–6): I (1845), 270) © British Library Board. All Rights Reserved. (12352.g.30)

a quarter of a century earlier: the phenomenology of shame and humiliation.

Suicide rates in Paris, which increased dramatically during the July Monarchy as the population of Paris grew, confirm Buret's thesis. Those most at risk came from opposite ends of the social spectrum, and lived in cities rather than in the provinces; professionals, men of leisure, and military officers also attempted suicide more often than average. One of the groups at highest risk of suicide consisted in those without profession or of unknown profession, precisely the type of individual whom Champfleury and Vallès typically term eccentric (see Fig. 13).[55] In an autobiographical text, Vallès recounts his own fantasies of suicide when a military friend left his pistol in his lodgings (JV2: 713). His *irréguliers* commit prolonged self-immolation in full view of the indifferent bourgeoisie. Their fate was often interpreted as a symbolic punishment for the hubris believed to accompany any form of eccentricity, whether in the salon or the street. But it is not only their stubbornness that keeps them in Bohemia. Obtaining exploitative work as a journalist or tutor

[55] Corbin 1987*a*: 593.

remains possible only before the *réfractaire* is 'branded' by misery (JV1: 146). If he goes without a meal for longer than a day he will be forced to sell his shirt; unable to return to respectable company, he becomes a 'man overboard', engulfed in an ocean of degradation.

Stressing the effort that *réfractaires* devoted to retaining their dignity, Vallès provides a startling reinterpretation of eccentricity of appearance. In July-Monarchy Bohemia, bizarre clothing symbolized the parodic humour of the Jeune-France. In contrast, Vallès's subjects, marked out by their strange hats, shoes, and coats, use eccentricity to deflect attention from their indigence. Its real meaning cannot be concealed from fellow marginals, who are staged as cunning urban detectives:

To hide their poverty and not wear it like a yoke, they bear it like a whim, they take on the air of a visionary or an eccentric, a clown or a puritan,—Diogenes or Brutus, Escousse or Lantara. They hide their anguish and their shame beneath a veil of oddity [originalité], even at the price of cutting holes in their new boots to excuse the holes in previous pairs and in those yet to come. They even agree to be taken as madmen, provided that they appear less poor . . . their eccentricity makes their poverty acceptable, it throws a mantle of flowers over their rags. They laugh, and therein lies their courage and their virtue; often, it is so they do not cry.   (JV1: 140)

The passage resonates with Vallès's descriptions of the shame he experienced at being badly dressed as a child, and his ludicrous attempts as an impoverished young man to survive with a disintegrating hat.[56] It concludes by evoking the figure of the sad clown. In a striking image, the *réfractaire* is compared to a paranoid, never-closing eye; his sense of pride renders him acutely sensitive to any hint of condescension.[57]

The gender of compassion

The cause of downfall for such Bohemians was often, Vallès believed, other men of letters, in particular those who purveyed romantic lies about Bohemia. His grotesque subjects are termed 'victims of the book', a phrase which evokes the figures of Don Quixote and Emma Bovary. If mythologizing depictions of Bohemia were particularly dangerous for idealistic young readers, Vallès's own account of the *réfractaire*, which he claimed to have been inspired to write on the occasion

---

[56] JV2: 681–3.   [57] '[H]is pride wide open like a fiery eye' (JV1: 154).

of Murger's funeral,[58] served as an antidote to this flood of textual poison. The text has a dual function, seeking both to save young writers and to transform the consciousness of its bourgeois readers, countering the prevailing association of indigence with effeminate moral weakness.[59]

His readers' responses are carefully controlled. Many depictions of eccentrics assume that readers will acquiesce with the narrator's patronizing attitude towards his subjects. In Vallès's work, the narrator attempts to recruit readers for his revalorization of marginality, implicitly appealing to their residual Christian sensibility. Belief in the posthumous fame awaiting the undiscovered genius echoed religious belief in the rewards awaiting the humble in heaven. Vallès compares the *réfractaire* to the victim burned at the stake, describing his unworldly subjects as having their feet in the gutter and their eyes fixed upon the heavens. Imagery of martyrdom, a common theme in writing about the Romantic artist, alternates with that of damnation, transforming Bohemia into Dante's hell.[60]

At times Vallès's rhetoric is more direct; he highlights the shared class origins of the eccentric and the bourgeois reader in order to encourage identification, describing the former as 'your old school friend' (JV1: 147). The degree of opposition to this enterprise of rehabilitation is evident from the work's reception. The text entitled 'Les Réfractaires', a polemical statement at the head of the collection, was published on the front page of the conservative newspaper *Le Figaro* in 1861. Conservatives typically responded that Bohemians were themselves to blame for their situation; lacking in self-discipline, their hubris was responsible for their misery.[61] An ambivalent review by Paul de Saint-Victor in 1866 criticizes Vallès for promising to portray men heroically fighting fate but in fact portraying vagabonds and maniacs:

Such a book would be intolerable... if one sensed only the cold hand of the specialist or the steel of the surgeon's scalpel in the treatment of these ulcers and open wounds. But these sardonic tales by M. Vallès are not without heart; we hear it beating beneath his sarcastic remarks, and sometimes a bitter and long restrained tear falls from the artist's eye onto the grotesque, miserable individual

---

[58] Recounted in *L'Insurgé* (JV2: 889).
[59] On this period in Vallès's political evolution, see Münster 1974: 76–80, 152–4. The writer stood in 1869 as the 'candidate of misery', which some observers interpreted as evidence of his 'eccentricity' (GD15: 748–9).
[60] See JV1: 154; 1256, and 197–8. [61] e.g. Veuillot 1867: 64–5, 85–6.

whose profile he worries away at or whose rags he sketches. Clearly, this book has been lived.[62]

But the author's compassion, Saint-Victor argues, is tainted by the perverse pleasure he takes from having escaped poverty himself. Enjoining bourgeois readers to identify with *réfractaires*, he suggests, is tantamount to encouraging them smugly to contemplate their superiority.[63]

Vallès repeatedly defended his sentimental descriptions of grotesque Bohemian eccentrics on the grounds that a stridently political tone would alienate bourgeois readers, whilst humility allows his images to penetrate their defences (and escape the attention of Napoleon III's censors) (JV1: 1272). His most explicit self-justification occurs in a letter to the critic Albert Rogat:

I would not have spoken of monsters had I been able to aim higher! But since it was forbidden to question those who drive the chariot, I turned to those the chariot jostles as it drives past…I collected some of [society's] victims from the streets and said to it, pushing them before it: 'take a good look at yourself!' I served the cause of the poor and downtrodden in my own way and as best I could. I took on the role of their historian, but with a certain bias and, in writing their story, I perhaps sketched a page of a new type of history [l'histoire nouvelle] … No one can be sure, nowadays, that they will not die of poverty…The unconventional individual [l'irrégulier] is not the exception but the rule. I did not choose the location, I merely dared to hold up the mirror. I witnessed a debacle and, as well as I could, sketched portraits of some of those who had been swept into the gutter.   (JV1: 921)

The metaphor of victims crushed by the carriage of civilization recalls the celebrated opening paragraphs of Balzac's *Le Père Goriot*, evoking the novelist's moral vision of Paris as a forest in the New World. In the brutal zoology of the *Comédie humaine*, framed in terms of the Manichean absolutes of the melodrama, ravenous tigers and lions are pitted against helpless lambs and doves. The most powerful rhetorical strategy deployed by Vallès is his attempt to widen the concept of misery in hypothetical mode, by reminding his bourgeois readers that they might one day be forced to join those whom they exclude. Vallès's emancipatory vision of 'a new type of history' consists in giving cultural

---

[62] Reproduced in JV1: 1257.
[63] Marotin argues that *La Rue* was more overtly political than *Les Réfractaires*, hence aroused more negative critical responses (1997: 231–5); Gille, in contrast, considers the latter more 'serene' (1941: 158–9). It certainly does not evoke bodily suffering with the same intensity as *Les Réfractaires*.

voice to the experience of the marginal, all those whom Charles Yriarte pathetically termed, in his study of eccentrics, 'the infinitely small' [les infiniment petits] (1868: 12).

Finally, Vallès relies upon the rhetoric of literary realism. If his texts are mirrors, then he is not responsible for what they reflect.[64] They are also mirrors in which comfortable readers must contemplate the unseen consequences of their wealth.[65] As for Champfleury and Courbet, realism becomes directly linked to eccentricity, transforming the seemingly insignificant into topics of aesthetic importance. Vallès was viewed by his contemporaries as the main 'historiographer' and 'photographer' of Parisian eccentrics.[66] Reversing the objectification and distance present in these labels, he uses characteristically religious imagery to stress his sense of identification with his subjects: 'I, who have been saved, am going to write the history of those who have not, of the beggars who did not find their bowls' (JV2: 889).

Some of the ambivalent responses elicited by Vallès's writing on social marginality arose from its gender implications. Compassion was culturally feminized; women's greater concern for others was supposedly evident in both the ease with which hysterical girls were moved to tears by the fate of fictional characters, and the empathy felt by mothers towards their children. In France, as in Britain, philanthropy was one of the few public arenas in which respectable women could become involved.[67] The highly popular genre of sentimental fiction was gendered as feminine, and predominantly associated with women authors and readers. Yet this mode of writing was increasingly contrasted with the allegedly greater robustness of the new male realists, a symptom of a wider tendency in mid-nineteenth-century French culture to devalue femininity.[68] Vallès's appeals to his readers' compassion risk undermining his masculinity, as the image of him weeping over his text suggests.[69] Insinuations of sentimentality appealed to conservatives, who argued that the wretched of Bohemia were lacking in manly skills such as energetic resourcefulness and self-reliance (one, for example, contrasts 'pathological' eccentrics to 'the useful man').[70] Vallès's use of heroic metaphors of truth-to-life attempts to grapple with the double

---

[64] He refers to a journal he founded as a 'mirror of seven sous' (JV1: 921, 936); the mirror metaphor underpinned much realist discourse.
[65] See JV1: 921.   [66] e.g. Clarétie, cited in JV1: 1477.
[67] See H. Mills 1991.   [68] See Schor 1993 and M. Cohen 1999.
[69] The metaphor was common; see e.g. Richepin 1872: 39.
[70] Pontmartin 1867: 84, 87.

symbolic violence inflicted upon the man of letters, construed not only as a prostitute but also as emasculated in his (self-) pity. The rhetoric of heroic stoicism functioned, for other analysts of urban wretchedness such as Baudelaire, as a necessary response to this crisis of masculinity.

Portable fairground booths in print

'I had other portraits to put in this museum, but I lacked the space' (JV1: 156). Vallès's desire to collect and exhibit eccentric individuals overlaps with a number of popular discursive genres. Similar collections by writers such as Champfleury, Nerval, Yriarte, Larchey, and Delvau evidently struck a chord with bourgeois readers, though they have been largely neglected by historians and critics. These galleries of eccentricity functioned as portable fairground booths in print, again appealing to the disavowed bourgeois fascination with the Parisian underworld.[71]

Their origins must be sought in the compendia of bizarre occurrences known as *mirabilia* which constituted the classical genre of paradoxography.[72] In English culture during the early decades of the nineteenth century, publications such as *Kirby's Wonderful and Eccentric Magazine*, the *Eccentric Magazine*, the *Eccentric Mirror*, and the *Cabinet of Curiosities* ('being a selection of extraordinary legends . . . and a variety of other eccentric matter') juxtaposed natural and supernatural prodigies with tales of psychological and anthropological difference.[73] The clumsily written prefaces of such magazines deploy the language of the fairground charlatan to entice paying customers; one describes itself as a 'panacea'.[74] Direct equivalents of English eccentric magazines did not materialize in France, with the partial exception of a review founded by Lorédan Larchey in 1855,[75] whose title was changed in 1860 to *Revue anecdotique des excentricités contemporaines*, foregrounding eccentricity. The fairground metaphors of the English galleries nonetheless underpinned subsequent French collections. French writers proved indifferent to the natural wonders that filled English collections, focusing instead on sketches of marginal figures and the borderline insane. They were also

[71] Adapted from Hunter 1990: 176.   [72] See Daston and Park 1998: 23–4.
[73] Cowlishaw terms them 'freak books' (1998: 165).
[74] Kirby 1803: I, p. iii. These texts are not, as Cowlishaw suggests, early versions of the Parisian physiology: rather than reassuring urban readers, as the physiology primarily does, they respond to a desire for defamiliarization and exoticism.
[75] Author of *Gens singuliers* ('Singular People') and a work on Parisian slang, *Les Excentricités de la langue française* (The Eccentricities of the French Language).

influenced by specifically French developments such as the legacy of the physiology, the metaphor of the human zoo, the doctrine of realism, and the biographical sketch popularized by Sainte-Beuve's literary portraits.[76]

Several overlapping subgenres arose. The first was the 'archive' of eccentricity. The metaphor of the collection could relate to either the writings of the insane or to biographical sketches of insane writers themselves; behind both stood the metaphor of the asylum. The first text in this tradition was Charles Nodier's *Bibliographie des fous: de quelques livres excentriques* (1833), or 'A Bibliography of Madmen: On Some Eccentric Books'. Its title poses the enigma of the relationship between insane minds and eccentric books but fails to resolve it. Nodier glosses his phrase *livres excentriques* as 'books that were written by madmen, in accordance with the common right of all men to write and to publish' (1993: 64). The connotations of the term 'eccentricity' are thus mainly of deviant textual production. Rather than the gallery or museum, textual metaphors of the library and archive predominate in subsequent writing about 'eccentric literature' and 'the eccentricities of the human mind'.[77] The concept of the *fou littéraire* was widened in the twentieth century to encompass all nineteenth-century published writings by those deemed insane or borderline insane,[78] though the exact relationship between eccentricity and the *fou littéraire*, as well as that between mental and literary eccentricity, remains vague.[79]

The second subgenre was the historical collection of originals and eccentrics, such as Nerval's *Les Illuminés, ou les précurseurs du socialisme* (1852) ('The Illuminati, or the Precursors of Socialism').[80] These

---

[76] See Goulemot and Oster 1992: 168–70.

[77] Examples include Philarète Chasles, 'Les Excentriques' (1834); Octave Delepierre, *Histoire littéraire des fous* (1860); Gustave Brunet, *Les Fous littéraires: essai bibliographique sur la littérature excentrique, les illuminés, visionnaires, etc* (1880) (Literary Madmen: A Bibliographical Esay on Eccentric Literature, Illuminati, Visionaries, etc); Avgoust Tcherpakoff, 'Les fous littéraires' (1883); Frédéric Loliée, *Le Paradoxe: essai sur les excentricités de l'esprit humain de tous les siècles* (1888) (Paradox: An Essay on the Eccentricities of the Human Mind Throughout the Ages).

[78] Queneau 2002 and Blavier 2001 form 20th-cent. continuations of this tradition; see also Popovic 2000 and 2001.

[79] Blavier seeks to differentiate the 'true' *fou littéraire* from the more 'banal' category of eccentric, though his criteria are arbitrary: he includes in the former only writers whom he personally considers amusing (2001: 171, 173).

[80] Also, for example, Paul de Musset, *Extravagants et Originaux du XVIIe siècle* (Extravagant and Original Characters of the Seventeenth Century) (1863), and Charles Monselet, *Les Originaux du siècle dernier: les oubliés et les dédaignés* (The Originals of Last Century: The Forgotten and the Despised) (1864).

attempts to reinterpret the past in terms of contemporaneous taxonomies were mirrored in the discourses of fashion (for instance, Barbey
d'Aurevilly's essays 'Les Lions d'autrefois' (The Lions of Bygone Days)
and 'Un dandy d'avant les dandys' (A Dandy before the Dandies))
and medicine; the genre termed 'retrospective medicine' by Emile Littré entailed scouring the past for symptoms to re-interpret from the
perspective of contemporaneous medicine.[81] The final subgenre consisted in the real-life sketch of eccentric characters such as those of
Champfleury and Vallès or Lorédan Larchey's *Gens singuliers* (1867).
Both textual archives and historical galleries lacked the realistic detail
of sketches set within Bohemia. Some authors positioned their sketches
within a frame of narratorial commentary, whilst others recycled anecdotes in the third person. Different degrees of sympathy and disdain
were manifested towards eccentric subjects, whose discourse was only
rarely reproduced.[82]

Whilst it is tempting to see only the patronizing objectification
present in textual collections of eccentricity,[83] responses such as ridicule
typically concealed more troubling emotions, and hinted at an anxious
obsession with acting out fantasies of superiority. The texts themselves,
some of which were extremely popular, also contributed to the increasing visibility of marginality and insanity in French culture, for they
suggested that the Parisian underclass constituted a vast reservoir of
neglected biographical subject matter.[84] The best-known eccentrics circulated in both the intertextual space between collections and everyday
Parisian discourse, a realm of gossip and anecdote. The regularity with
which certain figures reappear in different collections suggests they were
known to a wide audience, passing into the mythology of the city and
its topography.[85]

---

[81] See Goldstein 1987: 369–70.

[82] One of the few critics to have analysed this body of texts, José-Luiz Diaz proposes
that sketches of Bohemian eccentrics conform to the genre that Starobinski has termed
the 'portrait of the artist as a *saltimbanque*' (2003: 187). However, this underestimates
the frequent sense of distance in writers, who occupy a position of far greater symbolic
power in such encounters.

[83] Tyers's response is representative of this tendency (1998: 77–9).

[84] Including, in addition to those mentioned, 'E.C.P.', *Les Fous célèbres* (Famous
Madmen) (1834); the Marquis de Belloy, *Les Toqués* (Crackpots) (1860); Charles Yriarte,
Paris grotesque: les célébrités de la rue (Grotesque Paris: The Celebrities of the Street)
(1868); Alfred Delvau, *Les Lions du jour: physionomies parisiennes* (Lions of the Day:
Parisian Physiognomies) (1867). Many of these texts have recently been republished by
Plein chant.

[85] See e.g. Yriarte 1868: 94.

Retrospective portraits of eccentrics also testify to a sense of nostalgia, as commentators compared their own era to a supposedly more colourful past. In a text entitled *Les Excentriques disparus* (1890) (The Eccentrics of Yesteryear), Firmin Boissin suggests that eccentricity became a historical impossibility in the aftermath of the Franco-Prussian War, the Commune, and a new climate of utilitarian values: 'Those rare eccentrics who survived these events remained, until their deaths, mere shadows of their former selves, disoriented and helpless' (1890: 7). Boissin depicted harmless mystics whose originality lay in their lives rather than any specific achievements. These predominantly unproductive characters highlighted the puzzling relationship between eccentricity in life and in art.

Self-made monsters: Baudelaire and Poe

In discourse on the avant-garde, the term 'excentricité' was used to describe experimental artworks. Critics reacted violently to the work of Gustave Courbet, one of the most overtly oppositional Bohemians, finding his work to be shockingly and disagreeably eccentric.[86] Discussions of unconventional artists sought to establish parallels between the singularity of the artworks and that of their creators. Maxime Du Camp, for example, drew on the vocabulary of mental illness to describe the *Salon des refusés*: 'These works . . . are immensely disturbing to study, for they attest the strange abnormalities that nourish the human mind.' He also suggested that their creators could have been included in a contemporaneous psychiatric treatise by Ulysse Trélat, entitled *La Folie lucide* (Lucid Madness).[87] Du Camp's rhetoric implies that avant-garde artworks are the involuntary self-portraits of their diseased creators, to be gaped at like monsters in a fairground booth. The metaphor of monstrosity, and by implication voyeuristic curiosity, became prominent as the notion of the avant-garde gained currency. In his *Salon de 1875*, for instance, the writer Jules Clarétie described innovative artists as 'these experiments of artists, whose eccentricity may be excused and justified by the fact that they are attempting something new and fighting in the *avant-garde*' (1876: 338). His vocabulary of monstrous incompletion betrays evidently mixed feelings. Indeed, the vexed relationship between genius, eccentricity, and creativity became a cultural

---

[86] See Leduc-Adine 1984: 155–60.   [87] Du Camp 1863: 917.

preoccupation as the notion of innovation was foregrounded in aesthetic debate.

By the mid-nineteenth century, it had become a received idea that the figure of the genius was prone to eccentric behaviour. Yet it seemed equally self-evident that not every eccentric on the streets of Bohemian Paris was a genius, despite the fact that many made claims to this effect. The semantic ambivalence of eccentricity was particularly evident in discussions of genius. In addition to having both strong negative and positive connotations, the term could denote behaviour that was involuntary or feigned. Debate revolved around three questions. How many geniuses suffered from eccentricity, neurosis, or madness? (Any response evidently supposed prior judgement about the contentious boundaries of madness.) How many Bohemians who behaved strangely were frauds of the type flourishing in the fairground, feigning eccentricity in order to persuade observers of their genius? And finally, how many such figures were simply the victims of delusions of grandeur, eccentric or insane but without real talent? These questions, extensively discussed by European psychiatrists in the last quarter of the nineteenth century,[88] were also addressed by writers and artists themselves.

The definition of genius which prevailed in mid-nineteenth-century Paris was influenced both by European Romanticism, with its sacralization of the act of writing, and by a French tradition reaching back to Diderot's equivocal portrait of the Neveu de Rameau, an early Bohemian 'original' of uncertain sanity living in the shadow of his uncle, a composer of genius. Rameau's undeniable talents find their only outlet in ephemeral performances of mimicry, making him an emblem for those nineteenth-century Bohemian eccentrics whose gifts failed to translate into durable achievements.[89] Champfleury evokes Rameau in the preface to *Les Excentriques*: 'How many *Rameau's nephews* are this very day walking around on the city's pavements? And what do these unknown geniuses lack? A man of genius skilled in stenography' (1877: 9). His claim that the eccentrics he portrays are geniuses is evidently disingenuous—unlike his own desire to be a genius stenographer. In a planned preface to a second volume of eccentrics, Champfleury compares himself to Diderot's *philosophe*, observing the antics of the Neveu

---

[88] See 'The medicalization of genius' in Ch. 8 below.
[89] Compare Barbey's review of *Les Réfractaires*: 'Diderot...wrote the story of that *réfractaire*, Rameau's nephew'; 1964: 69. See Murat 2001: 72 and Diaz 2003: 173 for further instances of the trope.

de Rameau with an ironic inner smile.[90] He distinguishes between eccentricity as a writer, to which he aspires, and an eccentric *persona*, to which he does not. A biographical sketch of Champfleury nonetheless dismisses his claims to have created an original artistic style in the manner of Courbet, Wagner, or Murger, comparing him to a *saltimbanque*: 'In the field of literature and the arts, not just anyone can be eccentric...he's a man whom nature made to walk upright, but who puts himself to infinite trouble to dislocate his limbs' (GD3: 898). The article also compares him to the 'eccentric' Rousseau. This contradiction arose from confused recognition that, despite the myth of the identity between *l'homme* and *l'œuvre*, being an eccentric and creating eccentric works were not synonymous. Diderot's text is notably ambiguous, shifting between the equally compelling visions of the rational *philosophe* and the outrageous Rameau.

The conservative argument against Vallès's *réfractaires*, propounded by figures such as Louis Veuillot, was that they were deluded and without talent. Since the new myth of the genius implied that the visionary imagination was often incomprehensible within the codes of its own time, however, any eccentric might later be hailed as a misrecognized genius. Jules Vallès uses this key uncertainty to his advantage. He stresses the impossibility of genius flourishing in the midst of poverty, since, in Paris, appearances are everything: 'Place a man in the street with a coat that is too loose, trousers that are too short, without a proper collar, hosiery, or any money, and, even if he were here to have the genius of Machiavelli or Talleyrand, he will sink into the gutter' (JV1: 201). He claims that genius has a high wastage rate, and argues that a precautionary principle is needed, since eccentricity can easily become the new norm: ' "Madmen!" some shout. But yesterday's madness is tomorrow's wisdom, yesterday's impiety today's religion' (202). Despite the suspicions he voices in 'Les Victimes du livre' (The Victims of the Book), Vallès reveals residual belief in the redemptive mission of the writer, able to save the souls of all the damned of Bohemia.

But discerning true genius was a difficult task. Indeed, Vallès spectacularly misjudged the future reception of the writer who subsequently became the most famous of nineteenth-century Bohemians. Vallès encountered Charles Baudelaire often, for they frequented the same cafés, but the poet made a bad impression on Vallès at their first meeting

---

[90] Cited in Troubat 1906: 212–13.

by asserting that he had suffered from the contagious condition of scabies: 'He had counted on making an impression and believed he had altogether succeeded with this singular debut' (JV1: 971). Vallès refuses to rise to the challenge, placing the poet in the uncomfortable position of a would-be dandy whose efforts to intrigue have met with a blank response. As Walter Benjamin noted, Baudelaire lacked the personal charisma required of a dandy, and his attempts to astonish were generally received as vulgar eccentricities.[91] These provocations became increasingly abrupt: during his stay in Belgium, he attempted to shock bourgeois acquaintances by loudly announcing that he was a spy and a homosexual.[92] Baudelaire inspires nothing but contemptuous pity in Vallès, whose description of the poet's physiognomy—bloated, flushed face, fat nose, simpering mouth, evasive gaze, insinuations of homosexuality[93]—evokes a repulsive specimen.

This becomes explicit when Vallès considers the poet's likely fate. Will his martyrdom in Bohemia be compensated by an eternity of fame?

Hardly! His admirers can hope, at best, that one day a curious or discriminating individual will house this madman in a work printed in a hundred copies, accompanied by some other filthy eccentrics [excentriques crottés]. Let us not ask any more for him, for he deserves nothing better. How many others have fallen who were more worthy of being embalmed in the pages of an Elzevir; but they died of tuberculosis rather than madness; they never suffered the terrible preoccupations or the petty torments that afflicted this glowering galley slave of eccentricity [forçat lugubre de l'excentricité] throughout his entire life.

(JV1: 972)

Baudelaire is imagined as an exhibit in a virtual museum of embalmed eccentrics, his grimaces compared to those of the *saltimbanque*. 'Baudelaire turned himself into a monster', he writes disapprovingly (JV1: 974).

The ferocity of Vallès's response requires deciphering. The figure of the *forçat*, a galley slave or convict, recurs in his reflections on the crushing power of social norms, generally evoking his compassion for society's victims.[94] The terms *excentrique* and *excentricité*, which play a key role in his overall attempt to redeem marginality, are also deployed

[91] Benjamin 1997: 96–7.   [92] See Kempf 1977: 35–6.
[93] The last of these according to E. Wilson (2000: 184–5).
[94] Barbey situates Vallès's *réfractaires* in the 'bagne du Mépris' (prison of Contempt); see Marotin 1997: 234.

in this passage in an uncharacteristically negative sense. Examples of such inconsistency could be multiplied; in his writings on aesthetics, Vallès uses the term 'excentrique' in a positive context to characterize both Gustave Courbet and Pétrus Borel, describing the latter without hostility as a 'monster of eccentricity'.[95] What differentiates Borel as a monster of eccentricity from Baudelaire as a self-made monster, or Courbet the heroic eccentric from Baudelaire the galley slave of eccentricity?[96]

One possible answer lies in Vallès's ambivalence about Bohemia and its tendency to trade in superficially shocking exhibitionism. Like an increasing number of Second Empire writers, Vallès idealized 'manly' literary labour as a means of justifying his departure from bourgeois norms.[97] His sketch manifests aversion to both insanity and to Baudelaire's self-consciously perverse Satanism. In a moralizing reflex strikingly similar to the responses of the bourgeoisie he so often attacks, Vallès perceives madness as a sign of moral weakness, for he mistakenly interprets as insanity the aphasia from which Baudelaire suffered following a fall and which resulted in his death. Vallès does so despite the fact that he had, as a young man, been forcibly incarcerated by his father in direct response to his republican activism before 1848.

Vallès's diagnosis of Baudelaire's eccentricity must be contrasted to the poet's reflections on eccentricity in his writings on aesthetics. Baudelaire was intrigued by the ability of eccentricity to transcend dominant nineteenth-century oppositions between classicism and Romanticism, realism and idealism. In Romanticism, eccentricity was linked to *fantaisie* and the cult of originality; in the realist movement, to the valorization of the marginal and trivial; in the avant-garde, to the desire to shock. (The term would resurface in *fin-de-siècle* decadence as a synonym of the self-consciously perverse.) In its semantic proximity to *bizarrerie*, however, eccentricity also incarnated many of the positive values which Baudelaire associated with modernity, defined in relation to the ephemeral contingencies of urban life. '*Beauty is always bizarre*', he famously asserted, proposing that the differences which arise from variation in climate, custom, race, religion, and temperament, collectively constitute 'this dose of bizarreness which constitutes and

[95] JV1: 825, 524.
[96] Vallès opposed eccentricity in aesthetic terms, which he identified with novelty, to the truth-to-life of realism (e.g. 'it's not that I have a mania for the novel or eccentric'; JV1: 882–3).
[97] See e.g. Goulemot and Oster 1992: 143.

defines individuality'.[98] He also suggested that loneliness and the 'rage for friendship' were common in what he termed *les castes excentriques* or eccentric castes (implicitly of Bohemia). Such comments countered the stereotype of the artist as an egocentric individualist, precisely one of Vallès's criticisms of Baudelaire.[99]

Most suggestively, Baudelaire uses the term to denote the genuinely modern artist in an essay from the *Salon de 1846*, 'Des Écoles et des ouvriers' (On Artistic Schools and on Labourers), though his praise of individuality is nuanced.[100] The essay distinguishes between the modern conception of the artist as an individual working in isolation and previous models of artistic production as a communal enterprise. Baudelaire criticizes this development, describing the mass of mediocre nineteenth-century artists as '*artistic* monkeys' who illustrate the levelling consequences of democracy, although they would have made excellent workmen.[101] The essay initially appears to take issue with the modern equation of individuality with genius. But Baudelaire partially redeems individuality with reference to eccentricity:

This glorification of the individual necessitated the infinite division of the territory of art. The absolute and divergent freedom of each person, the division of effort and the splitting up of human will brought about this weakness, this doubt and this paucity of invention; a small number of sublime and suffering eccentrics [quelques excentriques, sublimes et souffrants] are but poor recompense for this disorder which swarms with mediocrity. Individuality,— that small property,—has devoured collective originality.   (CB2: 492)

For Baudelaire, the symbol of such 'sublime and suffering eccentrics' was Edgar Allan Poe, to whom he devoted several critical essays.

Baudelaire also used the term in the context of a Romantic vocabulary of intensity, wildness, and genius. The original astronomical meaning of the term 'eccentricity' denoted the deviation of a planet from a circular orbit. In America, Baudelaire notes, Poe was commonly seen as 'an *erratic* being, a planet *flung out of its usual orbit*' (CB2: 251; emphasis in original). Baudelaire writes of Poe's eccentricity in the context of metaphors of natural wonder and Satanism: 'This eccentric and stormy writer'; 'his eccentric and dazzling literary destiny'; 'this accursed

---

[98] CB2: 578–9; see also 695. On the specificity of French *modernité*, see Descombes 1993: 44–64.

[99] e.g. CB1: 973.

[100] On Baudelaire's aesthetic beliefs during this period, see Howells 1996: 26–63.

[101] He also uses the term 'excentrique' to denote romantic artists and innovators generally (CB2: 494, 572).

eccentric'.[102] Eccentricity is also associated with Poe's reflexive interest in the outcast: 'what will be to his eternal credit is his preoccupation with all the really important subjects, the only ones worthy of the attention of the spiritual man: probabilities, mental illness, the sciences of conjecture . . . analysis of the eccentrics and pariahs of terrestrial life [la vie sublunaire], and directly symbolic clownishness.'[103] Baudelaire's reading of Poe intersects significantly with critical essays on Poe written in the late 1850s by Barbey d'Aurevilly. As I have argued, Barbey and Baudelaire harboured different conceptions of the relationship between dandyism and eccentricity. For Barbey, true dandyism stopped short of overt eccentricity; for Baudelaire, the two could coincide, despite—and often in considerable tension with—his emphasis on the dandy's imperturbability. Thus, unsurprisingly, Barbey's judgement of the extravagantly eccentric Poe is more negative than that of Baudelaire, who added sceptical marginalia to his copy of Barbey's essay.

Barbey's account initially laments Poe's complicity with the American values Barbey detests, primarily Protestantism, capitalism, and egalitarianism. He associates these values with Poe's sensationalist style, which is interpreted as a concession to the American mass audience and its clamour for spectacle. Barbey's negative judgement recedes strikingly in the course of the essays, however, upon reading a biographical essay on Poe by Émile Hennequin which documents the writer's suffering in his home country. Barbey subsequently transforms Poe into an oppositional artist and victim of American society, though the writer's mental pathology remains a more important theme for him than it is for Baudelaire (despite the fact that both French writers shared a predilection for Satanism and 'moral teratology').

Barbey multiplies epithets similar to those of Baudelaire in his attempt to make sense of Poe, describing him as 'the American eccentric', 'this strange and eccentric literary individuality', the Hoffmann of America, the Byron of Bohemia, and even the king of Bohemia.[104] Poe's exceptional status is attributed to an oxymoronic combination of sickness and aesthetic brilliance, nervous illness (suggestive of hysteria and hypochondria) and genius: he is 'this sturdy and sickly genius' (1890: 388). Finally, Poe is described as a *saltimbanque*: 'This vigorous and singular two-headed genius was not, for all that, a freak sufficiently

---

[102] CB2: 289, 260, 303.   [103] CB2: 289; see also 272.
[104] Barbey also multiples adjectives such as 'bizarre', 'original', 'singulier', and 'mystificateur'.

monstrous to excite the gargantuan appetite of those devourers and gob-
blers of freaks whose applause he sought to elicit, and he *failed* during his
lifetime as a freak. What he needed were Barnums, those *manufacturers*
of notoriety in his home country' (1890: 398; emphasis in original).
That Vallès was offended by Baudelaire's mystifications, and that Barbey
remained ambivalent in the face of Poe's extravagant persona, illustrates
the suspicion of fraud that habitually arose in relation to the eccentric's
claim to genius.

The themes of dissimulation and mystification were prominent in
French cultural life from the July Monarchy onwards. A whole range
of social types generated uncertainty about the relationship between
subjective experience and external behaviour and appearance, including Jeune-France and Bousingots, false geniuses, fraudulent fairground
monsters, sad clowns, dandies, actresses and courtesans, hysterics, coun-
terfeiters, confidence men, and social climbers.[105] Deciphering the
connections between surfaces and their hidden meanings preoccupied
legions of urban interpreters, including novelists, journalists, phys-
iognomists, phrenologists, and alienists. The bourgeoisie experienced
profound anxiety about being duped in the anonymity of the city,
where a local community could no longer guarantee the truth behind
appearances.[106]

Two Parisian eccentrics of the July Monarchy were particularly suspected of fraud. The Baron de Saint-Cricq was, in the popular imagination, the emblem of extravagant eccentricity. Anecdotes of his bizarre
actions were circulated, like the legend of Nerval walking his lobster in
public. The baron's behaviour proved difficult to interpret because he
was not a Bohemian, and because he engaged in reckless expenditure
contrary to the bourgeois logic of self-interest. His most celebrated
antics included disrupting performances of Scribe's plays at the theatre
by offering to pay the bourgeois playwright vast sums on the condition
that he cease writing; ordering eight baths to enjoy the discomfort of the
delivery boys; asking for ice-cream at the Café Tortoni and placing it in
his boots; mixing ink and coffee; using hot chocolate as a salad dressing;
and giving extravagant gifts to the poor. Saint-Cricq delighted in being
noticed, yet no one was certain whether he was acting out deranged
fantasies or attempting to mystify his observers. Incarcerated in a *maison
de santé* at the request of his scandalized family, it was rumoured that,

---

[105] See e.g. Jones 1984: 123–4.   [106] See Prendergast 1986: 87–96.

Fig. 14. Carnevale, the Parisian eccentric. (Yriarte 1868: 209) © British Library Board. All Rights Reserved. (12350.g.11)

deprived of the audience of the Parisian street, he became depressed and died two years later.[107]

An Italian language teacher who dressed in extraordinary costumes, Carnevale was also catalogued in several galleries of Parisian eccentrics (see Fig. 14).[108] His sartorial monomania was widely interpreted as a sign of insanity deriving from unrequited love, but one writer cynically suggested that the Italian's eccentricity was feigned in order to attract students: 'to impress the crowd with eccentricities which, by in no way blemishing his probity and his character, could gain him entry everywhere.'[109] If this was his strategy, however, it was self-defeating according to Charles Yriarte:

---

[107] Yriarte 1868: 66.
[108] Including Champfleury 1877, Yriarte 1868, and Delvau 1867*b*: 65–8.
[109] Yriarte 1868: 98.

the Parisian is indulgent towards monomaniacs and visionaries. Though he does not show towards them the profound respect of the Arabs, who view such individuals as having been touched by the hand of Allah, he willingly grants them the indifference of a jaded public no longer attracted by eccentricities of language, behaviour, or dress. Have we not seen *Carnevale* walk through the crowd twenty times without people so much as turning their heads? To pay attention to these bizarre figures would be to show oneself to be a provincial or foreigner.   (Yriarte 1868: 123)

Eccentricity could be feigned for a variety of reasons. In Bohemian culture, the most common included the desire to assert one's intellectual distinction or aesthetic beliefs; the need to earn a living; and the urge to discomfort particular categories of people, primarily the bourgeoisie.[110] Bourgeois spectators were particularly infuriated by situations in which they were unable to decide whether behaviour was sincere or feigned.[111] This explains both why eccentricity was so frequently regarded with suspicion by this class, and why it proved, in certain contexts, a potential site of symbolic resistance and struggle.

This chapter has analysed the progressively more negative meanings attached to eccentricity in the context of Parisian Bohemia, from its association with provocative self-fashioning during the July Monarchy to its role as a cipher of misery during the late Second Empire. Due to the increasingly close identification between writers and those who lived with them in Bohemia, the realities of life at the bottom of the Parisian hierarchy began to be addressed with a new concern born of indirect self-pity. The implicit narcissism behind the publication of many 'galleries' of eccentrics did not detract from an important cultural shift: growing documentary interest in lives previously deemed unworthy of representation, and the Utopian project that Jules Vallès termed 'l'histoire nouvelle' or the 'new history'.

Fascination with the 'eccentricities' of the sideshow and gutter, whether real or fraudulent, was not restricted to popular and literary culture, for enquiry into mental and physical eccentricity simultaneously grew in various branches of French science after 1848. In the rapidly evolving field of natural history, scientists constructed

---

[110] Bourgeau, for example, warns that feigned eccentricity is rife in the salon (1864: 235–6).

[111] This accounts for perhaps the most sustained literary attempt of the period to confront bourgeois readers with uncertainty: Flaubert's fiction, underpinned by his youthful love of mystification (see Culler 1974: 157–65).

elaborate theories to account for physiological malformations, 'monstrosities' which appeared to lay observers to violate the conventions of nature in much the same way that Bohemian eccentrics violated the conventions of bourgeois life. The figure of the monster gained new prestige from depictions of the Bohemian genius yet simultaneously became the object of intense anxiety in a culture preoccupied with heredity, inspiring complex rhetorical responses in both scientists and writers.

PART IV

SCIENCE

7

Monsters

> I enjoy the company of your Monsters and am learning a good
> deal from them. They are likeable and frank prattlers, who
> speak knowledgeably of the marvels of organization, never failing
> to make pertinent comments about what is both possible and
> impossible.
>
> Corréa de Serra[1]

Throughout the nineteenth century, the concepts of eccentricity and
monstrosity were closely intertwined. The former represented departure
from the norms of convention and custom, and the latter, departure
from the norms of nature. The distinction between custom and nature
was often blurred: in polite society and the salon, unconventional behaviour and female self-assertion were branded 'monstrous' and 'unnatural'
departures from tradition; in the *demi-monde*, monstrosity was associated with the *femme excentrique* and the confusion of social categories
for which she was held responsible; in the fairground, the term 'monstre'
denoted the deformed bodies of the sideshow; and in Bohemia, imagery
of monstrosity was used to suggest social marginality, madness, and the
experimentations of the avant-garde. In the discourses of science and
medicine the concept of monstrosity was examined in an ostensibly
literal manner, as the new discipline of teratology sought to understand
the causes of physical deformity. The remit of teratology was subsequently extended to include madness and criminality, ascribed by many
scientists to organic malformations and thus believed to be susceptible
to physical explanation.

Despite scientists' desire for a neutral and objective language in
which to conduct their enquiries, the tropes of deviance which circulated in French culture at large continued to influence their thinking.
Writers and alienists drew on metaphors of natural wonder to describe
eccentrics; teratologists based some of their most important theories

---

[1] Cited in É. Geoffroy Saint-Hilaire 1827: 119 n. 2.

upon aesthetic criteria; and theorists of heredity blurred the boundaries between physical malformations and moral perceptions of 'unnatural' and 'perverse' behaviour. In her account of the cultural construction of the early twentieth-century American New Woman as an androgyne, pathologized by doctors as a hermaphrodite yet hailed by feminists as the symbol of a new order, the cultural historian Carroll Smith-Rosenberg has argued that 'during moments of intense confrontation, politically opposing groups adopt identical metaphors and images', terming this 'a rare but fascinating phenomenon' (1986: 246.) The trajectory of anomaly in mid-nineteenth-century Parisian culture suggests that such semantic reversibility is intrinsic to the concept of monstrosity, which, like androgyny, can be deployed in both a rhetorically positive and negative way.[2] The history of monsters 'encodes a complicated and changing history of emotion', amongst the most multifaceted and ambivalent of all those sedimented around eccentricity.[3]

Nature's laws and society's habits

The history of monsters in Western culture is inseparable from the rise of the modern scientific paradigm. One common narrative holds that monsters and natural wonders were originally viewed as divine portents (evoking the etymological derivation of 'monster' from the Latin *monere*, to warn); that they were subsequently seen as entertaining novelties, the 'sport' of nature (evoking an alternative derivation from *monstrare*, to show); and that the process concluded around the start of the eighteenth century with the emergence of a scientific perspective, in which monsters were seen as meaningless errors of nature and ceased to evoke such violent responses.[4] Georges Canguilhem, for example, compares the trajectory of monstrosity in nineteenth-century teratology to Foucault's history of madness: in both accounts, medieval tolerance of anomaly gives way to segregation and confinement (1965: 178). In contrast to the deterministic world of nature in the scientific age, he concludes, the imagination alone remains capable of limitless 'eccentricity', becoming the sole repository of creative freedom.[5] This narrative

---

[2] To adapt Jeanneret 1980: 67.   [3] Davidson 1991: 64.
[4] Daston and Park 1998: 176.
[5] On the products of the imagination as monsters, see Huet 1993.

portrays scientific understanding of the 'monster' and aesthetic explorations of 'monstrosity' as mutually exclusive (184).

The historians Katherine Daston and Lorraine Park have challenged such teleological accounts, citing the chronological coexistence of different paradigms for interpreting monstrosity. Instead, they propose three contextually variable 'complexes': horror, in which monsters are seen as portents, and 'against nature'; pleasure, in which they are seen as entertainment, and the 'preternatural' sport of nature; and impassivity or repugnance, in which they are seen as errors of nature. They concede that two attitudes became prominent in educated circles during the eighteenth century: the belief that monsters must be explained by reference to unchanging natural laws; and the replacement of nature by culture as the arbiter of order: 'What had once been nature's habits hardened into inviolable laws; what had once been irregular and unpredictable public conduct hardened into a regimen of propriety and social rules' (214). Monsters continued to shock, but for the same reason that eccentricity was seen as increasingly unacceptable in the salon.

The identification of the modern scientific paradigm with the third of these complexes, that of impassivity, continues to shape histories of monstrosity in the post-Revolutionary period (evident in the view, for example, that the framing of the anomalous body in nineteenth-century science 'can be characterized simply as a movement from a narrative of the marvellous to a narrative of the deviant').[6] Such statements converge with the narrative of the 'disenchantment of reality' proposed by Max Weber in his analysis of science and rationalization.[7] They also coincide with two other accounts of paradigm shift. First, historians of science have noted the decreasing importance of symbolic meaning in intellectual enquiry after the Renaissance.[8] Second, the concept of singularity is widely held to have lost its prestige in modern scientific culture, leading to growing scientific intolerance of the monster's apparent failure to fit into taxonomic categories. The early modern cabinet of curiosities, in which monstrous and singular objects were displayed, was the locus of seemingly irrational juxtaposition; but it ceded to the

---

[6] Thomson 1996: 3–4.
[7] The 'disenchantment of the world', a concept dating to Schiller, is explored in Weber 1948: 155 and Adorno and Horkheimer 2002: 2, 11; see also Outram 1995: 263–4.
[8] Pickstone 2000: 60.

eighteenth-century scientific collection which focused upon comprehensive coverage, and thereafter to the taxonomies of the natural history
museum.[9]

All three narratives of decline (of wonder and enchantment; symbolic meaning; and singularity) emphasize the distinctive psychic structures required of the scientist, in particular objectivity unclouded by
emotion. This shift often elicits mourning in cultural theory, for it is
seen to represent the loss of the numinous and the rise of oppressive
systems that are insensitive to particularity. One school of thought
concludes that attempts to master monstrosity are doomed to fail:
'Monsters cannot be announced', writes Jacques Derrida; 'One cannot
say, "here are our monsters", without immediately turning the monsters
into pets' (1989: 80). The domesticated monster is simultaneously
an emasculated monster, or, as Derrida's comment suggests—drawing
on the view that the monster is inherently a 'boundary-breaker' and
'category destabilizer'—no longer a real monster at all. Such poststructuralist accounts posit the monster as the eternal 'other' of the logic of
classification.[10]

The changing shape of responses to monstrosity in nineteenth-
century French culture suggests both that science failed to disentangle itself from myth and that it failed to domesticate monstrosity.
Though the Idéologues had placed great importance on purifying the
language of science around the turn of the nineteenth century, the
boundaries between scientific and everyday language remained porous.
The terminology of natural history was often transferred into the discourses of social life, a process evident in phenomena as diverse as
early nineteenth-century social reformers' discussions of 'social physiology' and the social 'organism', the rhetoric of social hygiene in the
aftermath of the French Revolution, the literary 'physiology' of the
July Monarchy, and the realist movement of the Second Empire; all
demonstrated the continuing cultural prestige of scientific vocabulary.[11]
In turn, nineteenth-century scientists were influenced, often uncon-
sciously, by everyday language. The emotional complexes linked to
horror, wonder, and pleasure continued to operate on a subterranean

[9] See Foucault 1966: ch. 5, Impey and MacGregor 1985: pp. xvii–xviii, and Hooper-
Greenhill 1992: 92.
[10] See J. Cohen 1996: 1–20. They echo postmodern accounts of madness as the
eternal 'other' of reason, which can obscure both the continuum between 'madness'
and 'sanity' and the view that the hypertrophy of reason can itself constitute a form
of madness (see Ch. 8).
[11] See Haines 1978.

level, as did the association between monsters, 'unnatural' behaviour, and moral and political transgression.[12] Two developments particularly influenced these largely unconscious associations. The French Romantic movement of 1830, with its emphasis on originality and enthusiasm for the grotesque, initiated a cultural revaluation of monstrosity in all its forms.[13] In contrast, French social and political debates about the new doctrine of individualism stressed the negative consequences of rejecting the customs that underpinned the reproduction of the social order in the name of individual freedom and difference. Nineteenth-century scientists' determination to make the 'eccentricities of nature' submit to deterministic paradigms and taxonomies belay the fact that monsters were being imbued with new layers of mythological significance across literary and political culture.

One further nineteenth-century development shaped understandings of monstrosity: the reconceptualization of the mind–body relationship. Eccentricity, and by extension madness, were the psychic corollaries of physical monstrosity. The increasing prestige of organicist theories of mind after 1848 favoured the belief that eccentric behaviour originated in anomalies of the nervous system. The school of eighteenth-century medical philosophy known as Montpellier vitalism had pioneered the study of the links between mind and body, described from the Revolutionary period as 'anthropological medicine'.[14] It proved crucial in the shift, charted by Michel Foucault, from somatic to moral anomaly, from monstrosity of nature to monstrosity of conduct, and from the 'legal–natural' to the 'legal–moral'.[15] The metaphorical link between monstrosity and madness, already established in the cultural imagination, was thus gradually literalized and incorporated into scientific discourse. This led to the proliferation of what Foucault terms 'everyday', 'small', 'banal', and 'pale' monsters in theories of morbid heredity.[16] Alain Corbin notes that the scientific analysis of monstrous births rapidly resulted in the emergence of 'social teratology' which posited 'a fabulous array of monsters, freaks, and degenerates'.[17] Previously the province of a celebrated few—whether the 'monstrous' murderers and rapists that gripped the public imagination from the early nineteenth century, or the

---

[12] e.g. 'The child who is ungrateful towards his parents is a MONSTER' (GD11: 475); see also Baldick 1987: 14–21.

[13] See e.g. Hugo's 1827 preface to *Cromwell* in 1968 and Théophile Gautier 1853.

[14] See E. Williams 1994: 3, 7, 246.   [15] Foucault 1999: 68.

[16] Foucault 1999: 52–3 and 1976: 40.   [17] Corbin 1987a: 566.

gallery of famous biological 'monsters' discussed in scientific circles and popular culture alike—monstrosity became the fate of the multitude.[18]

Eccentrics and monsters of Gérard de Nerval

Gérard de Nerval was, from this perspective, a paradigmatic example of what Foucault terms a 'pale' or 'small' monster. Nerval was repeatedly described as an eccentric by his peers, in rhetoric which emphasized the term's connotations of borderline madness, whimsical imagination, and social isolation. Théophile Gautier, who devoted various biographical sketches to the poet, wrote for example of Nerval's 'eccentric life, outside almost all social circles [conditions humaines]' (1874: 148), and of the poet's relationship to the Romantic movement of 1830 which institutionalized certain forms of eccentricity:

In those days of literary eccentricity, amongst all the originalities [originalités], outbursts, and examples of voluntary or involuntary outrageousness, it was very difficult to appear extravagant; every type of madness seemed plausible, and the most sober amongst us would have seemed worthy of the Petites Maisons asylum. The pleasure we derived from irritating the philistines impelled us, like the German students, to carry out acts of concerted oddity [bizarreries] in the most dubious taste. Gérard's mental equilibrium had no doubt been disturbed for quite some time before any of us actually noticed.   (1875: 35–6)

As Gautier's description suggests, Nerval's sustained questioning of bourgeois norms did not fit neatly into the exuberant parody of his peers (some of whom, like Gautier, soon became members of the literary establishment), making him an outsider even within a movement of self-proclaimed outsiders.

Nerval's well-publicized experiences of mental breakdown and incarceration made him particularly sensitive to the phenomenology of objectification. Bohemian writers such as Champfleury, Baudelaire, and Vallès haunted the fairground to explore the potential affinity between bourgeois and monster. In Nerval's writing, the testing of fairground barriers proved inseparable from the potential dissolution of self and sanity, and was portrayed with particularly acute ambivalence. For despite his hostility to being labelled insane, Nerval, who like Flaubert

---

[18] See Martin 1880: 295–7.

was acquainted with the teratological research of Étienne Geoffroy Saint-Hilaire,[19] refused to accept that scientific advances were synonymous with the loss of wonder. This emerges strongly in two works that Nerval published in 1852, *Les Nuits d'octobre* (October Nights) and *Les Illuminés* (The Illuminati).

A first-person, implicitly autobiographical narrative first published in instalments, *Les Nuits d'octobre* belongs to the genre of domestic travel literature popular with bourgeois readers seeking to explore 'unknown Paris' from the safety of their homes. The text undermines any sense of security in the reader, though, oscillating between parodic high spirits and the representation of disturbing hallucinatory states. The narrative begins with a *badaud*, or Parisian spectator, acting as Virgil to the narrator's Dante, leading him round the nocturnal underworld and its tramps, labourers, and women of questionable virtue. The narrator self-consciously relates his enterprise to the physiology and English realist fiction, announcing that his aim is to 'daguerrotype the truth'.[20] Yet reality appears marvellous and unpredictable, impossible to capture with a neutral recording machine: 'Indeed, novels will never be able to render all the bizarre combinations of life. You invent man—but are incapable of observing him. What novels can vie with the comic—or tragic—stories contained in a police gazette?'[21] The narrator alludes to the *Gazette des tribunaux*, a precursor of the *fait divers* and a repository of shocking examples of moral monstrosity, whilst the phrase 'bizarre combinations' had long been used in natural history to denote malformed bodies.[22] Neither appears a likely beginning for a realistic narrative.

The interlocking concepts of social marginality, eccentricity, and physical monstrosity play a central role in the narrative.[23] The narrator's guide is described in terms of the Bohemian eccentrics portrayed in contemporaneous galleries: he chatters constantly, exposing his 'systems', and is implicitly compared to Diderot's monstrous *original*,

---

[19] e.g. in *Lorély*, GN3: 207.
[20] GN3: 335; Nerval 1999: 227. Compare Fournel 1867: 263, and Gautier, cited in Goulemot and Oster 1989: 25 n. 7.
[21] GN3: 314; Nerval 1999: 205, trans. modified   [22] e.g. Robinet 1768: 168.
[23] From a poststructuralist perspective, Sangsue (1987: 360–4) emphasizes the text's anti-realist use of parody and irony, but neglects the role attributed by the text to mental states in problematizing representation; he thus focuses on the text's 'subversive' aspects rather than the narrator's anxiety, and neglects Nerval's ambivalent relationship to pathology, a key theme of 1850s realism with which the text persistently engages (see e.g. Matlock 1995: 28–30).

the Neveu de Rameau. The *badaud* then narrates an anecdote concerning the celebrated Parisian eccentric Saint-Cricq, banished from the Café Anglais for his peculiar behaviour. The narrator responds, perhaps ironically, by rehearsing conventional wisdom: 'Polite society could not tolerate his eccentricities.—Let's enjoy ourselves, but within bounds. Words to the wise.'[24] The jovial tone of the passage presents eccentricity from a bourgeois perspective as simultaneously amusing and tiresome, though Saint-Cricq was, like Nerval, incarcerated in a *maison de santé* when his eccentric behaviour became too disturbing for his family.[25]

When the narrator leaves the *badaud* to take the train to Meaux, daylight, fresh air, and the countryside appear to signify an end to the phantasmagoria of nocturnal Paris. Yet the marvellous lurks in the most implausible places. Upon entering a café, the narrator is struck by an enormous red poster:

> WONDER OF WONDERS
> One of the most bizarre occurrences in Nature:
> A WOMAN OF GREAT BEAUTY
> With a head of chestnut hair
> That is in fact
> THE FLEECE OF A MERINO.[26]

The exhibit is an 18-year-old Venetian woman, whose hair grows like a plant; two branches rise up on her forehead 'like horns'. Using typical fairground techniques, the poster claims that this 'phenomenon' has baffled the medical faculties of Paris and Montpellier and has even been shown to Queen Victoria.[27] The exhibition of mixed-race individuals, particularly those with anomalies of skin or hair, was common in fairgrounds (see Fig. 15). A metaphorical fusion of woman, sheep, and tree, the woman recalls the *femmes sauvages* exhibited in cages; she appears to illustrate the nineteenth-century view that women are closer to nature than men, like animals or even plants.[28]

Nerval's narrator wishes to verify the 'phenomenon' for himself by attending the spectacle. But this last attempt to bolster the realist project collapses in the face of the incomprehensibility of anomaly. After the show, the narrator is overcome by strange sensations; his subsequent

---

[24] GN3: 318; Nerval 1999: 209, trans. modified.
[25] See Yriarte's account (1868: 66).   [26] GN3: 336; Nerval 1999: 228.
[27] On Nerval's depiction of *saltimbanques*, see Stierle 1993: 671–86.
[28] See respectively Proudhon 1966: 274 and 1982: III, 5–6 and Hegel 1991: 206–7.

Fig. 15. A human 'phenomenon' characterized by her extraordinary hair. (Escudier 1875: 85) © British Library Board. All Rights Reserved. (12330.i.l)

nightmare illustrates Nerval's belief that dreams and madness are closely linked. In the dream, the narrator circles around corridors and stairs, loses his sense of time, and guiltily concludes he is being punished for his desire for the monster. A crowd of tiny German gnomes unscrew his skull and attempt to sweep out his brain, symbolically cleansing him from his transgression; they scold him for believing in the reality of the monster, suggesting that she was a fraud.[29] The prospect of sexual union with a monster threatens the structure of the narrator's self, positioning him as spectator to his own mental disintegration, which he links to Fichte's idealist philosophy and the agonizing experience of self-consciousness.

Waking from the dream, the narrator expresses a desire to purify his mind: 'Let's...try to extricate ourselves from this awful hotchpotch of comedy, dream, and reality.'[30] He seeks to re-establish the boundaries separating genres and perceptual states, both destabilized by the

[29] GN3: 338–9; Nerval 1999: 230–1.   [30] GN3: 340; Nerval 1999: 232.

boundary-defying figure of the monster. The narrator decides, again paradoxically, that the reality principle can only be regained by renouncing literary realism. He adds his voice to a common criticism of the realist movement, namely that it is overly focused on pathology, citing 'an article containing an entirely justified philippic against those bizarre imaginings [imaginations bizarres] that today go under the name of the *école du vrai*, or True-to-Life School'.[31] Echoing the phrase 'bizarre combinations' used at the start of the narrative, the passage implies that the monstrous subject matter of realist writers is the product not of reality but of their own deranged imaginations. The narrator thus implicitly repudiates realism as a form of communally induced madness. Realism is not the only literary movement cast under suspicion in the course of the narrative. In the penultimate scene, the narrator has a second nightmare in which he is placed on trial for his literary tendencies and accused of 'fantaisisme' and essayism, in addition to realism.[32] All three are suggestive of monstrosity. *Fantaisisme* is linked in the text to the 'worship of monsters',[33] whilst the generically hybrid form of writing known as essayism etymologically denotes the 'assay' or experimental foray, a concept with evident affinities to the notion of the monster as an experiment of nature.

When he finally recounts the exhibition of the *femme mérinos*, the narrator is in demythologizing mood, as if he has mastered the threat of monstrosity. He notes ironically that many bourgeois husbands would be delighted to have wives with woollen hair: furnishing them with raw material for their clothing, it would lower household costs. Yet strangeness creeps back into his description, which unsettles for many reasons:

Her eyes are almost red and have that meek look of sheep—even her voice seems to have something bleating to it. Her hair, if you can call it that, would frustrate any comb. It's a tangle of small cords, not unlike the butter-soaked braids worn by Nubian women. Her skin was none the less unmistakably matt white in colour, and her hair was a fairly light chestnut brown (see the poster). I think there must have been some sort of cross-breeding: a Negro—perhaps Othello himself—must have married some Venetian, thus creating this local variant several generations down the line.[34]

---

[31] GN3: 342; Nerval 1999: 234.
[32] GN3: 348; Nerval 1999: 241. On 'fantaisisme', an aesthetic of the fantastic and the imagination, see Diaz 2003.
[33] GN3: 349; Nerval 1999: 241.   [34] GN3: 344; Nerval 1999: 236.

The woman's hair frustrates the comb, just as she frustrates medical science, and just as Nerval, the *badaud*, Saint-Cricq, and others labelled eccentric confused alienist and bourgeois alike.

Erotic attraction and identification are fused, for as well as being an object of desire the *femme mérinos* functions as a projection of his deepest fears.[35] She symbolizes the poet's fear of being publicly ridiculed as an eccentric by members of the already marginal community of men of letters. Nerval knew very well what it meant to be exhibited in public: in 1841 Jules Janin had humiliatingly publicized one of Nerval's episodes of insanity in an article in the *Journal des Débats*. Alexandre Dumas followed suit in *Le Mousquétaire* in 1853.[36] Both articles deeply wounded the poet, eliciting passionate self-justification.[37] In his response to Alexandre Dumas—the preface to *Les Filles du Feu* (Daughters of Fire) published in 1854—Nerval cites a revealing comment by Brisacier, a fictitious seventeenth-century alter ego. Brisacier has been excluded from the theatrical troupe in which he worked, following a very public mental breakdown in the middle of a performance. 'Be so kind as to welcome me back', he pleads to the leading actress, 'if only as a monster, a freak, a victim of ringworm [*calot*] able to draw in the crowds' (GN3: 458).

The spectre of identification with the anomalous outcast in *Les Nuits d'octobre* threatens to dissolve the boundaries between reality, dream, and fantasy altogether. Nerval's incongruous Shakespearean reference, together with the possibility that the 'phenomenon' is a fairground fraud, assimilates the woman to the realm of fiction and implicitly aligns the narrator with the racial outsider Othello and his transgressive love affair. In his preface to Alexandre Dumas, Nerval would later explain that his so-called madness stemmed from his tendency to identify excessively with fictional characters (GN3: 450). The woman evokes the classical and medieval concept of the 'monstrous races', and her 'horns' have diabolical undertones. The narrator's expressions of sexual desire evoke fabulous copulations between humans, animals, and plants, whilst recalling the magical world of the Parisian physiology and its anthropomorphized animals. The woman merges with the absent figure

---

[35] The speaker also compares himself to the *saltimbanque* who exhibits her (GN3: 340).

[36] 1 March 1841; 10 December 1853. Nerval described the latter as 'a little eccentric', attempting to defuse its hurtful effect (GN3: 837).

[37] Namely, ironic dedications of *Lorély* and *Les Filles du feu* to Janin and Dumas respectively. Some missed the irony, e.g. Delvau 1865.

of the mother which haunted Nerval's writing: the narrator compares
her to the pale and spiritual Madonnas painted by the seventeenth-
century artist Carlo Dolci.[38] Finally, she incarnates the principle of
unpredictability, since bizarre variations may suddenly recur after generations of normality. The ambiguous *femme mérinos*, imbued with many
layers of imaginary significance, is presented as the ultimate rebuke to
realists who believe that grotesque subject matter provides privileged
access to reality.

Naturalists of the human soul

Nineteenth-century alienists attempted to understand mental illness by
means of analytical language and precise taxonomy. The following passage by J.-J. Moreau de Tours, however, reveals the semantic instability
that can result from the incursion of metaphor. Moreau was an unusual
alienist who, in addition to his preoccupation with genius, encouraged
artists to experiment with hashish and proposed that madness and
dream were similar if not identical mental phenomena, a view shared by
Nerval.[39] He here frames eccentricity in terms of racial heterogeneity:

> just as a state of *real madness* may be reproduced through heredity merely in the
> form of *eccentricity*, only transmitting itself from ancestors to descendants in
> half-shades (if I may put it thus), in tones which have been softened to varying
> degrees, so too a state of simple eccentricity in the parents, a state which is
> limited to certain peculiarities of the character and singularities of mind, may
> become, for the children, the source of veritable insanity.   (1859: 187)

Lurking and ready to leap out, like Nerval's evocation of Othello's
blackness, eccentricity symbolizes the mysterious workings of heredity.
Moreau multiplies racial metaphors: eccentrics are 'the crossing of
races, transported into the moral sphere' and 'true intellectual *half-
castes* [*métis*] who contain elements of both the madman and the reasonable man, or indeed of both of these to differing degrees' (211).
Moreau is at pains to dismiss the suggestion that monstrosity is merely
an analogy: eccentrics are 'a type of blending, a genuine mixture
(not a fictional or metaphorical one)' (212). Nonetheless, he evokes
their hybridity with a series of lyrical metaphors: the eccentric is
'this alloy of lead and gold', an 'incredible alloy', and a 'psychological

---

[38] GN3: 344; Nerval 1999: 236.
[39] See Jeanneret 1980. On Moreau's career, see Dowbiggin 1991: 54–75.

monstrosity' which excites 'extreme astonishment'.[40] The existence of the diseased within the healthy recalls the enveloping of precious metals in a base substance, and the 'melting' together of healthy and morbid elements.[41]

Forming a significant stage in the psychiatric attempt to understand borderline insanity, Moreau's text inaugurated a new category, 'l'état mixte', to be applied to figures such as the eccentric. At the centre of this theory lay the organicist view that the eccentric had a malformed nervous system, but also an aesthetic vision of monstrosity. Moreau cites Horace's description of a monster in the latter's *Ars Poetica*, which functions as a warning to classical poets to avoid mixing stylistic registers; like Nerval's *femme mérinos*, part woman and part sheep, Horace's monster combines the head of a beautiful woman with the tail of a hideously black fish. Moreau's discussion of eccentricity aims to demonstrate that madness and genius are inseparable, like madness and dream or drug-induced intoxication.[42]

Nerval's *Les Illuminés*, a collection of sketches of historical visionaries, formed an idiosyncratic contribution to the genre of the 'gallery' of eccentrics that flourished during the Second Empire.[43] The relationship between Nerval as an eccentric and his portraits of eccentrics intrigued contemporaneous critics. Some argued that Nerval was attempting to refute the view that his *illuminés* were mad, interpreting the text as a sustained exercise in self-justification;[44] others viewed it as a self-portrait, likening his autobiographical account of madness and mysticism, *Aurélia*, to a chapter added to *Les Illuminés*.[45] Indeed, *Aurélia* is premised upon interpretive uncertainty, simultaneously affirming and contesting the objective status of the narrator's mystical visions as well as that of his 'malady'.[46] Nerval appears to authorize connections between the two genres when, in *Les Illuminés*, he praises the genres of biography, confessions, and travel writing: 'the life of each man becomes in this way a mirror in which each person can study himself' (GN2: 1038). The eccentric subjects whose lives he narrates implicitly bind together narrator and readers in a journey of self-examination, and are intended to generate a sense of identification.

[40] J.-J. Moreau 1859: 218, 215, 217 respectively.
[41] J.-J. Moreau 1859: 211, 217.   [42] See Dowbiggin 1991: 55–60.
[43] See Ch. 6 above.   [44] See e.g. Mirecourt 1858: 86–7.
[45] GD8: 1209; see also Delvau 1865: 91–2.
[46] See Jeanneret 1980: 68–9, 72; for a well-known if less convincing reading of this aspect of *Aurélia*, see Todorov 1970: 42–5.

Both Nerval and his critics associated eccentricity with natural wonder. Alfred Delvau suggests, in his review of *Les Illuminés*, that '[t]he
frenetic evolutions of thought, that moral comet . . . leave you breathless
[anhélant], anxious and burning with curiosity. The spectacle of these
sublime eccentricities, these instances of heroic insanity and foolish
extravagance, trouble your reason . . . madness is contagious' (1865: 97).
In a strikingly Gothic image, Delvau portrays Nerval opening up the
minds of his eccentrics for his readers, just as Nerval had dreamed of
German gnomes opening his own skull:

> he also wanted—by entering and making his reader enter with him into
> these damaged, crazed, half-open brains, into which rain falls, in which night
> reigns and intelligence struggles breathlessly [haletante] and desperately beneath
> hideous spider's webs—he also wanted to see and to show to others, to the
> sane, the wise and the healthy alike, the causes of these disturbances and mental
> disorders. This sick man was once a doctor; this confused brain was once lucid.
>
> (95)

The metaphor of breathlessness linking the two passages implies that
madness can be inhaled, evoking the choking that characterizes hysterical crisis. Delvau represents readers as both alarmed and excited
by eccentricity, with a vocabulary of the sublime which persisted into
later psychiatric accounts of eccentricity.[47] In contrast, others wished to
believe that impassive neutrality prevailed in investigations of eccentrics,
as the rhetoric of scientific experimentalism was transposed onto literary investigations. A critical appraisal of Champfleury's collection *Les
Excentriques* compares the text to a work of natural history. Since it
is acceptable to study toads, birds, reptiles, and bats, the critic Ernest
Prarond proposes, science should make room for human 'originals';
he compares Champfleury's interest in eccentrics to the natural historian's fascination with teratological 'specimens'.[48] Nerval was repeatedly
framed as an ambiguous Janus-figure, a peculiar compound of madman
and alienist, monster and teratologist. Champfleury, for example, writes:
'Even whilst he was committing the wildest eccentricities, there was
always a curious observer at work inside Gérard, making a note of
strange events and recalling them later' (1861: 194).[49]

---

[47] Cullerre, for example, likens eccentrics to tempests, comets, and natural catas-
trophes (1888: 158–9).

[48] Prarond 1852: 143–4.

[49] Champfleury patronizingly portrays realism as vigorously masculine 'saviour' to the
morbidly introspective and feminized Nerval (220–1). See also Murat 2001: 131.

Nerval's preface to *Les Illuminés* constitutes a rare nineteenth-century vision of non-pathologizing enquiry into unconventional minds. Premised upon the notion of resurrecting eccentrics, and linked to the genre of retrospective taxonomy,[50] Nerval multiplies analogies to describe his task. First, the biographer of eccentrics from previous eras is portrayed as a book-lover rescuing mouldy, gnawed books from a forgotten library (GN2: 886). Second, he is the restorer of damaged art works, and by extension a painter:

It is not granted to everyone to write the *Praise of Folly*; but even if one is not Erasmus,—or Saint-Évremond, we can take pleasure in pulling some peculiar figure out of the jumble of past centuries, whom we will attempt ingeniously to bring back to life,—in restoring old canvasses whose strange composition and scratched paint make the ordinary amateur [*amateur vulgaire*] smile. In this age, in which literary portraits enjoy some success, I wanted to paint certain philosophical *eccentrics* [*certains excentriques* de la philosophie].

(GN2: 885)[51]

Third, he is a natural historian: 'Analysing the stripes of the human soul, that's moral physiology—and just as worthwhile as the work of a naturalist, palaeographer or archaeologist' (886). Nerval emphasizes the vulnerability of the remains—old books and paintings, archaeological debris, fossil remains—evoking the sensitivity needed to reconstruct the psychic structures of deceased eccentrics. This hybrid discipline, Nerval implies, constitutes a naturalism of the human soul that differs equally from the perspective of the 'ordinary amateur' (perhaps the journalist like Champfleury who sketches eccentrics from a position of patronizing superiority) and from that of the alienist.

Nerval's imagery of painstaking excavation resonates with a passage in *Les Nuits d'octobre* in which anomaly is portrayed, unusually, as the object of reverential fascination. The Parisian *badaud* is shown conversing with workers who had formerly participated in Cuvier's archaeological excavations in the quarries of Montmartre: 'These blunt yet knowledgeable fellows will sit there for hours in the flickering torchlight, listening to the history of the monsters whose remains they continue to uncover, fascinated by the account of the earth's prehistoric upheavals.'[52] The mysterious 'antediluvian monsters' of the past function, like the

---

[50] See Ch. 6 above.
[51] Compare Vallès in *Les Réfractaires*: 'I simply wanted to paint an eccentric' (JV1: 196 n.).
[52] GN3: 316; Nerval 1999: 207.

femme mérinos, as symbols for the eccentrics of the present. Both humble and spellbound, the workers constitute the audience that both eccentrics and monsters deserve.[53] Nerval's use of scientific rhetoric in the preface to *Les Illuminés* has been dismissed as an aberration, given his evident hostility to the naive positivism of the realist movement.[54] Yet in his writing he repeatedly returns to the myth-making, re-enchanting possibilities of natural history. Metaphors of monstrosity, caught between wonder and repugnance, also allow him to explore his ambivalence about the meanings of eccentricity.

For although Nerval rejects the pathologization of madness, his preface to *Les Illuminés* describes his uncle's library of mystical works as 'this food which is indigestible or unhealthy for the soul', a comment which implicitly positions him as the poisoner of his readers (GN2: 886).[55] In particular, the final section of Nerval's sketch of Restif de la Bretonne, perceived as the emblematic eighteenth-century eccentric, reveals that monstrosity retains some of its negative connotations in his writing.[56] The narrator argues that Restif's life has pedagogic significance because it instructs the reader about the moral causes of revolutions, compared, like Restif's character, to natural prodigies:

Nature's great upheavals bring to the surface of the earth unknown substances, obscure residues, monstrous or abortive combinations. Reason is astonished at the sight, curiosity avidly devours them, and bold speculation sees in them the seeds of a whole world. It would be insane to establish a false foundation upon what is merely an efflorescent, sickly decomposition, or a sterile mixture of heterogeneous substances, which future generations would believe to be firm ground. Human intelligence would then become like those lights which flutter over marshes and seem to light up the green surface of an immense prairie, yet which in fact only conceal a foul and stagnant mire.   (GN2: 1074)

Nerval's conclusion is that genius can no more exist without 'good taste' than character without morality; he hints that Restif, whose eccentricity

---

[53] This forms a contrast to the narrator's nightmare of a trial by hostile judges (GN3: 348–9).

[54] e.g. Tyers 1998: 77, who (mistakenly in my view) reads the reference as purely ironic.

[55] Rigoli claims that in *Les Illuminés* Nerval shows *no* desire to pathologize eccentricity (2001: 545 n. 314), citing Mirecourt 1858. But Nerval introduces the possibility of degrees of pathology, and himself links eccentricity to pathology; furthermore, Mirecourt's view was by no means universally shared.

[56] Restif's *Nuits de Paris* is a key intertextual reference in Nerval's narrative.

is stressed five times in the sketch, may be too pathological a monster to constitute a 'true genius'. The imagery of natural wonder is cast into suspicion, shown as providing a false sense of aesthetic satisfaction—though its fascination remains evident.[57]

Four years after Nerval's death by suicide, Moreau de Tours interpolates Nerval's description of Restif into his own analysis of eccentricity and theosophy: 'Let us cite the beautiful and wise words of Gérard de Nerval, about those sickly minds which, alas! his own so sadly resembled' (224). (Nerval was diagnosed by doctors as suffering from 'démonomanie' and 'théomanie', severe instances of the tendency known as 'religious eccentricity'.[58]) Moreau seizes upon Nerval's ambivalent description of Restif as unambiguous evidence of the writer's own mental pathology, retrospectively sealed by his suicide. He declines, however, to cite the rest of Nerval's passage, which turns from Restif to the realist movement, to attack:

this school of observers and sub-standard analysts which, today, has so many members and which only studies the lowly and sickly facets of the human mind. Its adherents delight in investigating suspect pathologies, in which the hideous anomalies of decomposition and illness are cultivated with that love and admiration which a naturalist typically devotes to the most seductive varieties of regular creations. (GN2: 1074)

Nerval's unflattering description applies equally to the physiologist and doctor, figures on whom realist writers such as Champfleury modelled themselves. Moreau's attempt to direct Nerval's condemnation of Restif back towards the poet himself is a rhetorical move already anticipated by Nerval's implicit pathologization of those who are perversely interested in decay. Yet the poet simultaneously reveals his own hesitation about the value of eccentric bodies and minds. Nerval's meditations on eccentricity emerged in a cultural context in which madness was widely viewed as evidence of a moral flaw. Having partially internalized this belief, his struggle against attempts to medicalize his own 'malady' gave rise to painful inner conflict.[59]

---

[57] Nerval's disapproval of popular culture is closely related; see Bony 1990: 145–6.

[58] See Bowman 1979: 75, 84–5. 'Théomanie' was more accurate, according to contemporaneous criteria; see Murat 2001: 74–5.

[59] See Murat 2001: 117.

Teratology and its metaphors

Nerval's explorations of the link between eccentricity and monstrosity occurred in the context of the emergence of both teratology, the new science of malformations, and new theories of hereditary insanity. The trajectory of monstrosity in natural history must be reconstructed in order to understand the wider resonance of such theories in literary culture.

Teratology emerged in early nineteenth-century France amidst tension between two forces: in the one instance, the attempt to retain the unity of the broad research areas known as the *sciences de la vie* (life sciences) and the *sciences de l'homme* (human sciences), and in the other, the rise of specialization.[60] At the cost of losing sight of connections between disciplines, the latter, which rapidly triumphed, promised to provide ever-greater clarity within clearly delineated fields of enquiry. The discipline of teratology was founded by Étienne Geoffroy Saint-Hilaire in the 1820s, and the term itself coined by his son Isidore in the early 1830s. Étienne Geoffroy's theories were premised upon a sexualized relationship to an implicitly female 'Nature', whose monstrous productions were described with many of the synonyms subsequently used to define eccentricity: 'When, at the beginning of my career, I was struck by the spectacle of such numerous monstrosities that were bizarre to the point of extravagance, it seemed to me that I was contemplating Organization on its days of Saturnalia, exhausted at that moment from having laboured so industriously for so long and seeking distraction by abandoning itself to its whims' (1822: 539). Elsewhere, he implies that he has violated a modest woman's privacy, catching her in a state of undress: 'Indeed I glimpse an entirely different drama, that of organization in its irregular acts and nature overcome by agitation, embarrassed amidst its evolutions, indeed surprised in its moments of hesitation and impotence' (1827: 103). Geoffroy exaggerates the novelty of his scientific approach, which already characterized eighteenth-century analyses of monstrosity, but his writing hints at a new, distinctively post-Revolutionary concern with the proper place of women. His metaphors attempt to dissociate Nature from public life and the destabilizing forces of the carnival, linking her instead to the home and to bourgeois sobriety.

[60] See Haines 1978: 23.

Geoffroy's approach to teratology derived from his preoccupation with the doctrine of the 'unity of organic composition'. This held that all animals demonstrated the same relationship between their different parts, thereby emphasizing the 'analogies' between different species.[61] (The extreme version of this claim was the view that there was only one archetypal animal on which all others were variations.[62]) Monsters, Geoffroy argued, demonstrated the universality of the unity of composition: 'a certain order still rules amidst all this disorder. The irregularities scarcely affect anything other than the creature's form, and, though extreme, they never go so far as to change the relationship between its parts' (1822: 21).

The 'artificial' approach to biological classification associated with Linnaeus and subsequently Charles Bonnet and Georges Cuvier proposed discontinuity between forms of life. In contrast, 'natural' classification, adopted by Buffon and subsequently Robinet, Lamarck, and Étienne Geoffroy himself, proposed that different forms of life were linked through continuities, and related as natural families. Adherents of natural classification tended to view monsters as transitional forms binding together the chain of beings and helping the 'correct' combinations to emerge over time.[63] The common notion that monsters furnished a comparative standard against which normality could be judged had both religious and aesthetic implications. The writer François-René de Chateaubriand, for example, argued that monsters served as reminders of the chaos that would exist without God, whilst museums such as the anatomy gallery at the Paris medical school used the principle of contrast to heighten the neoclassical appeal of regular animals: 'through a carefully staged contrast, formal perfection and purity are everywhere opposed to these aberrations' (see Fig. 16).[64]

Teratology investigated the definition, classification, and causes of malformations. All three of these domains proved contentious. First, ordinary language seemed to hinder the project of understanding malformation. The boundaries between terms such as 'monstrosity', 'anomaly', 'deformity', and 'variation' remained unclear, and the term 'Monstre', a frequently capitalized personal noun, had simultaneously sinister and comic anthropomorphic resonance. Towards the end of the century, tolerance for linguistic slippage decreased: 'the words

[61] Today termed 'homologies'. See Darwin 1998: 351.　[62] See HB1: 8.
[63] See Robinet 1768: 198, Canguilhem 1965: 179.
[64] Chateaubriand 1978: I, 150; Texier 1852: 192.

Fig. 16. Normal and monstrous bodies juxtaposed: the gallery of comparative anatomy at the Paris medical school. (Texier 1852–3: I (1852), 92) © British Library Board. All Rights Reserved. (574.m.13)

monstrosity and *monster* lack scientific precision, for their generally recognized meaning cannot be entirely stripped from them', complained J. Davaine, amongst others.[65] Some teratologists were more tolerant of variety than others; extremes of height, polydactyly and club feet, for example, formed contentious borderline cases. Consider Isidore Geoffroy's influential definition: 'Monstrosity is a very serious form of anomaly, which makes the accomplishment of one or many functions impossible, or which produces amongst affected individuals an aberrant physical structure [conformation vicieuse] very different from that which its species ordinarily presents.'[66] Key terms ('ordinarily', 'very serious', 'very different') prove impossible to circumscribe.

---

[65] Davaine 1875: 205; see Guinard 1893: 4–5. [66] Cited in Guinard 1893: 3.

The classification of monsters presented other difficulties. Taxonomy had grown steadily in prestige since the eighteenth century within the field of natural history, yet the rise of Romanticism, and the differentiation of both society and scientific disciplines, had simultaneously increased awareness of irreducible particularity. How could these two trends be reconciled, realizing the paradoxical desire for a taxonomy of the *sui generis*? In the early modern period, monsters were divided into 'monstres par excès' (monsters through excess, namely individuals with more than the ordinary number of body parts such as conjoined twins), and 'monstres par défaut' (monsters through lack, namely individuals lacking the ordinary number of body parts). The natural historians N. Adelon and F. Chaussier concluded that monsters were impossible to classify in general terms: 'the contemplation of monsters throws us into endless differences, and obliges us to describe as many genera of monstrosities as there appear to be monsters—since not one of them fails to present something unique' (1819: 170). É. Geoffroy identified thirty new genera of monsters, though some of his peers believed that his classificatory project would entail adding a new category for every new, unique monster.[67] By 1847 his son Isidore had added fifty more, arranging monsters in twenty-three families and subsuming monstrosities under the heading of 'anomaly', in what rapidly became, and remained, the dominant taxonomic model. The ancient Greek names given to the genera—such as Déradelphe, Xiphodyme, and Mélomèle—evoked fabulous mythological creatures, undermining the presumed neutrality of scientific language.

Finally, beliefs about the aetiology of monsters were inseparable from a paradigm shift in embryology: the decline of orthodox eighteenth-century preformationism,[68] a doctrine which held that the fully grown adult of a species exists in miniature in the 'germ' as a 'homunculus', and the concomitant emergence of the theory of epigenesis, which proposed that organic structures were formed from the gradual differentiation of globular masses (later termed cells). Preformationists argued, within a religious framework, that monstrosity was caused by a 'perversion' of the germ that was already present at the Creation. Epigenesists, in contrast, argued that the germs from which monsters developed were healthy, attributing their deviation from the norm to accidental damage before birth.[69] A committed epigenesist, Geoffroy argued that monstrosities

[67] See Andral 1826: 442.
[68] In the term's pre-Darwinian sense of the ontogenesis of the embryo.
[69] The subject of a famous 18th-cent. controversy; see Tort 1980.

were caused by 'shocks' that occurred during the gestation of the embryo and which altered blood flow to the placenta. This theory was linked to the belief that there were no differences between human 'monsters' and normal animals lower down the chain of being.[70] Following Geoffroy's stance, most French teratologists of the first part of the nineteenth century denied the influence of heredity in the production of 'monsters', an optimistic stance destined to be strikingly reversed after 1848.

The theory of arrested development suggested that all 'normal' human beings have passed through a stage of monstrosity.[71] But how could it account for 'monsters through excess', which seemingly suffered from excessive rather than insufficient development? Étienne Geoffroy tried to meet this challenge by drawing upon speculative theories of 'elective affinities' developed by his disciple Étienne Serres. Serres exploited the concept of eccentricity in its pre-figurative, spatial meaning of deviation from a circle, elaborating a new theory dubbed by Isidore Geoffroy 'la belle Théorie du devéloppement excentrique' ('the beautiful Theory of eccentric development'; 1832: 19). All organs were originally double in the developing embryo, Serres argued, and gradually formed into a single organ by moving from the periphery towards the centre and fusing. He cited as an example the view that the heart was formed by the merging of two identical components. The union of body parts is heavily eroticized: 'By progressing from the outside to the inside, these two analagous halves are brought into contact; once they reach this point, they mesh with each other and are intimately joined, in such a way that the two organic parts henceforth only form one' (1832: 3). Conjoined twins such as Ritta-Christina, on whom Serres wrote a monograph (and who, prior to their death, kidnap, and dissection, were shown for profit to crowds of curious Parisians),[72] were simply examples of development that had been arrested before this fusion could be completed, their organs eternally frozen in a position of 'eccentricity'.[73]

Isidore Geoffroy endowed his father's 'Loi de l'Affinité ou de l'Attraction de soi pour soi' ('Law of Affinity or of the Attraction of self to self') with quasi-mystical significance, describing the process as 'a sort of intimate attraction . . . which, though almost inexplicable, and though

---

[70] The 'théorie des analogues' (see e.g. Andral 1826: 468), later formalized in Ernst Haeckel's notorious 'biogenetic law' that ontogeny recapitulates phylogeny.

[71] Canguilhem 1965: 179.   [72] See Howard 1977: 30.

[73] Serres 1832: 17; see also É. Geoffroy Saint-Hilaire 1827: 131, 140 and 1822: 457–8.

Fig. 17. Frozen in the process of merging: an image of 'eccentric development' portrayed in Isidore Geoffroy Saint-Hilaire's scientific treatise on teratology. (I. Geoffroy Saint-Hilaire 1832–7: III (1837), plate XIV) © British Library Board. All Rights Reserved. (973.h.15–17)

its workings are forever incomprehensible, is proved by the facts'.[74] It had enormous imaginative potential, recalling Plato's erotic vision of the *Symposium*.[75] The iconography of 'double monsters' contributed to the covert association of monstrosity with narcissism and perverse desire (see Fig. 17).

The anthropomorphic connotations of the phrase 'attraction of self to self' [soi pour soi] were highlighted by the scientist Dugès, who rephrased the law to comic effect, and Isidore's displeasure, as an egocentric 'affinity of I for I' [moi pour moi].[76] Precisely because of its tendency to metaphorical slippage, perhaps, the law fell from favour. J. Davaine later dismissed it as product of Serres's imagination (1875: 247).

---

[74] I. Geoffroy Saint-Hilaire 1847: 302–3.
[75] A metaphor given fictional expression by Goethe, a keen follower of French natural history, in his novel *Die Wahlverwandtschaften* (Elective Affinities) (1809).
[76] I. Geoffroy Saint-Hilaire 1847: 303 n. 1.

Early French biology, in summary, witnessed a proliferation of theories positing links between monsters and natural 'laws', whether of organic composition, balance, similar union, affinity, or eccentric development. Davaine was in one sense right: such speculative constructions (together with his own equally speculative contributions) were essentially imaginative attempts to account for the mysteries of heredity and generation. Enormous stress was placed by French scientists upon the neoclassical aesthetic principles of symmetry, equilibrium, and harmony, all of which were opposed to eccentricity. Beauty and truth, it was hoped, would prove inseparable. To this combination Étienne Geoffroy added two similarly emotive concepts, justice and compassion, in a striking attempt to redeem monsters within a culture which disparaged and feared them.

The rhetoric of rehabilitation: Étienne Geoffroy Saint-Hilaire

The aim of teratology was to prove that, in the words of Étienne Geoffroy, 'Monsters are merely normal beings; or rather, there are no Monsters, and nature is one.'[77] Breaking down the boundaries between normal and pathological also removed the psychological barriers separating monsters from nineteenth-century observers, however, suggesting that all normal beings had, as embryos, resembled the monsters displayed in sideshows and anatomy theatres.

Monsters were entangled in a web of sinister metaphors, and described by most nineteenth-century scientists with terms such as 'germes', 'lésions', and 'stigmates' that were laden with reference to the fall. Monsters through deficit and excess were said 'to err [pécher] through too little or too much organization'; monstrosities were seen as 'defects [vices] of physical structure' or 'defects of situation';[78] and deviations from organic norms were termed 'perversions'.[79] In the absence of a convincing scientific theory of the aetiology of malformations, lay culture implicitly saw them as signs of hidden moral defects.[80]

Étienne Geoffroy attempted to counteract such negative publicity. He used a number of rhetorical strategies to persuade his readers that breaking down the barriers between norm and anomaly was not in fact

---

[77] Cited in I. Geoffroy Saint-Hilaire 1847: 260.
[78] É. Geoffroy Saint-Hilaire 1827: 111, Andral 1826: 461.
[79] Andral 1826: 441.   [80] See M. Perrot 1987*a*: 269–70.

threatening. First, he dramatizes his research, claiming he was initially reluctant to work on monstrosity since he worried that it would distract him from topics for which he felt more 'taste' and 'ability'. Yet he is soon 'highly excited', 'swept away' on a tide of passionate interest (1827: 112). The reader is exhorted to participate in the dramatic 'adventure' of teratology, rich in philosophical significance.[81] Second, Geoffroy frames his monstrous subjects as misunderstood victims. Was Nature so cruel as to create these creatures for no purpose? 'We presumed that she created beings ready for any metamorphosis, *made to live and to die at the same moment, and worthy at the very most to be placed in our cabinets*, their claim on our attention consisting in their status as singular jests of nature.'[82] Monsters, he suggests implicitly, possess dignity of their own.

His third strategy is to exhort readers not to view monsters as failed specimens of normal organization, but rather to judge them as 'a wholly different type of creation' with its own rules (1822: 104). Romantic aesthetics, in which the unfinished sketch was gaining in prestige against the highly finished academic painting, served as a model (the term *ébauche*, or sketch, was repeatedly used to denote monsters). Confusion has arisen, Geoffroy argues, because scientists assume that monsters ought to resemble human beings merely because they are born to human females: 'We went to this being to ask it to show us something it simply did not possess' (1827: 110). Once the scientist ceases to impose impossible demands, monsters are revealed as benevolent, '*precious* fragments to study', 'an *unhoped-for* set of diverse complications, unusual associations and methodical disorders'.[83] The metaphor of listening plays a key role. 'We asked organic deviations to tell us all that it seemed to us desirable to know', writes Étienne Geoffroy. He cites his correspondent Corréa de Serra who describes monsters as 'likeable and frank prattlers, who speak knowledgeably of the marvels of organization, never failing to make pertinent comments about what is both possible and impossible' (1827: 119). Geoffroy believes the monster and the standard being to be '*two perfect works*, if they are judged in themselves, by themselves, and in conformance with their first givens'; and monsters demonstrate what is 'without doubt an

---

[81] É. Geoffroy Saint-Hilaire 1822: pp. xxxiii–iv; my emphasis.
[82] É. Geoffroy Saint-Hilaire 1822: 104; my emphasis.
[83] É. Geoffroy Saint-Hilaire 1827: 151; 1822: 104; my emphasis.

admirable form of order.[84] Finally, he approvingly cites a comment by the sixteenth-century essayist Montaigne: '*Les monstres ne le sont pas à Dieu*' ('Monsters are not monsters to God') (1827: 151). The phrase suggests that it is merely ignorance that breeds suspicion of monsters, and implicitly (when appropriated by Geoffroy) that the enlightened scientist who values monsters has attained a quasi-divine perspective on creation.

Elements of Étienne Geoffroy's rehabilitation of monsters lingered even in the more pessimistic scientific climate after 1848. In his taxonomy of 1875, J. Davaine expressed to his readers his emotional and aesthetic repugnance at the thought of placing in the same category the individual who, whilst he had hidden physiological anomalies, was regular in external appearance, and the obviously 'hideous and deformed' monster (204). His taxonomic system thus distinguishes between the symmetrical 'anomaly' and the asymmetrical 'abnormity' (*abnormité*), the latter held to characterize the physiology of degenerates (228). He marshals two types of monsters as proof: the cyclocephalus, a monster with one central eye, represents pleasing symmetry, whilst the anencephalus, a monster without a brain, represents hideousness. The most curious aspect of Davaine's system is the need he evidently shares with Étienne Geoffroy to rehabilitate monsters—but in his case by opposing 'good' monsters to 'bad' and 'degenerate' monsters, the latter becoming the repository of all the negative emotions attributed to monsters in French culture at large.

Predictably, it is the neoclassical properties of harmony and symmetry that redeem Davaine's 'good' monsters. Étienne Geoffroy had sought to introduce alternative aesthetic vocabularies to science as part of his attempt to overcome the defensive mechanisms of his readers; his writing suggests that monsters are at their most compelling when associated with a Romantic vision of wild and untrammelled nature. Attempting to describe the crucial moment of monstrous deviation, for example, Geoffroy considers but then rejects an abstract mathematical metaphor, preferring to compare the developing embryo to a river into which an avalanche has fallen:

from then on, instead of a calm, continuous current, [the waters] begin to swirl ... either they surge back, if the avalanche has filled their basin, and spill over into the surrounding countryside; or, rising up like the intervening

---

[84] É. Geoffroy Saint-Hilaire 1822: 123; my emphasis.

obstacle, they go over the top of it and come crashing down beyond it, and then behave as they did before, having returned to their usual speed.

(1822: 106–7)

He concludes that the passage demonstrates the new spirit of teratology, from which the 'vague and chimerical' have been excluded. But his style exploits precisely such lyrical associations, just as imagery of the sublime intervenes in his son's writing on monstrosity.[85]

Étienne Geoffroy's attempts to make monsters submit to the laws of nature were laden with cultural significance. Gustave Flaubert, for instance, linked scientific developments to his interest in the aesthetics of the grotesque. A letter from 1853 reveals keen awareness of the adaptability of Étienne Geoffroy's Romantic teratology to other domains: 'Aesthetics awaits its Geoffroy Saint-Hilaire, this great man who has demonstrated the legitimacy of monsters.'[86] Though the term 'legitimacy' has political and moral connotations, Flaubert's interest centres upon the legitimacy of Romantic values in a culture still saturated with neoclassical assumptions.[87] Étienne Geoffroy's doctrine of the unity of nature appealed to many other writers and intellectuals, including Balzac, Sand, and Quinet. By proposing that monsters deserved to be 'listened' to, Geoffroy appropriated the rhetoric used to assert the natural rights of marginalized groups. Indeed, he was seen by the public as a liberal hero linked to the July Revolution and a flamboyantly eccentric *Naturphilosoph*, in contrast with Baron Cuvier, framed as a pedantic specialist and a scheming apologist for the Restoration.[88]

One important feature of Étienne Geoffroy's research on teratology with potential political implications was his rejection of the view that heredity was a determining factor in the transmission of congenital defects. As part of his desire to prove that monsters were formed as a result of environmental influences, he attempted to induce monstrosities in hen's eggs by interfering with their gestation. Though his experiments were frequently cited by his supporters as having proven that monstrosity could not be caused by monstrous 'germs', they were in reality of equivocal value, since many of the embryos died. In any case, teratogeny could not prove that heredity was *never* at work in

---

[85] See I. Geoffroy Saint-Hilaire 1832: 1, 7–8.   [86] Letter of 12 October 1853.

[87] See esp. Flaubert 2001: 1035 and Seznec 1943: 195 n. 4.

[88] See Appel 1987: 122, 145; as Rehbock notes, however, Étienne Geoffroy was in reality more an Enlightenment materialist and Deist than an Idealist *Naturphilosoph* (1990: 149).

the reproduction of anomaly. Subsequent French scientific theories of monstrosity and eccentricity, indeed, would come to a diametrically opposed conclusion.

Monsters within: theories of teratological heredity

Monsters have not always been assigned the same space in the cultural imagination. In the medieval period, the 'monstrous races' were depicted on maps as warnings to travellers who went beyond the known. From the early sixteenth century, monsters began to be sighted within Europe, creeping towards the familiar and everyday.[89] A still more radical shift occurred in the modern age when monstrosity was internalized. This new type of monstrosity, which Alain Corbin associates with early French attempts to communicate the first-person experience of insanity, threatened to dissolve the very foundations of the self.[90] This internalized monster dwelt in a territory as uncharted as before, posing an immense challenge to new cartographers in the form of psychiatrists, neurologists, and criminal anthropologists.

During the first part of the century, the affinities between eccentricity and anomaly were mainly metaphorical. At times the link was more explicit (as in Serres's 'law of eccentric development'), but the metaphor was only fully literalized with the emergence of teratological theories of insanity, which argued that psychological eccentricity was actually caused by 'monstrous' malformations of the nervous system. After the defeat of preformationism, there was a new willingness to address teratological heredity in a secular context, without reference to the Creation—though medical discussions of the 'innate perversity' and 'stigmata' of degenerates turned out to be remarkably similar to the rhetoric of original sin.

The tendency to conflate eccentricity with monstrous miscegenation, evident in Nerval's *femme mérinos* and Moreau de Tours's vision of eccentric 'half-castes', was echoed in scientific analyses of race and degeneration. From the origins of teratology until the 1840s, it was believed that severe cases of monstrosity such as conjoined twins were not transmissible, unlike 'simple' anomalies. The insistence of Prosper Lucas that *all* forms of monstrosity were hereditary marked the start

[89] See Daston and Park 1998: 173.   [90] Corbin 1987*a*: 566.

of a new paradigm. His treatise on heredity, the *Traité philosophique et physiologique de l'hérédité naturelle* (1847–50), includes a lengthy analysis of whether 'double monsters' (conjoined twins) were unitary or binary, formed by one 'germ' or two. Isidore Geoffroy had suggested it was possible that one 'part' of a double monster might produce normal offspring. Lucas, in contrast, insisted that they were inextricably bound together in their pathology. In a sinister image, he concludes that monstrosity is inescapable for both 'parts' of the monster (just as their non-white ancestry was thought to lurk in mixed race individuals): 'each of the two parts conceals the monster in all its force, each of the two is capable of regenerating it' (1847: 337).

Like many of his peers, Lucas was interested in the intersections between teratology and racial science. Albinism was widely viewed in natural history as a sign of degeneration, and it was established that pigmentation was added to the foetus late in its development. Were the white races in fact monsters suffering from arrested development? Lucas responds with indignation to this suggestion, attributed to Isidore Geoffroy, describing it as an attempt to pathologize the Caucasian race: 'it must be recognized that, in these varieties, white coloration has physiological causes which are compatible with all the perfection of life's characteristics: one must, in short, recognize, in addition to *abnormal* albinism, the existence of *normal* albinism which is very distinct from the former' (1847: 300). When required, this passage demonstrates, monstrous variation could quickly be redefined as normal. Focusing on melanism (excess rather than deficit of pigmentation), Lucas further claims that the human race was originally white; after a number of cases in which the foetus was accidentally exposed to too much pigment, the black race separated to form a new race (1847: 317). The dark-skinned become 'monsters through excess'.

B.-A. Morel's comments on monstrosity occur at a crucial point in his *Traité des dégénérescences* (1857) where he, like Lucas, attempts to define and police the parameters of acceptable diversity. Following Buffon, Morel attributes racial diversity to the influence of environment (the plump Eskimo is contrasted to the famished African, the lazy inhabitants of Oriental harems to energetic Europeans). These differences are seen as harmless, however, when compared to the very source of pathology, namely degeneration (1857: I, 25–6). One of Morel's most influential contributions was the suggestion that monstrosity was no longer external and visible. 'Stigmata', or physiological signs of degeneration, could consist in hidden 'vices de conformation intérieure' (defects of internal physical structure), whose symptoms included bizarre and eccentric behaviour:[91]

> The conditions of degeneration . . . are revealed not merely in typical external characteristics that are more or less easy to identify, such as the smallness or misshapenness of the head, the predominance of sickly temperament, particular deformities, anomalies in the structure of the organs, or sterility; they are also evident in the strangest aberrations of the intellectual faculties and moral sentiments.   (1857: I, 62)

Morel's belief that moral depravity originated in minute physical deformations characterized mid-century writings on heredity, though in 1875 Prosper Despine claimed to be the first fully to integrate the moral and physical domains (584). Despine approaches what he terms 'moral teratology' with the language of original sin. Perversity is innate in man, he argues; it originates in 'seeds' already planted in him at birth (579). The central term 'germes' is polysemic, denoting a seed, an embryo, and an infectious germ (the last sense dating from 1860); it provides a rhetorical bridge between preformationists' belief in monstrous seeds created by God and degeneration theory's model of hereditary transmission. Despine portrays perversity as a type of poison, and the moral instincts as a beneficial 'antidote' and 'precious seed' that must be nurtured. In this dramatization of a battle of good and bad 'seeds', the absence of the former is considered the source of all perversity.[92] By locating monstrosity in absence—implicitly the absence of conscience—Despine implicitly qualifies all criminals as 'monsters through deficit'. When discussing famous criminals he conflates criminality with 'originality', and places eccentrics next to murderers and rapists (639).

Individual and social deviance became increasingly tightly enmeshed, culminating in Charles Féré's *La Famille névropathique* (The Neuropathic Family), subtitled 'A Teratological Theory of Heredity' (1894). Féré attempts to collapse the entire concept of degeneration into that of teratology, arguing that 'somatic malformations, which, since Morel, have been known as the stigmata of degeneration . . . are in fact teratological deviations'. The text concludes by exhorting his fellow Frenchmen to rid society of its unwanted misfits and deviants by following nature and 'eliminating' these monstrosities.[93] Monstrosity is portrayed as existing in sinister webs of contagion. So comprehensive is the

---

[91] See Dallemagne 1885: 173.   [92] Despine 1875: 583, 585, 588.
[93] Féré 1898: 191, 229.

interpretive paradigm established by Féré that falsification is impossible: physical stigmata are present in all insane individuals, but may only come to light after an autopsy; the apparently healthy man who fathers defective offspring must harbour hidden defects. In Féré's system, the figure of the eccentric is cited as a typical example of such scarcely perceptible but nonetheless deeply alarming forms of monstrosity (1898: 19, 62). Féré rejected the view that 'stigmata' represented atavistic reversions to an earlier stage of development, claiming they proved that degenerates no longer belonged to the human race.[94] A chapter entitled 'Teratological stigmata of degeneration' uses photographs of minutely deformed body parts to illustrate arrested development. His work forms the most extreme manifestation of an underlying tendency in *fin-de-siècle* medical and scientific thought to conflate eccentricity of mind and morals with physical deformity.

Not all appraisals of eccentricity in the context of natural history were negative, particularly in the case of writers who focused on the purely aesthetic qualities of natural forms. In *Les Animaux excentriques*, a work of popular science for children first published in 1903, Henri Coupin eulogizes 'the inventive spirit of nature, which often—very often—takes delight in producing eccentricities, in creating types of monsters, as much in their form…as in their behaviour' (1912: vi). Rejecting Étienne Geoffroy's vision of Nature as a dutiful bourgeoise, he refashions her as a capricious *fin-de-siècle* Parisienne for pedagogic purposes.

In conclusion, Nerval's literary explorations of the links between physical and mental eccentricity were published at a juncture in which monstrosity was the subject of extraordinary cultural interest, a tendency equally evident in the realist movement's vocabulary of scientific experimentation and in the appropriation of the discipline of teratology by the new theoreticians of heredity. Though the founder of teratology, Étienne Geoffroy Saint-Hilaire, promoted liberal and Romantic values in his richly figurative attempts to dissipate the stigma surrounding 'monsters', his successors increasingly used teratological discourse as a means of legitimating underlying social anxieties, in a discursive sphere characterized by metaphorical slippage between monstrosity, perversity, sin, criminality, madness, and racial difference. The concept of eccentricity, which like that of monstrosity was highly polysemic and

---

[94] See Genil-Perrin 1913: 24.

associated with the violation of expectations, was drawn into these debates on a number of levels.

'Monsters', or 'eccentricities of nature', frustrated efforts to separate science from the wider cultural imagination, and gave rise to diverse and often powerfully ambivalent responses across both erudite and popular culture throughout the century. In particular, a growing tendency to locate monstrosity within the individual was much in evidence in theories of teratological evolution, heredity, and mental medicine. This process of internalization inevitably influenced representations of the socially marginal writer, threatened by madness and social ostracism and associated in the post-Romantic period with the aesthetics of the sublime and grotesque. The monstrous eccentric and the insane genius constituted psychological enigmas that nineteenth-century alienists became determined to decipher.

8

Madness and Medicine

No instance of physical or moral misery, no wound, however corrupt, should frighten he who has dedicated himself to the science of man. By forcing him to see everything, the sacred ministry of medicine also allows him to say everything.

Ambroise Tardieu[1]

French beliefs about the relationship between eccentricity and madness evolved considerably between 1830 and the *fin de siècle*. The notion that eccentricity might constitute a form of borderline madness was first explored during the July Monarchy, where it was linked to the fashionable new doctrine of monomania. After 1848 there was a significant evolution in attitudes towards borderline insanity or 'demi-folie', as French alienists concluded that madness was far more prevalent than had hitherto been assumed. Eccentric individuals appeared emblematic of an insidious form of pathology undermining society, and were pursued by alienists seeking both to expand their professional role and to counteract fears of social dissolution and national degeneration.

In contrast with well-known historical categories such as hysteria which in their extreme forms also challenged the boundaries between madness and sanity, eccentricity has received little attention in the history of French psychiatry.[2] This is partly because eccentricity was mainly discussed as a symptom of other disorders rather than in specialist psychiatric monographs, and partly, perhaps, because its broader cultural associations have tended to distract from its more restricted medical appropriation.[3] Nonetheless, the category was implicated in

---

[1] 1859: 2–3.

[2] I use the terms 'psychiatry' and 'psychiatric' in this study for the sake of convenience, though they are anachronistic since they were popularized only in the early 20th cent. in France. Previously, the dominant terms were *la médecine mentale* and *l'aliénisme*.

[3] There is very little scholarship on the medicalization of eccentricity in England, with the exception of the anthologization of brief excerpts from 19th-cent. writing on the subject (e.g. Skultans 1975 and Taylor and Shuttleworth 1998).

the rhetorical strategies of two of the most influential alienists active during the Second Empire, B.-A. Morel and J.-J. Moreau de Tours. Since it constantly called into question the ability of doctors to differentiate between sanity and insanity, furthermore, it constitutes a paradigmatic case study of nineteenth-century attempts to negotiate the elusive boundaries between norm and anomaly. The pathologization of eccentricity represents one of the most extreme attempts to medicalize deviance, for it restricted notions of normality and sanity to an increasingly narrow set of norms.

The relationship between eccentricity and madness will be approached primarily in the context of recurrent rhetorical tropes, and in relation to two discursive fields. First, from the July Monarchy to the Second Empire, eccentricity was associated with monomania and intellectual obsession in popular and literary culture. Analysing the connotations the concept initially accrued in non-medical culture (of which subsequent alienists were well aware) allows its semantics in later medical discourse to be understood. Second, the medicalization of eccentricity occurred mainly after 1848, primarily in relation to the influential new paradigm of degeneration. The concept became implicated in medical debates about psychiatric taxonomies, national decline, and the nature of genius.

Monomania, collecting, and the *idée fixe*

The 1830s, when eccentricity was first popularized as a French term, was a period of intense activity in mental medicine. As part of their ongoing efforts to raise the prestige of the psychiatric profession, Philippe Pinel and his disciple Étienne Esquirol sought to purify the terminology of the discipline. Specialized terms were substituted for everyday terms that had accumulated numerous connotations: *folie*, for instance, was replaced by *aliénation*, and *mélancolie* by *lypémanie*. The French term *excentricité* was not widely used in alienism until the 1850s. During the July Monarchy, Second Republic, and early Second Empire, however, the semantic fields of madness and eccentricity frequently overlapped in literary and journalistic discourse.

The idealized and paradoxical vision of England as a 'club of unclubable individuals' initially provided a point of contrast by which

French writers could evaluate attitudes towards madness in their own culture. The French author of a compendium of British 'singularities' published in 1814 summarized a common view: 'That which anywhere else would be perceived as an act of madness, or the ravings of an unregulated imagination, is here viewed indifferently, judged coldly, and perceived as the fruit of the excessive liberty which each individual enjoys in every class of society.'[4] In an article of 1834 which combines the genres of essay, fantasy, and travel writing, the French journalist Philarète Chasles similarly describes eccentricity as an instance of 'the inviolable strength of the *individual self*, the cult of this *self*' in English culture (1834: 509). Through a process of cross-cultural ventriloquism, Chasles explores a French fantasy of Englishness through the voice of an imaginary and francophobic English eccentric named Wordem, a self-styled historiographer of eccentricity. Expressing anxiety that English eccentricity will be lost through contact with the Continent, Wordem contrasts it with French conformism: 'For you, *originality* is a synonym of madness; for us, it is a term of praise and honour' (506).

Wordem's conception of eccentricity as a form of heroic individualism is disingenuous in a number of respects. He admits that English eccentrics are influenced by journalism's dissemination of oddities, making them less original than they initially appear. His planned encyclopaedia of eccentricity, each devoted to a different theme, also anticipates later psychiatric taxonomies, albeit in comic mode:

I.   To religious eccentrics.
II. To travelling eccentrics.
III. To learned eccentrics.
IV. To original women.
V.   To the peculiarities of poets.
VI. To the originalities of painters.
VII. To bourgeois originalities.
VIII. To famous eccentrics.
IX. To the biographies of English eccentrics, etc.   (510–11).

His imaginary compendium suggests the semantic elasticity of eccentricity, a label applied to different sexes, occupations, and classes. A number of these categories proved important in later medical debates about eccentricity and madness, particularly 'religious' and 'erudite'

---

[4] Verneur 1814: p. v.

eccentrics, and artists such as painters and poets. And despite his dissociation of eccentricity from insanity, Wordem employs terms like 'demi-démence' and 'nuance de folie' ('half-insanity', 'hint of madness') which gesture beyond the binary opposition between madness and sanity.[5]

Honoré de Balzac similarly evoked the greater freedoms permitted to English eccentrics. In 'Les Martyrs ignorés' (The Unknown Martyrs), an unfinished dramatic dialogue, one character narrates the story of a rich English aristocrat who believed that thought was a luminous substance, and attempted to perform chemical experiments on other people's minds (a view with certain similarities to Balzac's own beliefs in the early 1830s).[6] 'You are perhaps unaware that in English society there are many madmen who are not incarcerated and who are termed eccentrics', the narrator of the anecdote explains, terming them 'people with bizarre ideas'. He contrasts the deranged but wealthy chemist, attended by private doctors, to the poor London cobbler on whom the chemist conducts his experiments. Although the latter suffers from a very similar form of insanity, he is incarcerated. 'One must be rich to become an eccentric', the narrator asserts (737–9)—but his anecdote ends mysteriously, with the suggestion that the chemist's experiments were genuine. The text arguably authorizes many of the narratives in the *Études philosophiques* section of Balzac's *Comédie humaine* to be read as tales of mystical eccentricity, and suggests that 'bizarre ideas' might signify superior intellectual insight rather than madness.[7] Balzac also used the term to describe other forms of madness. 'Jealousy was the foundation of this character full of eccentricities, a word found by the English to denote the madness not of small but of large households', his narrator writes of the unmarried Cousine Bette, a character consumed by envy and spite.[8] As this suggests, Balzac situated eccentricity in relation to the new French concept of monomania, part of a growing cultural trend.

The doctrine of monomania, originally elaborated in the research of Esquirol and Étienne Georget, was the locus of the most advanced debate in French mental medicine during the July Monarchy. The

---

[5] Chasles 1834: 530, 511, 544.
[6] On Balzac's theory of the occult, see H. Hunt 1959: 34–58, Nykrog 1965: 73–121, and Evans 1951.
[7] Balzac's *Louis Lambert* admits both a 'mystical' reading, which accepts the truth of Lambert's supernatural visions, and a 'medical' reading which views these as symptoms of insanity (see Rigoli 2001: 493–503); Nerval's *Aurélia* creates similar indeterminacy.
[8] HB7: 207; see also HB7: 80, 85 and HB3: 387.

category suggested for the first time that insanity need not be complete, nor affect all mental faculties simultaneously. This greatly expanded the professional remit of alienists and the *médecins légistes*; the latter were increasingly called upon in court to testify to the mental state of the defendant.[9] Why did the monomania diagnosis prove so remarkably successful at this particular historical moment? As Jan Goldstein notes, Esquirol was highly sensitive to the relationship between monomania and the social fluidity of post-Revolutionary society: 'It corresponded to—indeed, it magnified and even caricatured—a salient mind-set and behavioural pattern of early bourgeois society, with its new possibilities for "self-making"', favouring characteristics such as single-mindedness and goal directedness (1987: 161–2). Monomania thus had an ambiguous relationship to the notion of individualism: in the one instance, it appeared an emblem of excessive individualism, of the type which the conduct manual advised should be concealed on pragmatic grounds; but in the other, it undermined the notion of the unified self.[10]

Monomania was linked to eccentricity in a typically humorous fashion in Parisian journalism and the physiology, and was used as a pretext for linguistic play; amateur art-collectors were termed *tableauxmanes*, for example, and lovers of music, *mélomanes*, on the model of the collector of antiquarian books, the *bibliomane*. The eccentric collector was portrayed as the archetypal monomaniac, his activities modelled upon erotic obsession. In a physiological sketch entitled 'Les Collectionneurs', Horace de Viel-Castel suggests that collectors have been 'caught...in *flagrant délit* of originality' (1840: 122), as if surprised in a guilty embrace. They inspire in observers a desire to collect *them* as peculiar specimens, suggesting that collecting is contagious: 'We would need not one volume, but rather hundreds of volumes to describe and analyse the different passions of collectors...these eccentric men, these Diogenes-figures shut up in their barrels and asking nothing from the world but to leave them to freely enjoy the object of their affection, their taste, their *Dada*, their monomania' (1840: 126). The sketch differentiates between fraudulent and genuine collectors, concluding that the latter are destined for full-blown madness.

[9] See Goldstein 1987: 152–96.
[10] On the cultural importance of the latter point, see Goldstein 2005: p. xi. Van Zuylen's thoughtful literary study of monomania only briefly considers the medical history of the concept, termed a 'point of departure' (2005: 3), nor does it engage with the concept's function in popular writing.

A celebrated literary example written shortly afterwards provided an archetype for the deranged collector for the rest of the century: Balzac's *Le Cousin Pons* (1846–7), the tragic narrative of an antique collector whose unsuspected wealth leads him to be cruelly exploited by his family.[11] The narrator uses the terms 'eccentric', 'monomaniac', and 'original' almost interchangeably, though they still evoke national differences such as the contrast between French sociability and looser erotic codes, in the one instance, and English spleen and misanthropy, in the other:

> Of all the cities in the world, Paris is the one which harbours the greatest numbers of such strange figures [originaux], so devoted to their particular religion. The eccentrics in London always grow tired of their enthusiasms in the end, just as they grow tired of life itself, whereas your Parisian monomaniac goes on living with his fantasy in blissful spiritual concubinage.
>
> (HB7: 598; Balzac 1968: 146)

Balzac's description of Pons's monomania is emblematic of the psychological structures underpinning the *Comédie humaine*, in which intense passion—whether sexual desire, financial acquisitiveness, ambition, or love—is portrayed as having a single, non-transferable object.[12] Whilst there have been few attempts to historicize the affinity of these representations with contemporaneous understandings of monomania as a specifically medical category, they suggest a 'remarkably tight correlation between the elements of Balzacian realism and those of psychiatric discourse'.[13]

Certain forms of monomania that were explicitly described as eccentric, such as collecting, were extreme forms of culturally sanctioned activities. Others hinted at more dangerous and even perverse desires. In 'Le Dessin de Piranèse' ('The Drawing of Piranesi'), an essay of 1833, the writer Charles Nodier attached different connotations to the term, using two anecdotes to illustrate 'an imagination which has reached the highest possible degree of eccentricity' (1996: 159). In one a wealthy Italian bachelor, who has had the interior of his castle decorated in imitation of a fantastically labyrinthine drawing by Piranesi, retires to the dungeon where he slowly and deliberately starves himself to death; in the other, a brilliant but reclusive young man withdraws

---

[11] On Pons, see Barberis 1972: 257–63 and Biasi 1988: 79–88.

[12] See Watson 1992: 129–33.

[13] Rothfield 1992: 63; he rightly criticizes Fredric Jameson's analysis of Balzacian 'appetency' (1971) for its anachronism (1992: 206 n. 36).

to live amongst his mechanical contraptions, and kills himself during an experiment. The latter was culled from the *Anecdotes de médecine*, which Nodier portrays as a vast archive of similar narratives collected by *médecins philosophes*. Nodier nuances their assumption that insanity is responsible, however, by relating eccentricity to the higher cultural purposes of martyrdom and asceticism: 'What I am seeking to understand is this strange form of madness which leaves untouched all the other faculties of a great mind, and which has no other object than to impose unimaginable torture on the material husk of the soul' (1996: 161) He concludes: 'This mystery is great and sublime, for it encompasses the whole secret of man's destination' (161). Nodier thus uses the term 'eccentricity' to denote an implicitly eroticized and masochistic variant of monomania.

Since he was dissatisfied with contemporary medical definitions of monomania, Nodier proposed his own. In an essay entitled 'De la Monomanie réflective' ('On Reflective Monomania'), he differentiates between 'explicit but harmless monomania', a medical issue; 'militant and sometimes murderous monomania', a legal issue; and 'reflective monomania', the more complex form which afflicts the eccentric characters of his anecdotes as well as many other highly gifted individuals (1993: 48–9). The duality of the condition is repeatedly highlighted: if channelled properly, it may result in heroic achievement, but if the subject is meditative and isolated from society, it will lead to the introverted insanity of the 'private madman' or *fou intime* (1993: 54). In contemporary society, he argues, the condition usually ends in suicide. The reflective monomaniac, whose symptoms closely resemble those of melancholia, is symbolized by the Janus's head, an emblem of ambivalence: 'a coin struck with one sole blow, which shows on one side the immortal head of the great man, and on the other the infirm head of the maniac' (53). Eccentricity is a malady of excessive individualism; but, as for the German Romantic movement which influenced Nodier, social and psychological isolation is simultaneously tragic and a sign of distinction. A notable feature of his writing on eccentricity is its emphasis upon order: 'By hijacking Esquirol's term and injecting it with a mystical aura', Marina van Zuylen notes, 'Nodier extracted from "reflective" monomania the promise of a new secular religion, one that would restore control to madmen and eccentrics by bestowing upon them a sense of divine control' (2005: 17). Indeed, a preoccupation with systematization was found in many cultural representations specifically related to eccentrics.

Intellectual passions and narrative pathos

During the July Monarchy, eccentric individuals were widely depicted as thinkers, theorizers, and mystical 'systematizers'. They therefore overlapped with the figure of the bibliomaniac which so fascinated Nodier.[14] Widely discussed in literary culture, this social type did not escape the attention of doctors and alienists.[15] In *La Médecine des passions* by J.-B.-F. Descurets (1841), for instance, the category of 'intellectual passions' is divided into five categories: mania for study, music, order, collecting, and 'political, artistic, and religious fanaticism'. Citing Nodier's essay on bibliomania, Descurets argues that the mania for collecting books is the most widespread, seductive, and harmful of all forms of morbid collection (1844: 752). Collecting functioned as a central metaphor for intellectual pursuits in the nineteenth century, since, as Walter Benjamin noted, '[c]ollecting is a primal phenomenon of study: the student collects knowledge' (1999: 210). Indeed, Descurets sees even apparently healthy intellectual passions as being prone to morbid hypertrophy. Study, for example, is the 'nourishment of the mind', but can be rapidly transformed into a 'veritable poison' (1844: 716) associated with hypochondria and male nervous disorders. His analysis anticipates the belief of many subsequent alienists that although eccentric individuals were often intelligent, they typically directed their talents to destructive or useless ends.[16]

Figures who fell under Descurets' category of 'political, artistic, and religious fanaticism' were portrayed in a number of texts about eccentricity. A link between radicalism and mystical sects, including freemasonry, Swedenborgianism, Martinism, and Mesmerism, was an important feature of the French political scene during the 1840s.[17] In an article entitled 'Les Excentriques de la littérature et de la science' (1846), which focuses mainly on a militant vegetarian, Alphonse Esquiros proposes that the post-Revolutionary period as a whole gave free rein to 'a thirst for chimerical well-being, felt by all unhappy beings and all those swept away by their imaginations'. He casts doubt on the sanity of such eccentric figures by terming them 'floating minds' (*raisons flottantes*), though he carefully distinguishes between 'innocent' and 'dangerous'

---

[14] On his notion of the 'eccentric book', see Ch. 6.   [15] See Desormeaux 2001.
[16] On the pathologization of collecting in French psychiatry, see Saisselin 1985: 63–8; B.-A. Morel, for example, linked collecting to madness (1852: I, 412–13, 433–5).
[17] See Wilkinson 1996: 8, 113–15 and Bowman 1988.

varieties (1846: 837–8). Writers continued to allude to the connections between eccentricity, political radicalism, and mysticism. Nerval's historical gallery of 'philosophical eccentrics', *Les Illuminés* (1852), was subtitled 'the precursors of socialism'.[18] And in a lengthy study entitled *La France mistique: tablau des excentricités religieuses de ce tems* [sic] (1855) (Mystical France: A Tableau of the Religious Eccentricities of the Age), Alexandre Erdan catalogued an array of tendencies from Swedenborg and mesmerism, turning tables, and the thought of Ballanche and Lamennais to Saint-Simonianism, Fourierism, communism, and positivism, using the phrase 'religious eccentricity' to encompass them all.[19] After the failure of the 1848 Revolution it was easier to pathologize and objectify such figures, though they continued to elicit some sympathy and increasingly also nostalgia.

Champfleury's sketches in *Les Excentriques* portray many Parisian characters of the July Monarchy who are preoccupied by extraordinary schemes to improve society. Intermittently invoking medical rhetoric, Champfleury calls for the expansion of popularizing psychiatric texts (1877: 102–3). He avoids sustained analysis of the relationship between madness and eccentricity, despite the fact that many of his subjects display symptoms such as hallucinations and delusions of persecution. But his terminological qualifications prefigure subsequent medical interest in the gradations of insanity: 'he is not mad . . . but scarcely any better', the narrator's friend concludes of one eccentric; Champfleury labels his subjects 'the almost mad'; and individual cases are described as 'a little mad' and 'perhaps mad'. Occasionally they 'pass beyond the boundaries of eccentricity'.[20] 'Were I mad', begins the self-justificatory monologue of one eccentric, his conditional tense striking a characteristic note of uncertainty (104). Champfleury's work was seen by many reviewers as a perfect illustration of the theory of medical realism, a psychiatric textbook capable of 'transporting the reader to Bicêtre'.[21] This medical rhetoric did not meet with universal approval.[22] Champfleury's subsequent preface responded to criticism of the first edition, which, he states, largely concerned 'the bizarreness of the characters, their lowly position and above all the unhealthy aspect of their minds' (1877: 1).

[18] The subtitle needs to be interpreted cautiously; see Tyers 1998: 9–11 and Lokke 1987: 31.
[19] As Erdan acknowledges (1855: I, p. xxx).
[20] Champfleury 1877: 239, 20, 157, 197, 208.
[21] Prarond 1852: 145; see also Émile Chasles 1856: 463–4.
[22] See Prarond 1852: 145.

Just as the boundary between fairground freaks and bourgeois observers at times proved fluid, reflexive parallels between eccentrics and those who analysed them emerged in medical discourse. Writers and readers such as Champfleury who collected anecdotes of eccentricity legitimated their enquiry with reference to the model of the doctor, a collector of diseased bodies and minds. At times the two domains overlapped: English asylums were termed 'Museums for the Collection of Insanity', whilst the Salpêtrière was labelled a 'living pathological museum' by Jean-Martin Charcot. Bourgeois visitors could tour asylums in both nineteenth-century England and France, ostensibly for pedagogic purposes.[23] Dr Spitzner, the owner of popular waxworks, included in his displays a group of figures labelled 'The Lesson of Dr Charcot',[24] and some psychiatrists retained the skulls of deceased patients for their personal displays.[25] Yet collecting itself was strongly codified as an eccentric and obsessive activity, raising the question of whether doctors could consider themselves exempt.

If the figure of the eccentric collector tended to merge reflexively into that of the collector of eccentrics, intellectual eccentrics could also be seen as parodic mirror images of alienists, for both were fixated on rival visions of over-interpretation and the creation of all-encompassing explanatory systems.[26] Charles Bussy's *Les Toquades* (1858), for example, exploits this theme for comic effect. The figure it examines, namely the 'toqué'—'crackpot' or 'loony'—was a synonym of 'excentrique' in a lower, comic register, though it figured in some *fin-de-siècle* medical writing.[27] In the text, an imaginary head of the Parisian asylum of Charenton, Dr Muller, suffers from a mania for seeing borderline insanity everywhere outside the asylum.[28] The text lists a heterogeneous assortment of eccentric characters, including *l'homme à projets* (man of projects), *l'homme à systèmes* (man of systems), monomaniacs, thinkers, and prophets of the type portrayed by Nerval, Erdan, and Champfleury, as well as inventors, hypochondriacs, bluestockings, and feminists. Such figures are used to illustrate the thesis that everyone has a 'grain of madness'. Anecdotes are interspersed with illustrations

---

[23] On the carnivalesque origins of such tours, see Altick 1978: 44–5.
[24] Francis Scott, cited in Scull 1982: 186 n.; Didi-Hubermann 1982: 275, 33.
[25] Rigoli 2001: 192–205.
[26] See e.g. J.-J. Moreau 1859: 215–16, 227, HB12: 677; Morel 1860: 546, Tissot 1877: 83
[27] See Azam 1891.
[28] See Bussy 1858: 160–2. Leuret famously questions the distinction between bizarre ideas inside and outside the asylum (1834: 41–2).

Fig. 18. An obsessive collector of engravings, part of a series of *toqués*, or crackpots, by Gavarni. (Bussy 1858: 57) © British Library Board. All Rights Reserved. (12352.g.18)

by Gavarni (see Fig. 18), mainly of figures suffering from mono-mania or obsession. 'The madman belongs to tragedy, the *crackpot* to the vaudeville,' Dr Muller asserts (38), in a text which evinces a strong desire to render these potentially threatening figures harmless by casting them in amiable and anodyne roles. It nonetheless highlights genuine anxieties about the potential mirroring between 'intellectual' eccentrics and obsessive alienists. Similar uncertainties are evident in the writing of some alienists themselves.[29]

Most eccentrics whose sanity was called into question in literary and psychiatric discourse were male, owing to the concept's early association with culturally masculine preoccupations such as collecting and

---

[29] e.g. J.-J. Moreau 1859: 227.

research.[30] Female monomaniacs were discussed in medical literature as well as in fiction, but their form of monomania rarely relates to the field of intellectual enquiry. An element of the pathetic tended to intrude to a greater degree in their depiction, rather than the odd mixture of humour and contempt which coloured descriptions of male eccentrics. Two literary texts of the Second Empire portray equivocal cases of female insanity with notable pathos, suggesting that gender codification could significantly inflect representations of psychological oddity.

In 1852 the influential human palaeontologist Boucher de Perthes published an epistolary novel entitled *Emma, ou quelques lettres de femme* (Emma, or Some Letters from a Woman), whose central theme is female monomania. The novel, which recounts the descent into homicidal monomania of a beautiful English aristocrat, Emma de North***, seeks to undermine the nineteenth-century tendency to conflate insanity and immorality. (Étienne Esquirol had discussed such cases in detail, arguing that they demonstrated the localized nature of monomania.[31]) Characteristic of homicidal monomania, it proposes, is the inexplicable desire to murder one's family or friends. The narrative form of Boucher's novel, like the implied author's view of female insanity, is highly unusual, for it represents Emma's experience of insanity in the first person. A preface by an unnamed individual functions as a textual frame. Alerting readers to her 'malady', it proves curiously uncertain about its aetiology and meaning. It describes her as having 'a nature set apart from others' [un caractère à part], and concludes that, given her medical circumstances, 'we can scarcely be surprised at her eccentric manners' (1852: p. x). Nonetheless, it suggests both that the thirst for blood is more likely to afflict women and that it might be socially contagious, citing the example of the well brought up girls who manifested murderous violence during the political upheavals of 1814–15 in the South of France (1852: pp. v–vi). The alarming possibility that all women are latent murderers haunts the narrative, rather undermining its sympathetic portrayal of the heroine.

In the narrative, Emma's devoted French suitor, Jules de P**, becomes the object of her repeated attacks, which she responds to in lucid intervals with confusion and remorse. When one attack becomes public, despite Jules's willingness to collude in hiding her secret, she is obliged to choose between facing trial or being declared insane and thereby

---

[30] The writing of some female equivalents ('folles littéraires') are excerpted in Blavier 2001.

[31] See e.g. Esquirol 1838: II, 802.

being deemed unfit for marriage. Eventually she chooses to withdraw to a convent. Eccentricity typically functions as a warning sign: as one of Jules's friends reminds him, 'it is an inherited illness, and therefore an incurable illness. You know, as I do, of the death of her father and the eccentricities of her forebear' (107). Nonetheless, the text implies that her homicidal outbursts are wholly outside the remit of her will, for they are carried out in a state of somnambulistic trance. She repeatedly accuses herself of being a monster,[32] but others reject this conclusion. The narrator of the novel, indeed, repeatedly emphasizes that Emma suffers from a hereditary condition for which she is not responsible. In an age of psychiatric advance, the novel implies, observers can no longer take comfort in narratives of wickedness, hence the tragic aporia created by the malady: 'Though recognized as innocent, the [homicidal] monomaniac is banished from humanity, as the leper once was' (p. vii). The masochistic self-sacrifice of Jules, who is perceived by others as irrational and even unbalanced in his refusal to abandon Emma, hints that the text simultaneously tells a second story, that of contagion.[33] Emma's insanity has perhaps contaminated the strangely feminized Jules in the manner so anxiously evoked in the preface.

A poetic depiction of a female momonaniac written shortly after Boucher de Perthes's novel dramatizes similar ambiguities about innocence and guilt. Whilst wandering amongst the Parisian crowds, the narrator of Baudelaire's *Spleen de Paris* is accosted by the monomaniac Mademoiselle Bistouri, or 'Miss Scalpel', in the prose poem of that title. Bistouri's delusion consists in erotic fixation upon doctors and gruesome surgical operations. In the unshakeable belief that the narrator is a doctor, she invites him to her miserable home, lavishing affection upon him. He decides to follow because he sees her as a human puzzle, 'this unhoped-for enigma'.[34] The speaker compares his own obsession with interpreting Bistouri to the latter's monomania, terming this his own 'idée fixe'. He thus implicitly positions himself, as has been noted, as her mirror image;[35] in some respects, he appears akin to the intellectual monomaniacs portrayed by doctors of the period. By creating a parallel between Bistouri and the speaker, the text reworks the widespread cultural association between the eccentric and the obsessive Bohemian

[32] Morel 1852: 60, 82.   [33] Morel 1852: 136, 183.
[34] CB1: 353; Baudelaire 1970: 95.
[35] See Van Zuylen 2005: ch. 4; though the author pertinently analyses the parallels between the speaker and Bistouri, she does not link the speaker's *idée fixe* to the specific historical category of intellectual monomania, nor to the *chimère*.

eccentric-hunter, and positions the poetic speaker as a collector of
human oddities.

Baudelaire's text concludes with a meditation on the prevalence of
peculiarity in the city:

What oddities [bizarreries] does one not find in big cities when one knows how
to roam and how to look? Life swarms with innocent monsters. You, my God,
You the Creator, you the Master; you who have made both Law and Liberty;
you the sovereign who permits, you the judge who pardons; you who contain all
motives and all causes, and who, perhaps, have put a taste for the horrible in my
mind in order to convert my heart, like the cure at the point of the knife; Lord
have pity on, have pity on mad men and mad women! O Creator! can monsters
exist in the eyes of the One who alone knows why they exist, who alone knows
how they *have been made* and how they could *not have been made*?[36]

Bistouri's lucid form of 'bizarrerie' is emblematic of the type of borderline insanity that was found increasingly threatening by nineteenth-
century alienists, for it could remain concealed within the anonymity of
the city. The Salpêtrière asylum in which Bistouri is, precisely, *not* incarcerated, was described by Charcot as a 'living pathological museum'; in
Baudelaire's poem, conversely, the city becomes a vast open-air asylum.
Yet the moral deficiency often associated with insanity by Baudelaire's
contemporaries is called into question by his startlingly oxymoronic
phrase 'innocent monsters'. The speaker frames God as one of the sur-
geons in whom Bistouri has such irrational confidence, operating on the
soul of the speaker; their voluntary submission to a greater power creates
a further parallel between the two, echoing the masochistic fantasies of
other poems in the collection.[37] In an allegorical poem in the same
collection entitled 'Chacun sa chimère' (To Every Man his Chimera),
the speaker portrays affliction by a dominant obsession as being the lot
of *all* human beings. He personifies obsession as a mythological monster
of ambiguous sex, a chimera; the term was often used to denote the *idées
fixes* of eccentrics, and had connotations of delusion and insanity. The
poem once again implicitly blurs the boundaries between his readers,
his poetic persona, and 'bizarre' figures such as Bistouri.

Like Étienne Geoffroy Saint-Hilaire, who approvingly cited Montaigne's conclusion that 'Monsters are not monsters to God', or Gustave Flaubert, who proclaimed the 'legitimacy of monsters', Baudelaire's
poem suggests a powerful desire to redeem the marginal in the face of

---

[36] CB1: 355–6; Baudelaire 1970: 98, trans. modified.
[37] This perspective differs from Stephens' argument in 1999: 146 n. 82.

bourgeois disdain. In the narratives of both Boucher de Perthes and Baudelaire, female characters with bizarre behaviour are granted the paradoxical status of 'innocent monster', despite both the unsettling emotions they elicit in the male narrators.

The concept of eccentricity as a form of borderline insanity thus evolved significantly between 1830 and the early Second Empire. It soon ceased to evoke the alleged English refusal to medicalize strange behaviour, and instead became associated with the popular French category of monomania, particularly in relation to collecting, 'intellectual passions', and theoretical systems. This gave rise to a potential homology between the eccentricity of the alienist and writer, in the one instance, and that of the peculiar figures they examined with their real or metaphorical 'scalpels', in the other. Though the terms 'excentricité' and 'excentrique' retained their connotations of madness in some literary and journalistic contexts well after 1848, attempts to analyse the exact nature of the relationship between the two moved into the province of professional alienists in the latter part of the century.

Eccentricity in psychiatric taxonomies

Increasing medical interest in eccentricity arose at a crucial juncture in the evolution of the psychiatric profession, for which three related reasons may be suggested. First, the dominant paradigm of Pinel and Esquirol, which viewed madness from a moral and social perspective, was increasingly challenged from the early 1850s by the paradigm of degeneration initiated by Prosper Lucas and B.-A. Morel and subsequently popularized by Valentin Magnan. Often characterized as organicist and biological, and ascribing madness largely to hereditary lesions of the nervous system, this new framework made degeneration the hermeneutic master key to a vast network of pathologies. It also repudiated Pinel's 'moral treatment', since insanity was held to result from incurable physiological defects.

The 'medical concept of national decline' responded to the crisis of liberal optimism after 1848, and was progressively exacerbated by defeat in the Franco-Prussian War, the Commune, and fears concerning colonial expansion and the declining French birth rate.[38] The success of hereditarian thought largely arose from its psychic efficacy; it 'offered

[38] See Nye 1984.

emotional assurance and intellectual comfort in the face of phenomena that frightened bourgeois sensibilities and mystified middle-class
ideologues'.[39] The differences between the two paradigms should not
be overstated: a distinct physiological focus was present in discussions
of monomania before 1850, whilst strong spiritual awareness under-
lay B.-A. Morel's vision of decline. A change of conceptual focus was
nonetheless crucial to the self-description of many alienists during the
latter part of the century.

Second, the 1850s witnessed concerted expansionism in French
psychiatry. Having gained professional confidence through attaining
a near-monopoly in the treatment of full madness, alienists turned
their attention to mastering various types of 'partial' or 'incomplete'
madness, seen as an extension of their earlier, highly successful research
on monomania. (Jan Goldstein terms this process the 'appropriation of
the *demi-fou*'; 1987: 331–8.)

Finally, in the course of the century, the medical profession replaced
the structuring division of health and disease with that of normal
and pathological, and attempted to define the second pair through
quantitative measurements, which were supposedly objective and value-
free. Normality was framed in terms of a statistical biological norm,
any departure from which was labelled pathological. Since the normal
nonetheless assumed a qualitative and normative character, the opposition readily mapped on to a realm of purely social norms, creating metaphorical connections with other forms of deviance, including
eccentricity.[40] By situating the pathological on a continuum with the
normal, the theories of the physiologist Claude Bernard undermined
the idea that a binary opposition separated disease from health, and by
extension madness from sanity.[41] Degeneration theory thus encouraged
the blurring of distinctions between mental, physiological, moral, and
social deviance, as the concept of pathology was mapped onto those
of immorality, criminality, and violence.[42] The normal–pathological
opposition also merged with the aesthetic opposition between the
neoclassical values of harmony and moderation, central to Bernard's

[39] Dowbiggin 1991: 158; see also Castel 1976: 149–56 and Pick 1989. Most recent
accounts of the history of French psychiatry have been significantly influenced by Michel
Foucault 1961, though his study does not consider the delicate conceptual relationship
between madness and eccentricity. Foucault's subsequent analyses of 'abnormality' (1999)
are more helpful in illuminating evolving 19th-cent. attitudes towards such problematic
and liminal categories.

[40] See Canguilhem 2003: 18–51, Foucault 1983: 35–6, and Nye 1984: 46–8.

[41] See Goldstein 1987: 332–3.   [42] Nye 1984: 48.

theory of equilibrium, and the Romantic values of heterogeneity and intensity.

As a liminal state already linked to monomania in the literary imagination, eccentricity was a natural candidate for psychiatric attention.[43] In psychiatric discourse the personal noun *un excentrique* was often used interchangeably with others such as the *monomane*, *original*, *illuminé*, *instable*, *maniaque*, and later the *dégénéré supérieur* (superior degenerate) and *déséquilibré* (unbalanced individual)—and, in a more popular register, the *détraqué*, *cerveau brûlé*, and *cerveau fêlé*, variations on the theme of the *toqué* or crackpot. Distinctions between 'an' eccentric and eccentric behaviour were blurred, since many subcategories of the insane might commit eccentric acts: 'an imbecile can simultaneously be an eccentric', and is probably other things as well, the *fin-de-siècle* medical popularizer Alexandre Cullerre complained, giving voice to a lengthy tradition of anxiety about the use of popular language in medical writing.[44] The process of renaming served to side-step actual analysis of borderline insanity, creating an alarming degree of conceptual vagueness. Linguistic proliferation undermined scientific neutrality, and created networks of subliminal associations.

Eccentricity was diagnosed on the basis of potentially minute infractions of mental and social norms. Claude Bernard's theories again influenced psychiatric discourse: his model of equilibrium, the first modern elaboration of homeostasis, staged the body in a constant drama, consisting in its efforts to maintain its 'internal environment'. Bernard famously noted of the organism that 'its equilibrium results from a continuous and *delicate* compensation established by the most *sensitive* of balances' (my emphasis).[45] Alienists increasingly appealed to Bernard's metaphor of delicacy, together with a heightening of the rhetoric of interpretative skill which had characterized the profession from the outset.[46] Eccentricity could occur in any semiotic system: ways of feeling, willing, imagining, and judging, for example, or modes of appearance and self-presentation, 'whether in an external habit, in the way in which one is dressed, does one's hair, walks, writes, or talks, or in a bizarre movement, expression, tic, or

---

[43] Eccentricity fulfils Ian Hacking's four 'vectors' characterizing an 'ecological niche' for transient mental illness (1998: 1–2).

[44] Cullerre 1888: 51; see also 226.

[45] Bernard 1878: 113. On the concept of equilibrium in Bernard, see Schiller 1967: 172–200.

[46] See Rigoli 2001: 19–33.

grimace'.[47] The alienist, in consequence, styled himself as sensitive interpreter of signs that were increasingly difficult to grasp.[48] Insanity and sanity were frequently construed as adjoining lands whose borders were fluid. The point of contact between the two was portrayed as shifting (*delicate limits*; *imperceptible line*s; *something equivocal, fluid, and uncertain*).[49] 'Modern' psychiatric sensitivity towards the existence of more subtle forms of madness was often contrasted with outmoded belief in fixed categories (*mathematical delimitations*; *fixed and precise limits*).[50] Occasionally eccentric patients were described in cartographical and ethnological terms as minds that were 'out of line' and 'outside the frame', belonging to an 'intermediary' class, state, or race.[51] Implicitly drawing upon the opposition between art and science, alienists appropriated the intuitive finesse of the artist to characterize their research, yet endowed it with scientific legitimacy.

Despite such dramatizations of hermeneutic uncertainty, nineteenth-century French psychiatry devoted considerable effort to constructing and revising its taxonomic systems, and these formed the context for analyses of eccentricity. Alexandre Cullerre provided a retrospective analysis of the struggle of alienists to define 'semi-madness' throughout the century. The categories they devised, he suggested, were merely a series of variations upon Pinel's inaugural category of *folie raisonnante* or reasoning madness (1888: 25–7). As a proponent of the organicist model, Cullerre interprets this taxonomic struggle in terms of a narrative of incipient chaos, in which categories proliferate (for example, reasoning (mono)mania, madness of acts or *folie des actes*, lucid madness, moral insanity, and conscious madness). The endless play of naming and renaming substituted for real analysis. Only the success of the organicist theory of mind propagated by B.-A. Morel and J.-J. Moreau de Tours, he holds, in a typically whiggish narrative, finally created consensus, and conceptual mastery of the elusive field of borderline insanity.

The category of eccentricity interested these alienists, both active during the transitional period of early Second Empire alienism, partially owing to its strong cultural connection to monomania, a doctrine which they attempted to dislodge from its prominent position in mental

---

[47] J.-J. Moreau 1859: 211; Régis 1906: 406, the latter also cited in Dallemagne 1885: 592.
[48] See Tardieu 1880: 152.
[49] Respectively Morel 1860: 543 n. and Cullerre 1888: 7 and 24 (my emphasis).
[50] Legrand du Saulle 1864: 54 (my emphasis).
[51] Ball 1885: 73, J.-J. Moreau 1859: 211–12, 242.

medicine. In *La Psychologie morbide* (1859), J.-J. Moreau de Tours formulated the concept of the *état mixte* or 'mixed state' (205–6), exemplified by the eccentric, but sharply distinguished this category from monomania. The latter entailed the mere 'juxtaposition' of healthy ideas with diseased ideas in relation to one specific subject; the mixed state, in contrast, was evoked through imagery of inextricable fusion and the monstrous disruption of categories.[52]

In his *Études cliniques* (1852), Morel cautioned that the eccentric's astonishing behaviour distracted people from understanding its true causes, and warned that it was particularly difficult to diagnose madness in eccentric individuals of high rank. He attempts to defuse potential objections to his pathologizing drive: 'I will always be able to distinguish between a sickly, bizarre, eccentric character, and a confirmed state of insanity.' Nonetheless, he adds a cautionary note. Were the force of general reason not to keep such individual aberrations in check, the deleterious consequences of eccentricity—principally the shame and suffering of the eccentric's relatives—would be 'incalculable' (1852: I, 406). Morel became one of the most high profile critics of the category of monomania during 1853–4, and his interventions in psychiatric debate contributed to the concept's demise. Perhaps surprisingly, therefore, he advocated retaining the term to describe eccentrics as late as 1860: 'It is these men that I would above all like to be labelled as *monomaniacs*, a term which should be erased from the legal medicine of the insane' (1860: 31 n. 1). Rather than implying that eccentricity, like monomania, could be localized, Morel's writings suggested that it functioned as a sign of future perturbations of the nervous system, like smoke indicating imminent conflagration. He subscribed to Moreau's view that '*madness* and *eccentricity* are two *pathological* states . . . with a common origin'—namely heredity.[53]

Morel uses the term 'excentrique' so widely in his psychiatric writing that it has been interpreted as merely a general synonym for insanity.[54] Like Moreau, however, Morel associated eccentricity with a range of more specific traits, including mysticism, systematizing thought, and bibliomania. He also illustrates his accounts of eccentricity with historical and literary material, showing awareness of dominant cultural codes of oddity.[55] Morel's descriptions of female eccentrics, however,

---

[52] See Ch. 7 above. [53] J.-J. Moreau 1859: 188. [54] Rigoli 2001: 199.
[55] La Rochefoucauld and La Bruyère, he proposes, satirized 'the eccentricities of weak and feeble minds' (1852: I, 409). See Morel 1860: 31 n. 1 and 532 for further examples.

stand in sharp contrast to the 'innocent monsters' of Boucher de Perthes and Charles Baudelaire. Three of Morel's case histories placed under the heading of 'unhealthy tendencies towards eccentricity', for example, narrate the stories of decidedly guilty female monsters whose mothers had been insane.

Morel claimed that the hereditary transmission of pathology was 'more complete' for women than for men (1860: 555); indeed, metaphors of feminine perversity and the archetype of Eve underpin his analyses.[56] Madame Charlotte P., for instance, is marked out from an early age by 'eccentric dispositions' which are indulged by her parents. These include engaging in masculine activities such as drinking, vigorous physical exercise, and having a 'passionate character'. Upon marrying at twenty, her eccentricity becomes full insanity, evident in her avoiding her familial duties: 'People hoped that the new conditions created by motherhood would modify such eccentric tendencies, but nothing of the sort transpired…She went to Paris, where she frequented famous authors, eccentric men and scheming women. She made herself into an author, and published novels whose style, ideas, and sentiments reflected the sickly dispositions of her mind' (1860: 556). Once confined to the asylum and the care of Morel, she continues such feverish intellectual activity, contesting her incarceration, writing letters and dossiers to prove she is not mad, and finally, upon converting to Catholicism, winning a literary competition. All are interpreted as pathological symptoms.

Madame C. was also 'disposed to eccentricity' from an early age, and once again this tendency is exacerbated after marriage. Accusing her husband of what Morel considers 'implausible things', namely secret debauchery, she denounces him to his superiors for financial impropriety in order to make him lose his position. Though considered incapable of bringing up her children, she appears disconcertingly lucid when questioned by magistrates.

Finally, Madame X. is, like Charlotte P., marked out from an early age by her brilliant intellectual gifts. Marriage again precipitates her decline; she becomes indifferent to her household and children's education, and damages the family business by ignoring customers. Once in the asylum, she turns her intellectual gifts to helping the other inmates contest their incarceration: 'She listened to their complaints and demands, wrote

---

[56] For an overview of the complex relationship between gender and madness, see Tombs 1994: 55–61.

letters and reports on behalf of her companions in misfortune just as the best lawyer might have; she analysed and interpreted the motives behind their actions, and at times corrected their errors of judgement with astonishing lucidity and reasonableness' (1860: 559). In Morel's narratives of all three women, the terms 'excentrique' and 'excentricité' play an important role in creating an impression of pathology, for what is at stake is precisely the moral character of the women and their refusal, or inability, to conform to the codes of bourgeois domesticity. His chronology clearly implies that marriage is the trigger that makes supposedly latent eccentricities erupt into full insanity. With circular logic, he argues that it is further proof of their malady that it persists *even* when married.[57]

The persistent moralism which surrounded fictional discussion of eccentricity thus filtered into real-life dramas. The term 'excentrique' had performative force such that it could help justify incarceration where few other grounds existed. It contributed to the alienist's quasi-novelistic framing of the patient's moral character, as we see from the case of Marie Esquiron, who was wrongfully incarcerated by her husband and brother.[58] In a document that she sent in 1893 to the Minister of Justice whilst confined to a *maison de santé*, she contested the diagnosis of insanity reached by three alienists, including the influential Valentin Magnan. In a typical example of the ingenious interpretive strategies pathologized by Morel and many of his peers, she cites passages from their diagnosis, two of which concern eccentricity, in order to contest them. In one citation, the alienists evoke a descent from eccentricity into full insanity: 'These preoccupations had deep roots in her past. It was not only a matter of one isolated act, it was merely one episode to be added to many others in a life whose peculiarities, eccentricities, and delirious beliefs [la bizarrerie, les excentricités, les conceptions délirantes] are too numerous to be counted.'[59] Another excerpt she cites concerns her relationship to the public gaze: 'She believed herself an object of hatred and contempt for everyone in the country where she had all her possessions; she believed herself to be

---

[57] i.e. when they become sexually active, a state held to lessen female susceptibility to hysteria.

[58] Esquiron's case could be contrasted with Hersilie Rouy, who, also contesting her incarceration, describes eccentricity as a deliberate strategy she uses to draw attention to her plight and hence avoid being forgotten (Rouy 1883: 170–1). I am grateful to Susannah Wilson for these references.

[59] Cited in Esquiron 1893: 8.

persecuted, without realizing that the losses she suffered had no other cause than the eccentricity of her behaviour and language' (10).

Esquiron's response is typical of the struggles to control interpretation which intensified during the 1880s with the advent of an 'anti-alienist' movement.[60] She turns their accusations back against them, accusing them of disordered interpretation:

The alienist gentlemen give free reign to their fertile imaginations; without having known me in the past, without ever having met me, they maintain that there were *numerous episodes*, *peculiarities* on my part, *eccentricities*, and *delirious beliefs*. That is easy to say. It is a well-established fact that alienists see madmen everywhere . . . To which delirious beliefs are they referring? These are empty, meaningless words. That much is obvious.   (Esquiron 1893: 8)

Her criticism of both the terminological vagueness of medical discourse and of doctors' mania for identifying hidden madness had been anticipated both by writers hostile to mental medicine and by alienists themselves, suggesting that the latter were uneasily aware of the coherence of her position.[61] Medical discussions of eccentric character were clearly influenced by novelistic notions of plausibility, such as assumptions about the feminine vocation of marriage and maternity.

The distance travelled since the widespread equation of the eccentric with the monomaniac and victim of the *idée fixe* during the 1830s is notable. Whilst both are forms of 'incomplete' madness, the idea of a single locus of mania, without any relationship to other faculties, was progressively abandoned in organicist psychiatry. Eccentricity, by implication, could no longer be contained and controlled. The interpenetration of cultural, religious, and medical imagery encouraged the widespread slippage of categories, as borderline insanity and moral perversity were increasingly conflated.   ʼ

On the brink of madness: eccentricity as 'superior degeneration'

Attempts to conceptualize eccentricity were shaped by specific narrative patterns. This was due largely to the influence of degeneration theory in the latter part of the century, whose proponents were fascinated by the chronology of dissolution and decay. Of the various narrative models which shaped writing on ambiguous forms of insanity, two

---

[60]   See Fauvel 2002: 207–16.
[61]   e.g. P. Janet 1867: 86 and J.-J. Moreau 1859: 212–14.

predominate: the theatrical notion of cathartic unveiling, and the biblical myth of the fall from grace. This appropriation of literary techniques was designed to render eccentricity legible. Alienists sought to reassure bourgeois readers puzzled by the apparent unpredictability of eccentric individuals by plotting out an orderly conclusion to their disorderly behaviour.

Eccentricity was portrayed in the writing of alienists in terms reminiscent of melodrama and sentimental fiction, and was linked to a dynamic tension between visibility and invisibility. Alexandre Cullerre proposed a taxonomic distinction between 'eccentric ideas' and 'eccentric acts' (1888: 121), which effectively reformulated Trélat's influential division between 'madness of speech' and 'madness of acts' in *La Folie lucide* (1861: pp. xii–xiii). One important consequence of either distinction was the view that explicit morbidity, easily 'readable' from the trail of astonishment and scandal it leaves in its wake, alternated with a more sinister form of concealed morbidity.

Alienists frequently exhorted their readers to apply medical theories to their personal experience. Their frequent use of generic 'one' and 'we' assumes that all readers have encountered eccentricity and are thus capable of recognizing it instantly.[62] Eccentrics endowed with rhetorical brilliance were, however, simultaneously represented as being adept at frustrating the interpretative efforts of family, friends, and colleagues. They were considered prone to violent outbursts in which the underlying sickness emerged, in scenes of cathartic unveiling. In the words of Morel, 'the veil is torn asunder, and the truth comes to light', and the many troubling instances of eccentricity that had baffled observers suddenly fall into place within the new framework of madness.[63] But as a sense of social menace intensified towards the end of the century, borderline insanity was increasingly framed as a condition that escaped detection.[64] Panic was aroused in the bourgeois reader at the suggestion that innocent public encounters might not be all they seemed. Ulysse Trélat argued, in 1861, that 'a great number of madmen live amongst us, meddling with our actions, our interests, and our affections' (6–7). Professor Ball took up the theme in his inaugural lecture at the Asile Sainte-Anne in 1885, which alarmingly concluded that there were some 600,000 borderline insane in France. He remarked that 'amongst our

---

[62] See e.g. Morel 1860: 543 n. 1; Cullerre 1888: 158–9.
[63] Morel 1852: I, 407; see Trélat 1861: 6–15.
[64] See Pick 1989, Dowbiggin 1991: 152–4.

fellow citizens whom we meet every day, whom we jostle at every moment in public places, there are many who … could quite easily pass for mad'.[65] Both alienists evoke physical proximity with imagery of nauseating bodily intimacy. The ability of the average bourgeois citizen to decipher eccentric behaviour was increasingly called into question, necessitating the intervention of medical experts.

Such 'concealed' eccentrics were a hundred times worse than true madmen, concluded the alienist Ambroise Tardieu, since their morbidity propagated unobserved and they left their families with no legal redress. His rhetoric precisely echoed contemporaneous descriptions of the clandestine prostitute as a menace a hundred times worse than the regulated *fille publique*.[66] Legal medicine repeatedly discussed the difficulties posed when seemingly sane individuals used rational means to justify 'eccentricities' such as unsuitable marriages and capricious testaments.[67] The eccentric was placed in a contradictory position, held to be both familiar and exotically alien. The alienist, in turn, promoted a hermeneutics of suspicion verging on paranoia.

In a popular work of 1885 which remained in print until 1923, Emmanuel Régis situated eccentricity in the category of 'disequilibrium', less severe than complete degeneration or physical monstrosity, but more severe than the 'désharmoniaque' who suffers from mood swings. Often, he writes,

[o]riginality is brought to light by an imperious and obsessive inclination which pushes the subject in a particular intellectual and moral direction to the detriment of every practical and useful occupation; for example to surround himself with birds, flowers, or cats, to collect insignificant objects … to become absorbed in research, calculations, ridiculous inventions. … [P]olitical and religious exaltation, eroticism, spontaneous deception, and the love of intrigue … are other inclinations which are frequently found in these individuals, whom the public vulgarly refers to as eccentrics, maniacs, and crackpots.   (1906: 406–7)

Though fairly broad, his description reiterates many of the previous cultural connotations of eccentricity, including collecting, intellectual obsession, and mysticism. Susceptible to a range of typically *fin-de-siècle* disorders such as neurasthenia, his eccentrics merge into the flux of city

---

[65] Ball 1885: 73; see Pick 1989: 43.
[66] See Tardieu 1880: 152 and Saint-Victor 1889: 95 respectively.
[67] Legrand du Saulle, for instance, narrates the legal struggles of two aristocrats of consistently eccentric behaviour to regain control over their financial affairs (see 1864: 48–62 and 1881: 406–13).

life, and, he notes, appear before the asylum or courts only when they cede to sudden and violent outbursts of madness.

In addition to discourses of cathartic unveiling, degeneration theory gave rise to a number of distinctive narrative trajectories to plot out the lives of vulnerable individuals. Claude Bernard's model of homeostasis implied a narrative of constant, subtle adjustments, as well as sudden ruptures in which the environment changed, followed by a new process of adjustment. Despite occasional suggestions that the tide could be reversed, the degeneration paradigm was based upon a narrative of progressive entropy. Taken together, these two models, in which decline was framed in terms of a gradual loss of equilibrium, greatly influenced discourse on eccentricity as a form of borderline insanity. In degeneration theory, eccentricity was construed as the sinister harbinger of full disintegration, the eccentric as a 'superior degenerate' occupying the first rung on the ladder of decline.[68] But if eccentricity was 'true madness in, as it were, an embryonic state',[69] or the first letter in the alphabet of madness, at what exact moment did precarious equilibrium shift into definitive disequilibrium?

Several narrative models existed in the latter part of the century. The fall could be abrupt. Describing the fate of 'degenerate eccentrics', Tardieu writes: 'They are not slow to debase themselves, and, since they find neither in their conscience nor in their judgement any brake which could restrain them, and since they are soon rejected from the company of honest and reasonable people, they fall from rung to rung to the lowest possible level of degradation' (1880: 153). This description of decline exemplifies the concept's over-determination. The 'fall' is charged with connotations at once moral, religious, biological, social, and economic. Those in the eccentric's social circle are, this time, credited with intuitive discernment of pathology, contradicting the view that the eccentric represents an insidious threat.

There was also, in contrast, a model of slow decline, the time-span of which could be a whole lifetime. B.-A. Morel argued that many eccentrics finished their lives by committing suicide, or suffering from imbecility or dementia (1860: 532). In a succession of bleak and quasi-novelistic anecdotes, he evokes the negative spiral of degeneration. An 'eccentric and erotic lady', for example, who at the age of 70 spent her fortune in marrying a young man, left to her daughter a 'bizarre, apathetic, indifferent, and disorderly character'. This daughter,

---

[68] Dallemagne 1885: 592.   [69] P. Moreau 1888: 207.

in turn, had six eccentric children: '[T]hey were all marked out by their eccentric, disorderly, and wild characters...by their delirious actions; and by the whole panoply of bad instinctive dispositions which have determined us to create a new category for these sad representatives of the hereditary transmission of bad character' (1860: 538–9). Elsewhere, he portrays the dynamic as slower, suggesting that the mental disequilibrium of the first generation becomes neurosis in the second, and in the third, an innate predisposition to 'dangerous and eccentric acts'. By the fourth generation, little can be hoped for.[70] Narratives of imperceptible decline raised anxieties about the weakening of hereditary capital, preoccupying families contemplating marital alliances.[71] Signs were often read in one member of a family and conclusions drawn about the likely fate of others.[72]

It was alternatively suggested that the fall from health could be warded off, at least for a time. J.-J. Moreau de Tours had proposed that madness could alternate unpredictably with eccentricity across generations, trapping the family in an oscillating pattern of contamination and dilution and transforming the eccentric into a metaphorical mixed-race child (1859: 187). A perpetual balancing act was also held to operate at the level of the individual self. Various suggestive metaphors evoked the eccentric's efforts to avoid the narrative closure of full insanity; on the brink of collapse, the mind still struggled to preserve its equilibrium. Legrand du Saulle described the borderline case in terms of architectural structure: 'in many cases, if the *self* has trembled, it has not yet crumbled to the extent that it is nothing more than a ruin' (1864: 53). Eccentrics were portrayed swaying tenuously at the top of the ladder of degeneration,[73] and lingering in a state of instability and nervous disequilibrium 'which is no longer illness, but not yet health'.[74] Such comments positioned the eccentric in permanent narrative limbo.

Homeostatic metaphors were taken furthest by Paul Moreau, the alienist son of the considerably more famous Jacques-Joseph Moreau de Tours, in *Les Excentriques* (1894). The text plagiarized significantly from existing medical literature, particularly his father's analysis of eccentricity from 1859, but its relentless emphasis on equilibrium was new:

---

[70] Cited in Cullerre 1888: 31.
[71] This anxiety was evident in the French tradition of obligatory medical examinations before marriage.
[72] e.g. J.-J. Moreau 1859: 189.   [73] Dallemagne 1885: 592.
[74] Cullerre 1888: 21.

'the eccentric is a perpetual candidate for madness, but he does not fall into it; he stops on the brink of the abyss', he argues (1894: 6), using a second striking image: 'the individuals who are the subject of this work belong to the group of madmen who keep their balance on the tightrope between reason and madness, leaning to the right, leaning to the left, but not falling' (20). The mind's ability to ward off external and internal threats to its 'internal environment' generates continuing dramatic suspense.

More pessimistically, there was a narrative of contagion which recalled the paradox of eccentricity as an imitative phenomenon. This narrative was also most explicit in Paul Moreau's study, which portrays episodes of incomprehensible behaviour such as eccentric journeys, marriages, duels, and testaments. One doctor commented that it resembled nothing so much as selected highlights from the daily newspapers,[75] and indeed Moreau blames the press for feeding an 'epidemic' of eccentricity by implicitly encouraging readers to emulate the bizarre actions they read about in the *fait divers* (1894: 22–4). His conclusion, though, suddenly strikes an alarming note. Whilst in times of political stability such episodes are of little social import, during periods of unrest 'the peaceable eccentrics we have just seen will be unleashed, will be transformed into wild beasts, thirsty only for blood and for massacre' (1894: 117). Paul Moreau distinguishes in this and other works between two forms of eccentricity. He considers genuine, 'morbid' eccentricity to be timeless, in an entry worthy of Flaubert's dictionary of received ideas: 'ECCENTRICITY—this mental disposition is assuredly too well known not to have been noticed in all historical periods, under whatever label it was known at the time' (1888: 207). In contrast, he argues that 'imitative' eccentricity is responsible for the contemporary epidemic of eccentricity that he suggests arose in 1889 (1894: 26). His distinction is evidently spurious, since he attributes even the imitative eccentric's impressionability to hereditary weakness of personality, and holds that it is this weakness that makes them vulnerable to political demagoguery. Whilst drawing on distinctively *fin-de-siècle* concepts, his argument effectively reformulates one of the most influential of the points his father had made in 1859: that those who participated in the Revolutionary turmoil of 1848 suffered from mental weakness and suggestibility. This theory elicited renewed interest amongst alienists after the Commune who sought to attribute this event to a 'vent de

[75] Dallemagne 1885: 593.

folie' ('gust of madness').[76] The language of hypnotism, suspicion of the crowd, and fear of weakness of character characterized much discourse on borderline insanity at this time, though few theoretical advances were made in French psychiatry in the last two decades of the century.[77]

Finally, despite the obsession with eccentricity as a harbinger of decline and entropy, some alienists proposed an unexpectedly optimistic narrative of salvation in which the eccentric was portrayed as a socially necessary source of innovation and creativity. This tendency, which drew on a parallel and often controversial strand of debate in mental medicine, deserves to be examined in more detail.

The medicalization of genius: Bohemian teratology

To many, the rambling 'systems' of nineteenth-century Parisian eccentrics, Bohemians, and visionary thinkers provided unequivocal evidence of madness, a debased form of originality with little in its favour.[78] Attempts to ascertain the exact relationship between genius, eccentricity, and madness became prominent in European psychiatric discourse from the 1860s to around 1920. These debates inevitably drew on the mythologies of the eccentric artist and 'great man' which had arisen in German and English Romanticism and in Parisian Bohemia.

The sociologist George Becker has influentially interpreted medical debate about the 'mad genius', a phrase not actually used at the time, in terms of labelling theory. Though Romantic artists self-consciously embraced eccentric lifestyles in order to proclaim their superiority to the rest of society, he argues, their strategy went awry during the latter part of the century, when their deviance was reinterpreted as pathology by the medical profession.[79] Many artists came to internalize the label, considering their own madness inevitable. Becker's distaste for the 'unsavoury' and self-conscious perversions of early Romantic writers colours his rather moralizing efforts to 'blame' artists for their

---

[76] J. Laborde (1872: p. iii), drawing on J.-J. Moreau 1859: 77. See Dowbiggin 1991: 154–6.

[77] See Dowbiggin 1991: 159.

[78] Even Raymond Queneau, who sought out forgotten 19th-cent. geniuses in the national archives with the aim of rehabilitating them, admitted to eventual disappointment at the tedious obsessiveness of his *fous littéraires* (2002: 16).

[79] Becker 1978: 55–6, 128.

own pathologization later in the century.[80] His chronology initially appears to capture the evolution of attitudes to genius in French culture, in which the flamboyant exploits of the Jeune-France and Bousingots of 1830 were almost immediately followed by the first attempts by alienists such as Lélut to interpret genius as a form of illness. But not all early Romantic theories of genius were as insouciant as his analysis suggests. Like that of pathology, furthermore, the label of eccentricity took on different meanings in different contexts, and literary representations continued to function as counter-discourses even at the height of medical suspicion of genius.

The romantic model of genius received its most compelling medical expression in J.-J. Moreau de Tours' *La Psychologie morbide*. Moreau's controversial assertion that genius, eccentricity, and pathology were inseparable was placed at the head of the volume in order to emphasize its importance: 'The mental disposition which leads one man to distinguish himself from others by the originality of his thoughts and ideas, by his eccentricity or the energy of his affective faculties, and by the transcendence of his intellectual faculties, stems from the same organic conditions of which *madness* and *idiocy* are the most complete expressions' (1859: p. v). Moreau underpins this claim with a proto-organicist theory of hereditary pathology, and illustrates it by means of a gallery of celebrated historical figures in whom he discerns eccentricities that reveal underlying pathology. Subsequent discussions of Moreau's work continue to stress the role of eccentricity in the debate, as in one gloss: 'Men of genius are subject to certain peculiarities, eccentricities, and distractions, which closely resemble madness and which can lead to it.'[81] Moreau's work was heavily criticized upon publication, however, and not reprinted.

Many of the criticisms levelled at Moreau's work concerned his attempts to link genius to eccentricity. For the philosopher Paul Janet, the key charges against Moreau's theory are lack of empirical rigour and the potential for fraud. 'He speaks of transcendence, of *superiority*, of *eccentricity*, of *originality*, etc', he writes, 'but those are merely words without any precise meaning' (1867: 86), his argument echoing the scientific suspicion of ordinary language which dated back to the Idéologues.[82] Since eccentricity is both ubiquitous and potentially

---

[80] Thus undermining his own allegedly 'agnostic' methodology; see Becker 1978: 55, 125. He also provides little socio-historical contextualization.

[81] Paul Janet 1867: 96; see also Genil-Perrin 1913: 191.

[82] See Jordanova 1984: 23.

fraudulent, he proposes, it is useless as a criterion for judging genius. When the painter Anne-Louis Girodet worked at night wearing a large hat covered with candles, for instance, his eccentricity constituted a Romantic 'mystification of the bourgeois' rather than madness. Janet concludes that Moreau has been overly influenced by the Romantic concept of genius. In *De la raison, du génie et de la folie* (1861) (On Reason, Genius, and Madness), Pierre Flourens is similarly critical. He defines the relationship between eccentricity and genius as circular: once it has been decided that a given artist is a genius, the smallest sign is marshalled as proof, whether '[t]he slightest eccentricity' or 'the most insignificant tendency towards apparent foolishness or distraction' (114).

The philosopher Albert Lemoine attacks Moreau on the grounds that that the latter's theory of genius is unable to account for the ubiquity of minor nervous troubles (1862: 266). He attempts to rehabilitate Socrates, famously diagnosed as suffering from pathological hallucinations in Lélut's 1836 study *Le Démon de Socrate*, as an individual whose eccentricities remain within the boundaries of normality:

> The figure of Socrates will remain forever shrouded in mystery ... Being mad or strange [singulier], bizarre or suffering from hallucinations, these are quite different things. Who, after all, is not bizarre, who is not strange? Nobody is made like everyone else, each person is an individual, and this is even truer of great men than of others. Every man has a grain of madness, said Aristotle, but is a touch enough to be mad ... and if a grain is not enough, is a gram? (292–3)

Lemoine's rejection of materialism coincides with willingness to accept the limitations of medical knowledge in the face of individual variation, contrasting sharply with dominant medical theories of decline.

Though more influential French theorists of morbid heredity did not contest Moreau de Tours's pathologization of genius, they appeared generally indifferent to the topic: 'neither Morel nor Magnan, the true fathers of degenerationism, was overly concerned with the deep psychology of the artist in the way that Moreau de Tours was.'[83] Moreau's work nonetheless achieved a substantial if dubious intellectual legacy in its influence on Cesare Lombroso's *Genio et follia* (Genius and Madness) (1864), a substantially revised edition of which was republished in 1888 as *L'uomo di genio* (The Man of Genius) and subsequently

---

[83] Magnan, for instance, critiqued Lombroso's portrait of the congenital criminal but ignored his theorization of the genius as a degenerate (Huertas 1993: 307).

translated into French in 1889 as *L'Homme de génie*. Lombroso's texts came to function as the classic affirmation of the identity of genius and madness. Why, then, had Moreau's work previously met with such a hostile reception in France, despite its apparent timeliness for wider European debates? French criticism of the work is marked, in part, by a desire to uphold the neoclassical ideal of rational genius associated with seventeenth-century culture and a rejection of the Romantic values of imagination and fantasy. Neoclassical aesthetics retained its prestige in many fields of nineteenth-century French culture, including prominent public forms of art such as architecture; indeed, a neoclassical emphasis on the need for harmonious moderation exerted a subterranean influence on much scientific rhetoric, including that of doctors and alienists. In addition, anxiety about national decline doubtless influenced the desire for a manly and robust model of creativity to dislodge the feminized figure of the Romantic artist.

The preface to the 1889 French translation of Lombroso's *L'Homme de génie*, by the French alienist Charles Richet, is typical of the ambivalence surrounding genius in French culture. Richet interprets genius within the framework of teratological science. A genius is a deviation from the norm ('an anomalous being, an *exception*'), a departure from the statistical average which, in the medical philosophy of Broussais, Comte, and Bernard, entails pathology *or* monstrosity.[84] A metaphor seals his argument: when sown, a handful of apparently identical grains will produce some shorter and some taller plants. 'Well! All of them, the large and the small alike, will be monstrosities and invalids.' Yet Richet is clearly uneasy with this image, for he suggests that rather than being termed a 'degenerate', the genius should be termed a *progénéré* (progenerate), an instance of excessive rather than arrested development (p. viii).[85] In terms of contemporaneous teratological theory, Richet's strategy was unconvincing, since 'monsters through excess', such as conjoined twins, were considered just as anomalous as 'monsters through lack', those lacking the usual number of body parts.

The conflation of authors and their works became more common as writers were diagnosed on the basis of their literary output in medical examples of 'pathography'. Lombroso notoriously placed Baudelaire, Rousseau, and Nerval in the company of figures such as Newton,

---

[84] Lombroso 1889: p. vii; see Canguilhem 2003: 85–91.
[85] A similar interest in 'progeneracy' arose in late 19th-cent. Russian psychiatry in relation to the literary genius; see Sirotkina 2002: 71–3.

Swift, Hoffmann, and Gogol, in order to illustrate the equation of genius with madness. Baudelaire's Byronic posturing and attempts to shock were evidence of congenital pathology, Lombroso suggested, in rhetoric strangely similar to that of Jules Vallès: 'Baudelaire appears in the portrait placed at the head of his posthumous works as the very type of the madman possessed by delusions of grandeur: a provocative stance and defiant glare, smugly satisfied with himself. He descended from a family of madmen and eccentrics. It was, therefore, unnecessary to be an alienist to certify that he was mad.'[86] 'He wanted, at any cost, to be original,' Lombroso concludes disapprovingly (1889: 94). Baudelaire himself explicitly rejected the conflation of originality in life and in art: 'the most inventive and surprising artists, those whose creations are the most eccentric, are often men whose lives are quiet and meticulously organized' (CB2: 572).

Medical studies increasingly drew on the literary and artistic sphere for evidence, both in the genre of the pathography popularized by Lombroso and in artists' fictional creations: 'numerous psychiatrists sought to find in numerous novels the data they needed for their research, data which they were apparently unable to find in real life'.[87] The links posited between literature and psychiatry culminated in Max Nordau's *Entartung* (Degeneration) (1892), a text which sought to base diagnoses of writers entirely on their literary output, equating literary decadence with medical degeneration.[88] Just as observers of Parisian Bohemia were preoccupied by the notion of fraud, Nordau sought in his later writing to differentiate between the true genius and the 'pseudo-genius'.[89] His distinction reformulated Paul Janet's insistence on the need to distinguish between true genius and the 'false genius, the sick genius who has gone astray'.[90] It also resonated with French teratologists' efforts to differentiate between 'good' and 'bad' monsters, or Richet's 'progenerates' and 'degenerates'. All such distinctions appear motivated more by aesthetic considerations than by rationality, revealing the polarization of scientific discourse by recurrent conceptual and axiological oppositions.

Though debates about genius, madness, and eccentricity occurred in a fairly specialized branch of mental medicine, they filtered into more

[86] 'discende da una famiglia di pazzi et di bizzarri' (Lombroso 1971 [1888]: I, 158), rendered in French as 'descendait d'une famille de fous et d'excentriques' (Lombroso 1889: 92–3).
[87] Huertas 1993: 308.   [88] See Becker 1978: 72–3.
[89] See Nordau 1897: 52 and Genil-Perrin 1913: 198.   [90] Janet 1867: 89.

general debates about borderline insanity. Thus the alienist Benjamin Ball concludes his alarming sketch of the hundreds of thousands of insane individuals allegedly living undetected in France by arguing that this group is often more intelligent than others: 'they possess powerful originality, for their brains swarm with absolutely novel ideas' (1885: 95). Alexandre Cullerre likewise claims that, were it not for the 'small grain of madness' provided by the borderline insane, civilization would perish from an excess of mediocrity.[91] Nowhere, perhaps, was the ambivalence aroused by eccentricity so finely balanced as in attempts to understand its relationship to genius: these could either subsume oddity into a broader narrative of pathology, or move towards a vision of the eccentric genius as a 'progenerate', even a more perfect model of the human being.

The tendency to conflate monstrous creations with their monstrous authors was also clearly in evidence in debates about eccentric genius in the literary sphere, including discussions of the eccentricity of Bohemian artists.[92] Though most of these revolved around male eccentrics, there were some exceptions. Rachilde's *Monsieur Vénus* (1884) was described in quasi-psychiatric terminology as *une excentricité cérébrale* ('a cerebral eccentricity') by the writer Maurice Barrès in his preface of 1889. '[H]ow can it be that these strange creations have sprung from this child of healthy upbringing?' Barrès asks. He then cites the psychologist Jules Soury's description of Restif de la Bretonne, the notoriously dissolute eighteenth-century eccentric:[93] 'Whoever produces such books is perhaps no more in possession of himself than is a two-headed monster; it is a fine case of teratology. The tomb and oblivion are only for the vulgar. He will have the honour of the dissection room and the Dupuytren museum.'[94]

Female sadism is so unthinkable that Barrès posits Rachilde as a two-headed monster, one head demurely feminine, the other perverted and cold. Labelled a 'monstre double', a phrase usually reserved for conjoined twins, Rachilde is implicitly positioned as a hermaphrodite—though differently gendered heads, rather than differently sexed genitals, are on display. Despite its ostensibly ironic tone, Barrès's dream of the

---

[91] Cullerre 1888: 9–10; the notion of the beneficial effects of a 'grain of madness' reworks Diderot's famous description of Rameau as a 'grain of yeast' who ferments society and restores individuality (1972: 333).

[92] See Ch. 6, 'Self-made monsters'.

[93] Nerval, for example, describes Restif as an eccentric and a monster (GN2: 885, 1074).

[94] Barrès in Rachilde 1926: pp. xxii–xxiii.

future dissection of Rachilde's singular imagination is clearly eroticized; she is imagined as a naked corpse in the Dupuytren museum in Paris, where anatomical malformations were housed.

Debate about eccentricity in mental medicine largely took place in the context of degeneration theory. The conceptual vagueness this model promoted was evident in the ease with which it lent itself to literary appropriation, and itself appropriated literary imagery and narratives. This vagueness had both advantages and disadvantages for its proponents. Degeneration was seen as 'an infinite network of diseases and disorders, and the patterns of return and transformation between them'.[95] Its polysemy allowed it to escape the narrow confines of medical science and attain a much broader status of cultural myth, evident for example in its pervasive imagery of monstrosity and perversity.[96] Yet the aetiology of a vast range of conditions became increasingly monolithic: morbid heredity, or at least hereditary susceptibility to environmental toxins. The overwhelming nosological coherence of the degeneration paradigm eventually undermined its interpretative power, for it was unable to grasp specificity, rapidly losing medical credibility in France around the start of the twentieth century.[97] Precisely the same may be said of eccentricity. Its polymorphous properties, and its ability to evoke multiple forms of deviance, were a distinct advantage in an era of perceived national vulnerability, leading directly to 'whole underworlds of political and social anxiety'.[98] But this very elasticity meant that it was in danger of coming to signify nothing in particular. The demise of both the psychiatric use of the term 'excentrique' and the degeneration paradigm in the early twentieth century were, significantly, contemporaneous.[99] After Darwinism filtered into French scientific culture from the early 1870s, it was suggested that eccentricity might be linked to beneficial variation of the type required by natural selection. A work of popular medicine defines eccentricity as 'spontaneous variations...which, if cultivated, may become the principle of new rules through the descent of the same beings'.[100] But although some alienists carved out a small space in which divergence from the norm was viewed as permissible, even beneficial, most remained as hostile

---

[95] Pick 1989: 50.   [96] See Huertas 1992: 403.
[97] See Genil-Perrin 1913: 275.
[98] Pick 1989: 10; see also Nye 1984: 132–70.
[99] The concept of 'personality disorder', one possible successor to eccentricity as a medical category, was popularized in the 20th cent. (Berrios 1993).
[100] Meunier 1889: pp. i–ii.

towards eccentrics as teratologists were towards those suffering from malformations.

In summary, the shifting relationship between eccentricity and madness was first examined in French literary and popular culture, and subsequently taken up in alienism during a period of professional expansion and increasing cultural and political influence. The category was successively caught up in the two of the most important psychiatric doctrines of the century, monomania and degeneration. Both doctrines testified to alienists' desire to 'appropriate' the mysterious territory of borderline insanity, and to master the infinite variety of human behaviour by constructing nosological categories capable of accounting for the slightest deviations from expected norms of behaviour, speech, and appearance.

Writers proved particularly sensitive to the ambiguities surrounding eccentricity as a form of borderline or indeterminate madness, and to the pathos (and comedy) to which it could give rise. In turn, alienists drew consistently on accumulated layers of cultural meaning in their investigations of the eccentricity as a simultaneously individual and collective pathology. In particular, eccentricity was interpreted with imagery of instability and imbalance, drawn from Claude Bernard's influential model of homeostasis; with metaphors of innocence and guilt; with narratives of cathartic unveiling; and with models of more or less rapid decline. Finally, despite widespread fear of the social consequences of 'disequilibrium', many alienists continued to maintain that a grain of madness was an essential component of creativity, partly on account of the persistent association between eccentricity, genius, and madness which had been established in both mental medicine and Parisian Bohemia in the earlier part of the century. Concepts, narratives, and metaphors thus migrated rapidly between alienism and literary and popular culture, though were put to quite divergent ideological ends in each field.

Epilogue: Eccentricity in European Perspective

It is never a waste of time to study the history of a word.

Lucien Febvre[1]

This study has sought to reconstruct the different meanings attached to eccentricity in Parisian culture from the early nineteenth century to the *fin de siècle*. It has charted the trajectory of the terms 'excentrique' and 'excentricité' in social, literary, and intellectual life from their initial introduction to French culture during the early July Monarchy to their 'frenchification' and naturalization by the *fin de siècle*. Though eccentricity has been a neglected topic, overshadowed in previous historiography by apparently more determinate categories such as genius and madness, its semantic elasticity enables it to illuminate central features of Parisian culture during a period of rapid social and ideological change. The attitude of the bourgeoisie towards eccentricity during this time, I have argued, was characterized by marked ambivalence. This ambivalence was in the first instance rooted in the prehistory of the concept in eighteenth-century French culture, and in the negative connotations of originality and singularity within the codes of neoclassicism and courtly *honnêteté*. In the post-Revolutionary period a number of tendencies contributed to differentiating French from English representations still further.

In particular, the rapid succession of regimes and repeated reconfigurations of the social order in nineteenth-century France made challenges to convention appear more threatening than they did in comparatively stable societies such as Victorian England. Revolution entails the dismantling not only of political structures but also those of custom. The spectre of such collective transformations was potentially present

[1] 1973: 219.

on an imaginary level even in minor acts of eccentricity. These suggested that entrenched habits could be broken and new cultural forms conceived, a prospect which some held to be synonymous with social disorder or even anarchy. Eccentricity forms one strand in the history of individualism, and was thus shaped by many of the same forces that made the latter so contentious a concept in post-Revolutionary France. French thinkers were unusually critical of the destabilizing and fragmenting consequences of individualism as a political and economic doctrine; in contrast, they stressed the need for order and conformism. The common tendency of French political theorists and legislators to privilege the needs of the collectivity over those of the individual was echoed in everyday life, especially in relation to the minutiae of self-presentation and ideals of good taste. A desire to ensure social cohesion, for instance, underpinned the 'ritualization' of bourgeois behaviour, symbolized by the etiquette manual's disapproval of eccentricity and its quest for discreet, almost invisible conformism.

Eccentricity was at times more overtly identified with political subversion, though again largely on the level of the cultural imagination. The term was widely used to describe the poor and marginal figures that peopled the Bohemian underworld, whose misery brought them into both geographical and symbolic proximity to the 'dangerous classes'. The failed 1848 Revolution led to a significant reappraisal of unconventional behaviour in France across many cultural fields, from Bohemia to mental medicine, as well as to the progressive medicalization of deviance. The 'medical model of national decline' and resultant politics of national defence became influential in the latter part of the century, in conjunction with the interpretive paradigm of degeneration. This process was implicated in growing intolerance of all forms of nonconformism across French society and its institutions. Eccentricity was portrayed as a symptom of underlying mental and physical pathology, and linked to anxious fantasies about the spread of congenital malformations, criminality, and insanity at a time of perceived national insecurity.

I have noted in the course of this study that ambivalent attitudes towards eccentricity point to a deeper structural contradiction in post-Revolutionary bourgeois identity, one highlighted in recent historical scholarship. Though the French bourgeoisie was hostile to unfettered individualism, often associated with anarchy and egotism, it simultaneously sought to remove obstacles to individual freedom, including those imposed by custom and convention. The dominant model of the bourgeois self was thus inherently 'Janus-faced'.[2] The efforts of the bourgeoisie to reconcile its desire for order with its desire for freedom generated a fascination with the psychic dynamics of ambivalence and a recurrent need to test the boundaries of the permissible. For, despite the widespread hostility to non-conformism that I have outlined, Parisian culture was undoubtedly more tolerant of *certain* forms of eccentricity than Victorian culture.

Paris was the centre of the world fashion industry throughout the nineteenth century, a phenomenon which was implicated in positive evaluations of the creative imagination and eccentricity across a wide body of cultural commentary. Fashion illuminated the logic of capitalism, for it was premised on a restless cycle of innovation and obsolescence. Both significantly undermined the empire of custom and habit, replacing it with the cult of permanent novelty. As greater importance was placed on the cultivation of an individual 'style', a carefully calculated degree of eccentricity was required in order to differentiate oneself from others and capture public attention. This rhetoric of fashionable individualism was popularized for mass audiences in genres such as the *physiologie* and journalism. Moreover, new fashions were largely determined by *femmes excentriques*, courtesans who were free to experiment with audacious novelties in a way not permitted to 'respectable' women or ordinary prostitutes. From this conjunction arose a widespread tendency to associate eccentric fashions with the peculiarly Parisian institution of the *demi-monde*, the fluid hierarchy of courtesans, kept women, and fallen women. By extension, the concept of eccentricity eventually came to evoke the powerful erotic and aesthetic phantasmagoria generated by this social constellation in men and women of the leisure classes, functioning as a symbol of the perceived irrationality of both fashion and female sexuality.

Finally, the second wave of French Romanticism around 1830 was largely favourable to the reappraisal of eccentricity. The extreme cultural significance ascribed to individuality and genius in English and German Romanticism was initially slow to infiltrate French culture, owing to the social conservatism of the Restoration and continuing hegemony of neoclassicism. France was subsequently at the forefront of developments in European aesthetics, in relation to phenomena as diverse as literary Bohemia, realism, early responses to urban modernity, the avant-garde,

---

[2] Goldstein's term (2006: paragraph 6 of 26; see also paragraphs 2–3 and Goldstein 2005: 179–81).

and artistic experimentalism. These discursive configurations encouraged debate about three interrelated types of eccentricity: the shocking originality of artworks; the borderline insanity and bizarre personae of the artists who created them; and the marginal role of the artist in society. Eccentricity was widely discussed in art criticism, debates about genius, and a growing body of discourse on Bohemian marginality, in which men of letters explored their real and metaphorical connections with other groups of stigmatized individuals.

This combination of factors, I believe, largely accounts for the peculiarly ambivalent feelings that eccentricity aroused in the Parisian bourgeoisie. Eccentricity also, of course, crystallized tensions which traversed European bourgeois identity as a whole, including the vexed relationship between individual freedom and collective welfare, the boundaries between masculine and feminine identity, and the troubled fascination of middle- and upper-class subjects with their numerous, omnipresent 'others'. Finally, eccentricity was inseparable from emergent attitudes to spectatorship, self-consciousness, and the public gaze, namely the prehistory of phenomena now often understood in terms of Foucault's concept of panopticism. It thereby cut across the distinction between public and private. Though related to public spectacle in both the salon and the fairground, eccentricity was simultaneously implicated in discourse about the very intimate experiences of shame, anxiety, and vanity. Conversely, though the causes of eccentricity were located by alienists deep within the mind and body, these internal processes and hidden pathologies became the subject of public debate (and, it was hoped, would eventually reveal themselves to anxious bourgeois spectators in cathartic scenes of unveiling). In all these ways and doubtless many others, responses to eccentricity proved to be as complex as bourgeois identity itself.

The meanings of eccentricity in Parisian culture varied significantly across different contexts. This is even more obviously the case when the multiple trajectories of eccentricity in European cultural history are juxtaposed. Though detailed semantic and historical contextualization would evidently be required in order to understand changing responses to the concept across different traditions, the dependence of eccentricity on 'local' factors is immediately evident when even small samples of discourse are considered. To conclude, I will suggest that uncertainty about one recurrent cluster of associations, the relationship between eccentricity and madness, was prominently highlighted in other European traditions of the same period, but in quite culturally specific ways. I will draw on discussions of eccentricity by two nineteenth-century novelists, Mary Elizabeth Braddon and Fyodor Dostoevsky, as miniature case histories.

Liberalism in peril in Victorian England: Mary Elizabeth Braddon

Throughout the nineteenth century, Continental observers referred, often for rhetorical purposes, to the freedom and tolerance of English society; this, they alleged, was exemplified by the English dislike of medicalizing unconventional behaviour. The precise relationship of eccentricity to madness nonetheless proved highly contentious in Victorian fiction and political thought. Indeed, English alienists' understanding of the relationship between eccentricity and madness increasingly converged with that of French alienists towards the *fin de siècle*, though in the context of specifically English debates about liberty.

Lady Audley's Secret (1862), a novel by Mary Elizabeth Braddon (1837–1915), explored a plot type that was to become common in subsequent English sensation novels of the 1860s and 1870s: an assertive heroine breaks with the norms of femininity and her sanity is consequently called into question.[3] Lady Audley attempts to conceal the existence of her first husband and their child from her new aristocratic husband, Sir Michael. When her first husband returns from abroad and threatens to expose her, she attempts to murder him and plots to accuse Robert, his friend and her new husband's nephew, of insanity to prevent her crime from being discovered. In a process of interrogation that mimics legal procedure, she attempts to induce her stepdaughter Alicia to admit that Robert, together with his father and mother, show alarming signs of eccentricity:

'But you recollect your uncle, I suppose?'

'My Uncle Robert?' said Alicia. 'Oh, yes, I remember him very well indeed.'

'Was *he* eccentric—I mean to say, peculiar in his habits, like your cousin?'

'Yes, I believe Robert inherits all his absurdities from his father. My uncle expressed the same indifference for his fellow-creatures as my cousin; but as he was a good husband, an affectionate father, and a kind master, nobody ever challenged his opinions.'

---

[3] There is extensive feminist commentary on this text: see e.g. Showalter 1985: 71–2, Cvetkovich 1992: 45–70, and Voskuil 2001, esp. 614–26.

'But he *was* eccentric?'

'Yes; I suppose he was generally thought a little eccentric.'

'Ah,' said my lady gravely, 'I thought as much. Do you know, Alicia, that madness is more often transmitted from father to son than from father to daughter, and from mother to daughter than from mother to son? Your cousin Robert Audley is a very handsome young man, and I believe a very good-hearted young man; but he must be watched, Alicia, for he is *mad*!' (1987: 278)

The reader is, naturally, encouraged to be suspicious of Lady Audley's devious attempts to reclassify eccentricity as a dangerous form of pathology.

Despite her attempt to use wrongful incarceration for her own ends, it is Lady Audley herself who is eventually sent to a *maison de santé* in Belgium, with the collusion of the alienist Dr Mosgrave. This 'burial alive' serves as a punishment for her attempted murder of her first husband, as well as an attempt to save Sir Michael's reputation. For in a crucial scene, Dr Mosgrave explicitly rejects the notion that Lady Audley has inherited insanity from her mad mother. He diagnoses her, albeit with notable equivocation, as suffering from a form of borderline, incipient pathology: 'The lady is not mad; but she has the hereditary taint in her blood. She has the cunning of madness, with the prudence of intelligence . . . She is dangerous!' (1987: 379). At least three divergent interpretations of the text are therefore possible: first, that it affirms the common Victorian view that hereditary insanity was transmitted through the mother, the 'standard explanation for any act of feminine passion, self-assertion, or violence';[4] second, that it undermines this common view through Mosgrave's insistence on differentiating perversity from insanity (though he only does so slightly); and third, that it construes Lady Audley as sane, merely acting out the repressed fantasies of multitudes of dissatisfied Victorian women. Incarcerated though she is not unambiguously mad, after having tried to persuade her family that the 'eccentric' Robert should be incarcerated though he is seemingly harmless, Lady Audley's fate highlights uncertainties in English discourse about the relationship between sanity and morality similar to those expressed in French medicine. The passage also suggests that a gender symmetrical approach is required, since Lady Audley's characterization must be juxtaposed with repeated references to Robert's melancholia, even his borderline madness. '[H]ow many minds', writes

---

[4] Showalter 1980: 326.

the narrator, implicitly referring to him, 'must tremble upon the narrow boundary between reason and unreason' (205).[5]

In 1830 the influential alienist John Conolly cautioned his readers not to confuse eccentricity with madness, placing the former under the heading 'Inequalities, weaknesses, and peculiarities of the human understanding, which do not amount to insanity'. His analysis is framed in the language of classic English liberalism: it is 'repugnant to every idea of that rational freedom which all ought to enjoy, that a man should not do as he chooses with his time, or his property, so long as he does not inflict direct injury on others' (1964: 139). A survey of English psychiatric literature from the mid-nineteenth century reveals that this attitude was increasingly qualified. Lady Audley's 'condition' is characterized by depravity of actions together with alarming rhetorical and intellectual ingenuity. It is therefore close to the alienist J. C. Prichard's influential category of 'Moral Insanity', defined in 1835 as moral perversion 'without any illusion, or the belief of any unreal and imaginary fact'.[6] Whilst those suffering from moral insanity are often reputed to have a 'singular, wayward, and eccentric' character, Prichard argues, eccentricity in itself 'can hardly be said to constitute sufficient evidence' of moral insanity.[7]

In 1842, however, Prichard takes a harsher stance, claiming that 'it is to no purpose to shut our eyes against the evidence' that eccentricity and insanity are 'closely allied', indeed almost without exception related (64). He portrays eccentricity as an insidious contaminant and a hereditary menace. The notions of possessive liberalism and bourgeois conformism again intervene: so long as a jury determines that the eccentric can be entrusted with the care of himself and his property, and govern his conduct with propriety, there should be no interference. Yet, Prichard immediately adds, the evidence shows that this is hardly ever the case (66–7).[8]

The courts became theatres for collective judgement of the boundaries of acceptable eccentricity, particularly where money or property was at stake. One of Prichard's case histories narrates the life of 'I. K.', sent to an asylum soon after inheriting a large estate. Though

[5] This aspect of the novel is recognized by Cvetkovich (1992: 65–8), though she does not relate the text to contemporaneous alienism.
[6] Prichard was influenced by French alienism and the category of 'manie sans délire' or mania without delirium; see Berrios 1999.
[7] Prichard 1835: 12, 23.
[8] Berrios's claim that moral insanity had *no* 'moral' connotations in the modern sense (1999: 112) is sharply contradicted on a performative level by Pritchard's rhetoric of moral repugnance.

incarcerated with the unanimous judgement of a panel of physicians, a jury subsequently 'attributed his peculiarities to eccentricity', and he was released (1842: 45). In a lawsuit of 1846, *Frere v Peacocke*, Mrs Peacocke contested her brother's will on the grounds that 'the deceased evinced evident gratification in causing inconvenience and annoyance to others'. The jury rejected her suit, finding her brother 'eccentric, not insane'.[9] Other alienists manifested concern at potential abuses. In 1858 John Bucknill and Daniel Tuke distinguished between two types of eccentric: one is manly and vigorous, the other feminized, of weak and impressionable character—but still only potentially mad and rarely harmful. They note with evident disapproval that 'the Diagnosis of Eccentricity is only likely to be required in cases of disputed will, or in criminal trials where eccentric conduct is seized upon to support the plea of insanity' (312).

The infringements of law and liberty exemplified by Lady Audley's stratagems became the subject of increasing public alarm, evident in the convening of parliamentary select committees to examine wrongful confinement in 1858–9 and 1876–7. Victorian novels and newspaper accounts provided lurid descriptions of the ploys used by the unscrupulous to incarcerate those from whom they could profit. Prichard's invention of the suggestive category of 'moral' insanity, together with the success of the middle-class puritan moral code in shaping the social norms of all classes, sharply reduced tolerance of any form of difference. The slightest examples of eccentricity, which would have passed unchallenged during the eighteenth century, became subjects for medical and legal intervention—especially deviations from the strict codes regulating sexual morality, or from gender or class norms.[10] Far from being the natural home of eccentricity, Victorian England appeared ever more inimical to it.[11]

Within England, conflict between the founding ideals of liberal theory, a repressive moral climate, and the rise of legal medicine were examined by John Stuart Mill in a well-known section of his tract *On Liberty* (1859). Mill expresses outrage at the 'contemptible and frightful' tendency for those who depart from convention to be declared unfit to manage their affairs: 'All the minute details of his daily life are pried into, and whatever is found which ... bears an appearance unlike absolute

---

[9] Cited in Porter 1991: 188–90.   [10] See McCandless 1981: 239–45.
[11] The conclusion of Cowlishaw 1998: ch. 4, though he does not discuss Victorian alienism.

commonplace, is laid before the jury as evidence of insanity, and often with success' (1974: 134 n.). He presents eccentricity as the object of nostalgia, under threat from the mass public, religion, alienism, and the courts. It represents, in Mill's vision, the threatened spirit of masculine greatness:

Precisely because the tyranny of opinion is such as to make eccentricity a reproach, it is desirable, in order to break through that tyranny, that people should be eccentric. Eccentricity has always abounded when and where strength of character has abounded; and the amount of eccentricity in a society has generally been proportional to the amount of genius, mental vigour, and moral courage which it contained. That so few now dare to be eccentric, marks the chief danger of the time.   (1974: 132)

His assertion is perhaps marked by anxiety at the consequences of the Evangelical revival.[12] Mill's version of liberalism is primarily associated with the political doctrine of negative freedom, which emphasizes freedom from constraint. But there is, this passage recognizes, a potential chasm between freedom from political, economic, and religious interference, and freedom from the equally potent yet far more nebulous constraints of custom.

Despite Mill's attempt to dissociate eccentricity from madness, eccentricity was increasingly medicalized as the influence of degeneration theory was felt in the writing of Henry Maudsley, J. F. Nisbet, and many others.[13] Nisbet argues, for example, that when 'an "eccentric" man' marries a 'healthy woman' and has four children, 'the eldest son is sound, the daughter is weak-minded, the second son is also weak-minded, and the third is eccentric and ailing' (1891: 42). In a story published in 1905, Arthur Conan Doyle's detective Sherlock Holmes provides a turn-of-the-century expression of this newly fashionable Continental paradigm:

There are some trees, Watson, which grow to a certain height, and then suddenly develop some unsightly eccentricity. You will see it often in humans. I have a theory that the individual represents in his development the whole procession of his ancestors, and that such a sudden turn to good or evil stands

---

[12] See Gilmour 1993: 76.

[13] On Maudsley's views on eccentricity, see Skultans 1975: 217–18. Eccentricity began to be linked to paranoia in turn-of-the-century England, as in France: Stoddart divides paranoids into eccentrics and egocentrics (1908: 346–7), whilst Hollander claims 'Many people who go through life as eccentrics are possibly only aborted cases of paranoia' (1912: 256). See Sully 1898: 461–2, Cole 1913: 72, 140, and Taylor and Shuttleworth 1998: 282, 340, 350 for further usage.

for some strong influence which came into the line of his pedigree. The person becomes, as it were, the epitome of the history of his own family.

(Doyle 1981: 494)

Eccentricity is held to have a potential for good and evil, framed in terms of a potentially Romantic aesthetic of ugliness.[14] In further comments, however, Holmes argues that it is through attempting to stand out as a genius that one risks falling below the level of human to that of ape. His partially scientific metaphor echoes the moralizing view of eccentricity as hubris that was widespread in French culture. Like their French colleagues, furthermore, Victorian alienists became pre-occupied by cartographical metaphors. In his influential work of 1875 entitled *The Borderlands of Insanity*, for example, Andrew Wynter proposed ominously that there was a 'vast army of undiscovered lunatics', 'always eccentric both in thought and action'.[15] In the latter part of the nineteenth century, pessimistic attitudes to eccentricity prevailed in Victorian medicine and across many aspects of Victorian culture.

Eccentric individuality in Imperial Russia: Fyodor Dostoevsky

In contrast to the growing suspicion of eccentricity in Victorian England, eccentricity was imbued with extreme cultural value in late nineteenth-century Russia, particularly in the fiction of Fyodor Dostoevsky (1821–81). Dostoevsky reworked a number of existing cultural traditions to forge a highly personal vision of the historical and social significance of eccentricity. The label of eccentricity is frequently used to describe his characters, and at times forms part of their self-designation. The English term 'eccentric' could be rendered in two different ways in nineteenth-century Russian. The standard translation was the Slavic personal noun *čudak*, etymologically linked to the Russian terms for 'marvel' and 'monster', and often positive in connotation.[16] There was also a Latinate equivalent, *èkscentrik*. The latter was higher register and probably confined to the Francophone upper

---

[14] Watson greets the suggestion with typically English empiricism: see Pick 1989: 155–6.

[15] Cited in Taylor and Shuttleworth 1998: 281, 280 respectively.

[16] See Buckler 2006: 302, though she does not discuss the Latinate terms. Her analysis, which focuses on non-fictional portraits of urban eccentrics, is to my knowledge the only work on the subject.

classes; it rapidly faded from use in the twentieth century after the 1917 Revolution and exile of the intelligentsia.[17] As in French and English, both terms were accompanied by a range of synonyms including *strannyj* and *original'nyj* (strange and original). Dostoevsky typically alternates between *čudak* and *èkscentrisk* in his depictions of eccentric types; at times he places the former in inverted commas, perhaps to signal its 'popular' linguistic status.

A number of wider cultural contexts shaped the semantic field of eccentricity in Dostoevsky's writing. Some relate to the role of norms and conventions in the Russian elite, whose behavioural codes were governed by the appropriation of a French model of exquisite politeness (the tyrannical 'comme il faut'), yet were simultaneously marked by a peculiar fascination with *poshlost'*. This untranslatable term evoked banality, boredom, and everyday routine as well as vulgarity, ugliness, obscenity, and sexuality.[18] A range of mythologies also coalesced around the *čudak* in the latter part of the century, as Julie Buckler has shown. This figure, associated with urban spectacle, the notion of 'living museums', and fashionable dandyism, had important thematic affinities with the models of eccentricity previously elaborated in England and France.[19]

A further distinctively Russian concept which influenced perceptions of the relationship between eccentricity, individuality, and madness was that of the holy fool or *jurodivyj*. Though the *jurodivyj* and the stylized figure of the urban *čudak* were certainly not interchangeable types,[20] they shared the same general semantic field of oddity, strangeness, and eccentricity.[21] The unkempt, filthy appearance and behaviour of many holy fools, typically interpreted as a sign of their uncommon spiritual insight, constituted a systematic inversion of dominant norms. The figure generated uncertainty about what the diagnosis of madness really meant, in a cultural climate which readily allowed other forms of non-conformism such as political dissidence to be relabelled as symptoms

---

[17] See Martinovskij and Kovalevskij 1892: 585 and Dal' 1909: 1369, 1550.

[18] See respectively Boym 1994: 56–8 and 41–3.   [19] See Buckler 2006.

[20] Buckler proposes that to link the two figures would be 'specious', since 'true eccentrics', unlike the holy fool, are not 'an identifiable form of difference bearing a specific historical function' (2006: 302–3), a view with affinities to Sangsue 1988: 53–5. I find the notion of the 'true' eccentric dating from the 16th cent. (which Buckler adopts from David Weeks) problematic on the grounds of anachronism, and am more concerned with the broader semantics of eccentricity than with the figure of 'the' eccentric.

[21] In addition to its specifically religious meaning, the term *jurodivyj* could 'sometimes' be used more generally to denote the 'foolish, unreasoning, thoughtless' individual (Dal' 1909: 1369–70).

of serious illness.[22] Early Russian psychiatrists attempted repeatedly to pathologize holy fools, and the figures were recurrently associated with fraud, creating an unstable continuum between 'ascetics masquerading as fools and madmen, madmen allegedly venerated as holy men, and madmen treated as madmen'.[23] They nonetheless retained extraordinary support amongst both the populace and many in the social elite. Despite some notable thematic convergences, then, Russian culture conceptualized the relationship between madness, sanity, and eccentricity quite differently from contemporaneous French and Victorian culture.

Peculiar figures understood as holy fools became, to some extent, a 'site of resistance' to what Dostoevsky dismissed as an age of scientific positivism, in the context of his well-known hostility towards the new discipline of scientific psychology.[24] As Mikhail Bakhtin notes, eccentricity is a central attribute of all of Dostoevsky's main characters: 'Dostoevsky's mode of artistic thinking could not imagine anything in the slightest way humanly significant that did not have certain elements of *eccentricity* [*čudačestva*]' (1984: 150). The philosopher cites the novelist's best-known portrait of a holy fool, Prince Myshkin, as the exemplary instance of this tendency, but includes 'all' of Dostoevsky's major heroes, namely Raskolnikov, Stavrogin, Versilov, and Ivan Karamazov, in this category. Their eccentricity, he suggests, lies in their 'ridiculousness' and their affinity with the carnivalesque figure of the wise fool (1984: 150). Bakhtin thus associates eccentricity exclusively with Dostoevsky's male protagonists, and predominantly with the comic mode of the ridiculous. Both these assumptions can be questioned if Dostoevsky's linguistic usage is considered in more detail.

First, Dostoevsky himself repeatedly foregrounded the eccentricity of his female characters. In *The Idiot* (1869), for example, the semantic field of eccentricity largely relates to female characters rather than to Prince Myshkin. Its meaning oscillates between deliberate, mischievous violation of the codes of polite society, in the one instance, and involuntary peculiarity verging on borderline insanity, in the other. As an example of the first of these tendencies, Dostoevsky portrays Lizveta Prokofievna, a socially eccentric but nonetheless socially esteemed figure, as a woman preoccupied by the potential similarities between herself and her free-spirited daughters ('Most of all she was tormented

---

[22] Thompson 1987: 44–5; on medicalization, see also Murav 1992: ch. 2.
[23] Murav 1992: 3–4.   [24] Murav 1992: 8.

by the suspicion that her daughters were becoming the same sort of "eccentrics" ["čudački"] as she').[25] In contrast, he emphasizes the eccentricity of Nastasya in the context of extreme norm violations and the threat of madness, which emerges ever more strongly in the course of the narrative ('She's an astonishing woman, you see, an eccentric woman [èkscentričeskaja], I'm so afraid of her I can hardly sleep').[26] Eccentricity is often feminized within *The Idiot*, and has more or less threatening connotations depending on which character it is used to describe.

Dostoevsky explicitly addressed what Bakhtin terms the 'special and vital *historical* significance of eccentricity' in the preface to his last novel, *The Karamazov Brothers*.[27] The focus of his discussion is Aleksei Fyodorovich Karamazov, a character strongly coded as a holy fool.[28] Dostoevsky's original terms for 'odd' and 'eccentric' in this passage are *strannyj* and *čudak* respectively:

One thing, however, is indisputable: he is an odd, not to say eccentric, figure. But oddity and eccentricity, far from commanding attention, are calculated to undermine reputations, especially at a time when everybody is striving to unify what is disparate and to find some kind of common meaning in our universal chaos. And in most cases the eccentric is the very essence of individuality and isolation, is he not? Should you not agree with this last thesis, however, and reply, 'It is not so', or 'not always so', then I might perhaps take heart over the significance of my hero, Aleksei Fyodorovich. For not only is an eccentric 'not always' a man apart and isolated, but, on the contrary, it may be he in particular who sometimes represents the very essence of his epoch, while others of his generation, for whatever reason, will drift aimlessly in the wind.

(1994: 5)

The passage stages an imaginary three-way debate (between the narrator, the wider community hostile to eccentric individuality, and a thoughtful reader who might potentially dissent from the dominant view), which serves to welcome the isolated eccentric into a Utopian counter-community of odd souls. The concluding image portrays the masses of conventional individuals ceding their agency to wider historical

---

[25] Dostoevsky 2002: 328; amongst others, see also e.g. 327 ('She constantly scolded herself with being a "foolish, indecent eccentric" [čudačkoj]') and 328 ('in society Lizaveta Prokofyevna was indeed considered an "eccentric" ["čudačkoj"]; but for all that she was indubitably respected').

[26] Dostoevsky 2002: 314; Nastasya is also described as being prone to 'overstep the bounds of reasonable conduct by some extraordinary eccentricity [sliškom èkscentrično]' (42; translation modified).

[27] Bakhtin 1984: 150.   [28] See Murav 1992: 15.

forces, whilst the eccentric stands firm, becoming the sole repository of historical meaning and value.[29]

The world-historical significance that Dostoevsky ascribes to eccentricity in his preface appears to be echoed by the universal, even cosmic significance that Bakhtin later assigned to the carnival (and by extension to eccentricity as a 'special category of the carnival sense of the world'; 1984: 123). However, the passage brings out a second point of contrast between Dostoevsky and Bakhtin's respective visions of transgression. Dostoevsky underscores the general isolation and stigmatization of the eccentric individual; and he dramatizes himself as disheartened and precariously dependent upon his readers' interest in eccentricity. In many of his novels, the oddity of his main characters is portrayed in relation to the omnipresent threat of madness and a nightmarish vision of chaos, together constituting a 'demonic' inversion of the carnivalesque.[30]

The potentially tragic and sacrificial associations of eccentricity as a form of extreme isolation call into question both Bakhtin's socialized model of the carnival, whose symbolic locus is the real or metaphorical marketplace, and his characteristic optimism (implicit in his conflation of eccentricity with a type of comic absurdity). These ideological tensions are perhaps indicative of broader uncertainties. Dostoevksy's effective normalization of psychic eccentricity may be interpreted as an extreme instance of the 'sublimation' and privatization of transgression, the fundamental shift in nineteenth-century bourgeois culture described by Stallybrass and White. As these authors note, however, Bakhtin never satisfactorily accounted for this process of internalization in his writings on nineteenth-century culture (1986: 180), leaving a strange and perhaps revealing gap in his analyses of the carnivalesque.

As we have seen, then, French representations of eccentricity and madness have a complex relationship to those which emerged in contemporaneous European traditions, including but by no means only those of England and Russia (eccentricity was also depicted, for example, in a number of nineteenth-century Spanish texts).[31] These

---

[29] Petr Viazemsky (1792–1878), who chronicled Russian eccentrics over many decades, also attributed profound historical significance to these figures; see Buckler 2006: 306.

[30] Murav 1992: 111.

[31] As Robert Bly has shown, Benito Pérez Galdós's fictional portraits of eccentrics in the last two decades of the century were influenced by the French physiology, the typologies of English and French realist fiction, and mental medicine (see Bly 2004: 10, 18, 23, 187 n. 4, 198 n. 4).

different traditions exemplify what Ludwig Wittgenstein termed the 'complicated network of similarities overlapping and criss-crossing' typical of family resemblances, the theoretical model which best accounts for the diversity of concepts such as eccentricity.[32] Patterns of cross-cultural influence arose in many directions. Just as English attitudes towards oddity shaped early French depictions of eccentricity, French discourses associated with the literary physiology, realist fiction, the journalism of urban life, and mental medicine were subsequently transplanted to other European cultures, where they shaped new discourses of eccentricity. Other influences related to archetypes elaborated over many centuries across elite and popular European culture, including the wise fool, madman, and idiot. Similar forms of divergence and convergence would undoubtedly also emerge in cross-cultural comparisons of eccentricity in relation to other themes such as monstrosity, fashion, and genius. Common to all the traditions I have considered, however, is an uneasy awareness of the ambivalence that arises when nineteenth-century bourgeois subjects encounter eccentricity.

Eccentricity, ambivalence, and postmodernity

The notion of ambivalence, which is repeatedly highlighted in Bakhtin's analysis of eccentricity, has reappeared in recent debates in cultural theory. The term 'ambivalence' originally denoted the experience of feeling conflicting emotions towards the same object, but more broadly construed it includes an inability to categorize phenomena and uncertainty about which approach to adopt in any given situation. The social theorist Zygmunt Bauman defines ambivalence, for example, as 'a situation with no decidable solution, with no foolproof choice, no unreflective knowledge of "how to go on" ' (1991: 244–5). He views ambivalence as an unwanted but ineradicable by-product of modernity's preoccupation with order, classification, and categorization. But he concludes that although ambivalence has traditionally been perceived as intolerably threatening, even constituting the 'the main affliction of modernity and the most worrying of its concerns' (1991: 15), it is gradually becoming accepted as a structuring principle of contemporary society. We can

---

[32] Wittgenstein 1997: 32.

do little else but make our peace with the 'others' of order, including unremitting ambiguity, confusion, and undecidability.[33]

As well as revaluing ambivalence, cultural theory in the aftermath of structuralism and poststructuralism has proved famously critical of traditional models of unified and autonomous bourgeois selfhood, proposing competing theories of decentred subjectivity and heralding a new era of 'post-humanism', 'post-subjectivity', and 'post-identity'.[34] As a phenomenon which is historically inseparable from the rise of classical doctrines of individual liberty and autonomy, eccentricity would appear from this perspective to be increasingly anachronistic. Not only have conceptions of selfhood radically altered, there is no longer any dominant 'centre' to which eccentricity can be opposed, but rather a seemingly endless series of plural and competing perspectives.[35]

Nonetheless, it would be inaccurate to suggest that eccentricity has become a completely meaningless concept. For various difficulties are raised by the popular narrative of contemporary culture's emancipation from both the oppressive social conventions of previous generations and the defunct vision of bourgeois subjectivity that underpins them. The dynamic interplay of norm and transgression, or of the closely related conceptual dyad of constraint and freedom, creates many paradoxes and puzzles. Self-consciously oppositional subcultures can prove to be even more rigid in policing deviance than are the dominant cultures they oppose; the most shocking avant-garde artistic and intellectual movements can be almost instantaneously institutionalized; adherents of liberal pluralism can prove intolerant and monologic in promoting their own system of values; and freedom of choice can become an oppressive and unwanted burden. And whilst Freud's case histories have convinced many that an excessively conformist society can generate neurosis, a line of sociological thought dating back to Émile Durkheim suggests that a society with diluted and weakened norms can generate the potentially life-threatening malady of *anomie* (derived from the Greek *a-nomos*, or 'lawless').[36]

Theoretical challenges to bourgeois individualism also coexist with a barely suppressed yearning for this ideology in everyday life and the

[33] Bauman 1991: 25, 7. For an overview of ambivalence in contemporary critical theory, see also Smart 1999: 1–34.

[34] See Jameson 1991: 15.

[35] Though Hutcheon 1988 seeks to co-opt eccentricity as a key value of postmodernity, as I note in the Introduction, it is difficult to maintain that postmodernism is perpetually decentred when it has become so institutionally mainstream.

[36] See Durkheim 1972: 173–88.

cultural imagination. As the critic Timothy Melley argues, for example, much postmodern fiction, film, and theory is fascinated by paranoia and 'agency panic', consisting in generalized suspicion and fear of manipulation by vast and impersonal forces.[37] The intense hostility to the de-individuating influence of institutions such as government, corporations, and the mass media which emerges in many recent artworks tends to trigger nostalgia for the heroic individual self, portrayed (rather like Dostoevsky and John Stuart Mill's lone eccentrics) as the last remaining outpost of resistance to a debased social order. Thus the same cultural currents which promote decentred subjectivity can simultaneously foster anxiety at the political consequences of relinquishing autonomy and agency, and the figure of the nonconformist individual continues to be imbued with redemptive power.[38]

Contemporary Western culture is, in short, still grappling with its heritage of individualism, without which both subjectivity and political engagement are seemingly impossible for many to imagine in a meaningful way. Eccentricity may indeed be less provocative a concept today than it was for the nineteenth-century bourgeoisie. But given the stubborn persistence of the individual as a category, together with the ineradicable nature of at least some norms within particular communities and local contexts, the ability of eccentricity to provoke ambivalent and Janus-like reactions appears unlikely to disappear just yet.

[37] Melley 2000: 15, 40–1.   [38] Melley 2000: 23, 34.

Bibliography

Orthography has been standardized to modern French, and the date of original publication is given in square brackets after the title. Unless otherwise stated, all translations in the study are my own.

PRIMARY SOURCES (FIRST PUBLISHED BEFORE 1915)

Adelon, N. P., and F. Chaussier (1819), 'Monstruosités', *Dictionnaire des sciences médicales*, 60 vols. (Paris: Panckoucke, 1812–22), XXXIV (1819), 154–263.

Alhoy, Maurice (1841), *Physiologie de la lorette* (Paris: Aubert).

—— Taxile Delord, and Edmond Texier (1854), *Mémoires de Bilboquet recueillis par un bourgeois de Paris*, 3 vols. (Paris: Librairie nouvelle).

Ancelot, Virginie (1840), 'Une femme à la mode', in *Les Français peints par eux-mêmes*: I, 57–64.

Andral, G. (1826), 'Monstruosités', in *Dictionnaire de médecine*, 21 vols. (Paris: Béchet, 1821–8), XIV (1826), 438–88.

Anon. [n.d.], *Les Lorettes, les grisettes et les amoureux: types, mœurs et excentricités* (Paris: Desloges).

Anon. (1832), 'Le Flâneur à Paris, par un flâneur', in *Paris, ou Le Livre des Cent-et-Un* (1831–4): VI, 95–111.

Anon. (1841*a*), *Le Nouveau catéchisme des amants, art de jouir des douceurs légitimes et excentriques de l'amour* (Paris: Les marchands de nouveautés).

Anon. (1841*b*), *Physiologie des physiologies* (Paris: Desloges).

Anon. (1844), 'Le Batteur de pavé', in *Paris comique*, 16 [unpaginated].

Anon. (1882), *Les Usages du monde, le savoir-vivre et la politesse* (Paris: T. Lefèvre).

Arago, Jacques (1841), *Physiologie du protecteur* (Paris: Charpentier).

Ashe, Thomas (1819), *The Charms of Dandyism, or, Living in Style: By Olivia Moreland, Chief of the Female Dandies, and Edited by Captain Ashe* (London: [n.pub.]).

Aubert, Constance (1865), *Encore le luxe des femmes: les femmes sages et les femmes folles* (Paris: Dentu).

Audebrand, Philibert (1905), *Derniers Jours de la Bohème: souvenirs de la vie littéraire* (Paris: Calmann Lévy).

Audouard, Olympe (1865*a*), *Le Luxe des femmes: réponse d'une femme à M. le Procureur général Dupin* (Paris: Dentu).

Audouard, Olympe (1865*b*), 'Le Luxe effréné des hommes: discours tenu dans un comité de femmes' (Paris: Dentu).

Augier, Émile (1866), *La Contagion* (Paris: M. Lévy).

——and Édouard Foussier (1884), *Les Lionnes pauvres; La famille de Puiméné* (Paris: A. Lemerre).

Azam, Eugène (1891), *Entre la folie et la raison des toqués* (Paris: Alcan).

Ball, Benjamin (1885), *La Morphinomanie; Les frontières de la folie; Le dualisme cérébral; Les rêves prolongés* (Paris: Asselin et Houzeau).

Balzac, Honoré de (1968), *Cousin Pons* [1847], trans. Herbert J. Hunt (Harmondsworth: Penguin).

Barbey d'Aurevilly, Jules (1859), *L'Amour impossible, chronique parisienne* [1841] (Paris: Bourdilliat).

——(1890), *Littérature étrangère* (Paris: Alphonse Lemerre).

——(1964–6), *Le XIXe siècle: des œuvres et des hommes*, ed. Jacques Petit, 2 vols. (Paris: Mercure de France), I (1964), II (1966).

——(1979), *Lettres à Trébutien*, 4 vols. (Geneva: Slatkine).

——(1986), *The She-Devils*, trans. Ernest Boyd (London: Dedalus).

Barrière, Théodore de (1883), *Les Filles de marbre* [1853] (Paris: Lévy).

Baudelaire, Charles (1970), *Paris Spleen*, trans. Louise Varèse (New York: New Directions).

Baudrillart, H. (1878), *Histoire du luxe*, 4 vols. (Paris: Hachette, 1878–80), I (1878).

Belloy, Auguste (1860), *Les Toqués* (Paris: M. Lévy).

Belmontet, Louis (1858), *Le Luxe des femmes et la jeunesse de l'époque* (Paris: Aymot).

Bernard, Claude (1878), *Leçons sur les phénomènes de la vie communs aux animaux et aux végétaux* (Paris: Baillière).

Bertillon, Alphonse (1883), *Ethnographie moderne: les races sauvages* (Paris: G. Masson).

Bernard, Pierre, and Louis Couailhac (1841), *Physiologie du jardin des plantes* (Paris: L. Curmer).

Bescherelle, Louis-Nicolas (1861), *L'Usage du monde, ou Conseils sur l'art de plaire en société* (Paris: Garnier).

Boissin, Firmin (1890), *Excentriques disparus* (Paris: A. Savine).

Boitard, Pierre (1851), *Guide-Manuel de la bonne compagnie* (Paris: Passard).

Boucher de Perthes, Jacques (1852), *Emma, ou quelques lettres de femme* (Paris: Treuttel and Würtz).

Bouchot, Henri (1901), 'Le Costume', in *La Vie parisienne à travers le XIXe siècle: Paris de 1800 à 1900 d'après les estampes et les mémoires du temps*, ed. Paul van Cleemputte, 3 vols. (Paris: Plon-Nourrit et Cie, 1900–1), II (1901), 334–6.

Bourgeau, Th. (1864), *Les Usages du monde, ou Ce qui s'observe dans la bonne compagnie* (Poitiers: H. Oudin).

Brachet, Jean-Louis (1844), *Traité complet de l'hypochondrie* (Paris: Baillière).

—— (1847), *Traité de l'hystérie* (Paris: Baillière).

Braddon, Mary Elizabeth (1987), *Lady Audley's Secret* [1862] (Oxford: Oxford University Press).

Briquet, Pierre (1859), *Traité clinique et thérapeutique de l'hystérie* (Paris: Baillière).

Broca, Paul (1879), *Instructions générales pour les recherches anthropologiques: à faire sur le vivant* (Paris: G. Masson).

Brunet, Gustave (1880), *Les Fous littéraires, essai bibliographique sur la littérature excentrique, les illuminés, visionnaires, etc., par Philomneste junior* (Brussels: Gay et Doucé).

Bucknill, John Charles, and Daniel H. Tuke (1858), *A Manual of Psychological Medicine* (London: J. Churchill).

Burani, Paul (1879), *Guide-Manuel de la civilité française, ou Nouveau code de la politesse et du savoir-vivre* (Paris: Le Bailly).

Buret, Eugène (1840), *De la misère des classes laborieuses en Angleterre et en France*, 2 vols. (Paris: Paulin).

Burney, Fanny (1782), *Cecilia, or Memoirs of an Heiress*, 5 vols. (London: T. Payne).

—— (1796), *Camilla: or, A Picture of Youth*, 5 vols. (London: T. Payne).

—— (1814), *The Wanderer; or, Female Difficulties*, 5 vols. (London: Longman, Hurst, Rees, Orme, and Brown).

Bussy, Charles de [Charles Marchal] (1858), *Les Toquades, illustrées par Gavarni: étude de mœurs* (Paris: P. Martinon).

Cabinet of Curiosities: or, Mirror of entertainment. Being a selection of extraordinary legends [...] *authentic and remarkable anecdotes* [...] *and a variety of other eccentric matter* (1810) (London: Burkett & Plumpton).

Carlier, Félix (1887), *Études de pathologie sociale: les deux prostitutions* (Paris: E. Dentu).

Cavé, Marie-Élisabeth (1863), *La Femme aujourd'hui, la femme autrefois* (Paris: Plon).

Challamel, Augustin (1873), *L'Ancien boulevard du Temple* (Paris: Librairie de la Société des gens de lettres).

—— (1875), *Les Amuseurs de la rue* (Paris: Ducrocq).

—— (1881), *Histoire de la mode en France: la toilette des femmes depuis l'époque gallo-romaine jusqu'à nos jours* [1875] (Paris: Hennuyer).

Champfleury [Jules François Feìlix Husson] (1861), *Grandes Figures d'hier et d'aujourd'hui: Balzac, Gérard de Nerval, Wagner, Courbet* (Paris: Poulet-Malassis et de Broise).

—— (1877), *Les Excentriques* [1852] (Paris. M. Lévy).

Champfleury (1997), 'Les Excentriques, nouvelle série', in *Maître Palsgravius: et autres inédits*. (Paris: Kimé).

Champfleury (1871), *Histoire de la caricature moderne* (Paris: Dentu).

Chapus, Eugène (1844), *Théorie de l'élégance* (Paris: Comptoir des imprimeurs-unis).

—— (1877), *Manuel de l'homme et de la femme comme il faut* [1861] (Paris: Decauax).

Chasles, Emile (1856), Review of 'Les Excentriques' by Champfleury, *Athenaeum français*, 13 May: 463–64.

Chasles, Philarète (1834), 'Les Excentriques [anglais]', *Revue des deux mondes*, 1 September: 497–558.

Chateaubriand, François-René de (1978), *Essai sur les Révolutions; Génie du Christianisme*, ed. Maurice Regard (Paris: Gallimard).

Clarétie, Jules (1876), *L'Art et les artistes français contemporains* (Paris: Charpentier).

Coffignon, A. (1888), *Paris vivant: la corruption à Paris* (Paris: Librairie illustrée).

Cole, R. H. (1913), *Mental Diseases: A Text-Book of Psychiatry for Medical Students and Practitioners* (London: University of London Press).

Comte, Stéphane (1854), *Les Saltimbanques jugés, ou Considérations sur l'influence pernicieuse exercée par les charlatans, saltimbanques et chanteurs ambulants sur les mœurs sociales* (Grenoble: Redon).

Conolly, John (1964), *An Inquiry Concerning the Indications of Insanity* [1830] (London: Dawsons).

Constantin, Marc (1854), *Almanach des belles manières* (Paris: Desloges).

Coupin, Henri (1905), *Les Bizarreries des races humaines* (Paris: Vuibert et Nony).

—— (1912), *Les Animaux excentriques* [1903] (Paris: Vuibert).

Cullerre, Alexandre (1888), *Les Frontières de la folie* (Paris: Baillière).

Dal', V. I. (1903–9), *Tolkovyj slovar' živogo velikorusskogo jazyka* [*Defining Dictionary of the Living Russian Language*], ed. I. A. Boduen De Kurtene, 3rd edn., 4 vols., IV (1909).

Dallemagne, Jules (1885), *Dégénérés et déséquilibrés* (Paris: Alcan).

Dangennes, Berthe [Mme Blanchard] [n.d. (a)], *Pour vivre sa vie, ce que toute jeune fille doit savoir* (Paris: Nilsson).

—— [n.d. (b)], *La Jeune fille et l'émancipation* (Paris: Nilsson).

—— (1919), *Ce qu'il faut que toute jeune femme sache* (Paris: Nilsson).

—— (1920), *La Femme moderne: pour vivre sa vie, ce que toute femme moderne doit savoir* (Paris: Nilsson).

Darwin, Charles (1998), *On the Origin of Species by Means of Natural Selection, or the Preservation of Favoured Races in the Struggle for Life* [1859] (Oxford: World's Classics).

Dash, Comtesse [Anne de Poilloüe de Saint-Mars] (1860), *Le Livre des femmes* (Paris: Bourdilliat).

—— (1868*a*), *Comment on fait son chemin dans le monde: code du savoir-vivre* (Paris: Lévy).

—— (1868*b*), *Les Femmes à Paris et en province* (Paris: Lévy).

Daudet, Alphonse (1879), *Les Rois en exil: roman parisien* (Paris: E. Dentu).

Davaine, Casimir-Joseph (1875), 'Monstres', in *Dictionnaire encyclopédique des sciences médicales* (Paris: Masson and Asselin, 1864–89), second series, ix (1875), 201–64.

Delécluze, Jean-Baptiste (1832), 'Les Barbus d'à-présent et les barbus de 1800', in *Paris, ou Le Livre des Cent-et-Un* (1831–4): VII, 61–86.

Delepierre, Octave (1860), *Histoire littéraire des fous* (London: Trübner).

Delord, Taxile (1840), 'La Femme sans nom', in *Les Français peints par eux-mêmes*: I, 245–56.

—— Arnould Frémy, and Edmond Texier (1854*a*), *Paris-gagne-petit* (Paris: E. Taride).

—— (1854*b*), *Paris-saltimbanque* (Paris: E. Taride).

Delvau, Alfred (1848), *Grandeur et décadence des grisettes* (Paris: Desloges).

—— (1865), *Gérard de Nerval: sa vie et ses œuvres* (Paris: Bachelin-Deflorenne).

—— (1867*a*), *Dictionnaire de la langue verte: argots parisiens comparés* [1866] (Paris: Dentu).

—— (1867*b*), *Les Lions du jour, physionomies parisiennes* (Paris: Dentu).

—— (1867*c*), *Les Plaisirs de Paris* (Paris: Faure).

Démar, Claire (1833), *Appel d'une femme au peuple sur l'affranchissement de la femme; suivi de Ma loi d'avenir* (Paris: L'auteur).

Deriège, Félix (1842), *Physiologie du lion* (Paris: Delahaye).

Descurets, Jean-Baptiste-Félix (1844), *La Médecine des passions ou Les passions considérées dans leurs rapports avec les maladies, les lois et la religion* [1841] (Paris: Labé).

Despaigne, H. (1866), *Le Code de la mode* (Paris: Chez l'auteur).

Despine, Prosper (1875), *De la folie au point de vue philosophique, ou plus spécialement psychologique, étudiée chez le malade et l'homme en santé* (Paris: F. Savy).

Diderot, Denis (1972), *Le Neveu de Rameau* [1762] (Paris: Gallimard).

—— (1938), *Lettres à Sophie Volland*, ed. André Babélon, 2 vols. (Paris: Gallimard).

Dondey, Auguste-Marie (1875), *Lettre inédite de Philothée O'Neddy...sur le groupe littéraire romantique dit des Bousingos* (Paris: P. Rouquette).

Dostoevsky, Fyodor (1994), *The Karamazov Brothers* [1880], trans. Ignat Avsey (Oxford: Oxford University Press).

—— (2002), *The Idiot* [1869], trans. Richard Pevear and Larissa Volokhonsky (London: Everyman's Library).

Doyle, Arthur Conan (1981), *The Penguin Complete Sherlock Holmes* (Harmondsworth: Penguin).

Drohojowska, Comtesse Antoinette (1858), *La Vérité aux femmes sur l'excentricité des modes et de la toilette, par le chevalier A. de Doncourt* (Paris: Périsse).

Drohojowska, Comtesse Antoinette (1861), *De la politesse et du bon ton, ou Devoirs d'une femme chrétienne dans le monde* [1860] (Paris: Sarlit).

Du Camp, Maxime (1863), 'Salon de 1863', *Revue des deux mondes*, 15 June: 886–918.

—— (1875), *Paris, ses organes, ses fonctions et sa vie dans la seconde moitié du XIXe siècle* [1866–75], 6 vols. (Paris: Hachette).

—— (1984), *Souvenirs littéraires* [1892] (Paris: Balland).

—— and Gustave Flaubert (1987), *Par les champs et par les grèves*, ed. Adrianne J. Tooke (Geneva: Droz).

Dubarry, Armand (1897), *L'Hermaphrodite* (Paris: Chamuel).

Duff, William (1767), *An Essay on Original Genius* (London: Edward and Charles Dilly).

Dugas, Ludovic (1898), *La Timidité, étude psychologique et morale* (Paris: F. Alcan).

Dumanoir, Philippe and Théodore de Barrière (1856), *Les Toilettes tapageuses* (Paris: M. Lévy).

Dumas, Alexandre (père) (1956), *Le Comte de Monte-Cristo* [1846]. (Paris: Garnier).

Dumas, Alexandre (fils) (1898), *Théâtre complet avec préfaces inédites*, 8 vols. (Paris: Calmann Lévy).

Edgeworth, Maria (1801), *Belinda*, 3 vols. (London: J. Thomson).

Erdan, Alexandre [Alexandre-André Jacob] (1855), *La France mistique, tableau des excentricités religieuses de ce tems* [sic], 2 vols. (Paris: Coulon-Pineau).

Escudier, Gaston (1875), *Les Saltimbanques, leur vie, leurs mœurs* (Paris: M. Lévy).

Esquirol, Étienne (1838), *Des Maladies mentales: considérées sous les rapports médical, hygiénique et médico-légal*, 2 vols. (Paris: J.-B. Baillière).

Esquiron, Marie (1893), *Mémoire adressé à Monsieur le Ministre de la Justice par Madame Esquiron [...] Où elle réfute elle-même l'imputation d'aliénation mentale et le rapport de MM. Les aliénistes Mottet, Magnan et Voisin* (Paris: Imprimerie de Hénon).

Esquiros, Alphonse (1846), 'Les Excentriques de la littérature et de la science: M. Gleïzès et le Régime des Herbes', *Revue des deux mondes*, July–September: 837–57.

—— (1859), 'L'Angleterre et la vie anglaise: V. Les Industries excentriques: les musiciens des rues de Londres, les exhibiteurs forains et les acteurs des campagnes', *Revue des deux mondes*, 1 March: 105–54.

Eyma, Louis Xavier (1860), *Excentricités américaines* (Paris: Lévy).

Féré, Charles (1898), *La Famille névropathique: théorie tératologique de l'hérédité et de la prédisposition morbides et de la dégénérescence* [1894] (Paris: Alcan).

Feydeau, Ernest (1866), *Du luxe, des femmes, des mœurs; de la littérature et de la vertu* (Paris: Clichy).

—— (1988), *Théâtre complet*, 4 vols. (Paris: Bordas).

Flaubert, Gustave (2001), *Œuvres de jeunesse*, ed. Claudine Gothot-Mersch and Guy Sagnes (Paris: Gallimard).

Flourens, Pierre (1861), *De la raison, du génie et de la folie* (Paris: Garnier).

Foa, Eugénie (1833), 'La Femme à la mode et la femme élégante en 1833', in *Paris, ou Le Livre des Cent-et-Un* (1831–4): XI, 273–82.

—— (1834), *La Femme à la mode; roman* (Paris: Delongchamps).

—— (1841), 'Le Fat', in *Les Français peints par eux-mêmes*: III, 297–304.

Forgues, E. D. (1862), *Gens de bohême et têtes fêlés, scènes de la vie excentrique, imités de l'anglais* (Paris: J. Hetzel).

Fournel, Victor (1867), *Ce qu'on voit dans les rues de Paris* [1858] (Paris: E. Dentu).

Les Français peints par eux-mêmes (1840–2), 8 vols. (Paris: Curmer), I (1840), II (1840), III (1841), V (1842).

Frémy, Arnould (1836), 'Le Roi de la mode', *Revue de Paris*, 15 October.

—— (1861), *Les Mœurs de notre temps* (Paris: Librairie Nouvelle).

Fresne, Baronne de (1858), *De l'usage et de la politesse dans le monde* (Paris: Taride).

Gallais, Alphonse (1909), *Les Enfers lubriques: curiosités, excentricités et monstruosités passionnelles* (Paris: J. Fort).

Gautier, Théophile (1853), *Les Grotesques* [1844] (Paris: M. Lévy).

—— (1874), *Histoire du romantisme* (Paris: Charpentier).

—— (1875), *Portraits et Souvenirs littéraires* (Paris: Châtillon-sur-Seine).

—— (1995), *Les Jeunes France* [1833] (Paris: Séguier).

Gavarni, P. et al. (1845–46), *Le Diable à Paris: Paris et les Parisiens à la plume et au crayon*, 4 vols. (Paris: J. Hetzel), I (1845).

Gay, Sophie (1833), *Physiologie du ridicule, ou suite d'observations, par une société de gens ridicules* (Paris: C. Vimont).

Genil-Perrin, Georges-Paul-Henri (1913), 'Histoire des origines et de l'évolution de l'idée de dégénérescence en médecine mentale' (Paris: medical thesis).

Geoffroy Saint-Hilaire, Étienne (1822), *Philosophie anatomique: des monstruosités humaines* (Paris: L'auteur).

—— (1827), 'Monstre', in *Dictionnaire classique d'histoire naturelle*, 17 vols. (Paris: Rey et Gravier/Baudouin, 1822–31), XI (1827), 108–51.

Geoffroy Saint-Hilaire, Isidore (1832–7), *Histoire générale et particulière des anomalies de l'organisation chez l'homme et les animaux [...] ou Traité de tératologie*, 4 vols. (Paris: Baillière), I (1832), III (1837).

—— (1847), *Vie, travaux et doctrine scientifique d'Étienne Geoffroy Saint-Hilaire* (Paris: P. Bertrand).

Ginos, L. (1889), *La Guerre contre les Kroumirs: les Fuégiens au Jardin d'acclimatation* (Paris: Villefranche-de-Rouergue).

Girardin, Delphine de (1856), *Lettres parisiennes* [1843], 3 vols. (Paris: Librairie nouvelle).

——(1857), *Le vicomte de Launay: lettres parisiennes*, 4 vols. (Paris: M. Lévy).

Goncourt, Edmond and Jules de (1959), *Journal: mémoires de la vie littéraire*, 4 vols. (Paris: Fasquelle et Flammarion).

Gourdon, Édouard (1841), *Physiologie du Bois de Boulogne* (Paris: Charpentier).

Grandville, J. J. [Jean Ignace Isidore Gérard] (1844), *Un Autre monde: transformations, visions, incarnations, etc.* (Paris: Fournier).

Guinard, Louis (1893), *Précis de tératologie, anomalies et monstruosités chez l'homme et chez les animaux* (Paris: Baillière).

Guinot, Eugène (1840), 'La Lionne', in *Les Français peints par eux-mêmes*: II, 9–16.

Hartenberg, Paul (1901), *Les Timides et la timidité* (Paris: F. Alcan).

Hays, Mary (1796), *Memoirs of Emma Courtney*, 2 vols. (London: G. G. and J. Robinson).

Hazlitt, William (1825), *The Spirit of the Age: or, Contemporary Portraits* (London: Henry Colburn).

Hegel, G. W. F. (1991), *The Philosophy of Right* [1821], ed. Allen W. Wood, trans. H. B. Nisbet (Cambridge: Cambridge University Press).

Hetzel, Pierre Jules (ed.) (1842), *Scènes de la vie privée et publique des animaux*, 2 vols. (Paris: J. Hetzel).

Hill, Aaron (1743), *The Fanciad: An Heroic Poem* (London: J. Osborn).

Hollander, Bernard (1912), *The First Signs of Insanity, their Prevention and Treatment* (London: Stanley Paul & Co).

Huart, Louis (1841*a*), *Physiologie du flâneur* (Paris: Aubert).

——(1841*b*), *Muséum parisien: histoire physiologique, pittoresque, philosophique et grotesque de toutes les bêtes curieuses de Paris et de la banlieue, pour faire suite à toutes les éditions des œuvres de M. de Buffon* (Paris: Beauger).

Hugo, Victor (1968), *Cromwell* [1827] (Paris: Garnier-Flammarion).

Huysmans, Joris-Karl (1907), *À Rebours* [1884] (Paris: Fasquelle).

Janet, Paul (1867), *Le Cerveau et la pensée* (Paris: G. Baillière).

Jesse, William (1854), *The Life of George Brummell, Esq., commonly called Beau Brummell* [1844] (London: Clarke and Beeton).

Jourdan, Louis (ed.) (1860), *Le Causeur, Revue hebdomadaire des lettres, des sciences et des arts* [1859–61], 6 vols., II (1860).

Jouy, Étienne (1815), *L'Hermite de la Chaussée-d'Antin ou Observations sur les mœurs et les usages parisiens au commencement du XIXe siècle*, 5 vols. (Paris: Pillet, 1815–17), I (1815).

Karr, Alphonse (1860), *Les Femmes* [1853] (Paris: Lévy).

Kirby, R. S. (1803–15), *Kirby's Wonderful and Eccentric Museum; or, Magazine of remarkable characters, etc.* [previously entitled *The Wonderful and Scientific Museum: Or Magazine of Remarkable Characters*] (London: [n.pub.]).

Kock, Charles Paul de (1844), *La Grande ville: nouveau tableau de Paris, comique, critique et philosophique* [1842], 2 vols. (Paris: Marescq).

La Bédollière, Émile de (1858), *Histoire de la mode en France* (Brussels: Office de la publicité).

Laborde, J. V. (1872), *Fragments médico-psychologiques: les hommes et les actes de l'insurrection de Paris devant la psychologie morbide: lettres à M. le docteur Moreau (de Tours)* (Paris: Germer-Baillière).

Larchey, Lorédan (1861), *Les Excentricités du langage français* (Paris: Bureaux de la Revue anecdotique).

—— (1867), *Gens singuliers* (Paris: F. Henry).

Le Roux, Henri (1889), *Les Jeux du cirque et la vie foraine* (Paris: E. Plon, Nourrit).

Léca, Victor (1908), *De l'amour et du sang: volupté excentrique* (Paris: J. Fort).

Lecour, Charles-Jérôme (1870), *La Prostitution à Paris et à Londres, 1789–1869* (Paris: Asselin).

—— (1874), *De l'état actuel de la prostitution parisienne* (Paris: Corbeille).

Legrand du Saulle, Henri (1864), *La Folie devant les tribunaux* (Paris: Savy).

—— (1878), *Étude clinique sur la peur des espaces (agoraphobie, des allemands)* (Paris: Delahaye).

—— (1881), *Étude médico-légale sur l'interdiction des aliénés et sur le conseil judiciaire* (Paris: Delahaye et Lecrosnier).

Lélut, Louis-Françisque (1836), *Du démon de Socrate: spécimen d'une application de la science psychologique à celle de l'histoire* (Paris: Trinquart).

Lemoine, Albert (1862), *L'Ame et le corps, études de philosophie morale et naturelle* (Paris: Didier).

Lemoine, Henry, and James Cauldfield (eds.) (1812), *The Eccentric Magazine; or, Lives and Portraits of Remarkable Characters*, 2 vols. (London: G. Smeeton).

Leuret, François (1834), *Fragments psychologiques sur la folie* (Paris: Crochard).

Littré, Émile (1877), *Dictionnaire de la langue française: suppleìment* (Paris: Hachette).

—— (1885), *Dictionnaire de la langue française*, 5 vols. (Paris: Hachette, 1878–89), II (1885).

Loliée, Frédéric (1888), *Le Paradoxe: essai sur les excentricités de l'esprit humain dans tous les siècles* (Paris: A. Savine).

Lombroso, Cesare (1889), *L'Homme de génie*, trans. Colonna d'Istria, preface by Charles Richet (Paris: F. Alcan).

—— (1971), *L'Uomo di genio* [1888; 5th expanded edn. of *Genio et follia*, 1865], 2 vols. (Rome: Napoleone).

Loüis, Gustave (1867), *Physiologie de l'opinion* [1855] (Paris: Dentu).

Louyer-Villermay, Jean-Baptiste (1816), *Traité des maladies nerveuses en vapeurs, et particulièrement de l'hystérie et de l'hypocondrie*, 2 vols. (Paris: Méquignon).

Lucas, Prosper (1847–50), *Traité philosophique et physiologique de l'hérédité naturelle dans les états de santé et de maladie du système nerveux*, 2 vols. (Paris: Baillière), I (1847), II (1850).

Lytton, Edward Bulwer (1828), *Pelham, or the Adventures of a Gentleman*, 3 vols. (London: Henry Colburn).

Maigron, Louis (1911), *Le Romantisme et la mode d'après des documents inédits* (Paris: Champion).

Marie, Anna (1842), 'La Belle-mère', in *Les Français peints par eux-mêmes*: V, 232–8.

Martin, Ernest (1880), *Histoire des monstres depuis l'Antiquité jusqu'à nos jours* (Paris: Reinwald).

Martynovskij and Kovaevskij (eds.) (1892), *Novejshij polnyj slovotolkovatel' i ob'jasnitel' 150,000 inostrannyx slov, vošedšix v russkij jazyk s privedeniem kornej i izsledovaniem o proisxoždenii ix*, 2nd edn. (Moscow: P. E. Astaf'ev's Printing Office).

Marx, Karl and Friedrich Engels (1950), *Selected Works*, 2 vols. (London: Lawrence & Wishart).

Maturin, Charles (1820), *Melmoth the Wanderer: A Tale*, 4 vols. (London: Hurst Robinson).

Maugny, Albert de (1892), *Le Demi-monde sous le Second Empire: souvenirs d'un sybarite* (Paris: Kolb).

Mazade, Charles de (1866), 'La Jeune littérature', *Revue des deux mondes*, 1 October: 763–5.

Meilhac, Henri and Ludovic Halévy (1867), *La Vie parisienne* (Paris: M. Lévy).

Meilheurat, Alphonse de (1864), *Manuel du savoir-vivre, ou l'Art de se conduire selon les convenances et les usages du monde* [1852] (Paris: Desloges).

Mérimée, Prosper (1957), *Romans et nouvelles*, ed. Henri Martineau (Paris: Gallimard).

Meugy, Jules (1865), *De l'extinction de la prostitution, pétition au Sénat* (Paris: Garnier).

Meunier, Victor-Amédée (1889), *Les Excentricités physiologiques* (Paris: E. Dentu).

Mill, John Stuart (1974), *On Liberty* [1859] (Harmondsworth: Penguin).

Mirecourt, Eugène de (1857), *Lola Montès* (Paris: Havard).

—— (1858), *Gérard de Nerval* [1854–55] (Paris: G. Havard).

Monselet, Charles (1864), *Les Originaux du siècle dernier: les oubliés et les dédaignés* (Paris: M. Lévy).

—— (*c.*1870), *Le Musée secret de Paris* (Paris: Michel-Lévy frères).

More, Hannah (1777), *Essays on Various Subjects, Principally designed for Young Ladies* (London: T. Cadell).

Moreau (de Tours), Jacques-Joseph (1846), *Du hachisch et de l'aliénation mentale* (Paris: Fortin Masson).

—— (1859), *La Psychologie morbide: dans ses rapports avec la philosophie de l'histoire ou De l'influence des névropathes sur la dynamisme intellectuel* (Paris: V. Masson).

Moreau, Paul (1888), *La Folie chez les enfants* (Paris: Baillière).

—— (1894), *Les Excentriques: étude psychologique et anecdotique* (Paris: Société d'éditions Scientifiques).

Morel, Bénédict-Auguste (1852), *Études cliniques: Traité théorique et pratique des maladies mentales*, 2 vols. (Nancy: Grimblot and Raybois).

—— (1857), *Traité des dégénérescences physiques, intellectuelles et morales de l'espèce humaine*, 2 vols. (Paris: Baillière).

—— (1860), *Traité des maladies mentales* (Paris: Masson).

Morgan, Lady Sydney (1831), *France in 1829–30*, 2 vols. (London: Saunders and Otley).

Mortemart-Boisse, Baron de (1858), *La Vie élégante à Paris* [1857] (Paris: Hachette).

Murger, Henry (1869), *Scènes de la vie de Bohème* [1852; 4th edn. of *Scènes de Bohème*, 1848] (Paris: M. Lévy).

Musset, Paul de (1863), *Extravagants et Originaux du XVIIe siècle* (Paris: Charpentier).

Nadault de Buffon, Henri (1869), *Notre ennemi le luxe* [1868] (Paris: Furne, Jouvet et Cie).

Nerval, Gérard de (1999), *Selected Writings*, trans. Richard Sieburth (Harmondsworth: Penguin).

Neufville, Étienne de (1842), *Physiologie de la femme* [1841] (Paris: Laisné).

Nisbet, J. F. (1891), *The Insanity of Genius* (London: Ward and Downey).

Nodier, Charles (1993), *L'Amateur de livres* (Paris: Castor astral).

—— (1996), *De quelques phénomènes du sommeil* (Paris: Castor astral).

Nordau, Max (1897), *Psycho-physiologie du génie et du talent*, trans. Auguste Dietrich (Paris: F. Alcan).

Parent-Duchâtelet, A.-J.-B. (1857), *De la prostitution dans la ville de Paris: considérée sous le rapport de l'hygiène publique, de la morale et de l'administration* [1836], 2 vols. (Paris: Baillière).

Paris-Guide, par les principaux écrivains et artistes de la France (1867), 2 vols. (Paris: Librairie internationale).

Paris, ou Le Livre des Cent-et-Un (1831–4), 15 vols. (Paris: Ladvocat).

Pascal, Blaise de (1963), *Pensées*, ed. Louis Lafuma (Paris: Seuil).

Pavot, T. (1897), 'Changement du sens du mot "excentrique"', *Intermédiaire des chercheurs et des curieux*, XXXVI, 148.

Poisle-Desgranges, Joseph (1869), *Nouveau manuel du savoir-vivre, ou l'Art de se conduire dans le monde et dans toutes les circonstances de la vie* (Paris: Vresse).

Pommier, Amédée (1831), 'Charlatans, jongleurs, phénomènes vivants, etc.', in *Paris, ou Le Livre des Cent-et-Un* (1831–4): II, 195–228.

Pommier, Amédée (1832), 'Les Fêtes publiques', in *Paris, ou Le Livre des Cent-et-Un* (1831–4): IV, 95–128.

Ponson du Terrail, Pierre-Alexis (1963–5), *Rocambole: les drames de Paris* [1859], 5 vols., I (1963), II (1964*a*), IV (1964*b*) (Monaco: Édition du Rocher).

Pontmartin, Armand de (1867), *Nouveaux samedis*, 20 vols. (Paris: M. Lévy, 1865–81), III (1867).

Prarond, Ernest (1852), *De quelques écrivains nouveaux* (Paris: M. Lévy).

Prichard, J. C. (1835), *A Treatise on Insanity, and Other Disorders Affecting the Mind* (London: Sherwood, Gilbert, and Piper).

—— (1842), *On the Different Forms of Insanity, in Relation to Jurisprudence* (London: H. Baillière).

Privat d'Anglemont, Alexandre (1846), *Le Prado* (Paris: Paulier).

—— (1861), *Paris inconnu* (Paris: Delahays).

—— (1984), *Paris anecdote: les industries inconnus* [1854] (Paris: Éditions de Paris).

Proudhon, Pierre-Joseph (1966), *Qu'est-ce que la propriété?* [1840] (Paris: Garnier-Flammarion).

—— (1982), *De la justice dans la Révolution et dans l'église* [1858], 4 vols. (Geneva: Slatkine).

Rachilde [Marguerite Eymery] (1926), *Monsieur Vénus* [1884] (Paris: Flammarion).

Raisson, Horace-Napoléon (1836), *Nouveau manuel de la politesse, du ton, et des manières de la bonne compagnie* (Paris: Rue du Paon).

—— (1853), *Code civil: manuel complet de la politesse, du ton, des manières de la bonne compagnie* [1828] (Paris: B. Renault).

Régis, Emmanuel (1906), *Précis de psychiâtrie* [3rd expanded edn. of *Manuel pratique de médecine mentale*, 1885] (Paris: O. Doin).

Régnier, E.-P.-P. (1896), *Éreuthophobie* (Bordeaux: medical thesis).

Renneville, Viscomtesse [Olympe de Lascaux] (1852), *Le Livre de la toilette, guide des dames et des demoiselles* (Paris: Ploche).

Richepin, Jean (1872), *Les Étapes d'un réfractaire: Jules Vallès* (Paris: Lacroix and Verboeckhoven).

Richet, Charles (1880), 'Les Démoniaques d'aujourd'hui: étude de psychologie pathologique', *Revue des deux mondes*, 15 January: 340–72.

Ritter, Eugene (1905), *Les Quatre dictionnaires français* (Geneva: H. Kündig).

Robinet, Jean-Baptiste-René (1768), *Considérations philosophiques de la gradation naturelle des formes de l'être* (Paris: C. Saillant).

Robinson, Mary (1806), *The Poetical Works*, 3 vols. (London: Richard Phillips).

Rocqueplan, Nestor (1857), *Regain; La vie parisienne* [1853] (Paris: Librairie nouvelle).

Ronteix, Eugène (1829), *Manuel du fashionable, ou Guide de l'élégant* (Paris: Audot).

Rostaing, Jules (n.d.), *Manuel de la politesse des usages du monde et du savoir-vivre, par madame J.-J. Lambert* (Paris: Delarue).

Rousseau, Jean-Jacques (1997), *Les Confessions* [1778] (Paris: Gallimard).

Roussel, Pierre (1775), *Système physique et moral de la femme* (Paris: Vincent).

Rouy, Hersilie (1883), *Mémoires d'une aliénée* (Paris: Ollendorff).

Saint-Céran, Marquise de (1865), *Lettre de Mme la Mise de Saint-Céran à M. le procureur général Dupin* (Paris: Josse).

Saint-Victor, Paul de (1889), *Le Théâtre contemporain: Émile Augier, Alexandre Dumas fils* (Paris: C. Lévy).

Salle de Gosse, Isidore (1847), *Histoire naturelle, drôlatique et philosophique des professeurs au jardin des plantes* (Paris: G. Sandré).

Sand, George (1879), *Histoire de ma vie* (Paris: Calmann-Lévy).

—— (1960), *Lélia* [1833] (Paris: Garnier).

—— (1993), *Jeanne* [1844] (Grenoble: Glénat).

Sandras, C.-M.-S. (1851), *Traité pratique des maladies nerveuses*, 2 vols. (Paris: Baillière).

Sarcey, Francisque (1860), *Le Mot et la chose* (Paris: M. Lévy).

Sardou, Victorien (1889), *La Famille Benoîton* [1866] (Paris: C. Lévy).

Scott, Walter (1823), *St. Ronan's Well*, 2 vols. (London: Whittaker & Co).

Serres, Étienne (1832), *Recherches d'anatomie transcendante et pathologique* (Paris: Baillière).

Simmel, Georg (1971), *On Individuality and Social Forms: Selected Writings*, ed. Donald Levine (Chicago: University of Chicago Press).

Smollett, Tobias (1771), *Humphry Clinker*, 2 vols. (Dublin: A. Leathley, J. Exshaw, and H. Saunders).

Soulié, Frédéric (1846?), *Physiologie du bas-bleu* [1830] (Paris: Aubert).

Staël, Germaine de (1862), *Considérations sur les principaux événements de la Révolution française*, 2 vols. (Paris: Charpentier).

Staffe, Baronne Blanche de (1891), *Usages du monde: règles du savoir-vivre dans la société moderne* [1889] (Paris: Havard).

Stendhal [Henri Beyle] (1948–52), *Romans*, ed. Henri Martineau, 2 vols. (Paris: Gallimard), I (1948), II (1952).

—— (1971), *Lamiel*, in *Œuvres de Stendhal*, Cercle du Bibliophile, 50 vols. (Geneva: Edito-Service S.A., 1967–74), XL (1971).

Stern, Daniel [Marie de Flavigny, Comtesse d'Agoult] (1880), *Mes Souvenirs* [1877] (Paris: Calmann Lévy).

Sterne, Laurence (1983), *The Life and Opinions of Tristram Shandy* [1760] (Oxford: World's Classics).

Stoddart, William (1908), *The Mind and its Disorders* (London: Lewis).

Sully, James (1898), *Outlines of Psychology* [1892] (London: Longmans Green).

Tallemant des Réaux, Gédéon (1834–5), *Historiettes*, 6 vols. (Paris: A. Levavasseur), V (1834).

Tardieu, Ambroise (1859), *Etude médico-légale sur les attentats aux mœurs* [1857] (Paris: J. B. Baillière).

—— (1880), *Étude médico-légale sur la folie* [1872] (Paris: Baillière).

Tcherpakov, Avgoust Ivanovitch (1883), *'Les Fous littéraires': rectifications et additions à l'Essai bibliographique sur la littérature excentrique, les illuminés, visionnaires, etc.* (Moscow: W. G. Gautier).

Texier, Edmond (1852–3), *Tableau de Paris*, 2 vols. (Paris: Paulin et Le Chevalier), I (1852), II (1853).

Tissot, Joseph (1877), *La Folie considérée surtout dans ses rapports avec la psychologie normale* (Paris: Marescq).

Trélat, Ulysse (1861), *La Folie lucide étudiée et considérée au point de vue de la famille et de la société* (Paris: Delahaye).

Trollope, Fanny (1985), *Paris and the Parisians* [1836] (Gloucester: Alan Sutton).

Troubat, Jules (1906), *Une amitié à la d'Arthez: Champfleury, Courbet, Max Buchon* (Paris: L. Duc).

Uzanne, Baron Octave (1894*a*), *La Femme à Paris: nos contemporaines* (Paris: May).

—— (1894*b*), *La Française du siècle: la femme et la mode* [1892] (Paris: May).

—— (1895), *Coiffures de style: la parure excentrique, époque Louis XVI* (Paris: Rouveyre).

—— (1898), *Les Modes de Paris, variations du goût et de l'esthétique de la femme, 1797–1897* (Paris: May).

—— (1910), *Études de sociologie féminine: Parisiennes de ce temps en leurs divers milieux, états et conditions* (Paris: Mercure de France).

Veuillot, Louis (1867), *Les Odeurs de Paris* (Paris: Palmé).

Verneur, J. T (1814), *Singularités anglaises, écossaises, et irlandaises*, 2 vols. (Paris: Delaunay).

Véron, Pierre (1868), *Phénomènes vivants* (Paris: A. de Vresse).

—— (1875), *La Foire aux grotesques* (Paris: M. Lévy).

Viel-Castel, Horace de (1840), 'Les Collectionneurs', in *Les Français peints par eux-mêmes*: I, 121–8.

Virey, J.-J. (1815), 'La Femme', in *Dictionnaire des sciences médicales*, 15 vols. (Paris: Panckoucke, 1812–22), XIV (1815), 503–72.

—— (1823), *De la femme sous ses rapports physiologique, moral et littéraire* (Paris: Crochard).

Virmaître, Charles (1893), *Trottoirs et lupanars* (Paris: Perrot).

Warton, Thomas (1774–81), *The History of English Poetry from the Close of the Eleventh to the Commencement of the Eighteenth Century*, 4 vols. (London: Dodsley, J. Walter, and T. Becket).

Wey, Francis-Alphonse (1845), *Remarques sur la langue française au dix-neuvième siècle, sur le style et la composition littéraire*, 2 vols. (Paris: Firmin Didot).

Wilson, Henriette (1825), *Mémoires d'Henriette Wilson*, 8 vols. (Brussels: P. J. de Mat).

Young, Edward (1759), *Conjectures on Original Composition* (London: A. Millar and R. J. Dodsley).

Yriarte, Charles (1868), *Paris grotesque: les célébrités de la rue* [1864] (Paris: E. Dentu)

Zola, Émile (1960), *La Curée* [1872] (Paris: Gallimard).

SECONDARY SOURCES

Adams, Rachel (2001), *Sideshow USA: Freaks and the American Cultural Imagination* (Chicago and London: University of Chicago Press).

Adorno, Theodor and Max Horkheimer (2002), 'The Concept of Enlightenment', in *Dialectic of Enlightenment: Philosophical Fragments* [1944], trans. Edmund Jephcott (Stanford: Stanford University Press), 1–34.

Altick, Richard D. (1978), *The Shows of London* (Cambridge, Mass. and London: Belknap).

Appel, Toby A. (1987), *The Cuvier–Geoffroy Debate: French Biology in the Decades before Darwin* (Oxford: Oxford University Press).

Ardagna, Yann, and Gilles Boëtsch (2002), 'Zoos humains: le "sauvage" et l'anthropologue', in Bancel et al. (2002): 55–62.

Auslander, Leora (1996), *Taste and Power: Furnishing Modern France* (Berkeley and London: University of California Press).

Babcock, Barbara A. (ed.) (1978), *The Reversible World: Symbolic Inversion in Art and Society* (Ithaca: Cornell University Press).

Baguley, David (2000), *Napoléon III and his Regime: An Extravaganza* (Baton Rouge: Louisiana State University Press).

Bakhtin, Mikhail (1981), *The Dialogic Imagination: Four Essays*, trans. Caryl Emerson and Michael Holquist (Austin: University of Texas Press).

——(1984), *Problems of Dostoevsky's Poetics*, ed. and trans. Caryl Emerson (Manchester: Manchester University Press).

Bal, Mieke (2002), *Travelling Concepts in the Humanities: A Rough Guide* (Toronto: University of Toronto Press).

Baldick, Chris (1987), *In Frankenstein's Shadow: Myth, Monstrosity, and Nineteenth-Century Writing* (Oxford: Clarendon Press).

Bancel, Nicolas, Pascal Blanchard, Gilles Boëtsch, Eric Deroo, and Sandrine Lemaire (eds.) (2002), *Zoos humains: de la Vénus hottentote aux reality shows* (Paris: Édition la Découverte).

Baratay, Eric and Elisabeth Hardouin-Fugier (2002), *Zoo: A History of Zoological Gardens in the West* (London: Reaktion).

Barberis, Pierre (1972), *Mythes Balzaciennes* (Paris: A. Colin).

Barker, Christopher and Dariusz Galasinski (2001), *Cultural Studies and Discourse Analysis: A Dialogue on Language and Identity* (London: Sage).

Barrow, Susanna (1981), *Distorting Mirrors: Visions of the Crowd in Late Nineteenth-Century France* (New Haven and London: Yale University Press).

Bartky, Sandra Lee (1990), *Femininity and Domination: Studies in the Phenomenology of Oppression* (New York and London: Routledge).

Bauman, Zygmunt (1991), *Modernity and Ambivalence* (Cambridge: Polity).

—— (2001), *The Individualized Society* (Cambridge: Polity).

Beauvoir, Simone de (1950), *Le Deuxième sexe* [1949], 2 vols. (Paris: Gallimard).

Becker, George (1978), *The Mad Genius Controversy: A Study in the Sociology of Deviance* (Beverly Hills and London: Sage Publications).

Bellet, Roger (1977), *Jules Vallès, journaliste du Second Empire, de la Commune de Paris et de la IIIe République (1857–1885)* (Paris: Les Éditeurs français réunis).

Benchuza, Robert (1994), 'Discourses on Misery', in Dennis Hollier and R. Howard Bloch (eds.), *A New History of French Literature* (Cambridge, Mass.: Harvard University Press, 1994), 687–92.

Bénichou, Paul (1971), 'Jeune-France et bousingots', *Revue d'histoire littéraire de la France*, 3: 439–62.

—— (1973), *Le Sacre de l'écrivain, 1750–1830: essai sur l'avènement d'un pouvoir spirituel laïque dans la France moderne* (Paris: José Corti).

Benjamin, Walter (1997), *Charles Baudelaire: A Lyric Poet in the Era of High Capitalism*, trans. Harry Zohn (London: Verso).

—— (1999), *The Arcades Project*, trans. Howard Eiland and Kevin McLaughlin (Cambridge, Mass. and London: Belknap).

Bennett, Tony (1995), *The Birth of the Museum: History, Theory, Politics* (London: Routledge).

Berger, John (1972), *Ways of Seeing* (Harmondsworth: Penguin).

Bernheimer, Charles (1989), *Figures of Ill Repute: Representing Prostitution in Nineteenth-Century France* (Cambridge, Mass: Harvard University Press).

Berrios, German E. (1993), 'European Views on Personality Disorders: A Conceptual History', *Comprehensive Psychiatry*, 34: 14–30.

—— (1999), 'J. C. Prichard and the Concept of "Moral Insanity"', *History of Psychiatry*, 10 (37): 111–16.

Biasi, Pierre-Marc de (1988), 'Système et déviances de la collection à l'époque romantique', *Romantisme*, 59: 77–93.

Blanchard, Pascal, Nicolas Bancel, and Sandrine Lemaire (2002), 'Les Zoos humains: le passage d'un "racisme scientifique" vers un "racisme populaire et colonial" en Occident', in Bancel et al. (2002): 63–71.

Blanckaert, Claude (1995), 'Le Système des races', in Poutrin (1995): 5–41.

Blavier, André (2001), *Les Fous littéraires* [1982] (Paris: Editions des cendres).

Blum, André Salomé and Charles Chassé (1931), *Histoire du costume: les modes au XIXe siècle* (Paris: Seine-et-Oise).

Bly, Peter Anthony (2004), *The Wisdom of Eccentric Old Men: A Study of Type and Secondary Character in Galdós's Social Novels, 1870–1897* (Montreal and Ithaca: McGill-Queen's University Press).

Bogdan, Robert (1988), *Freak Show: Presenting Human Oddities for Amusement and Profit* (Chicago: University of Chicago Press).

Bony, Jacques (1990), *Le Récit nervalien: une recherché des formes* (Paris: J. Corti).

Boudon, Jacques-Olivier (1995), 'Les Générations libérales', in Poutrin (1995): 313–41.

Boulenger, Marcel (1930), *La Païva* (Paris: Trémois).

Bourdieu, Pierre (1980), *Le Sens pratique* (Paris: Minuit).

—— (1983), 'Vous avez dit "populaire"?', *Actes de la recherche en sciences sociales*, 46: 98–105.

—— (1998), *La Domination masculine* (Paris: Seuil).

Bowman, Frank Paul (1979), 'Une Lecture politique de la folie religieuse ou "théomanie"', *Romantisme*, 24: 75–87.

—— (1988), 'La Marginalité en religion', *Romantisme*, 59: 31–40.

Boym, Svetlana (1994), *Common Places: Mythologies of Everyday Life in Russia* (Cambridge, Mass.: Harvard University Press).

Brooks, Peter (1969), *The Novel of Worldliness* (Princeton: Princeton University Press).

—— (1976), *The Melodramatic Imagination: Balzac, Henry James, Melodrama, and the Mode of Excess* (New Haven: Yale University Press).

—— (1993), *Body Work: Objects of Desire in Modern Narrative* (Cambridge, Mass.: Harvard University Press).

Brown, Marshall (1978), 'The Eccentric Path', *Journal of English and Germanic Philology*, 77 (1): 104–12.

Buck-Morss, Susan (1983), 'Benjamin's Passagen-Werk: Redeeming Mass Culture for the Revolution', *New German Critique*, 29: 211–40.

—— (1986), 'The Flâneur, the Sandwichman and the Whore: The Politics of Loitering', *New German Critique*, 39: 99–140.

Buckler, Julie (2006), 'Eccentricity and Cultural Semiotics in Imperial Russia', in Andreas Schönle (ed.), *Lotman and Cultural Studies: Encounters and Extensions* (Madison: University of Wisconsin Press, 2006), 297–319.

Burke, Peter (1988), 'Bakhtin for Historians', *Social History*, 13 (1): 85–90.

Burton, Richard (1991), *Baudelaire and the Second Republic: Writing and Revolution* (Oxford: Clarendon Press).

—— (1994), *The Flâneur and his City: Paris 1815–1851* (Durham: Durham University Press).

Canguilhem, Georges (1965), *La Connaissance de la vie* [1952] (Paris: J. Vrin).

Canguilhem, Georges (2003), *Le Normal et le pathologique* [1966] (Paris: Quadrige/Presses universitaires de France).

Carassus, Emilien (1971), *Le Mythe du dandy* (Paris: Colin).

Carroll, Victoria (2006), 'Science and Eccentricity in Early Nineteenth-Century Britain', unpublished Ph.D. manuscript, University of Cambridge.

Carroy, Jacqueline (1991), *Hypnose, suggestion, et psychologie: l'invention de sujets* (Paris: Presses Universitaires de France).

Castel, Robert (1976), *L'Ordre psychiatrique: l'âge d'or de l'aliénisme* (Paris: Minuit).

—— (1998), *La Querelle de l'hystérie: la formation du discours psychopathologique en France, 1881–1913* (Paris: Presses universitaires de France).

Catalogue de la Bibliothèque de l'Opéra: Le Cirque—iconographie (1969), Paris.

Cave, Terence (1985), *The Cornucopian Text: Problems of Writing in the French Renaissance* [1979] (Oxford: Oxford University Press).

—— (1999), *Préhistoires I: textes troublés au seuil de la modernité* (Geneva: Droz).

Certeau, Michel de (1990), *L'Invention du quotidien, 1: Arts de faire* (Paris: Gallimard).

—— Dominique Julia, and Jacques Revel (1993), 'La Beauté du mort' [1970], in Michel de Certeau, *La Culture au pluriel* (Paris: Christian Bourgois, 1980), 45–72.

Chambers, Ross (1971*a*), *L'Ange et l'automate: variations sur le mythe de l'actrice de Nerval à Proust* (Paris: Minard).

—— (1971*b*), 'The Artist as Performing Dog', *Comparative Literature*, 23 (4): 312–24.

—— (1985), 'Baudelaire's Street Poetry', *Nineteenth-Century French Studies*, 13: 244–59.

—— (1987), *Mélancolie et opposition: les débuts du modernisme en France* (Paris: Corti).

Chartier, Roger (1988), *Cultural History: Between Practices and Representations* (Cambridge: Polity).

—— (1998), *Au bord de la falaise: l'histoire entre certitudes et inquiétude* (Paris: A Michel).

Chevalier, Louis (1958), *Classes laborieuses et classes dangereuses à Paris pendant la première moitié du XIXe siècle* (Paris: Plon).

Clark, T. J. (1973), *The Absolute Bourgeois: Artists and Politics in France 1848–1851* (London: Thames and Hudson).

—— (1982), *Image of the People: Gustave Courbet and the 1848 Revolution* [1973] (London: Thames and Hudson).

—— (2003), *The Painting of Modern Life: Paris in the Art of Manet and his Followers* [1984] (Princeton: Princeton University Press).

Coblence, Françoise (1988), *Le Dandysme, obligation d'incertitude* (Paris: Presses universitaires de France).

Cohen, Jerome (1996), *Monster Theory: Reading Culture* (Minneapolis: University of Minnesota Press).

Cohen, Margaret (1999), *The Sentimental Education of the Novel* (Princeton: Princeton University Press).

Colin, Paul (1942), *Quelques visages du romantisme* (Brussels: Nouvelle société d'éditions).

Corbin, Alain (1978), *Les Filles de noces: misère sexuelle et prostitution (XIXe siècle)* (Paris: Flammarion).

—— (1987*a*), 'Cris et chuchotements', in M. Perrot (1987*c*): 563–610.

—— (1987*b*), 'La Relation intime ou les plaisirs de l'échange', in M. Perrot (1987*c*): 503–61.

—— (1987*c*), 'Le Secret de l'individu', in M. Perrot (1987*c*): 419–501.

—— (1991), *Le Temps, le désir et l'horreur: essais sur le XIXe siècle* (Paris: Flammarion).

Cowling, Mary (1989), *The Artist as Anthropologist: The Representation of Type and Character in Victorian Art* (Cambridge: Cambridge University Press).

Cowlishaw, Brian (1998), 'A Genealogy of Eccentricity', unpublished PhD manuscript, University of Oklahoma.

Culler, Jonathan (1974), *Flaubert: The Uses of Uncertainty* (Ithaca, New York: Cornell University Press).

Curran, Andrew (2001), *Sublime Disorder: Physical Monstrosity in Diderot's Universe* (Oxford: Voltaire Foundation).

Cvetkovich, Ann (1992), *Mixed Feelings: Feminism, Mass Culture, and Victorian Sensationalism* (New Brunswick, NJ: Rutgers University Press).

Danger, Pierre (1998), *Émile Augier, ou le théâtre de l'ambiguïté: éléments pour une archéologie morale de la bourgeoisie sous le Second Empire* (Paris: L'Harmattan).

Daston, Lorraine and Katherine Park (1998), *Wonders and the Order of Nature: 1150–1750* (New York: Zone Books).

Daumard, Adeline (1996), *La Bourgeoisie parisienne de 1815 à 1848* [1963] (Paris: A. Michel).

Davidson, Arnold I. (1991), 'The Horror of Monsters', in James J. Sheehan and Morton Sosna (eds.), *The Boundaries of Humanity: Humans, Animals, Machines* (Berkeley: University of California Press, 1991), 36–67.

DeJean, Joan (1997), *Ancients Against Moderns: Culture Wars and the Making of a Fin de Siècle* (Chicago and London: Chicago University Press).

Derrida, Jacques (1989), 'Some Statements and Truisms about Neologisms, Newisms, Postisms, Parasitisms, and Other Small Seismisms', in David Carroll (ed.), *The States of Theory* (New York: Columbia University Press, 1989), 63–94.

Descombes, Vincent (1993), *The Barometer of Modern Reason: On the Philosophies of Current Events* (New York and Oxford: Oxford University Press).

Desormeaux, Daniel (2001), *La Figure du bibliomane: histoire du livre et stratégie littéraire au XIXe siècle* (Paris: Nizet).

Diaz, José-Luiz (2003), 'Grotesques, originaux, excentriques: le spleen des fantaisistes', in J. L. Cabanès and J. P. Saïdah (eds.), *La Fantaisie post-romantique* (Toulouse: Presses Universitaires du Mirail, 2003), 171–90.

Didi-Hubermann, Georges (1982), *Invention de l'hystérie: Charcot et l'iconographie photographique de la Salpêtrière* (Paris: Macula).

Donzelot, Jacques (1997), *The Policing of Families* [1977], trans. Robert Hurley (Baltimore: Johns Hopkins University Press).

Dowbiggin, Ian (1991), *Inheriting Madness: Professionalisation and Psychiatric Knowledge* (Berkeley: University of California Press).

Durkheim, Émile (1972), *Émile Durkheim: Selected Writings*, ed. and trans. Anthony Giddens (Cambridge: Cambridge University Press).

Ebers, Nicola (1995), *'Individualisierung': Georg Simmel—Norbert Elias—Ulrich Beck* (Würtzburg: Königshausen and Neumann).

Edelman, Nicole (2003), *Métamorphoses de l'hystérique: du début du XIXe siècle à la Grande guerre* (Paris: Édition de la découverte).

Eichel-Lojkine, Patricia (2002), *Excentricité et humanisme: parodie, dérision et détournement des codes à la Renaissance* (Geneva: Droz).

Elias, Norbert (1994), *The Civilising Process: Sociogenetic and Psychogenetic Investigations* [1939] (Oxford: Blackwell).

Elkington, Margery (1929), *Les Relations de société entre l'Angleterre et la France sous la restauration: 1814–1830* (Paris: Honoré Champion).

Evans, Henri (1951), *Louis Lambert et la philosophie de Balzac* (Paris: J. Corti).

Farber, Paul Lawrence (1976), 'The Type-Concept in Zoology During the First Half of the Nineteenth Century', *Journal of the History of Biology*, 9 (1): 93–119.

Faure, Alain (1978), *Paris Carême-prenant: du Carnaval à Paris au XIXe siècle, 1800–1914* (Paris: Hachette).

Fauvel, Aude (2002), 'Le Crime de Clermont et la remise en cause des asiles en 1880', *Revue d'histoire moderne et contemporaine*, 49 (1):195–216.

Febvre, Lucien (1973), 'Civilisation: Evolution of a Word and a Group of Ideas' [1930], in Peter Burke (ed.), *A New Kind of History: From the Writings of Lucien Febvre* (New York: Harper & Row, 1973), 219–57.

Felski, Rita (1995), *The Gender of Modernity* (Cambridge, Mass.: Harvard University Press).

Fiedler, Leslie A. (1981), *Freaks: Myths and Images of the Secret Self* [1978] (Harmondsworth: Penguin).

Fillin-Yeh, Susan (ed.) (2001), *Dandies: Fashion and Finesse in Art and Culture* (New York: New York University Press).

Forth, Christopher (2004), *The Dreyfus Affair and the Crisis of French Manhood* (Baltimore and London: Johns Hopkins University Press).

Foucault, Michel (1961), *Folie et déraison: histoire de la folie à l'âge classique* (Paris: Plon).

—— (1966), *Les Mots et les choses: une archéologie des sciences humaines* (Paris: Gallimard).

—— (1976), *Surveiller et punir: naissance de la prison* (Paris: Gallimard).

—— (1983), *Naissance de la clinique: une archéologie du regard médical* (Paris: Presses Universitaires de France).

—— (1999), *Les Anormaux: cours au Collège de France (1974–1975)*, ed. Valerio Marchetti and Antonella Salomoni (Paris: Gallimard).

Fraisse, Geneviève and Michelle Perrot (eds.) (1992), *Histoire des femmes en occident: 4, le XIXe siècle* (Paris: Plon).

Freud, Sigmund (1953–74). *Standard Edition of the Complete Psychological Works of Sigmund Freud*, trans. and ed. James Strachey et al., 24 vols. (London: Hogarth), XVII (1955).

Garelick, Rhonda (1998), *Rising Star: Dandyism, Gender, and Performance in the* fin de siècle (Princeton: Princeton University Press).

Garrioch, David (1996), *The Formation of the Parisian Bourgeoisie, 1690–1830* (Cambridge, Mass. and London: Harvard University Press).

Gay, Peter (1984–98), *The Bourgeois Experience: Victoria to Freud*, 5 vols. (New York: Oxford University Press), V, *Pleasure Wars* (1998).

Gibbs, Jack P. (1981), *Norms, Deviance, and Social Control: Conceptual Matters* (New York and Oxford: Elsevier).

Gibson, Ralph (1989), *A Social History of French Catholicism 1789–1914* (London: Routledge).

Gill, Miranda (2006), 'Sketching Social Marginality in Nineteenth-Century Paris: Jules Vallès and his Contemporaries', *Modern Language Review*, 101 (2): 375–87.

—— (2007), 'The Myth of the Female Dandy', *French Studies*, 61 (2): 167–81.

Gille, Gaston (1941), *Jules Vallès, 1832–1885: Ses révoltes, sa maîtrise, son prestige* (Paris: Flammarion).

Gilmour, Robin (1993), *The Victorian Period: The Intellectual and Cultural Context of English Literature, 1830–1890* (London: Longman).

Ginzburg, Carlo (1990), 'Clues: Roots of an Evidential Paradigm', in *Myths, Emblems, Clues*, trans. John and Anne C. Tedeschi (London: Hutchinson Radius, 1990), 96–125.

Girardet, Raoul (1986), *Mythes et mythologies politiques* (Paris: Seuil).

Gluck, Mary (2005), *Popular Bohemia: Modernism and Urban Culture in Nineteenth-Century Paris* (Cambridge, Mass.: Harvard University Press).

Goldstein, Jan (1987), *Console and Classify: The French Psychiatric Profession in the Nineteenth Century* (Cambridge: Cambridge University Press).

Goldstein, Jan (2005), *The Post-Revolutionary Self: Politics and Psyche in France, 1750–1850* (Cambridge, Mass.: Harvard University Press).

Goldstein, Jan (2006), 'Response Essay', *H-France Forum* 1(1) <http://www.h-france.net/forum/forumvol1/Goldstein1%20Response.html> [accessed 1 March 2008]. 36 paragraphs.

Goulemot, Jean Marie, and Daniel Oster (eds.) (1989), *La Vie parisienne: anthologie des mœurs du XIXe siècle* (Paris: Sand).

—— (1992), *Gens de lettres, écrivains et bohèmes: l'imaginaire littéraire, 1630–1900* (Paris: Minerve).

Graña, César (1964), *Bohemian versus Bourgeois: French Society and the French Man of Letters in the Nineteenth Century* (New York and London: Basic Books).

Greene, Thomas M. (1982), *The Light in Troy: Imitation and Discovery in Renaissance Poetry* (New Haven and London: Yale University Press).

Greenhalgh, Paul (1988), *Ephemeral Vistas: A History of the Expositions Universelles, Great Exhibitions and World's Fairs, 1851–1939* (Manchester: Manchester University Press).

Grieder, Josephine (1985), *Anglomania in France: 1740–1789: Fact, Fiction, and Political Discourse* (Geneva: Droz).

Grosz, Elizabeth (1990), 'The Body of Signification', in Andrew Benjamin and John Fletcher (eds.), *Abjection, Melancholia, and Love: The Work of Julia Kristeva* (London: Routledge, 1990), 80–103.

—— (1996), 'Intolerable Ambiguity: Freaks as/at the Limit', in Rosemarie Garland Thomson (1996): 55–66.

Hacking, Ian (1986), 'Making Up People', in Thomas C. Heller, Morton Sosna, and David E. Wellbery (eds.), *Reconstructing Individualism: Autonomy, Individuality, and the Self in Western Thought* (Stanford: Stanford University Press), 222–36.

—— (1998), *Mad Travelers: Reflections on the Reality of Transient Mental Illnesses* (Charlottesville and London: University Press of Virginia).

Haines, Barbara (1978), 'The Inter-Relations Between Social, Biological, and Medical Thought, 1750–1850: Saint-Simon and Comte', *The British Journal for the History of Science*, 37: 19–35.

Harper, Paula Hays (1981), *Daumier's Clowns: les saltimbanques et les parades. New Biographical and Political Functions for a Nineteenth-Century Myth* (New York and London: Garland).

Harsin, Jill (1985), *Policing Prostitution in Nineteenth-Century Paris* (Princeton: Princeton University Press).

Hemmings, F. J. W. (1971), *Culture and Society in France, 1848–1898: Dissidents and Philistines* (London: Batsford).

—— (1987), *Culture and Society in France, 1789–1848* (Leicester: Leicester University Press).

—— (1993), *The Theatre Industry in Nineteenth-Century France* (Cambridge: Cambridge University Press).

Hooper-Greenhill, Eilean (1992), *Museums and the Shaping of Knowledge* (London: Routledge).

Hotier, Hugues (1972), *Le Vocabulaire du cirque et du music-hall en France* (Paris: Maloine).

Howard, Martin (1977), *Victorian Grotesque: An Illustrated Excursion into Medical Curiosities, Freaks and Abnormalities* (London: Jupiter).

Howells, Bernard (1996), *Baudelaire: Individualism, Dandyism, and the Philosophy of History* (Oxford: Legenda).

Huertas, Rafael (1992), 'Madness and Degeneration, I: From "Fallen Angel" to "Mentally Ill" ', *History of Psychiatry*, 4 (12): 391–411.

—— (1993), 'Madness and Degeneration: IV. The Man of Genius', *History of Psychiatry*, 3 (15): 301–19.

Huet, Marie-Hélène (1993), *Monstrous Imagination* (Cambridge, Mass.: Harvard University Press).

Hunt, Herbert James (1959), *Balzac's* Comédie humaine (London: Althone).

Hunt, Lynn (1986), 'French History in the Last Twenty Years: The Rise and Fall of the *Annales* Paradigm', *Journal of Contemporary History*, 21: 209–24.

—— (1987), 'Révolution française et vie privée' in Perrot (1987*c*): 21–51.

—— (ed.) (1989), *The New Cultural History* (Berkeley: University of California Press).

Hunter, J. Paul (1990), *Before Novels: The Cultural Contexts of Eighteenth-Century English Fiction* (New York and London: Norton).

Hutcheon, Linda (1988), *A Poetics of Postmodernism* (New York and London: Routledge).

Impey, Oliver and Arthur MacGregor (eds.) (1985), *The Origins of Museums: The Cabinet of Curiosities in Sixteenth- and Seventeenth-Century Europe* (Oxford: Clarendon Press).

James, Tony (1995), *Dream, Creativity, and Madness in Nineteenth-Century France* (Oxford: Clarendon Press).

Jameson, Fredric (1971), 'La Cousine Bette and Allegorical Realism', *PMLA*, 86 (2): 241–54.

—— (1991), *Postmodernism, or, The Cultural Logic of Late Capitalism* (Durham, N.C.: Duke University Press).

Jaton, Anne-Marie (1984), 'Énergétique et féminité (1780–1820)', *Romantisme*, 46: 15–25.

Jeanneret, Michel (1980), 'La Folie est un rêve: Nerval et le docteur Moreau de Tours', *Romantisme*, 29: 59–75.

Jolliffe, John (2001), *Eccentrics* (London: Duckworth).

Jones, Louisa E. (1984), *Sad Clowns and Pale Pierrots: Literature and the Popular Comic Arts in Nineteenth-Century France* (Lexington: French Forum).

Jordanova, Ludmilla (1984), *Lamarck* (Oxford: Oxford University Press).

Jordanova, Ludmilla (1989), *Sexual Visions: Images of Gender in Science and Medicine Between the Eighteenth and Twentieth Centuries* (London: Harvester Wheatsheaf).

Kelly, George Armstrong (1992), *A Humane Comedy: Constant, Tocqueville, and French Liberalism* (Cambridge: Cambridge University Press).

Kempf, Roger (1977), *Dandies: Baudelaire et Cie* (Paris: Seuil).

Kete, Katherine (1994), *The Beast in the Boudoir: Petkeeping in Nineteenth-Century Paris* (Berkeley and London: University of California Press).

Klein, Jean-René (1976), *Le Vocabulaire des mœurs de la vie parisienne sous le Second Empire: introduction à l'étude du langage boulevardier* (Louvain: Bibliothèque de l'université).

Koselleck, Reinhart (2004), *Futures Past: On the Semantics of Historical Time*, trans. K. Tribe (New York: Columbia University Press).

Krailsheimer, A. J. (1962), *Studies in Self-Interest: From Descartes to La Bruyère* (Oxford: Clarendon Press).

Lacroix, Michel (1990), *De la politesse: essai sur la littérature du savoir-vivre* (Paris: Julliard).

Langford, Paul (2000), *Englishness Identified: Manners and Character 1650–1850* (Oxford: Oxford University Press).

Laqueur, Thomas (1990), *Making Sex: Body and Gender from the Greeks to Freud* (Cambridge, Mass.: Harvard University Press).

Laver, James (1968), *Dandies* (London: Weidenfeld & Nicolson).

Lawrence, Paul (2004), 'Policing the Poor in England and France, 1850–1900', in Clive Emsley, Eric Johnson, and Peter Spierenburg (eds.), *Social Control in Europe, 1800–2000* (Columbus: Ohio State University Press, 2004), 210–25.

Leduc-Adine, Jean-Pierre (1984), 'A propos de Courbet, un champ sémantique: l'excentrique', in R. Mathé (ed.), *Actualité de l'histoire de la langue française, méthodes et documents* (Limoges: U.E.R, 1984), 149–60.

Lepenies, Wolf (1988), *Between Literature and Science: the Rise of Sociology* (Cambridge: Cambridge University Press).

—— (1992), *Melancholy and Society*, trans. Jeremy Gaines and Doris Jones (Cambridge, Mass. and London: Harvard University Press).

Levier, Daniel (1976), 'Anatomie de l'excentricité en Angleterre au XVIIIe siècle', in Plaisant (1976*a*): 9–24.

Levinson, Stephen C. (1983), *Pragmatics* (Cambridge: Cambridge University Press).

Le Wita, Béatrix (1994), *French Bourgeois Culture*, trans. J. A. Underwood (Cambridge: Cambridge University Press).

Lhéritier, Andrée (ed.) (1958), *Les Physiologies* (Paris: Université de Paris).

Limoges, C. (1980), 'The Development of the Muséum d'Histoire naturelle of Paris, 1800–1914', in Robert Fox and George Weisz (eds.), *The Organisation of Science and Technology in France* (Cambridge: Cambridge University Press, 1980), 211–40.

Lindfors, Bernth (1996), 'Ethnological Show Business: Footlighting the Dark Continent', in Thomson (1996): 207–18.

Lokke, Kari (1987), *Gérard de Nerval: The Poet as Social Visionary* (Lexington: French Forum).

Loliée, Frédéric (1920), *La Païva* (Paris: Tallandier).

Lukes, Stephen (1971), 'The Meanings of Individualism', *Journal of the History of Ideas* 32 (1): 45–66.

McCandless, Peter (1981), 'Liberty and Lunacy: The Victorians and Wrongful Confinement', in Scull (1981): 229–62.

Macfarlane, Robert (2007), *Original Copy: Plagiarism and Originality in Nineteenth-Century Literature* (Oxford: Oxford University Press).

Mackenzie, Fraser (1939), *Les Relations de l'Angleterre et de la France d'après le vocabulaire*, 2 vols. (Paris: Droz).

McKnight, Natalie (1993), *Idiots, Madmen, and Other Prisoners in Dickens* (New York: St Martin's Press).

Magendie, Maurice (1925), *La Politesse mondaine et les théories de l'honnêteté en France, au XVIIe siècle, de 1600 à 1660* (Paris: F. Alcan).

Mainardi, Patricia (2003), *Husbands, Wives and Lovers: Marriage and its Discontents in Nineteenth-Century France* (New Haven and London: Yale University Press).

Marcus, Sharon (1999), *Apartment Stories: City and Home in Nineteenth-Century Paris and London* (Berkeley: University of California Press).

Marotin, François (1997), *Les Années de formation de Jules Vallès: histoire d'une génération* (Paris: L'Harmattan).

Matlock, Jann (1994), *Scenes of Seduction: Prostitution, Hysteria, and Reading Difference in Nineteenth-Century France* (New York: Columbia University Press).

—— (1995), 'Censoring the Realist Gaze', in Margaret Cohen and Christopher Prendergast (eds.), *Spectacles of Realism: Gender, Body, Genre* (Minneapolis: University of Minnesota Press, 1995), 28–65.

Matoré, Georges (1951), *Le Vocabulaire et la société sous Louis-Philippe* (Geneva: Droz).

Maza, Sarah (2003), *The Myth of the French Bourgeoisie: An Essay on the Social Imaginary, 1750–1850* (Cambridge, Mass. and London, Harvard University Press).

Melley, Timothy (2000), *Empire of Conspiracy: Cultures of Paranoia in Post-War America* (Ithaca: Cornell University Press).

Merlin-Kajmann, Hélène (2001), *L'Excentricité académique* (Paris: Belles lettres).

Micale, Mark S. (1995), *Approaching Hysteria: Disease and its Interpretations* (Princeton: Princeton University Press).

Miller, Michael (1981), *The* Bon Marché: *Bourgeois Culture and the Department Store, 1869–1920* (London: Allen and Unwin).

Mills, Hazel (1991), 'Negotiating the Divide: Women, Philanthropy and the "Public Sphere" in Nineteenth-Century France', in Frank Talett and Nicholas Atkin (eds.), *Religion, Society and Politics in France since 1789* (London: Hambledon, 1991), 29–54.

Moi, Toril (1999), *What is a Woman? and Other Essays* (Oxford: Oxford University Press).

Monroe, Jonathan (1985), 'Baudelaire's Poor: The *Petits poèmes en prose* and the Social Reinscription of the Lyric', *Stanford French Review*, 9 (2): 169–88.

Montandon, Alain (1994), *Pour une histoire des traités de savoir-vivre en Europe* (Clermont-Ferrand: Association des publications de la Faculté des lettres et sciences humaines de Clermont-Ferrand).

Morazé, Charles (1957), *Les Bourgeois conquérants, XIX siècle* (Paris: A. Colin).

Moriarty, Michael (1988), *Taste and Ideology in Seventeenth-Century France* (Cambridge: Cambridge University Press).

Mortier, Roland (1982), *L'Originalité: une nouvelle catégorie esthétique au siècle des Lumières* (Geneva: Droz).

Moses, Claire Goldberg (1984), *French Feminism in the Nineteenth Century* (Albany: State University of New York Press).

—— and Leslie Walhl Rabine (1993), *Feminism, Socialism, and French Romanticism* (Bloomington: Indiana University Press).

Münster, Arno (1974), *Das Thema der Revolte im Werke von Jules Vallès: ein Beitrag zur Soziologie der Kommune-Literatur* (Munich: W. Fink).

Murat, Laure (2001), *La Maison du docteur Blanche: histoire d'un asile et de ses pensionnaires, de Nerval à Maupassant* (Paris: J. C. Lattès).

Murav, Harriet (1992), *Holy Foolishness: Dostoevsky's Novels & the Poetics of Cultural Critique* (Stanford: Stanford University Press).

Natta, Marie-Christine (1991), *La Grandeur sans convictions: essai sur le dandysme* (Paris: Félin, 1991).

Nye, Robert A. (1984), *Crime, Madness and Politics in Modern France: The Medical Concept of National Decline* (Princeton: Princeton University Press).

—— (1998), *Masculinity and Male Codes of Honor in Modern France* (Berkeley: University of California Press).

Nykrog, Per (1965), *La Pensée de Balzac dans* La comédie humaine: *esquisse de quelques concepts-clés* (Copenhagen: Munksgaard).

Outram, Dorinda (1995), 'New Spaces in Natural History', in *Cultures of Natural History*, ed. N. Jardine, J. Secord, and E. Spary (Cambridge: Cambridge University Press, 1995), 249–65.

Parkhurst-Ferguson, Priscilla (1994), *Paris as Revolution: Writing the Nineteenth-Century City* (Berkeley: University of California Press).

Parsons, Deborah (2000), *Streetwalking the Metropolis: Women, the City and Modernity* (Oxford: Oxford University Press).

Patterson, Lee (1996), 'Historical Criticism and the Claims of Humanism', in Ryan 1996: 92–102.

Perrot, Michelle (1987*a*), 'Drames et conflits familiaux', in M. Perrot (1987*c*): 264–85.

—— (1987*b*), 'En marge: célibataires et solitaires', in M. Perrot (1987*c*): 287–303.

—— (ed.) (1987*c*), *Histoire de la vie privée: de la Révolution à la Grande Guerre* (Paris: Seuil).

Perrot, Philippe (1981), *Les Dessus et les dessous de la bourgeoisie: une histoire du vêtement au XIXe siècle* (Paris: Fayard).

—— (1995), *Le Luxe: une richesse entre faste en confort, XVIII–XIXe siècle* (Paris: Seuil).

Phillips, Patricia (1984), *The Adventurous Muse: Theories of Originality in English Poetics, 1650–1760* (Uppsala and Stockholm: Almqvist & Wiksell International).

Pichois, Claude (1958), 'Le Succès des physiologies', in Lhéritier (1958): 59–66.

Pick, Daniel (1989), *Faces of Degeneration: A European Disorder, c.1848–c.1918* (Cambridge: Cambridge University Press).

Pickstone, John V. (2000), *Ways of Knowing: A New History of Science, Technology and Medicine* (Manchester: Manchester University Press).

Plaisant, Michèle (ed.) (1976*a*), *L'Excentricité en Grande-Bretagne au 18e siècle* (Lille: Université de Lille III).

—— (1976*b*), 'Bohème et poésie en Angleterre au XVIIIe siècle', in Plaisant (1976*a*): 117–36.

Pocock, J. G. A. (1996), 'Concepts and Discourses: A Difference in Culture? Comment on a Paper by Melvin Richter', in H. Lehmann and M. Richter (eds.), *The Meaning of Historical Terms and Concepts: New Studies on Begriffsgeschichte* (Washington, DC: German Historical Institute, 1996), 47–58.

Popovic, Pierre (2000), 'Hommages collatéraux: archéologie d'une catégorie indiscrète: le fou littéraire, l'excentrique (Nodier, Champfleury, Queneau, Blavier)', in Denis Saint-Jacques (ed.), *Que vaut la littérature?* (Québec: Nota Bene, 2000), 161–85.

—— (2001), 'Écrivains et philosophes à lier: Paulin Gagne, Descartes, Pascal, Rousseau, la folie et le positivisme', in Pierre Popovic and Éric Vigneault (eds.), *Les Dérèglements de l'art: formes et procédures de l'illégitimité culturelle en France (1715–1914)* (Montréal: Presses de l'Université de Montréal, 2001), 149–67.

Porter, Roy (1983), 'The Rage of the Party: A Glorious Revolution in English Psychiatry?' *Medical History*, 27: 35–50.

—— (1987), *Mind-Forg'd Manacles: A History of Madness in England from the Restoration to the Regency* (London: Athlone).

—— (ed.) (1991), *The Faber Book of Madness* (London: Faber and Faber).

Poutrin, Isabelle (ed.) (1995), *Le XIXe siècle: science, politique et tradition* (Paris: Berger-Levrault).

Prendergast, Christopher (1986), *The Order of Mimesis: Balzac, Stendhal, Nerval, Flaubert* (Cambridge: Cambridge University Press).

—— (1992), *Paris and the Nineteenth Century* (Oxford: Blackwell).

Prevost, John C. (1957), *Le Dandysme en France, 1817–1839* (Geneva: Droz).

Queneau, Raymond (2002), *Aux confins des ténèbres: les fous littéraires français du dix-neuvième siècle* (Paris: Gallimard).

Rehbock, Philip F. (1990), 'Transcendental Anatomy', in A. Cunningham and Nicholas Jardine (eds.), *Romanticism and the Sciences* (Cambridge: Cambridge University Press, 1990), 144–60.

Richardson, Joanna (1967), *The Courtesans: The Demi-Monde in Nineteenth-Century France* (London: Phoenix).

—— (1969), *The Bohemians: La Vie de Bohème in Paris, 1830–1914* (London: Macmillan).

Rieger, Dietmar (1988), ' "Ce qu'on voit dans les rues de Paris": marginalités sociales et regards bourgeois', *Romantisme*, 59: 19–29.

Rigoli, Juan (2001), *Lire le délire: aliénisme, rhétorique et littérature en France au XIXe siècle* (Paris: Fayard).

Rigolot, François (1994), 'The Invention of the Renaissance', in Dennis Hollier and R. Howard Bloch (eds.), *A New History of French Literature* (Cambridge, Mass.: Harvard University Press, 1994), 638–44.

Rivers, Christopher (1993), 'L'homme hiéroglyphié: Balzac, Physiognomy, and the Legible Body', in Elias Shookman (ed.), *Faces of Physiognomy: Interdisciplinary Approaches to Johann Casper Lavater* (Columbia, SC: Camden House, 1993), 144–60.

Rosario, Vernon A. (1997), *The Erotic Imagination: French Histories of Perversity* (New York: Oxford University Press).

Rothfield, Laurence (1992), *Vital Signs: Medical Realism in Nineteenth-Century Fiction* (Princeton and Oxford: Princeton University Press).

Ryan, Kiernan (ed.) (1996), *New Historicism and Cultural Materialism: A Reader* (London: Arnold).

Said, Edward (1995), *Orientalism* [1978] (Harmondsworth: Penguin).

Saisselin, Rémy G. (1985), *Bricabracomania: The Bourgeois and the Bibelot* (London: Thames and Hudson).

Sangsue, Daniel (1987), *Le Récit excentrique: Gautier—de Maistre—Nerval—Nodier* (Paris: José Corti).

—— (1988), 'Vous avez dit "excentrique"?', *Romantisme* 59: 41–57.

—— (2000), 'L'Excentricité fin de siècle', in Sylvie Thorel-Cailleteau (ed.), *Dieu, la chair et les livres* (Paris: Champion, 2000), 359–482.

Sartre, Jean-Paul (1971–2), *L'Idiot de la famille: Gustave Flaubert de 1821 à 1857*, 3 vols. (Paris: Gallimard), I (1971).

Schiller, Joseph (1967), *Claude Bernard et les problèmes scientifiques de son temps* (Paris: Cèdre).

Schneider, William H. (1982), *An Empire for the Masses: The French Popular Image of Africa, 1870–1900* (Westport, Conn. and London: Greenwood).

Schor, Naomi (1993), *George Sand and Idealism* (New York: Columbia University Press).

Schulman, Peter (2003), *The Sunday of Fiction: The Modern French Eccentric* (West Lafayette: Purdue University Press).

Schwartz, Vanessa R. (1998), *Spectacular Realities: Early Mass Culture in Fin-de-Siècle Paris* (Berkeley: University of California Press).

Scull, Andrew (ed.) (1981), *Madhouses, Mad-Doctors, and Madmen: The Social History of Madness in the Victorian Era* (London: Althone).

—— (1982), *Museums of Madness: The Social Organization of Insanity in Nineteenth-Century England* [1979] (Harmondsworth: Penguin).

Seigel, Jerrold (1999), *Bohemian Paris: Culture, Politics, and the Boundaries of Bourgeois Life 1830–1930* [1986] (Baltimore and London, Johns Hopkins University Press).

Sennett, Richard (1986), *The Fall of Public Man* [1977] (London: Faber).

Seznec, Jean (1943), 'Saint Antoine et les monstres', *PMLA* 58 (1): 195–222.

Shaya, Gregory (2004), 'The *Flâneur*, the *Badaud*, and the Making of a Mass Public in France, circa 1860–1910', *The American Historical Review*, 109 (1): 41–77.

Showalter, Elaine (1980), 'Victorian Woman and Insanity', in Scull (1981): 313–36.

—— (1985), *The Female Malady: Women, Madness, and English Culture, 1830–1980* (New York: Penguin Books).

—— (1993), 'Hysteria, Feminism, and Gender', in Sander L. Gilman, Helen King, Roy Porter, G. S. Rousseau, and Elaine Showalter (eds.), *Hysteria Beyond Freud* (Berkeley: University of California Press, 1993), 286–344.

Sieburth, Richard (1984), 'Same Difference: the French Physiologies, 1840–1842', *Notebooks in Cultural Analysis*, 1: 163–200.

Sirotkina, Irina (2002), *Diagnosing Literary Genius: A Cultural History of Psychiatry in Russia, 1880–1930* (Baltimore and London: Johns Hopkins University Press).

Sitwell, Edith (1933), *English Eccentrics* (London: Faber and Faber).

Skinner, Quentin (2002), *Visions of Politics: 1: Regarding Method* (Cambridge: Cambridge University Press).

Skultans, Vieda (ed.) (1975), *Madness and Morals: Ideas on Insanity in the Nineteenth Century* (London and Boston: Routledge & Kegan Paul).

Sledziweski, Elisabeth G. (1992), 'Révolution Française: le tournant', in Fraisse and Perrot (1992): 43–56.

Smart, Barry (1999), *Facing Modernity: Ambivalence, Reflexivity, and Morality* (London: Sage).

Smith-Rosenberg, Carroll (1986), *Disorderly Conduct: Visions of Gender in Victorian America* [1985] (New York and Oxford: Oxford University Press).

Spary, Emma (1995), 'Political, Natural and Bodily Economies', in N. Jardine, J. Secord, and E. Spary (eds.), *Cultures of Natural History* (Cambridge: Cambridge University Press, 1995), 178–96.

Stallybrass, Peter and Allon White (1986), *The Politics and Poetics of Transgression* (Ithaca: Cornell University Press).

Stanton, Domna C. (1980), *The Aristocrat as Art: A Study of the Honnête Homme and Dandy in Seventeenth- and Nineteenth-Century French Literature* (New York: Columbia University Press).

Starobinski, Jean (1970), *Portrait de l'artiste en saltimbanque* (Geneva: Albert Skira).

—— (1999), *Action et réaction: vie et aventures d'un couple* (Paris: Seuil).

Stead, Évanghélia (2004), *Le Monstre, le singe et le fœtus: tératogonie et décadence dans l'Europe fin de siècle* (Geneva: Droz).

Steele, Valerie (1998), *Paris Fashion: A Cultural History* (Oxford: Berg).

Steig, Michael (1970), 'Defining the Grotesque: An Attempt at Synthesis', *Journal of Aesthetics and Art Criticism*, 29 (2): 253–60.

Steinmetz, Jean-Luc (1988), 'Quatre hantises (sur les lieux de la Bohême)', *Romantisme*, 59: 59–70.

Stephens, Sonya (1999), *Baudelaire's Prose Poems: The Practice and Politics of Irony* (Oxford: Oxford University Press).

Stierle, Karlheinz (1993), *Der Mythos von Paris: Zeichen und Bewusstsein der Stadt* (Munich: C. Hanser).

Swart, Koenrad W. (1962*a*), ' "Individualism" in the Mid-Nineteenth Century (1826–1860)', *Journal of the History of Ideas*, 23 (1): 77–90.

—— (1962*b*), 'The French: Are They Individualists?' *South Atlantic Quarterly*, 61: 1–12.

Taylor, Charles (1989), *Sources of the Self: The Making of the Modern Identity* (Cambridge, Mass.: Harvard University Press).

Taylor, Jenny Bourne and Sally Shuttleworth (1998), *Embodied Selves: An Anthology of Psychological Texts, 1830–1890* (Oxford: Oxford University Press).

Terdiman, Richard (1985), *Discourse/Counter-Discourse: The Theory and Practice of Symbolic Opposition in Nineteenth-Century France* (Ithaca: Cornell University Press).

Thétard, Henry (1934), *Coulisses et secrets du cirque* (Paris: Plon).

—— (1978), *La Merveilleuse histoire du cirque* [1947] (Paris: Juillard).

Thompson, C. W. (1997), *Lamiel, fille du feu: essai sur Stendhal et l'énergie* (Paris: L'Harmattan).

Thompson, Victoria (1996), 'Creating Boundaries: Homosexuality and the Changing Social Order in France, 1830–1870', in Jeffrey Merrick and

Bryant T. Ragan (eds.), *Homosexuality in Modern France* (Oxford: Oxford University Press, 1996), 102–27.

Thompson, Ewa M. (1987), *Understanding Russia: The Holy Fool in Russian Culture* (Lanham, Md.: University Press of America).

Thomson, Rosemarie Garland (ed.) (1996), *Freakery: Cultural Spectacles of the Extraordinary Body* (New York: New York University Press).

Todorov, Tzvetan (1970), *Introduction à la littérature fantastique* (Paris: Seuil).

Tombs, Nancy (1994), 'Feminist Histories of Psychiatry', in Mark Micale and Roy Porter (eds.), *Discovering the History of Psychiatry* (New York and Oxford: Oxford University Press, 1994), 348–83.

Tort, Patrick (1980), *L'Ordre et les monstres: le débat sur l'origine des déviations anatomiques au XVIIIe siècle* (Paris: Le Sycomore).

Tyers, Meryl (1998), *Critical Fictions: Nerval's* Les Illuminés (Oxford: Legenda).

Vanier, Henriette (1960), *La Mode et ses métiers: frivolités et luttes des classes, 1830–1870* (Paris: A. Colin).

Van Zuylen, Marina (2005), *Monomania: The Flight From Everyday Life In Literature And Art* (Ithaca: Cornell University Press).

Vincent, Andrew (1995), *Modern Political Ideologies* [1992] (Oxford: Blackwell).

Voskuil, Lynn M. (2001), 'Acts of Madness: Lady Audley and the Meanings of Victorian Femininity', *Feminist Studies*, 27 (3): 611–39.

Wagniart, Jean-François (1999), *Le Vagabond à la fin du XIXe siècle* (Paris: Belin).

Waller, Margaret (1993), *The Male Malady: Fictions of Impotence in the French Romantic Novel* (New Brunswick, NJ: Rutgers University Press).

Watson, Janell (1992), *Literature and Material Culture from Balzac to Proust: The Collection and Consumption of Curiosities* (Cambridge: Cambridge University Press).

Weber, Max (1948), 'Science as a Vocation' [1918–1919], in H. H. Gerth and C. Wright Mills (eds. and trans.), *Max Weber: Essays in Sociology* (New York: Oxford University Press, 1948), 129–56.

Wechsler, Judith (1982), *A Human Comedy: Physiognomy and Caricature in 19th-Century Paris* (London: Thames and Hudson).

Weeks, David (1995), *Eccentrics* (London: Weidenfeld and Nicolson).

Weigert, Andrew J. (1991), *Mixed Emotions: Certain Steps Towards Understanding Ambivalence* (Albany: State University of New York Press).

Weinberg, Bernard (1937), *French Realism: The Critical Reaction, 1830–1870* (New York: MLA).

Wilkinson, Lynn (1996), *The Dream of an Absolute Language: Emanuel Swedenborg and French Literary Culture* (Albany: State University of New York Press).

Williams, Elizabeth A. (1994), *The Physical and the Moral: Anthropology, Physiology, and Philosophical Medicine in France, 1750–1850* (Cambridge: Cambridge University Press).

Williams, Raymond (1977), *Marxism and Literature* (Oxford: Oxford University Press).

—— (1983), *Keywords: A Vocabulary of Culture and Society* [1976] (London: Fontana).

Williams, Rosalind H. (1982), *Dream Worlds: Mass Consumption in Late Nineteenth-Century France* (Berkeley: University of California Press).

Wilson, Elizabeth (1987), *Adorned in Dreams: Fashion and Modernity* (Berkeley: University of California Press).

—— (2000), *Bohemians: The Glamorous Outcasts* (London: I. B. Tauris).

Wilson, Susannah (2005), 'Voices from the Asylum: Four French Women Writers, 1850–1920', unpublished DPhil manuscript, University of Oxford.

Wing, Nathaniel (2004), *Between Genders: Narrating Difference in Early French Modernism* (Newark: University of Delaware Press).

Wittgenstein, Ludwig (1997), *Philosophical Investigations*, trans. G. E. M. Anscombe (Oxford: Blackwell).

Youngquist, Paul (2003), *Monstrosities: Bodies and British Romanticism* (Minneapolis: University of Minnesota Press).

Index

Bold numbers denote reference to illustrations.